THE MINUTES OF

Edinburgh Trades Council

1859–1873

edited by Ian MacDougall M.A.

★

★

EDINBURGH
printed for the Scottish History Society *by*
T. AND A. CONSTABLE LTD
1968

Printed in Great Britain

PREFACE

My thanks are due to Edinburgh Trades Council for permission to publish these minutes and to the Council of the Scottish History Society for its invitation to edit them. I am indebted to Professor S. G. E. Lythe of the department of Economic History in the university of Strathclyde for arrangements that enabled this work to be completed much sooner than would otherwise have been possible. Dr W. Hamish Fraser of the same department gave advice and information on several points and I am grateful also to him for allowing me to read his recent PH.D. thesis on trades councils. I did not read it until most of the present volume was already in proof, but as will be seen I have benefited from it at several points in the introduction. Mr W. H. Marwick kindly lent books to me and gave help in locating the obituaries of several of the delegates. Mrs N. Armstrong and her staff at the Edinburgh Room of Edinburgh Central Public Library were most helpful in providing local source material.

I. M.

Edinburgh
May, 1968

A generous contribution from the
Carnegie Trust for the Universities of Scotland
towards the cost of producing this volume
is gratefully acknowledged by the
Council of the Society

CONTENTS

———

ILLUSTRATIONS

Introduction

The task of writing the history of working class organisations and movements in Scotland before the late nineteenth century is made difficult by the frequent lack of documentary record. This problem certainly exists in the case of trade unionism. But the growth of unions in nineteenth-century Britain was accompanied in many towns by the formation of trades councils. These councils were purely local bodies of delegates from various unions and their aim was to promote the interests of working men. In their surviving records, therefore, is a body of written material revealing the activities and attitudes of at least a section of the working class. Although much has been written about the history of trade unions in Britain and several studies of particular trades councils have also been made,[1] this is the first attempt to put into print at length the original minutes of any trade union or trades council.

The records which follow are the earliest surviving minutes of Edinburgh trades council. Though the council was not one of the most important of its kind in Britain, the value of its minutes as a source of working class and trade union history is magnified by the extensive loss and destruction of other Scottish trades council and trade union records. Except for the recently discovered first minute book of Glasgow trades council for 1858-9, no other Scottish trades council minutes survive for this or any earlier period.[2] Even among

[1] E.g., K. D. Buckley, *Trade Unionism in Aberdeen, 1878 to 1900* (Edinburgh, 1955), G. Tate, *London Trades Council, 1860-1950* (London, 1950), J. Corbett, *Birmingham Trades Council, 1866-1966* (London, 1966). W. Hamish Fraser has made a general study in his unpublished PH.D. thesis, 'Trades Councils in England and Scotland, 1858-1897' (University of Sussex, 1967).

[2] Meetings of Glasgow trades council in the 1860s are, however, reported in the *Glasgow Sentinel*. The minute book for 1858-9 is in Mitchell Library, Glasgow (ref. 832300). No other minutes of the trades council exist before 1884 (Mitchell Library, 832301), and none of Aberdeen trades council, formed in 1868, before 1876 (Aberdeen university library, 124077). No records survive of the other trades councils in Scotland during the period: Dundee, formed about 1861 and re-formed in 1867, Greenock,

English trades councils, which were more numerous, the minutes of only two or three[1] exist for all or part of the period covered here. Similar losses have been suffered by Scottish trade union minutes, and only a dozen sets, some of them mere fragments, are known to survive from the whole of the first three-quarters of the nineteenth century. Of the thirty-one unions affiliated to Edinburgh trades council during 1859-73 the minutes of only five remain.[2]

The manuscript minutes of Edinburgh trades council are the property of the council and are kept in its offices in Albany Street, Edinburgh.[3] The minutes, which are contained in some thirty volumes strongly re-bound in recent years, run almost continuously from 1859 to the present day.[4] The first volume covers the years 1859-67 and the second 1867-76. The original intention of gathering the contents of both these volumes into the present publication had to be modified because of their bulk. The choice of December 1873, two-thirds of the way through volume ii of the manuscript, as the point at which to break off publication was not perhaps without some historical as well as practical justification. Not only was the trade union boom of the early 1870s then at its height, but also the date had some significance for the trades council since it was at the last meeting minuted below that the council for the first time appointed a delegate to attend the Trades Union Congress.

The minutes of 1859-73 were written by the dozen successive secretaries of the trades council.[5] Their spelling was often idiosyncratic and sometimes merely phonetic, and one or two of them had weak powers of expression. None the less it is clear that each wrote up his minutes conscientiously. The handwriting is generally easily legible, the layout of each page usually neat, and the accuracy of the

---

formed about 1859 and re-formed in 1872, and Kirkcaldy, formed in 1873. See W. H. Fraser, op. cit., 45, 58, 76-78, 92.

[1] London, Birmingham, and possibly some of those of Bristol trades council. W. H. Fraser, op. cit., 587.

[2] The National Library of Scotland, Edinburgh (hereafter NLS) has those of the tin-plate workers (Acc. 4050), printers (Acc. 4068), and bookbinders (Acc. 4395), and will shortly receive those of the cabinetmakers. Minutes of two branches of the joiners are at the union's Edinburgh district office, 1 Hillside Crescent.

[3] Permission has recently been given the National Library of Scotland to microfilm the minutes up to c. 1950.

[4] Those from November 1876 to July 1877 and from November 1903 to July 1906 are missing.   [5] Below, appendix I, p. 374.

minutes was not often challenged. The naïvely verbose style of John Beaton, who as secretary from 1861 to 1864 sometimes incorrectly dated his minutes, was fortunately not typical. On the contrary, the minutes too often lapse from the succinct into the cryptic. They will be seen to illustrate the conflict of interests between minute secretaries and historians, and from the point of view of the latter contain perhaps an unusually large share of inadequacies. Though the few surviving records of affiliated unions are slightly helpful and the contemporary press very much more so, it has not proved possible to identify or enlarge upon bare references to a number of persons, events or organisations. Any criticism of the shortcomings of the minutes as sources ought, however, to be tempered by three considerations. The men who wrote them were more accustomed to handling a hammer or a drill than a pen. All were voluntary office-bearers. Their secretarial duties had to be carried out in whatever time remained after employment at their trades for over or well over fifty hours a week, and in some cases in addition to work as office-bearers or activists within their own unions.

The minutes of the trades council have, it is believed, so far been consulted by only a handful of scholars. Of these only three appear to have quoted from the minutes in published works.[1] No full history of the council itself has yet been undertaken.

★

The history of the trades council in Edinburgh before 1859 is largely obscure. As early as 1825, the year following the repeal of the anti-combination laws, an anonymous journeyman bookbinder in Edinburgh published with the approval of his union a pamphlet in which he urged the formation of a local association of trades for mutual assistance.[2] He proposed that each trade should 'send a certain

---

[1] W. H. Marwick, especially in his *Economic Developments in Victorian Scotland* (London, 1936) and *Short History of Labour in Scotland* (Edinburgh, 1967); Miss A. Tuckett made use at least of the late nineteenth-century minutes in *The Scottish Carter* (London, 1967); H. McKinven based on the minutes his short brochure *Edinburgh and District Trades Council Centenary, 1859-1959* (Edinburgh, 1959).

[2] *A statement of the causes which led to the present difference between the Master and Journeymen Bookbinders of Edinburgh, with proposals to journeymen mechanics; drawn up by the authority of the Journeymen Bookbinders' Society, by a Journeyman* (Edinburgh, 1825), 15-16. NLS, Acc. 4395.

b

number as Committee Members, who shall represent the trade to which they shall belong at general committee meetings'. It has recently been discovered that these proposals were evidently carried out, at least during 1826-7, by a Mechanics' Institution in Edinburgh, which gave financial support to trade unionists on strike.[1] The appearance of the bookbinder's pamphlet reflected the growth by the early 1830s of a tendency in several towns in Britain to establish local joint committees or meetings of trade union delegates. Such a committee appears to have been formed, or perhaps re-formed, in Edinburgh about 1830, and the trades delegates, as they were generally termed, were active in the agitation for the Reform Bill of 1832. They led the great procession of trades through the city on 10 August 1832 to celebrate the passage of the Bill.[2] From October 1833 they issued the *Trades Monthly Journal*.[3] In 1834 and 1835 meetings of the trades delegates are reported in connection with the visits to the city of Earl Grey and Daniel O'Connell respectively.[4] Indeed dissension among the delegates and in their trades on both these occasions, as to whether demonstrations of welcome ought to be held, probably contributed, along with disagreements over political matter in the *Trades Monthly Journal*,[5] to the exclusion of 'politics' from the earliest of the trades council meetings minuted below. Whether the meetings in the 1830s were regular or merely *ad hoc* is not certain, but references in the contemporary press to the trades delegates' presidents and secretaries suggest that the delegates' organisation was a formal and regular one. While further research may establish that the delegates continued to function throughout the period of the Chartist agitation, no reference has been discovered to any meeting for fourteen years after 1839, when the bookbinders had called one to discuss a dispute in their trade in London.[6]

[1] W. H. Fraser, op. cit., 5.
[2] *Edinburgh Evening Courant*, 11 August 1832.
[3] Minutes, 27 August 1833, Edinburgh branch, Scottish National Union of Cabinet and Chair Makers, shortly to be deposited in NLS. No copies of this *Journal* are known to survive. Some scraps of information about it are contained in an article by the present writer on the cabinetmakers' union in a forthcoming issue of the *Book of the Old Edinburgh Club*.
[4] *Edinburgh Evening Courant*, 4 and 13 September 1834, 19 and 21 September 1835.
[5] *Poor Law Inquiry (Scotland), 1844*, appendix i, 179, evidence of John Wright.
[6] Minutes, Edinburgh Union Society of Journeymen Bookbinders, 5 February 1839. NLS, Acc. 4395.

It seems probable that the formation of a permanent trades council in Edinburgh took place in or about 1853. If this is correct then the Edinburgh council would appear to be the oldest existing trades council in Britain after that of Liverpool.[1] In October 1853 meetings of trades delegates re-emerge. The delegates appear as leaders of the local agitation for a Saturday afternoon holiday and payment of wages on Fridays instead of Saturdays.[2] Their secretary was James G. Bald of the plumbers' union, who was again a delegate to the trades council in 1859-61. Their meeting place was evidently Burden's Coffee House at 129 High Street, where the trades council regularly met between 1859 and 1867. At the latter date, it is true, the minutes refer to a minute-book 'now completed, commenced in 1849'.[3] But the context indicates that this is a reference to volume i of the surviving minutes, and the date should therefore read 1859, not 1849. Confirmation that it was probably in or about 1853 that the council was formed appears to lie in the minutes of 13 August 1861. At his retirement then, after a 'number of years' as a joiners' delegate, William Caw referred to 'the origination of the Council in the Saturday afternoon holiday movement, and subsequent emergence into the United Trades Council'.[4] Only two further references have been discovered to the existence of the council before the earliest surviving minute. On new year's day 1855 the trades delegates held in the Corn Exchange 'a grand fruit soiree and musical entertainment', in connection with the Saturday half holiday movement,[5] and four years later they held a similarly abstemious celebration to mark the centenary of Robert Burns.[6]

There may appear some ground for considering 1867 rather than about 1853 as the date of foundation of a permanent council. The council clearly passed through a crisis in the winter of 1866-7, evidenced by the absence of recorded meetings in February and March 1867, the subsequent reference to the then 'state of disorganisation' of the council,[7] and the reconstruction during the spring and early summer. On the other hand, the council had had its lowest attendances in some previous years too at that season.

[1] S. and B. Webb, *The History of Trade Unionism* (London, 1920), 225, n. 1.
[2] Rev. D. Jamie, *John Hope, Philanthropist and Reformer* (Edinburgh, 1900), 293-5.
[3] Below, p. 199.   [4] Below, p. 63.   [5] *The Witness*, 3 January 1855.
[6] Below, p. 3, n. 4.   [7] Below, p. 190, n. 2.

Moreover, the actual hiatus, perhaps caused by the withdrawal of the secretary by his union,[1] was brief, and there was continuity in the office of president. All this makes it seem an exaggeration to consider the crisis a complete break in the existence of the council.

The province of the council included Leith[2] as well as Edinburgh, though this fact was not clearly reflected in the earlier formal titles of the council. Until 1860 it described itself as the United Trades Delegates Association of Edinburgh and Vicinity. Its title was then altered to Council of United Trades Delegates and subsequently, at the reorganisation in 1867, to United Trades Council. The rules drawn up in 1867, however, specifically stated that the council should 'consist of Delegates elected by the various Trades and Professions in Edinburgh, Leith, and Vicinity'.[3] There was evidently a proposal in 1868 to establish a separate trades council in Leith, but this seems to have come to nothing at that time.[4]

Edinburgh and Leith had a considerable range of industries, but most were on a relatively modest scale and none was dominant. Individual firms were generally small. Printing with its allied trades was the staple industry of Edinburgh: some 3,000 inhabitants were engaged in printing, bookbinding and typefounding,[5] constituting the chief centre of these trades in Scotland. But the building and furnishing trades, in which some 7,000 were engaged,[6] employed the largest work force and this fact was shown in the composition of the trades council. Other leading trades and industries, in which however those engaged were numbered in hundreds rather than thousands, included coach-making, brewing and distilling, leather- and glass-making, brass-founding, and rubber manufacture. Among the more traditional consumption trades, bakers, tailors and shoe-makers were particularly numerous. Industrialisation was less exten-sive than in Glasgow, the most obvious city of comparison. Though their combined population of 200,000 in 1861,[7] rising to 240,000 in 1871,[8] was half that of Glasgow, Edinburgh and Leith had less than

---

[1] Below, p. 185.   [2] A separate burgh until 1920.
[3] *Laws for the Government of the United Trades Council* (Edinburgh, 1867), 3. NLS, Acc. 4068.
[4] Below, p. 234. One had, however, been formed at Leith by 1876. Minutes of Edinburgh trades council, 27 June 1876.
[5] *Census of Scotland, 1861*, ii, 85.   [6] Ibid., ii, 314.
[7] Ibid., i, 152-3.   [8] *Census of Scotland, 1871*, i, 160-1.

a third as many inhabitants engaged in manufacture.[1] Their share, of heavy industry was substantially smaller than Glasgow's engineering for example employing only about a quarter of the number in Glasgow.[2] Though surrounded by the coalfields of the Lothians, Edinburgh contained only a score of miners, Glasgow almost a thousand.[3] Ship-repairing at Leith continued to give some partly seasonal employment, but the shipbuilding industry there was comparatively small and moreover was in decline.[4] The textile industry was of practically no importance in Edinburgh.[5] This largely explained why far fewer women were employed in industry there than in Glasgow, and relatively fewer than in Dundee or Aberdeen.[6] Because of the sex distribution of the labour force, trade union organisation may have been less difficult to establish and maintain in Edinburgh than in the other main Scottish cities. Possibly also Edinburgh, with its distinctive industrial structure, may have offered more stable employment to its workmen. Certainly the trades council minutes contain very few references to recession or unemployment within the city. It is reasonable to suppose, however, that economic conditions affected the strength of the council to a considerable extent throughout the period.[7] In particular, the economic crisis of 1866-7 was probably partly responsible for the serious decline of the council at that time, and the economic expansion from the late 1860s until the mid-1870s helped to bring an increase in affiliations to the council.

The much higher proportion in Edinburgh than in Glasgow of such tradesmen as cabinetmakers, upholsterers and french polishers[8] was no doubt a consequence of the relatively high proportion in the capital of middle class and professional people, a notable feature of its class structure. As the ecclesiastical, legal and administrative centre of Scotland, it contained more ministers of religion than Glasgow, more physicians and surgeons, and two-and-a-half times as many members of the legal profession.[9] The abundance and organisation of some of these middle class elements seems occasionally

---

[1] *Census of Scotland, 1861*, ii, 78.   [2] Ibid., ii, 86.   [3] Ibid., ii, 318-19.
[4] D. Bremner, *The Industries of Scotland* (Edinburgh, 1869), 74.
[5] *Census of Scotland, 1861*, ii, 87-88.   [6] Ibid., ii, pp. lxx, 322-3.
[7] See below, pp. 377-8.   [8] *Census of Scotland, 1861*, ii, 314-17.
[9] In 1861 Glasgow had over 600 lawyers, advocates, judges and law clerks, Edinburgh over 1,500. Ibid., ii, 310-11.

in the earlier part of the period 1859-73, for example in 1862,[1] to have inhibited the council from taking action as a pressure group. The abundant middle class presence in the city may also have enlarged the desire of some of the delegates to the trades council to demonstrate their own 'respectability'.[2] It probably also explains why the council so often asked middle class people to preside or speak at its public meetings.[3]

How far trade union organisation existed among the trades and industries of Edinburgh and Leith in 1859-73 is a question to which it is difficult for lack of records to give a very precise answer. It seems certain, however, that unions existed, even if not perhaps in every case continuously, among almost all the skilled trades of any significance. Some of these unions had been established for many years. The Edinburgh Union Society of Journeymen Bookbinders had existed since 1822,[4] the plasterers' society evidently from 1827,[5] and the cabinetmakers' from 1836.[6] The printers' union, or Edinburgh Typographical Society, a branch of the Scottish Typographical Association, had been formed between 1826 and 1836.[7] On the other hand, one or two unions mentioned in the trades council minutes were formed, or perhaps re-formed, only during the period 1859-73. The tinplate workers, for example, founded their union in 1866[8] and the milling trades theirs in 1873.[9]

The extent of trade union organisation among unskilled or semi-skilled workers in Edinburgh and Leith is much more obscure. The carters evidently had a union in 1861, when it was reported to have offered help to Glasgow carters on strike.[10] In the trade union boom

---

[1] Below, pp. 109-11.   [2] Below, p. xl.   [3] Below, p. xl.

[4] Its minutes are preserved unbroken from 1822 to date. Those up to 1956 are in NLS, Acc. 4395.

[5] *Rules of Edinburgh United Operative Plasterers' Benefit Protection Society* (Edinburgh, 1875), 1. Scottish Record Office, Edinburgh (hereafter SRO), FS 7/22.

[6] Minutes, 1836-72, Edinburgh Cabinet and Chair Makers' Society. These and the minutes dated 1833-7 of the Society's predecessor are shortly to be deposited in NLS.

[7] S. Gillespie, *A Hundred Years of Progress: The Record of the Scottish Typographical Association 1853-1953* (Glasgow, 1953), 21. But union organisation among the Edinburgh printers can be traced back to the late eighteenth century. Gillespie, op. cit., 19.

[8] Minutes of the United Tinplate Workers of Edinburgh and Leith, 1866-1952. NLS, Acc. 4050.

[9] *Rules of the Edinburgh, Leith and District Milling Trade Friendly and Protective League* (Edinburgh, 1873). SRO, FS 7/36.

[10] *Scotsman*, 14 November 1861.

of early 1866 the gardeners formed in Edinburgh the Scottish
Gardeners' Protection Association which sought a minimum wage
of fifteen shillings a week.[1] The Leith dockers had a union in 1866
whose 'own funds were so large that they had refused an offered
contribution of £200 from the Glasgow union'.[2] There was also a
united labourers' society, with a numerous Irish element,[3] and it was
apparently this union which affiliated to the trades council in 1868.
Railwaymen appear to have formed a union in the city by 1872.[4]
On the whole it seems probable that trade unionism among the
unskilled or semi-skilled in Edinburgh, as elsewhere in Britain, was
much more limited and ephemeral than among the skilled workers.
Local trade unionism was predominantly though not exclusively
that of the skilled workers or labour aristocracy, and the composition
of the trades council illustrated this fact.

The minutes throw only a little light on the numbers and proportion of trade unionists in the city. Probably very few unions
could claim, as the glasscutters' delegate did at a meeting of the
council in 1861,[5] that non-unionists were a relatively small proportion in their trades. Alexander Fraser, blacksmiths' delegate, may
have been referring to the position in Scotland or Britain rather than
in Edinburgh when he remarked at the same meeting that 'the
proportion of non-society to society men in the most of trades were
as 3 to 1'. But John Gardner, tailors, bore out Fraser's assessment by
admitting that 'the unionists in his trade in Edinburgh bore the
proportion of one fourth'. No doubt proportions varied throughout
the period, particularly during the trade union booms in early
1866 and the early 1870s. But such statistics of membership as it
has been possible to obtain suggest that total union membership in
Edinburgh was markedly increasing between 1859 and 1873. The
membership of the local branch of the Amalgamated Society of
Engineers rose fairly steadily from a monthly average of ninety in
1859 to double that number in 1873, and much the same rate of

---

[1] *Scotsman,* 15 March 1866.

[2] *Scotsman,* 21 March and 16 May 1866.

[3] *Scotsman,* 19 November 1866, 25 August 1873.

[4] P. Bagwell, *The Railwaymen: The History of the National Union of Railwaymen*
(London, 1963), 62-63. The Amalgamated Society of Railway Servants for Scotland
had been formed in March of that year; its rules are in SRO, FS 7/30.

[5] Below, p. 65.

increase took place in the Leith branch founded in 1861.[1] The average membership of the Edinburgh Typographical Society for the five years up to 1861 had been 265,[2] but seems generally to have been around 650 between 1868 and 1874.[3] When the Associated Carpenters and Joiners Society was formed in 1861 its Edinburgh branch had 181 members,[4] but membership must have grown very considerably by the end of the decade, since the Society then had at least three branches in the city. Not all local trade unionists may have been included in the claim by the Edinburgh delegate to the St Martin's Hall trade union conference in London in 1867 that he represented 6,000 unionists.[5] On the other hand there was probably some exaggeration in the assertion by a delegate to the trades council in 1868 that there were 10,000 trade unionists in Edinburgh.[6]

Of the unions in the city there were three organisational types. Some, such as the cabinetmakers, coopers, tinplate workers and (until 1872) the larger of the two bookbinders' unions, were purely local societies. Others, including the blacksmiths, moulders, masons, and (from 1861) the joiners, were branches of Scottish unions. The third category consisted of branches of British unions, such as the engineers, glassmakers and coachmakers. It is not certain to which category every union affiliated to the trades council belonged. But over the period as a whole it seems that branches of Scottish unions formed the largest category, and the remainder divided fairly equally between purely local unions and branches of British unions. The growing strength of trade unionism and the increasing necessity for better organisation in strikes and lock-outs was reflected in the tendency for the purely local unions to merge into Scottish or British unions. Thus the joiners in 1861 and the tailors and slaters in 1866 merged into Scottish unions, and the bookbinders in 1872 into the existing Edinburgh branch of a British union. These differences of structure were not without significance in some of the

---

[1] *Monthly Reports of the Amalgamated Society of Engineers,* 1859-73. Mitchell Library, S.331.8812 AMA.

[2] Minutes of the Society, 13 July 1861. NLS, Acc. 4068.

[3] Minutes of the Society, 6 January 1869, 13 March 1874.

[4] S. Higgenbottam, *Our Society's History* (Manchester, 1939), 56.

[5] Below, p. 190, n. 2; W. J. Davis, *The British Trade Union Congress: History and Recollections* (London, 1910), 142.

[6] *Scotsman,* 12 March 1868.

discussions at the trades council, particularly on the questions of federation and the legalisation of unions.

The unions affiliated to the council were drawn from metal and engineering trades, building and furnishing, printing and book-binding, clothing and leather, and food, glass and several other miscellaneous crafts such as coachmaking. Thirty-one unions were represented in the years between 1859 and 1873. But as the engineers and bakers each at some time had two branches affiliated and the joiners three, the aggregate number of organisations represented was thirty-five. In any one year, however, the number of affiliates was very much smaller. The largest affiliation appears to have been twenty-three or twenty-four (in 1868), but only half a dozen organisations were affiliated in 1866, and the annual average was about fifteen. Only one union, the tailors, appears to have been continuously affiliated from 1859 to 1873. Their delegates, along with those of the blacksmiths, joiners, cabinetmakers, brassfounders, printers, bookbinders, and glasscutters, played the most active part in the affairs of the council. The joiners, tailors and blacksmiths indeed provided the president and the secretary of the council for most of the period.[1]

Some unions in Edinburgh and Leith were not affiliated to the trades council at any time in the period. They included the litho-graphic printers[2] and a small branch at Leith of the boilermakers.[3] It seems likely that unions of sawmillers, shipwrights, brushmakers, sailmakers, ropemakers and hatters also existed,[4] but if they did they were not affiliated to the council. There was, as already noted, no affiliation of any union of unskilled workers, apart from that of the labourers.

[1] Below, appendix I, pp. 373-4. Detail of affiliations is given below, appendix II pp. 377-9.

[2] Below, p. 204. They affiliated, however, in 1874. Minutes of trades council, 10 March 1874.

[3] Information kindly provided by Mr D. McGarvey, president, Amalgamated Society of Boilermakers. Unions of hairdressers (below, p. 275) and horseshoers (below, p. 245) also existed, and the latter affiliated to the trades council in 1874 (minutes of trades council, 12 May 1874).

[4] Representatives from these trades took part in the trades council processions in 1866 and 1873. *Edinburgh Evening Courant*, 19 November 1866; *Scotsman*, 23 August 1873. For sawyers, see also below, p. 335. The hatters affiliated to the trades council in 1875 (minutes of trades council, 27 April 1875).

The reasons for non-affiliation or for discontinuous affiliation were not completely summed up in the sour comment by the vice-president of the trades council in 1863, that the council was 'well known when any class wanted anything from us but unknown at any other time'.[1] The withdrawal of the Leith bakers was due to inability to find members willing or able to journey up to the High Street of Edinburgh in the winter.[2] The glassmakers also had difficulty in finding delegates.[3] Mutual rivalry may have caused the disaffiliation of what seem to have been two distinct groups of masons in 1859.[4] Withdrawal or non-affiliation was in some cases probably due to the weakening or collapse of the union, or the inability of some smaller unions to afford the affiliation fees. The most significant absence from the council was that before 1867 of the unions in the printing and allied trades. The reason for the printers' non-affiliation may have been a belief either that the council was not efficiently conducted or that it was too inclined to concern itself with political questions.[5]

If the comparatively modest number of unions affiliated in most years, especially before 1867, limited the effectiveness of the trades council, so did the irregular attendance of some delegates. Before 1867 representation may have been on a *pro rata* basis. Several unions, including the brassfounders and the bakers, not infrequently had three delegates present and on a few occasions the joiners and engineers had four. After the reorganisation of 1867 each affiliate was allowed a maximum of two delegates.[6] The absences of some delegates were numerous. None from the engineers seems to have attended during eight months in 1861. The plumbers' delegate J. G. Bald was present at only one-third of the meetings of the council in 1859 and the french polishers' delegate at even fewer. The largest recorded attendance of delegates appears to have been twenty-six.[7] Because of disaffiliations and poor attendances, meetings of the council were reduced on ten occasions before 1867 to the bare

---

[1] Below, p. 115.   [2] Below, p. 299.
[3] Below, p. 259.   [4] Below, pp. 17-18.
[5] 'The printers withheld their support from the Trades Council for many years and only became affiliated on the promise that it would reform itself.' Letter by 'O.K.' in *Scottish Typographical Circular*, July 1871, in NLS, Acc. 4068; below, pp. 323-4.
[6] *Laws for the Government of the United Trades Council* (Edinburgh, 1867), 4.
[7] Below, pp. 95-96, 284.

quorum of five and there were half a dozen other occasions in the same period when not even a quorum was present. The average recorded attendance of delegates throughout the years 1859-73 appears to have been only twelve. No doubt irregular attendance was due to the other commitments of some delegates and to the irresponsibility of one or two others. But it probably also reflected, at least on occasion, both weak organisation within some unions and a lack of effectiveness on the part of the trades council.

Some delegates were office-bearers in their union or branch. Thus J. S. Common was secretary of the Edinburgh Typographical Society. More notably, three general secretaries of important national Scottish unions were delegates for a time: James Hart, masons, John McWhinnie, tailors, and William Paterson of the Associated Carpenters and Joiners' Society. Their presence, or at least that of Paterson, increased the prestige and activities of the council.

Of almost all the 300 or so delegates to the council in 1859-73 nothing is known beyond what is recorded in these minutes. Biographical information, in some cases meagre, has been discovered for about a dozen only. Of these one was John Borrowman, president of the council in 1859. He was victimised in that year for his trade unionist activities and consequently set up in business as a joiner with his fellow-delegate William Caw.[1] Borrowman was a founder of St Cuthbert's Co-operative Association in Edinburgh in 1859 and until 1866 was its president. For the following five years he was the first president of the Edinburgh Northern District Co-operative Society.[2] Like Borrowman, William Caw, who was secretary of his union, was dismissed from his employment on account of his trade unionist activities.[3] He too was a founder of St Cuthbert's Co-operative Association and was its secretary from 1859 until 1862. A third joiners' delegate to the trades council was William Paterson. He was one of the most outstanding delegates. Born in Elgin in 1843, Paterson came to Edinburgh to work as a

---

[1] *First Fifty Years of St Cuthbert's Co-operative Association*, ed. W. Maxwell (Edinburgh, 1909), 27-28.

[2] Maxwell, op. cit., 257, 271-2. Borrowman's sons were also active co-operators: John was the first secretary of the Edinburgh Northern Society (Maxwell, op. cit., 272); for James see below, p. 343, n. 1.

[3] Maxwell, op. cit., 28, 259.

joiner.[1] He was elected branch secretary and in 1868 general secretary of the Associated Carpenters and Joiners' Society of Scotland. The trades council put him up as a candidate in the municipal election of 1870.[2] He was a member in 1881-2 of the parliamentary committee of the Trades Union Congress, and in the following year was appointed an assistant factory inspector, one of the first working men to hold the office. In his Edinburgh days he made himself an authority on fire-fighting and was firemaster of Glasgow from 1884 until his death in 1906.

Political activity was a characteristic of almost all the remaining delegates about whom something is known. John Cubie, elected secretary of the council in 1873, was born in Fife in 1840, the son of a miner.[3] He came to Edinburgh in the early 1860s and became a foreman cabinetmaker. An active Liberal who became a Unionist after 1885, Cubie was a town councillor in Edinburgh from 1891 until 1900 and was appointed registrar of the Canongate district shortly before his death in 1903. Much less is known about William Troup, tailors, who was president of the council from 1859 to 1867. He was also president in 1867-8 of the Edinburgh branch of the Scottish National Reform League.[4] In later minutes of the trades council[5] there is a reference to Troup from which it appears that he had by then fallen into poverty. The council declined, however, as a body to make any donation to him. Neil McLean, another tailors' delegate, later secretary of his union and from 1880 to 1887 of the trades council, was the author of a pamphlet entitled *The Sweating System in the Tailoring Trade*.[6] He was an official of St Cuthbert's Co-operative Association and in 1889 a candidate in Calton ward of the Labour Electoral Association. He died in 1895.[7] Two delegates, both upholsterers, whose political activities had begun in the Chartist movement were Henry Ranken and Gabriel Wallace. Ranken had been a leading Edinburgh Chartist and editor of the

[1] This note is based mainly on his obituary in *Glasgow Herald*, 18 December 1906.
[2] Below, p. 304. According to R. W. Postgate, *The Builders' History* (London, 1923), 261, Paterson had been a Liberal parliamentary candidate in 1866, but no confirmation of this has been found.
[3] Information from his obituary in *Scotsman*, 2 March 1903.
[4] *Scotsman*, 6 February 1868.
[5] 25 January 1876.
[6] 7 pp., Edinburgh, 1880. NLS, Acc. 1880. 27 (22).
[7] Mr W. H. Marwick has kindly provided most of this information about McLean.

North British Express when arrested in 1848, convicted of sedition and sentenced to four months' imprisonment.[1] He was secretary of the local Ernest Jones Memorial Committee in 1869. President of the Edinburgh Mechanics' Subscription Library in 1847 and vice-president in 1853, Ranken was its secretary from 1855 to 1880.[2] Along with Ranken, Gabriel Wallace was said to have 'suffered hardships and privations' in 1848 in their 'noble efforts to emancipate their class'.[3] Wallace subsequently became an energetic advocate of temperance, but remained an active radical and was president of an Edinburgh branch of the Irish nationalists when elected a town councillor in 1891. He died within a fortnight of his election, at the age of seventy-five.[4]

Political activity thus eventually carried several delegates into the town council but carried only one into the House of Commons. John Goundry Holburn, tinplate workers, elected president of the trades council in 1873, was an Englishman born in Durham thirty years earlier.[5] As a youth he had been on board a transport vessel in the Crimean War and 'saw the bloodshed of that strife'.[6] A Gladstonian Liberal, Holburn was a town councillor in Leith from 1890 to 1895. He was then elected Liberal and Labour M.P. for North-West Lanarkshire and held the seat until his death in 1899.

If Holburn of all the delegates to the council in 1859-73 climbed furthest up the ladder of respectability, one who fell off it altogether was James Hart, a delegate from Edinburgh lodge of the Scottish masons in 1862-5. Hart became general secretary of his union in 1862 and his leadership helped it to gain within four years the almost universal concession to its members of the nine hours' day.[7] Possibly the strain of waging this campaign contributed to Hart's fall from grace. From about 1865 his central committee suspected him of drunkenness, complained of his 'filthy language' and suspended him,

---

[1] *Edinburgh Evening Courant*, 16 November 1848.
[2] *Laws and Catalogue of the Edinburgh Mechanics' Subscription Library* (Edinburgh, 1874, 7th edn.), iii-iv, in Edinburgh Room, Edinburgh Central Public Library (hereafter EPL), YZ 921.E.23.M; Oliver and Boyd's *Almanac* (1880), 931.
[3] *Reformer*, 7 October 1871.
[4] *Scotsman*, 17 November 1891.
[5] *Who Was Who* (London, 1953), i, 345.
[6] *Scotsman*, 20 May 1873, reporting Holburn's speech at the peace conference in Glasgow (below, p. 360).
[7] R. W. Postgate, *The Builders' History* (London, 1923), 255-6; below, pp. xxxvii-viii.

but he was reinstated on appeal to the general membership. Hart then embezzled £179 of the union funds. According to the historian of the building trades unions, Hart on realising his detection was certain exclaimed 'the sooner I make a hole in the water the better', left the office and never returned. Press reports[1] show that Hart reappeared, however, two years later in Glasgow, where he was recognised by a member of his former union and handed over to the police. He was charged at the Edinburgh police court on 13 February 1869 with embezzling union funds, remitted to the High Court, granted bail there to secure evidence for his defence, but failed to re-appear and was declared an outlaw. About his subsequent career nothing has been discovered.

The trades council was not a wealthy organisation. The affiliation fees paid by unions to the council formed the most regular and so far as can be discovered the most important part of its income. The rate of annual subscription payable before 1867 is not known and possibly there was then no fixed rate, since a new or amended rule approved in 1860 recommended that affiliates 'should make quarterly subscriptions among their members or vote a portion of their Funds' to the council.[2] Fixed scales both of subscriptions and of admission money were included in the rules drawn up at the reconstruction of the council in 1867.[3] Some affiliates failed, however, to pay conscientiously; moreover the rate of subscription itself was described by 1869 as 'altogether inadequate'.[4] Consequently it was soon afterwards doubled, and the amended rules published in 1873 increased the amount of admission money.[5] Other sources of income to the council included charges or collections at public meetings, profit from the summer excursion, and in one year a donation of £10 by a Tory advocate.[6] The income of the council is known for only half of the fifteen years between 1859 and 1873. It was £47 in 1861[7] but only about half that amount in each of the years between 1867 and 1873.[8] These statistics bear out the frequent references in the minutes to the limited financial

[1] *Reformer*, 20 February and 27 March 1869.   [2] Below, p. 37.

[3] Below, pp. 193-4, 196.   [4] Below, p. 264.

[5] *Laws of the United Trades Council* (Edinburgh, 1873), 4. In trades council office.

[6] Below, p. 299.   [7] Below, p. 86.

[8] *Reformer*, 2 January 1869 and 2 September 1871; annual reports of the council for 1868-9, 1871-2 and 1872-3 (EPL, YHD 6661).

resources of the council. Lack of money occasionally hampered it in carrying out its objects, and in particular appears to have been a chief reason for its absence from representation at any of the first five Trades Union Congresses.

The objects of the trades council as set forth in the rules adopted at the reorganisation of 1867 were 'the advancement and protection of the rights of labour; as also the well-being of the working classes generally'.[1] These objects were to be carried out '(1) by assisting to organise Trade Societies for friendly and other purposes;[2] (2) by endeavouring to bring about an amicable adjustment in cases of dispute between Employers and Employed; or when such dispute cannot be amicably settled, by rendering sympathy, and devising means for the support of such as require assistance;[3] (3) by agitating for a reduction of the hours of labour, instituting holidays, etc; (4) by holding meetings, or taking other measures for the public advocacy of the just claims of labour; (5) by petitioning Parliament on such questions as may affect the rights and interests of the working classes of the kingdom; (6) by watching over proceedings in our Local or Law Courts affecting their rights; (7) by co-operating with similar Associations throughout the kingdom; (8) and by any other means which may from time to time be deemed advisable by the Council'. These formal objects probably differed little from those contained in the earlier rules of the council, of which no copy is known to survive. Possibly the chief difference was that if at the beginning of the period 1859–73 it had been 'contrary to the laws and constitution of the council to engage in Politics',[4] no such debarment existed under the rules of 1867.

A turning point in the council's attitude to political questions came in 1861. Although some delegates were politically active themselves,[5] the council evidently shared until then the widespread opposition among trade unionists 'to trades meetings being mixed with politics'.[6] This opposition was a result mainly of dissension and failures among earlier working class political movements, especially

---

[1] *Laws for the Government of the United Trades Council* (Edinburgh, 1867), 3-4.
[2] The last five words were deleted in the amended rules of 1873.
[3] The words 'in the opinion of the Council' were inserted before 'require assistance' in the amended rules of 1873.
[4] Below, p. 71.   [5] See *Scotsman*, 26 April 1859 and 16 April 1860.
[6] *Glasgow Sentinel*, 2 November 1861.

Chartism. If union was strength, politics were likely to be divisive. Their exclusion was perhaps partly also a relic of an earlier fear of prosecution for sedition.[1] But the issue by Glasgow trades council in November 1861 of an appeal to working men throughout the United Kingdom to demand political reform persuaded the Edinburgh council, despite the opposition of several delegates, to 'go into the reform movement'.[2] Even if shortly afterwards it declined to support the national conference in London on reform on the ground that 'as a body of trades delegates we do not meddle with politics',[3] and if the older suspicion of 'politics' continued to appear fitfully in later minutes, the council nevertheless after 1861 increasingly engaged in political activity. Its change of attitude reflected a general revival of political interest and agitation among the working class in Britain in the 1860s. The revival was partly a result of three international events to which there are some references in the minutes: the Italian risorgimento and particularly the visit in 1864 of Garibaldi to Britain, the American civil war, and the Polish revolt of 1863. But the political revival was also in effect the growth of working class demands for enfranchisement and for reform of laws affecting labour and the trade unions. As the *Address* of the Glasgow trades council had put it in 1861: 'We are aware that many [trade unionists] are opposed to trades meetings being mixed with politics; we cannot coincide with such views so long as Trades Societies are amenable to the law. There are several matters in law that affect them, such as those relating to combinations of workmen and the inequality of the law of master and servant. . . . By what means are these measures to be rectified or obtained but by political power, the want of which affects the whole labouring class?'[4]

In Edinburgh in 1866 it was the trades council which called a preliminary meeting to organise working class demand for reform.[5] There is some contradiction in the minutes as to whether or not the council then left this ad hoc meeting to carry on the campaign. But the council's members certainly took a prominent part in the subsequent agitation and its president presided over the ad hoc meetings.[6]

[1] H. A. Clegg, A. Fox and A. F. Thompson, *A History of British Trade Unions since 1889* (Oxford, 1964), 48.
[2] Below, p. 71.
[3] Below, p. 80.
[4] *Glasgow Sentinel*, 2 November 1861.
[5] Below, pp. 185-6.
[6] *Edinburgh Evening Courant*, 25 October 1866.

The demand put forward was for manhood suffrage[1] and the only reason the *ad hoc* meetings did not then form themselves into a branch of the Reform League, as had been done in Glasgow, was 'so as not to ask working men for money both for admission to the hall and to join the League'.[2] Although he dissented from the demand for manhood suffrage there was close co-operation with Duncan McLaren, the Radical M.P. for the city, whose middle class supporters undertook to pay for the cost of erecting platforms in Queen's Park for the huge working class reform demonstration on 17 November 1866.[3] Some 14,000 working men from over fifty separate trades or occupations marched in procession through the main streets, watched by between half and two-thirds of the population of the city. The crowd around the speakers' platform at Queen's Park was estimated at 40,000.[4] The chairmen were Independent Liberal[5] town councillors, but the speakers were workmen, several of whom were or later became delegates to the trades council, such as Dewar, blacksmiths, and McWhinnie, tailors.

Not surprisingly the political activities of the trades council increased after the passage of the Reform Act of 1867-8. In 1869 and again in 1870 the council put up its own candidates at the municipal elections. The minutes show clearly that throughout the period 1859-73 the sympathies of the council, or at least of a majority of its members, were normally Radical.[6] But in 1869 the council unanimously resolved that it would in 'future connect itself with none of the present pollitical Parties but confine itself to the representation of labour',[7] and supported John McWhinnie, a tailors' delegate, in Canongate ward in opposition to the Independent

[1] Ibid., 8 October 1866. [2] Ibid., 25 October 1866.
[3] Ibid., 8 November 1866. [4] Ibid., 19 November 1866.
[5] Party or group labels have been used in editorial matter as follows: all Liberal (or Whig) M.P.s have been described as Liberals unless the former are normally described in standard works as Radicals, in which case that term has been used here. In municipal politics, however, the allies and supporters of the Radical M.P. Duncan McLaren were almost always referred to at the time not as Radicals but as Independent Liberals and this latter term has been kept here.
[6] Only a handful appear to have been Tories or Tory sympathisers: Scott, glasscutters (below, p. 230), Lawson, tinplate workers (below, pp. 252, 254), Fleming, skinners, and Young, cabinetmakers. All except Lawson were members of a working men's committee which in 1867 presented an address to Disraeli. *Scotsman*, 26-31 October 1867.
[7] Below, p. 273.

c

Liberals. The 'political jugglery' of the Independent Liberals, which helped to bring about this notable though temporary break with them, may be followed below.[1] The initial decision by the council to put up a candidate in 1869 seems also, however, to have been a reaction against the town council's refusal to grant a wages increase to the city scavengers,[2] and possibly too a consequence of the earlier struggle to secure the appointment in Edinburgh of an inspector under the Workshops Regulation Act.[3] If the defeat of McWhinnie, who received 269 votes against 622 for the Independent Liberal and 655 for the Tory,[4] persuaded the council of the unlikelihood of returning working men candidates opposed by the Independent Liberals, it also persuaded the latter to come to terms with the trades council before the 1870 municipal elections. Consequently when the council, resolved into a Municipal Election Committee and with an understanding also with the Temperance Electoral Association, put up William Paterson in Canongate and J. H. Waterston in St Cuthbert's ward, no Independent Liberal stood against them. Waterston and Paterson were both defeated, Waterston heavily[5] but Paterson by only 923 votes to 872.[6] This was the last occasion in the period covered by these minutes on which the trades council put up its own candidates in municipal elections. But it learned some obvious lessons and afterwards pressed for the alteration of polling day from Tuesdays to Saturdays, and for extension of polling hours. These and a number of other demands, including the ballot, prohibition of canvassing and the use of cabs in elections, closing of public houses on polling day, and increased parliamentary representation for Scotland, became part of the programme of the Scottish Reform Union set up by the trades council municipal election committee at the end of 1870. Though the Reform Union promised to 'embrace every opportunity of securing a more extended representation of labour in civic bodies', it evidently did not attempt to run candidates of its own.[7]

Even in their 'non-political' days before the early 1860s, trade unions and trades councils had been ready to oppose 'the tyranny of any legislative enactments to coerce trade societies, or of a similar

[1] Pp. 271-3.   [2] Below, pp. 264, 267-8.   [3] Below, p. xxxvi.
[4] Scotsman, 3 November 1869.   [5] Below, p. 305, n. 2.
[6] Scotsman, 2 November 1870.   [7] Reformer, 17 December 1870.

character to the Masters and Servants Bill. . . .'[1] Much of the period
covered by the minutes below embraced a struggle by trade unions
over both their own legal position and the master and servant laws.
Under the latter a workman who broke his contract of service
committed a criminal act and was liable to fine or imprisonment,
whereas breach by a master could be the subject of only a civil
action for damages. In 1861 some 10,393 cases had been heard in
England and Wales and about 700 in Scotland.[2] Workmen doubted
the impartiality or competence of the bench in some cases dealt with
in justice of the peace courts, and believed that the master and servant
laws were used to break strikes.[3] In England a workman accused of
breach of contract could be and normally was summoned to appear
in court, but in Scotland he was invariably arrested.[4] For this reason
and because prosecutions were particularly numerous in the mining,
iron and pottery industries, of which Glasgow was a centre, it was
Glasgow trades council which in 1863 originated the national movement for the reform of the master and servant laws. Two of the
original Glasgow proposals were considered too mild by Edinburgh
trades council, which sent a letter of support to, but was not
represented at, the national conference of trade unionists held in
London from 30 May to 2 June 1864 and convened by Glasgow
trades council.[5] The conference set up a national master and servant
executive committee, which, with George Newton as secretary, was
virtually Glasgow trades council. Though the Edinburgh council
secured 3,000 signatures to a petition to parliament, it does not
appear to have conducted a particularly vigorous local campaign.
This was probably due partly to the reported absence of cases of prosecution in three of the main organised trades in the city (masons,
joiners and tailors).[6] Concern with its own reorganisation in the first

---

[1] S. and B. Webb, *The History of Trade Unionism* (London, 1920), 188-9, quoting
from a report by the London Committee of Trade Delegates to a national trade union
conference in 1845.
[2] *Scotsman,* 21 January 1865, quoting George Newton, Glasgow trades council.
[3] Daphne Simon, 'Master and Servant', in *Democracy and the Labour Movement,* ed.
J. Saville (London, 1954), 168.
[4] *Report of a Conference on the Law of Masters and Workmen under their Contract of Service*
(Glasgow, 1864), 5.
[5] A. E. Musson, *The Congress of 1868* (London, 1955), 12, n. 2; Daphne Simon, art.
cit., 177.
[6] Below, p. 175, though for a case concerning a joiner see also below, p. 97.

half of 1867 precluded the council from renewing the agitation during the passage of the Master and Servant Act of that year, which made some concessions to workmen but retained in certain circumstances punishment by imprisonment. Dissatisfaction with the Act doubtless largely explained the council's readiness to dissociate itself from the Glasgow executive committee's banquet for Lord Elcho, chairman of the select committee on whose report the Act had been based.

The council played a more energetic part in the struggle of 1866–1875 against those laws or legal doctrines and judgements which threatened the strength and effectiveness of trade unions themselves. The minutes contain no reference to the explosive event that precipitated the struggle, the Sheffield 'outrage' of October 1866 in which some members of the saw-grinders' union dropped a can of gun-powder down the chimney of a 'blackleg'.[1] Nor is there any mention of the case of *Hornby v. Close* in January 1867, in which the ruling of Queen's Bench that unions were in restraint of trade and therefore illegal removed from their funds the legal protection till then believed to be granted to them by depositing their rules with the registrar under the Friendly Societies Act of 1855. Its own 'state of disorganisation' prevented the council as such from being represented at the St Martin's Hall conference in London in March 1867, the purpose of which was to agitate for legal protection of trade union funds and to prepare the union case for the Royal Commission on trade unions set up after the Sheffield events. The minutes make only a few brief references to the Royal Commission itself and no representative of the council was called before it. The fresh legal difficulties raised for trade unionists by several prosecutions, including two in Scotland, arising from strikes or threats of strikes receive some notice, and on the leading case of *R. v. Druitt* the council held a public meeting addressed by George Druitt himself.[2]

Little explanation is offered in the minutes for the council's severe criticism of the two Bills to establish the legality of unions and protect their funds that were drawn up by the 'Junta' and its allies,

---

[1] S. and B. Webb, op. cit., 259–60. But at a public meeting held by the council on 5 July 1867 (below, p. 194, n. 1) a resolution was passed denouncing the Sheffield 'atrocities'.

[2] Below, pp. 192–4, 348.

who formed the Conference of Amalgamated Trades,[1] and were introduced into the Commons in 1868 and 1869 respectively. But the chief criticism of the more important of the two Bills, that introduced by Hughes and Mundella in 1869, appears to have been its withholding from unions of the power to sue or be sued.[2] Similar criticisms voiced at the United Trades Conference of Glasgow had been narrowly voted down.[3] The Edinburgh council rejected the view that the conferment on the unions of such power would have 'subjected them to constant and harassing interference by Courts of Justice'.[4] As dissatisfaction with the first of the 'Junta's' Bills had led the council to send a deputation to the Tory lord advocate 'to solicit him to draw up a bill',[5] so dissatisfaction with the Hughes–Mundella Bill led the council to take what was for it a notable initiative. It convened in Edinburgh from 8 to 11 February 1870 a national conference of Scottish trade union organisations. The conference was small. There were twenty-two delegates, drawn from Glasgow, Edinburgh and Dundee, and including at least two general secretaries. The only trades council represented was Edinburgh itself, though Dundee had signified 'hearty approval', and there were no representatives from any union, such as the engineers, which embraced the whole of Britain. The conference, which was said to represent 20,000 trade unionists, amended all but four of the sixteen clauses of the Hughes–Mundella Bill. The most important amendment was reversal of the clause which had withheld from unions the power to sue or be sued.[6] The amended Bill was subsequently revised for the trades council by the Tory advocate

---

[1] Below, p. 207. 'Junta' was the term applied by the Webbs to the group of general secretaries of 'new model' unions who formed in London 'a cabinet of the Trade Union Movement': Robert Applegarth of the Amalgamated Carpenters and Joiners, William Allan of the Amalgamated Engineers, Daniel Guile of the Ironfounders, Edwin Coulson of the Bricklayers, and George Odger (below, p. 280, n. 5). S. and B. Webb, op. cit., 233-41.

[2] Below, p. 260, n. 2. The *Reformer*, 19 June 1869, added: 'Such a bill may meet the views of . . . trade unions in England, where sick, funeral and trades contributions are all combined in one common fund; but in Scotland, where sick and funeral contributions are generally, and as we think properly, kept separate and distinct, . . . there is good reason for opposition to the Bill'.

[3] A letter from Edinburgh trades council in *Reformer*, 26 June 1869, upbraided Glasgow supporters of the Bill for 'worshipping the opinions of a few magnates in London'.

[4] S. and B. Webb, op. cit., 271.   [5] Below, p. 208.

[6] *Scotsman*, 9 and 10 February 1870.

Charles Scott[1] and was sent to the home secretary, to several M.P.s, and, in lieu of a delegate, to the Trades Union Congress held in London early in 1871. By that date the trade union Bill introduced by the government and based mainly on the Hughes–Mundella Bill marked a new stage in the struggle. The concession by the government Bill of full legal recognition to unions and protection for their funds was offset by the penal provisions of its third clause, subsequently enacted separately as the Criminal Law Amendment Act. By prescribing imprisonment for vaguely worded acts of molestation, obstruction, intimidation, and watching and besetting, it made picketing a hazardous undertaking for trade unionists. The trades council demanded deletion of this third clause.[2] But probably because of an absence of prosecutions in Edinburgh under the Act the minutes only occasionally reflect between 1871 and 1873 the growing agitation by trade unionists in Britain against 'this tyrannical and one-sided measure'.[3]

As a result of the London gas stokers' case at the end of 1872 the agitation broadened into one against all penal legislation covering trade disputes. The huge demonstration held by the trades council in Edinburgh on 23 August 1873, though preceded by several in England, was the first on the issue in Scotland. Almost 16,000 trade unionists from all over Scotland were estimated to have marched in the procession from Bruntsfield Links to the Queen's Park 'to the music of thirty-six bands and four gangs of pipers'.[4] At each of four platforms surrounded by large crowds at the Queen's Park resolutions were carried that demanded immediate repeal of the Criminal Law Amendment Act, protested against the criminal clauses of the Master and Servant Act and the application of the law of conspiracy in labour disputes, and urged support only for those parliamentary candidates pledged to press these demands. Among the speakers, who included several trades council delegates, was the miners' leader Alexander McDonald. Two of six Perth trade unionists who had been convicted and imprisoned under the Criminal Law Amendment Act also appeared on the platforms. The remarks

---

[1] *Scotsman*, 4 May 1870.
[2] Below, p. 314. The fifth clause, to which the council also objected, withheld from the courts power to enforce internal trade union agreements.
[3] Below, p. 362.   [4] *Scotsman*, 25 August 1873.

of several speakers reflected disenchantment with the Liberal government and many of its supporters in parliament, only five of whom, including John Miller, M.P. for Edinburgh, had sent letters of sympathy to the demonstration. It marked a parting of the ways between local trade unionists and Duncan McLaren, who was bitterly criticised by several speakers and described as 'the man who had put upon the statute book the picketing clauses of the Act', and, more bluntly, as 'a traitor to the working class interest'. Two local trade unionists at the demonstration urged the return of working men to parliament and one of them called on the unions to set up a fund to maintain a representative there. Despite the opposition to him, however, of trade unionists, some of whom including William Paterson of the joiners were associated with an anti-McLaren Advanced Liberal Association,[1] McLaren was re-elected at the general election of 1874. Miller, who had promised to support repeal of the Criminal Law Amendment Act, lost his seat to an ally of McLaren.[2]

Among other subjects of labour legislation referred to in the minutes were workmen's compensation, arrestment of wages, and the Factory Acts. Reform of the law of arrestment of wages in Scotland was a demand raised and pressed particularly by Glasgow trades council. The law, 'a very pernicious one',[3] whose effect on workingmen and their families was outlined in a petition to parliament by the Edinburgh council in 1870,[4] allowed a creditor to detain in the hands of third parties the goods of his debtor until the debt was paid.[5] In Glasgow there were some 30,000 cases a year.[6] George Anderson, elected as a Radical in Glasgow in 1868, pressed in parliament for reform and the consequent Act of 1870 exempted from arrestment wages up to twenty shillings per week. The Edinburgh council played a far more notable role locally in pressing for the enforcement of the Bakehouse Regulation Act of 1863 and the Workshop Regulation Act of 1867. The Bakehouse Act prohibited employment of young persons between 9 p.m. and 5 a.m. and dealt also with sanitation and cleanliness. It was supposed to be administered by the local sanitary authority, and the factory

---

[1] This seems not to have been the group of that title mentioned below, p. 354.
[2] J. B. Mackie, *Life of Duncan McLaren* (Edinburgh, 1888), ii, 53-57.
[3] Below, pp. 85-86.　　　　　　[4] Below, pp. 289-90.
[5] *Encyclopedia Britannica* (Cambridge, 1910), ii, 647.
[6] W. H. Marwick, *Economic Developments in Victorian Scotland* (London, 1936), 151.

inspectorate had no right of entry into bakehouses until 1878.[1] That the Act was virtually a dead letter in Edinburgh is indicated in the minutes. The Factory Extension Act of 1867, which extended control over most industries and over any manufacturing premises in which fifty or more persons were employed, and the Workshop Regulation Act, which applied to any manufacturing establishment in which fewer than fifty were employed, were at first 'ignored, or where the law was acknowledged, systematically violated in Edinburgh'.[2] The minutes show the trades council bringing considerable pressure upon the town council to appoint an inspector under the Workshop Act. Though a majority of the council at first resisted, an inspector was appointed some two years before the general unwillingness of local authorities elsewhere to operate the Act led to its administration being transferred to the factory inspectorate by the Factory Act of 1871.[3] The council also opposed proposed modifications of the factory and workshop regulations and pressed for the issue of a report by the inspector of workshops.

This agitation seems to have fathered the enquiry by the trades council into occupational diseases in Edinburgh, and a lengthy section of the council's annual report for 1867-8 was devoted to the reports from several affiliated unions.[4] In the minutes, however, working conditions receive comparatively slight notice. There are brief descriptions of those of the bakers and shoemakers. The succinctly recorded discussion on seamen's conditions that arose from the appeal by the Plimsoll Committee was expanded in the annual report of the council. 'During the debate which arose . . . facts were stated by some of the members who were conversant with the Leith and Baltic trade, which were both startling and appalling. Various instances were given of men being sent in vessels which were clearly overloaded, of some refusing to go in such vessels and being sent to prison in consequence; and those who were persuaded to go in their stead never being heard of again.' All working men were urged to support Plimsoll's agitation and 'so do away with a system which cannot be characterised in milder terms than "wholesale murder"'.[5]

[1] B. L. Hutchins and A. Harrison, *A History of Factory Legislation* (London, 1911), 247, n. 1.
[2] Edinburgh trades council *Annual Report*, 1868-9, p. 2. EPL, YHD 6661.
[3] Hutchins and Harrison, op. cit., 230.   [4] *Reformer*, 26 December 1868.
[5] *Annual Report, 1872-3*, 3, EPL, YHD 6661.

Strikes and lock-outs arising from working conditions are frequently reported in the minutes. Provision of help for workers involved in disputes was one of the chief functions of the trades council. Help took a variety of forms, but one of the most important, especially for the purely local or the small union or for non-unionist strikers, was provision of funds. The council's own funds were, as already indicated, distinctly meagre. The importance of its role lay not so much in what it could itself donate but in acting as a clearing house for applications to its affiliated unions. The council could not oblige these to meet any application it approved, but its endorsement made their response more likely. Moreover, it was easier for strikers or lock-outs, especially if outside Edinburgh, to direct an appeal through the council than to attempt to contact each local union or branch. The minutes show that applications for help were fairly frequent and came from affiliates, from unions or workers in other towns in Scotland, from England and indirectly in one case from Canada, and from non-unionists. The few rejections by the council of applications were the result mainly of the existence of too many other appeals or of its concentration upon its own re-organisation. Some local unions or branches, such as the glassmakers and moulders, affiliated to the council as a result of help given by it. How far the council's help enabled workers to win their disputes with employers it is not possible to say. But it must have been considered worth seeking.

Many of the strikes and lock-outs mentioned in the minutes were of only local significance. Of those that were not, one of the most notable was the nine hours movement. The London building trades dispute of 1859, which began the movement, was a seminal event in British trade union history. In Scotland it stimulated the building trades, particularly the masons and joiners, to demand the nine hours day or fifty-one hours week. The beginning and spread of the Scottish movement, 'the only important trade dispute that has taken place in Scotland for many years',[1] may be followed in the minutes below. By May 1861 the Edinburgh operative masons had become the first building trades workers in Britain to win the nine hours day. From Edinburgh the movement spread to other parts of

[1] H. G. Reid, 'Building Trades Disputes in Scotland 1861-2', in *Transactions of the National Association for the Promotion of Social Science* (London, 1863), 722.

Scotland and by 1869, according to a statement by a member of the union at a public meeting held by the trades council, the nine hours day had been won by almost 7,000 masons in thirty-eight towns, and only rather more than 1,100 other masons continued to work the formerly general fifty-seven hours week.[1] To the stimulus provided by the building trades dispute in London may also be attributed the formation in 1861 of the Associated Carpenters and Joiners of Scotland, six months after the collapse of the Edinburgh local union which had struck with the masons for the nine hours day. The Scottish joiners subsequently made less rapid progress than either the masons or the plasterers in gaining the shorter day, but large numbers of them had won it by 1870. A difference in working conditions between the building trades in England and those in Scotland is also brought out by the minutes, in the sequel to the London dispute when the employers in the south introduced payment by the hour instead of by the day or week.[2]

The spread in the later 1860s of the nine hours movement into the iron-working trades is outlined in the minutes. The agitation brought the trades council the first of its four direct contacts with the International Working Men's Association, or First International, formed in London in 1864 by George Odger and other labour leaders in which a leading role was soon assumed by Karl Marx.[3] The nine hours movement was given everywhere in Britain a powerful push forward by the successful strike in 1871 of the engineers on the north-east coast of England; and news of their victory at Newcastle was evidently first received by their leader, John Burnett, while he was addressing a public meeting called by the trades council in Edinburgh.[4] Of the trades affiliated to the council the blacksmiths, engineers, moulders, brassfounders, tinplate workers and cabinet-makers all gained during 1871-2 a fifty-one hours week, and the printers, bookbinders and typefounders a fifty-four hours week.[5]

---

[1] *Scotsman*, 11 March 1869.   [2] Below, pp. 59, 68.
[3] Below, p. 251. The minutes contain no reference to any contact there may have been with the International in 1866 when its general council sent two representatives to Edinburgh during the tailors' lock-out (below, pp. 178-9), to dissuade Danish and German tailors imported by employers from filling the places of the local journeymen. H. Collins and C. Abramsky, *Karl Marx and the British Labour Movement* (London, 1965), 70, 72; *Edinburgh Evening Courant*, 16 and 19 April 1866.
[4] Below, p. 327.   [5] *Annual Report, 1871-2*, 2.

An occasional outcome of strikes and lock-outs in the early and mid-Victorian period was the formation by trade unionists of productive co-operative associations. The minutes mention the successful one formed by the operative masons in Edinburgh in 1861, and show that it was later the subject of an enquiry from operative masons in Vienna.[1] A second outcome of disputes was discussion at the council of conciliation and arbitration. A copy of a parliamentary report on the subject was added to the council's library, and the advice was sought of Robert Applegarth, an advocate of arbitration. But much more of the council's time was given to discussion of how best trade unionists could combine to win strikes and resist lock-outs and almost every important dispute was followed by an examination by the council of the possibility of federation or confederation of unions. It took an initiative itself in 1860 in proposing a Working Man's Mutual Protection and Co-operative League. Among the relevant problems considered was whether such an organisation should embrace Britain or be limited to Scotland or even to Edinburgh. The council, however, took almost no direct part in the important development in the 1860s of national conferences of trade unionists. It was not represented at the master and servant conference of 1864, nor at the Sheffield conference of 1866 which created the United Kingdom Alliance of Organised Trades,[2] was only very indirectly represented at the St Martin's Hall conference in London in 1867, and sent no delegates to any of the first five Trades Union Congresses.

The minutes indicate how wide a range of questions was taken up during 1859-73 by the trades council. They had, however, a common source in the council's attempts to advocate, in the words of its formal objects, 'the just claims of labour' and to protect and extend 'the rights and interests of the working classes'. Thus it sent two delegates, each of whom read a paper defending trade unionism, to the congress in Glasgow in 1860 of the Social Science Association, whose report that year on trade unions helped make these seem more 'respectable'. The council co-ordinated and led the successful movement by unions in the city to establish two or three days' general annual holiday. It attempted to create a local labour newspaper. It raised considerable sums of money for the rebuilding of the Royal Infirmary. It concerned itself with matters of local amenity and tried

[1] Below, p. 277. [2] Below, p. 181.

to secure entry at reduced rates for working people to the Royal
Scottish Academy exhibition. It frequently pressed for the establishment of a public library in Edinburgh and carried on a particularly
vigorous agitation in 1867-8, which however evidently aroused
political disagreements among the delegates.[1] At least in the earlier
years covered by these minutes, the council ran its own small
library. It organised educational lectures. At the end of the period it
devoted much attention to proposed new uses for certain local
educational funds, and sent four of its members to give evidence
before the Endowed Schools Commission. It conducted an agitation
over housing in Edinburgh and a special committee of the council
carried out an investigation of living conditions in parts of the city.

Its manifold activities led the council into direct contact or correspondence not only with leading trade unionists in Britain, but
also with many members of the middle and upper classes. University
or college professors or lecturers were brought to lecture at meetings
organised by the council. Invitations to other meetings were issued
to those leading churchmen Dr Thomas Guthrie and Dr James Begg.
There was frequent contact between the council and the lord
advocates of the period, one of whom admittedly was an M.P. for
Edinburgh.[2] A Liberal lord advocate and his Tory predecessor both
agreed to become honorary presidents of the council. Of the score
of public meetings the council held between 1859 and 1873, at least
half were presided over by members of the upper classes. On one
occasion an invitation to preside was declined by the duke of
Buccleuch but accepted by the lord justice general of Scotland.[3]
The council was anxious to appear as a body of respectable working
men. The minutes show how earnestly the delegates conducted their
business. Their annual excursion to Glasgow included visits to
'Institutions, Warehouses, Works, Etc.'.[4] What could lend their
activities greater respectability than the association with them of
distinguished gentlemen? A masons' delegate had been applauded
when he read a paper at the trades council in which he spoke of the
desirability of 'raising the moral tone of Trades Unions in the
opinions of those whose good opinions and cooperations are really
worth having'.[5]

[1] Below, p. 223.   [2] Below, p. 79, n. 1.   [3] Below, p. 206.
[4] Below, p. 12.   [5] Below, pp. 107-8.

Temperance was considered an attribute of the respectable artisan and a delegate on one occasion defended trade unions as 'great checks to drunkenness and immorality'.[1] The choice of its regular meeting places reflected the attitude of the council. Though it took some inconclusive steps towards building a trades hall, the council met until 1867 in Burden's Coffee House in the High Street. The premises had a close association both with temperance and with Chartism. Opened originally in 1843 as a temperance coffee and lodging house by the Chartist Robert Cranston, who had also carried on there his business as a tailor, it had been a meeting place for Edinburgh Chartists. Cranston had sold the premises in 1848 to George Burden (about whom nothing has been discovered), and the latter and his family carried on the coffee house for many years.[2] The reason for the transfer in 1867 of the council's meetings from Burden's to Buchanan's Temperance Hotel, almost directly across the High Street, is not known. Buchanan's had opened in 1848 and its proprietor James Buchanan, who was evidently a radical in the 1860s,[3] may have been a Chartist. The trades council continued to meet at Buchanan's for twenty years after 1867.

Between 1859 and 1873 the importance of the trades council increased within Edinburgh, and for a few of the intervening years it was perhaps also the most important of the three or four trades councils that existed in Scotland. If in 1862 its application for entry to the columns of that treasury of local information, Oliver and Boyd's *Almanac*, had been treated with silent disdain,[4] by 1873 the trades council was being invited to give evidence before a royal commission. In the second half of the period the local press took more notice of the council, and on a few occasions in the early 1870s the minutes are simply press cuttings pasted into the minute book. The growth in the importance of the council was due primarily to the general expansion of trade unionism locally and nationally, and to the winning in 1867-8 of the franchise by the urban working class. Stronger and more representative of local skilled unions after 1867-8 than before it, the council acted with greater effectiveness in the later part of the period covered by the minutes below. Between 1866

---

[1] *Edinburgh Evening Courant*, 11 February 1870, quoting a paper read by W. Wilson, engineers.

[2] E. M. Mein, *Through Four Reigns: The Story of the Old Waverley Hotel and its Founder* (Edinburgh, n.d.), 3, 4.   [3] Below, p. 272.   [4] Below, p. 109.

and 1873 it successfully organised two of the largest public processions and demonstrations held in Edinburgh in the nineteenth century.[1] Its activities were similar to those of other trades councils. Some of these councils played roles of national importance in the development of trade unionism during the period. Glasgow trades council led the master and servant laws agitation in the mid-1860s, Sheffield trades council took the initiative in the creation in 1866 of the United Kingdom Alliance of Organised Trades,[2] Manchester and Salford trades council issued the circular that summoned in 1868 the first Trades Union Congress,[3] and London trades council provided for much of the period a measure of national leadership for trade unionists. Compared with these, Edinburgh trades council was of secondary importance. It took no initiative of national significance, and even although it did contain two or three general secretaries of trade unions the unions were Scottish only, and the power of their secretaries could scarcely be compared with that of the 'Junta' in London. Within Scotland the relative importance of Edinburgh trades council was perhaps greatest during the years between 1867 and 1871, when Glasgow trades council, to whose precedence the Edinburgh council had deferred in 1860,[4] was 'dormant'.[5] Its calling of the Scottish trade union conference in Edinburgh in 1870 may be regarded as marking the height of its influence in the period. Even if its importance in Britain was secondary and its hegemony in Scotland brief, within Edinburgh and Leith the trades council established itself during the period as the central organisation of the organised working class. Its existence and activities as a joint committee of delegates helped in some measure to diminish sectionalism among local trade unionists. It gave them an opportunity, or an additional opportunity, to discover and exercise whatever talents they had for discussion, organisation and political activity. Above all, it tried, even if not always successfully, to improve the working and living conditions not only of the skilled workers whom it predominantly represented, but also of the working class in general.

★

[1] Above, pp. xxix, xxxiv.   [2] Below, pp. 181-2.   [3] Below, p. 211.
[4] Below, p. 33.   [5] Below, p. 219, n. 3.

In editing the manuscript certain deletions, transpositions and other changes have been made. Some repetitious and purely formal matter has been deleted: the presence of the president in the chair, his or the secretary's signature of the minutes, the sub-headings in the margins, enumeration of paragraphs, declaration of the passage of a motion, adjournment of the council, and, except where they were questioned or challenged, approval of previous minutes. Since the council met until 1867 at Burden's and thereafter at Buchanan's, the address block has been retained only at the first meeting in each. Some tautological matter and verbiage have also been cut out from the minutes, and the adverb 'then' given some respite. In these ways the manuscript has been reduced in print by approximately one-sixth, but no subject raised, however unimportant, has been deleted. In the few cases between 1859 and 1867 where the list of delegates present was given at the end of minutes it has been transferred to the beginning in order to make easier the identification of delegates. The form of the lists themselves has been standardised. Where only the number of delegates present was given it has been placed in the first paragraph, except from October 1873 when the roll was called at the end of the meeting. In minutes or reports of public meetings, the place of meeting has been transferred from the body to the head of the minute wherever it was not already there.

It must be emphasised that spelling, however incorrect or inconsistent, has with a few exceptions been preserved as it was in the manuscript. The exceptions have been made in a relatively small number of cases where the misspelling was so bad as to be likely to puzzle the reader. Abbreviations in the manuscript have been printed out in full, except for commonplace cases such as M.P. Punctuation has been modernised throughout. Paragraphing has been largely altered or imposed. Omissions have been dealt with either by the insertion of the missing word or words in square brackets whenever the meaning was obvious, or where it was not by the insertion of three dots. Square brackets have been used in the minutes of 10 May 1859 to enclose topics referred to in the manuscript only by page and paragraph numbers, and have also been used in those of 4 December 1860 because of the difficulty of reproducing the original layout. The form of the date at the head of each minute has been standardised, but that of dates in the body of the minutes has been left untouched. Where minutes or reports were in the form of press cuttings pasted into the minute books this fact has been footnoted. One of the chief problems in editing the manuscript has been the difficulty of identifying some of the delegates and other persons mentioned. Each case of unknown or uncertain identity has been footnoted. Identification of persons belonging to more exalted social classes has generally been based on the *Concise Dictionary of National Biography*, Oliver and Boyd's *Edinburgh Almanac*, or the *Edinburgh and Leith Post Office Directory*.

1859-1863

Buxtew's Coffee House
129 High Street — 1st March 1859

The United Trades Delegates Association
of Edinburgh & its vicinity held their usual
fortnightly Meeting — (Place and Date as above)
President Mr John Borrowman in
the Chair

The Secretary having read the
Minutes of last Meeting — Mr Wm Troup
Moved that that section of the Minutes
which referred to soliciting Professor Donaldson
to give A Lecture for the Benefit of Mr Walter
Glover be not approved of — as he considered
the Sub committee appointed to get up A
Concert in honour of that individual had
been disrespectfully treated — in as much as
they had been superseded without any reason
being assigned for so doing

Mr Wm Caw replied
that Mr Troup and the Members of that Sub-
committee who thought with him, had entirely misunderstood his object in making the
Motion complained of — he himself con-
-sidered — and thought it was the opinion
of the Meeting also that it would be injudicious to get up A concert at this season — and
So he proposed the Lecture which would (he
thought) be A more safe and profitable
scheme — he denied that he had treated

Facsimile of Edinburgh Trades Council Minutes, 1 March 1859

1859

Burden's Coffee House
129 High Street
1 March 1859

The United Trades Delegates Association of Edinburgh and its vicinity held their usual fortnightly Meeting. President, Mr John Borrowman, in the Chair.[1] Delegates present: Brass Founders, Mr George Smith; Black-Smiths, Mr Alexander Fraser; Joiners, Messrs William Caw, John Borrowman, William Tait, William Thomson; French Polishers, Mr John Millar; Masons, Messers James Collins, Thomas Thomson; Tailors, Mr William Troup.[2]

The Secretary haveing read the Minutes of last Meeting, Mr William Troup Moved that that section which referred to soliciting Professor Donoldson[3] to give A Lecture for the Benefit of Mr Walter Glover[4] be not approved of, as he considered the sub committee appointed to get up A Concert in honour of that individual had been disrespectfully treated in as much as they had been superceded without any reason being assigned for so doing. Mr William Caw replied that Mr Troup and the Members of that Sub-Committee who thought with him, had entirely misunderstood his object in makeing the Motion complained of. He himself considered, and thought it was the oppinion of the Meeting also, that it would be injudicious to get up A concert at this Season, and so he proposed the Lecture which would, he thought, be A more safe and profitable

---

[1] For a few biographical details of Borrowman see above, p. xxiii.
[2] Alexander Taylor, tailors, the secretary of the trades council, was also present.
[3] John Donaldson, professor of music at Edinburgh 1845-65, died 1865.
[4] Walter Glover, a centenarian living at Craigmillar, near Edinburgh, former carrier between Dumfries and Edinburgh who had had a slight personal acquaintance with Robert Burns. Glover had recited *Death and Dr Hornbook* at the trades council Burns centenary fruit soirée. *Scotsman, 26 January 1859.*

scheme. He denied that he had treated the committee with disrespect; so far from that it was his impression that the same Sub-committee would have undertaken the arraingements for the Lecture had the Services of Professor Donoldson been obtained. After A lengthened discussion Mr James Colins Moved that that section of the Minutes haveing reference to Mr Glover be wholly resinded. This was agreed to, after which the Minute so amended was approved of. The question was then taken up of how was Mr Glover to be recompensed for his attendance at the Burn's Centenary Sioree. Mr James Colins Moved, Seconded by Mr John Millar, That Mr Glover be presented with One Pound from the funds of the association. Mr William Caw Moved, Seconded by Mr Alexander Taylor, That Two Pound be presented to him from said fund, and that while no promise be made to Mr Glover The Members consider themselves in honour bound to present Mr Glover with something more hand-some should the Trip of the ensueing Summer prove A successfull one.[1] As Mr Colins and another Member had retired, it was agreed not to take a vote till next Meeting.

The Sub committee appointed to Memoralise the Town Council on the propriety of Erecting Wells in East Princes Street Gardens then reported that the Memorial entrusted to them had been brought before the Town Council at their last Meeting and remitted to the Plans and Works Committee.

The Secretary then read A Letter from Mr McKinnon, M.P. for Lymington, in reply to the Letter of enquiry from this Association, stateing that his Conciliation Bill for this Season would be printed immediatly. Along with said letter A copy of last year's Bill had been received.[2] This was read and remitted for farther discussion till next Meeting, the delegates engageing to bring it before their respective Trades committees in the Interim. During the Evening A deputation from the Flint Glass Makers was received, whose case was, in Accordance with former agreement, remitted

---

[1] Below, p. 8.
[2] William Alexander Mackinnon, 1789-1870, Conservative M.P. for Dunwich 1830-1, for Lymington 1835-52 (from 1847 as a Liberal-Conservative), and Liberal M.P. for Rye 1852-65. His Bill to establish Councils of Conciliation and Arbitration was introduced on 24 February 1859 but subsequently lost through a procedural mishap. The 1858 Bill had been withdrawn at its second reading.

to the Committees of the respective Trades to whoom they have
appealed.[1]

15 March 1859

Delegates present: Brass-Founders, Mr George Smith; Joiners, Messr
John Borrowman, William Caw; Tailors, Messers William Troup,
Alexander Taylor.

The Secretary read A Letter from Mr John Sinclair[2] intimateing
that the communication from this association regarding the Wells
in East Princes Street Gardens had been considered by the Magistrates, who had resolved that the consideration be delayed in the
mean-time.

Oweing to the smallness of the Meeting it was agreed to remit
the rest of the Business on the Paper till next Meeting, Viz., The
Vote on the Grant to Mr Glover, and the consideration of the
Concilliation Bill. Mr John Borrowman then gave notice that he
would at next Meeting Move the consideration of the Propriety of
Establishing A Co-Operative Store in Edinburgh. Mr William
Troup also gave notice that he would Move the Propriety of haveing
A Library for the use of the Working Classes, with suitable ac-
comodation for the same.

29 March 1859

Delegates present: Black-Smiths, Mr Alexander Fraser; Brass-
Founders, Messers George Smith, John McDonold; French Polishers,
Mr John Millar; Masons, Mr James Collins; Joiners, Mr John
Borrowman; Tailors, Messers William Troup, Alexander Taylor.

In consequince of the absence of several Delegates, The Vote on
the Grant to Mr Glover and the consideration of Mr Mackinnon's
Conciliation Bill was again remitted till next meeting.

The propriety of Establishing A Co-Operative Store, of which
notice was given at last Meeting by Mr Borrowman, was then
taken up. After A lengthened discussion Mr Fraser Moved, Seconded
by Mr John Millar, That The Trades Delegates have discussed the

[1] The flint glass makers at Leith had been on strike since 19 February because of their
employers' refusal to recognise the union. *Edinburgh Evening Courant,* 24 February
1859.
[2] Conjunct city clerk of Edinburgh.

propriety of Establishing A Co-Operative Store and have resolved that it would be unwise for the Trades Delegates to take the initiative step in such A movement. Mr John McDonold Moved, Seconded by Mr George Smith, That The Trades Delegates, as Trades Delegates, recommend to their respective Trades Committees and Friends in general to take into their consideration the propriety of Establishing A Co-Operative Store in Edinburgh. On the Vote being taken the votes were equal, Mr William Troup haveing declined to vote. The President haveing given the casting vote in favour of Mr John McDonold's Motion, it was declaired carried. Mr Alexander Fraser then protested against any of the Funds of the association being appropriated in any way to advance the movement, and Moved that his protest be recorded on the Minutes. Mr James Collins Seconded the Motion, which was agreed to. The Motion in reference to A Trades Library, of which Mr Troup gave notice at last meetting, was then taken up. After A short discussion it was remitted for further consideration to next meeting.

12 April 1859

Delegates present: BlackSmiths, Mr Alexander Fraser; Brass Founders, Messers John McDonold, George Smith; Joiners, Messers John Borrowman, William Caw, William Thomson; Masons, Messers James Colins, James Fleming, Thomas Thomson; Plumbers, Mr J. G. Bald; Tailors, Messers William Troup, Alexander Taylor.

Messers James Reid and Richard Kay, Flint Glass Makers, were also present. They intimated that the dispute which had existed for some time between the Flint Glass Makers and their Employers was now satisfactaraly settled and that they, in accordance with A promise given to this association to join it so soon as that settlement was effected, were sent to represent their Trade. They also Stated that other two Delegates were also appointed, Viz., Messers William Watson and William Johnston, so as to enable two of their number to attend the Meettings while the other two were at work. The Secretary enrolled their Names accordingly.

The Secretary then read the Minutes of last Meetting. Mr James Fleming Moved, Seconded by Mr John McDonold, That that portion of the Minutes containing the Protest entered thereon by Mr Alexander Fraser be rescinded. Mr Alexander Fraser Moved the

Minutes be approved of entire, which not being seconded Mr
Fleming's Motion was declaired carried and the Minutes so amended
were approved of. Mr Alexander Taylor then reported that as the
usual Monthly Meetting of Tailors' Delegates did not meet this
Month neither he nor Mr Troup had as yet had an opportunity of
laying the finding of this Association in reference to A Co-Operative
Store before their Trade or its committee. Messers James Colins,
Mason, and George Smith, Brass-Founder, stated they had laid it
before their respective Trades Committees and that it had been
favourably received.

The Vote was then taken on the grant to Mr Walter Glover when
Mr Caw's Motion was carried. The Treasurer was authorised to pay
the Money to the Secretary, who agreed to see to the same being
paid to Mr Glover. The discussion on Mr Mackinnon's Conciliation
Bill was then resumed, but there being no probibility that the Bill
would be read A Second time this Session it was agreed to suspend
any active proceedings thereon till next Session. The Secretary was
instructed to intimate the same to Mr Mackinnon and requist A
Copy of the Bill for this year.

Mr Troup's Motion On the propriety of getting A Library for the
use of the Working Classes, with Suitable accomadeation for the
same, he subsequintly changed in course of discussion to the propriety of this association takeing into their consideration the best
means of Erecting A Suitable Trades Hall with Library attached.
It was after some discussion unanimously agreed that it should stand
an open question, the Delegates being requisted to bring it at their
earliest opportunity before their respective Trades and report their
suggestions to this association. The Delegates in so doing were
authorised to state to their respective Trades, that the Movement
had the association's unanimous approval.

Mr Fraser then reminded the Meetting that it would be expedient
to see to their Trip of this Summer at an early day. Mr William Caw
enquired if any farther steps were to be taken in carrying out the
resolutions passed in favour of Weekly Payment of Wages and
extension of the Half Holiday on Saturdays. It was agreed to
consider both questions at next Meetting. The Secretary then requisted the Delegates to furnish him at next Meetting with Slips
of Paper containing their Name and address with the Trade they

represented, in order to enable him to make A correct Committee list.

10 May 1859[1]

Delegates present: BlackSmiths, Mr Alexander Frazer; Brass Founders, Mr George Smith; Flint Glass Makers, Mr James Reid; Joiners, Messers William Caw, John Borrowman, William Thomson; Masons, Mr Thomas Thomson; French Polishers, Mr John Miller; Tailors, Mr William Troup.[2]

[Agreed that question of building a Trades Hall with library attached be laid before the first public meeting of the Trades, and that weekly payments and extension of Saturday half-holiday be taken up at first favourable opportunity.] Mr Alexander Frazer then moved, seconded by Mr William Caw, That arraingements be made for the Trades Annual Trip, which was agreed to and A Sub-Committee was appointed to make preliminary enquiries and report. Mr Caw Moved, Seconded by Mr Thomson, That in the event of any important Public Meeting happening to be held on the usual Meeting nights of this association The usual Meeting be held on the Evening of the first Thursday following. Agreed to. Mr Frazer suggested that the Secretary be instructed to write to Mr Black, M.P., and enquire Where and When would it be convenient for him to meet with the Working Classes, in accordance with promise, for the purpose of discussing or giveing an explanation of his sentiments on Trades Unions. Agreed to.[3]

24 May 1859

Delegates present: BlackSmiths, Mr Alexander Frazer; Brass Founders, Mr John McDonold; Flint-Glass-Makers, Mr James Reid; Joiners Association, Messers William Caw, William Thomson; Tailors, Mr William Troup.[4] Vice President[5] in the Chair.

---

[1] The meeting due on 26 April was cancelled because of a meeting of working men that night with Adam Black, M.P. for Edinburgh, and James Moncreiff, who was elected as second member for the city on 29 April.

[2] Alexander Taylor, the secretary, wrote the minutes and must have been present.

[3] Adam Black, 1784-1874, publisher, Liberal M.P. for Edinburgh 1856-65. His promise to discuss unions had been given at the meeting on 26 April. See below, p. 18.

[4] Alexander Taylor, the secretary, wrote the minutes and must also have been present.

[5] William Troup. For a few biographical details of Troup see above, p. xxiv.

The Sub Committee appointed to make enquiries relative to the Annual Excursion Trip haveing given their preliminary report, it was agreed that the Trip be to Glasgow; that the last Saturday of July next be fixed on if A Train can be had for that day; that Messers Alexander Fraser and William Caw be appointed to go to Glasgow to make the necessary arraingements and that their expenses be paid as formerly.

A Letter was then read from Adam Black, Esq., M.P., in reply to A Letter of enquiry addressed to him from this Association. Mr Alexander Frazer Moved, Seconded by Mr William Caw, that Mr Black's Letter be recorded on the Minutes and the Trades Delegates employ the interveneing period in collecting facts connectted with Unions both of Employers and Employed, to be placed in possession of said Delegates with such Copies of Rules, Etc., as may be deemed necessary and usefull, to enable the said Delegates to reply to or put such questions as may be considered calculated to illustrate or clear up the subject in hand. Agreed to. A conversation then followed in reference to Mr Black's requist to be furnished with copies of the Rules of different Trades Unions to assist him in his investigations. After some consideration it was deemed inexpedient to comply with said requist, as several Trades decline to give their Rules to any but their own members.

Copy of Mr Adam Black, M.P.'s, reply to A Letter addressed to him from this Association:

North Bridge
17 May 1859

Mr Alexander Taylor

Sir,

I do contemplate prepareing A Lecture on Trades Unions, but as I wish to discuss pretty fully the Subject of wages and the causes of their rise and fall, so as to make it useful I must take more time for it than I can command before the meeting of Parliment. In the mean time if you would be good enough to procure for me the regulations of as many of the Unions as you can to assist me in my investigations you will oblige, Sir,

Your obedient Servant,

A. Black

7 June 1859

Delegates present: Blacksmiths, Mr Alexander Frazer; Brass Founders, Messers George Smith, John McDonold; Joiners, Messers John Borrowman, William Caw, William Thomson, William Tait; Masons, Messers James Colins, James Fleming, Thomas Thomson; Tailors, Mr William Troup.[1]

Mr Alexander Fraser reported the arraingements that he and Mr Caw had made in Glasgow relative to the Trades Annual Trip, and submitted the offer of the Edinburgh and Glasgow Railway Company. Mr William Caw stated he had had A conversation with A party connectted with the Caledonian Railway Company respecting Trips, and suggested that before closeing with the offer now before them enquiry be made at said Company. Mr James Fleming Moved that the matter be remitted to the Sub Committee with powers. Mr James Colins Seconded the Motion. Agreed to. Names of Sub Committee: Messers Alexander Frazer, William Caw, William Thomson, John Borrowman and William Troup. Mr William Caw Moved that A Special Meeting to forward Trip Business be held this day week, the 14th inst. Agreed to.

21 June 1859[2]

A Special Committee Meeting was held for the purpose of forwarding buisness connectted with the Trades Annual Trip. The Sub Committee reported that after due consideration they had accepted and closed with the offer of the Edinburgh and Glasgow Railway Company.

21 June 1859

Delegates present: Black-Smiths, Mr Alexander Frazer; Brass Founders, Messers George Smith, and John McDonold; Clock-Makers, Mr George Latimer; Joiners, Messers John Borrowman, and William Caw; Masons, Messers James Colins, James Fleming, and Thomas Thomson; Tailors, Messers William Troup and Alexander Taylor.

Some routine buisness was disposed of relative to the Annual Trip,

---

[1] Alexander Taylor, the secretary, wrote the minutes and must have been present.
[2] The date should perhaps read 14 June 1859.

after which the Secretary enquired if he would write to Mr Adam Black, M.P., acknowledgeing his reply. It was agreed that it was unnecessary to take any further notice of the matter till the end of the Session. At the same time it was deemed requisite that A Sub Committee be appointed who should in the Interim collect all the information they could obtain concerning the Rules, Regulations, and objects of Unions, both of Employers and Employed, the causes of rise and falls in wages, Etc., in order that they might be prepared to oppose Mr Black should such A Step be found necessary. The following were forthwith appointed: Mr John Borrowman (President), Mr William Troup (Vice President), Messers Alexander Frazer, William Caw, James Fleming, and Alexander Taylor (Secretary). It was then agreed that the Trip Sub Committee meet this day week for the purpose of divideing the Tickets, Bills, Etc.

28 June 1859

The Trip Sub Committee met for Special buisness connectted therewith. The Tickets and Bills haveing been divided and Routine buisness dispatched, the Meetting adjourned.

5 July 1859

Delegates present: Black Smiths, Mr Alexander Frazer; Brass Founders, Messers George Smith, John McDonold; Clock-Makers, Mr George Latimer; French Polishers, Mr John Millar; Joiners, Messers John Borrowman, William Caw, William Thomson; Masons, Messers James Collens, James Fleming; Plumbers, Mr James Bald; Tailors, Mr Alexander Taylor.

The Question as to whether any steps should be taken this Session towards supporting Mr McKinnon, M.P.'s, Concilliation Bill was taken up. After some conversation it was considered unnesscessary to do so at present as there was no probibility that the Bill would be read A second time this Session. It was, however, agreed on the Motion of Mr Alexander Frazer, Seconded by Mr John Miller, That in the meantime the Secretary write to Mr Charles Cowan, late Member for this City,[1] and Solicit in Loan for A short time A

[1] Charles Cowan of Valleyfield, 1801-89, paper manufacturer, Liberal M.P. for Edinburgh 1847-59.

Copy of the *Report of the House of Commons Committee on Settlement of Strickes by Arbitration*.[1] Some Routine Buisness was then dispatched relative to the Annual Trip.

19 July 1859

Delegates present: Black Smiths, Mr Alexander Fraser; Brass-Founders, Messers George Smith, John McDonold; Clock Makers, Mr George Latimer; Joiners, Messers John Borrowman, William Caw, William Thomson; Masons, Messers James Colins, James Fleming, Thomas Thomson; Plumbers, Mr J. G. Bald; Tailors, Messers William Troup, Alexander Taylor.

The fittest time for the half-yearly Election of Office Bearers was discussed. Mr William Caw Moved, Seconded by Mr James Colins, that the Elections take place on the first Meeting nights in June and December, and as the former date is now past, to save further trouble at this time the present Office Bearers be requisted to retain Office till December. Agreed to.

The Secretary was further instructed to write to the Respective parties in Glasgow who have agreed to admit the Trades Delegates Excursionists to inspect their respective Institutions, Warehouses, Works, Etc., to remind them of the Date, Etc. After this some routine Trip Buisness was disposed of, the Sub Committee agreeing to meett for furtherance of Trip buisness on Tuesday the 26th, Thursday the 28th, and Friday the 29th inst., The full Committee to be in attendance on the last of these Meeting nights with all Tickets, Cash, Etc., by eight Oclock p.m. to facilitate the final arraingements.

2 August 1859

Delegates present: Black Smiths, Mr Alexander Frazer; Brass Founders, Messers George Smith, John McDonold; Clock Makers, Mr George Latimer; Joiners, Messers John Borrowman, William Caw, William Thomson; Masons, Messers James Colens, James Fleming; Plumbers, Mr James G. Bald; Tailors, Mr William Troup.[2]

---

[1] *Report from the Select Committee on Masters and Operatives (Equitable Councils of Conciliation)* (1856).
[2] Alexander Taylor, the secretary, wrote the minutes and must have been present.

This being the first time the Delegates had met after their Annual Trip, the greater part of the Evening was taken up in disposeing of the buisness connectted with the winding up of said affair. The Treasurer reported that after paying all demands connectted therewith there remained in his hands A Balance of £4 11s. 10½d. His report was approved of. Mr William Caw said He would at next Meetting Move that preliminary arraingements be entered on for A Course of Winter Evening Lectures. Mr Alexander Frazer intimated that he would Second the Motion when brought forward.

16 August 1859

Delegates present: Black Smiths, Mr Alexander Frazer; Clock Makers, Mr George Latimer; Flint Glass Makers, Mr James Reid; Joiners, Messrs John Borrowman, William Caw; Masons, Messrs James Collens, James Fleming; Tailors, Messrs William Troup, Alexander Taylor.

The Secretary reported that he had not as yet succeeded in procuring A Copy of the House of Commons Committee's *report on Settlement of Strickes by Arbitration*, and read Letters from Parties to whoom he had applied. Mr Alexander Frazer suggested To try Duncan McLaren, Esq.[1] Agreed to. Mr Caw then brought forward the Motion of which he had given notice. It was agreed to, and as A first Step the Secretary was instructed to apply by Letter to Mr Mathieson, office of her Majesty's Works,[2] to Solicit the use of that Chapel in North College Street, formerly belonging to Dr Alexander's Congregation,[3] for the purpose of Said Lectures being delivered in during the ensueing Winter.

30 August 1859

Delegates present: Brass-Founders, Messers George Smith, John McDonold; Flint Glass Makers, Mr James Reid; Joiners, Messers John Borrowman, William Caw, William Thomson; Masons, Messers James Collens, James Fleming; Plumbers, Mr J. G. Bald; Tailors, Messers William Troup, Alexander Taylor.

---

[1] Duncan McLaren, 1800-86, Radical M.P. for Edinburgh 1865-81; brother-in-law to John Bright.
[2] Robert Matheson, clerk or assistant surveyor of H.M. Works 1849-77.
[3] W. L. Alexander, D.D., minister of Argyle Square Congregationalist Church.

The Secretary read A Letter from Duncan McLaren, Esq., intimateing that the House of Commons Committee's Report enquired for by this Association might be had through the agency of A. & C. Black & Coy. The Secretary added that he had taken the liberty to order the same. His so doing was approved of and the Treasurer instructed to pay the same. In reference to the Chapel in College Street, the Secretary read A Letter from Mr Mathieson of Her Majesty's Works intimateing that the Chapel was not in his Charge. The Matter was remitted to the Secretary to make further enquirey, with power to summon A deputation if necessary. A conversation followed on the best means of promoteing the welfare of this Association, the principle points of which was remitted for further discussion. A Tray was then ordered for the Society's Box.

27 September 1859[1]

In Consequence of the sudden and unexpected death of Mr Alexander Taylor, Secretary, there were no minuets recorded of the previous meeting. Before entering into any other business Mr William Caw Moved, Seconded by Mr Alexander Frazer, That there be entred upon the Minuets a record of our respect and esteem for our late lamented Secretary Alexander Taylor for his kind, unwearied and invaluable services in behalf of this Assocation, And that our deep and heartfelt sympthy be convayed to his Widow. Other members having given expression to their concurrance in the Motion it was unanimously adopted.

On the question of a Winter Course of Lectures coming on for consideration It was agreed that Messers Borrowman, Caw and Troup wait upon Mr Knox and other leading Members of the Saturday Half-Holy-day Assocation[2] and assertain how far they would be prepared to assist in the getting up of said Lectures, and report to a future meeting.

On the Motion of John McDonald, Seconded by John Iverach,

---

[1] These and following minutes were written by John Iverach, tailors, who was formally appointed secretary on 11 October.
[2] Thomas Knox, 1818-79, head of a firm of glovers, master of the merchant company 1871-2, an active Independent Liberal and temperance advocate. The Saturday Half Holiday Association was formed in 1854 and arranged lectures and musical entertainments for working men; see, e.g. The Witness, 3 January 1855.

it was Resolved that a Public Meeting of the Working Classes be held on Thursday the 6th proximo in Buccleuch Street Hall, to protest against the Document issued by the Employers in the Bulding Trades of London for their Workmen to Sign before giving them employment.[1] And to consider what steps should be taken to aid their bretheren in their present position.

Resolved that a Copy of the *Glasgow Sentenal* be suplied weekly to the Assocation On the ground of its able advocacy of the rights of the Working Classes.[2] Moved by William Caw, Seconded by John McDonald. Mr Alexander Fraser was then appointed to draw up resilution to be submitted to the Public Meeting.

29 September 1859

A special Meeting was held. Vice President in the Chair. Resolved that 200 bills anouncing the Public Meeting to be held on the 6th proximo be printed, and that Mr J. G. Bauld be empowred to see the same exicuted. Messers Troup and Iverach appointed to engage the Hall.

4 October 1859

A special Meeting was held. The Edinburgh Lodge of the United Operative Masons Assocation of Scotland having given in their adhesion to the Assocaton of United Trades Delegates, Messers James McLeod and John Sutherland appeared to represent the Lodge. Resolved on the Motion of James Reid, Seconded by George Smith, that their names be recorded in the Minuet book.

The following Resilutions were then agreed to be submitted to the Public Meeting on the 6th inst.: 1st, That this Meeting is of opinion that the Document issued by the Employers in the Building Trades of London for their Workmen to Sign before giving them employment is an unjust and tyranical interferance with their rights as citizens and Freemen. 2nd, That this Meeting desire to record

---

[1] 'The Document' declared that the signatory was not and would not during his engagement become a member or supporter of a trade union. R. W. Postgate, *The Builders' History* (London, 1923), 172.

[2] The *Glasgow Sentinel*, 1850-77, the main working-class newspaper of the period in Scotland. Founded by Robert Buchanan, the Owenite missionary, it came under the control from 1860 of Alexander McDonald, the miners' leader; its industrial reporter and, from about 1863, editor was Alexander Campbell. W. H. Marwick, *Life of Alexander Campbell* (Glasgow, n.d.), 15, 17.

their sympathy with the Workmen of London for the Noble stand they have made in resisting the Masters' Document and hereby resolve to aid them by subscriptions among the Working Classes of Edinburgh. 3rd, That a Committee be appointed to Co-operate with the Trades Delegates to carry the above Resilutions into effect. The 1st Resilution to be Moved by John Iverach, seconded by William Troup. The 2nd to be moved by John McDonald, seconded by John Sutherland. The 3rd to be moved by George Campbell, seconded by John Millar.[1]

PUBLIC MEETING

Buccleuch Street Hall

6 October 1859

The Public Meeting called to protest against the Document issued by the Employers in the Building Trades of London for their Workmen to sign before they be employed, and to consider what steps should be taken to assist the men locked-out in their present position, was held. The President in the Chair. The Resilutions agreed to at a Meeting of the Committee were submitted to the Meeting and unanimously adopted. After considerable discussion upon the third resilution, the following Gentlemen were appointed to Co-operate with the Trades Delegates Committee for the purpos of raising subscriptions, it being understood that they be in no way committed by the ordinary business of the Trades Delegates. Names of Committee appointed and the Trades represented: Glass-cutter, Mr Andrew Brown; Slater, Mr Andrew Gourly; Joiners, Messers Gallin, George Gill, Robert Rae, Joseph McDonald; Printer, Mr John Bertim; Mason, Mr George Lorimer;[2] Tailor, Mr Thomas Young. After A Vote of thanks to the Chairman the Meeting separated.

11 October 1859

The following Notice from the Non-Society Operative Masons of Edinburgh was read:

---

[1] Campbell was an engineer, Millar a French polisher.
[2] Lorimer seems not to have been the master builder of the same name mentioned below, p. 49.

Masons' Hall, Lyons Close
High Street, Edinburgh
7 October 1859

The United Trades delegates Committee. At a Public Meeting of
the Masons of Edinburgh held in this Hall the following resolution
was proposed, seconded, and carried without dessent, Viz.: – 'Proposed that this meeting authorize the withdrawall of Messers
Fleming, Collins, and Thompson from the Committee of the United
Trades Delegates and Authorize the Chairman and Committee to
certify to the United Trades Delegates that the Non-Society Operative Masons of Edinburgh have no representatives at the said Committee'. We have the honour of intimating the above to you. James
Lyal, Chairman; John D. Sutherland, Secretary; John Trotter,
Treasurer.[1]

On the question of Electing a Treasurer in the place of Mr Colins,
it was moved by John Iverach, seconded by George Campbell, that
Mr Colins remain in office till nixt meeting of Committee. Carried
unanimously. Mr William Caw Moved, Seconded by Mr Alexander
Frazer, That we record a cordial vote of thanks to Mr Collins for
the able, diligent, and effecient manner in which he discharged the
various duties connected with the Office of Treasurer, and for his
kind and courtious conduct as a Delegate and a Man. Other
members having given expression to the high respect and esteem
in which they held Mr Collins, the Motion was cordialy adopted. Resolved on the Motion of William Caw, seconded by
George Smith, that John Iverach Act as Secretary untill December nixt, and that Mrs Taylor[2] receive a twelve months' sallery,
Viz., £1.

A good deal of discussion then took place regarding the best
manner of distributing the Subscription Sheets for behoof of the
Lock-outs in the Building Trades of London. It was ultimately
agreed that each Delegate take as many as he thought he could use-
fully distribute and that each adopt the plan best suited to his own

---

[1] It is not clear how non-society masons could be represented at the trades council.
The decision to withdraw the delegates was perhaps connected with the affiliation on
4 October of the lodge of the United Operative Masons.
[2] Widow of the late secretary.

B

Trade. Mr Tate[1] was then elected to act as Treasurer for the Subscriptions and Mr J. G. Bald as secretary.

25 October 1859

Delegates present: Joiners, Messers William Caw, John Borrowman,
Tait; French Polisher, Mr John Millar; Clock-Maker, George
Latimer; Brass Founder, George Smith; Flint-Glass-Makers, Messers
James Reid, William Johnstone; Engineers, Mr George Campbell;
Black Smiths, Mr Alexander Frazer; Tailors, Messers William Troup,
John Iverach. Vice President in the Chair.[2]

The Secretary read a communication from The Edinburgh
Lodge of United Operative Masons intimating the withdrawal of
their representatives. Mr Tait was then Elected Treasurer in the
room of Mr Collins, on the Motion of John Millar, Seconded by
James Reid. William Caw and William Troup then appointed
Adators. Alexander Frazer proposed, Seconded by George Campbell, that 10s. be paid to Mr Collins as a slight recognetion of his
services. William Troup and John Iverach instructed to pay Mrs
Taylor.

Resolved that the Secretarys of Trades not represented be communicated with, requesting them to attend A Delegate Meeting of
the Trades of Edinburgh on Saturday the 29th instant at 7 p.m. for
the purpose of Considering the propriety of having a Public Meeting
of the Working Classes so that they might have an oportunity of
replying to the Lecture delivered by Adam Black, M.P., upon Wages,
Trades-unions, and strikes, and to ascertain how far they would
assist in geting up said meeting.[3] Moved by Alexander Frazer,
Seconded by Mr Latimer.

29 October 1859

A special Delegate Meeting of the Trades of Edinburgh was held,
John Borrowman, President of the United Trades Delegates Assoca-

---

[1] William Tait, joiners.
[2] William Troup; but Borrowman, the president, was evidently present later.
[3] Black had delivered his lecture on 22 October in Edinburgh 'in accordance with a
promise given by him to the working classes in April'. *Edinburgh Evening Courant*,
24 October 1859. See above, p. 8, n. 3.

tion, in the Chair. Delegates present: Engineers, George Campbell;
Black Smiths, Alexander Frazer; Plumbers, J. G. Bald; Printers,
James Willkie; Painters, Robert Noble; Joiners, Flint Glass Makers,
Flint Glass Cutters, Cork Cutters, Watch Makers, French Polishers,
Tailors. The Secretary read the Minute refferring to the calling of
the Meeting. After an animated discussion in which the representatives of the Painters, Printers, and others not generaly represented
took part, and the expression of an opinion that their Trades
generaly would be willing to support the getting up of a Public
Meetting, the following, on the Motion of Alexander Frazer,
seconded by J. G. Bald, was unanimously agreed to: That the Trades
Delegates agree to Call a Public Meeting of the Working Classes
upon an early day, That they might have an opertunity of replying
to the Lecture delivered by Adam Black, M.P., upon Wages, Trades
Unions, and Strikes. A Committe was then appointed to make the
necessary arrangements and draw up Resolutions. The meeting then
adjourned till Tuesday 1st November.

1 November 1859

A Special Meeting of Trades Delegates was held, the Vice President
of the Trades Delegates in the Chair. The Secretary reported with
regard to the Waterloo Rooms that they could be had for Five
Ginues. Deputations were then appointed to look after some other
place for the Meeting. The deputations returned and reported as
followes: That the Queen Street Hall Could be had for £4 4s.;
Brighton Street Chaple – No reply could be given till Monday and
then a charge would have to be made at the doors or the admittance
be by ticket. Mr Andrew Brown[1] proposed, seconded by James
Reid, that the Queen Street Hall be taken, which was agreed to.
On the resolutions coming on for consideration, a good deal of
discussion arose upon the words, in the first resolution, 'The theory
of Supply and Demand as applied to the producers of labour'.
It was afterwards agreed to as submitted. The second and third
were likewise agreed to. The meeting adjourned till Saturday the
5th inst.

[1] Probably either a slater or a glasscutter.

5 November 1859

A Special Meeting of Trades Delegates held, Vice President in the Chair. Resolved that the Lord Provost[1] be requested to take the chair at the Public Meeting to be held on the 11th inst. A deputation appointed to wate upon his Lordship on Monday, and the Secretary instructed to send notice of the same to his Lordship by the first post on Monday and to inclose a Copy of the Resolutions proposed to be submitted to the meeting. A letter was received from an Assocation styling itself The Anti-Union Assocation, intimating a desire to disscuss publicly the question of the utility of Trades Unions. The letter was remitted for consideration to a future meeting.

8 November 1859[2]

Vice President in the Chair. Messers Campbell and Reid, the deputation appointed to wait upon the Lord Provost, reported that they, accompanied by the Secretary, waited upon his Lordship on Monday forenoon and were courtiously received. His Lordship expressed his willingness to preside at the meeting upon condition that some of the expressions in the 2nd and 3rd Resolutions were slightly modified. The deputation stated that they had no doubt but that the resolution would be modified by the committee. The Lord Provost then said that he would take a little more time to consider the mater and that he would send his annser in the course of the afternoon. The deputation thanked his Lordship for his Courtesay and retired. A letter from the Lord Provost was then read intimating that he would Preside at the meeting on the 11th inst. if the alterations sugested to the deputation who waited upon him were made in the resolutions. The resolutions were then considered and amended as sugested at the conference with the Lord Provost. The Delegates made the following arrangments with refrence to the Public Meeting: The 1st resolution to be moved by John Iverach, seconded by John Sutherland; 2nd resolution to be moved by Robert Gun, seconded by George Campbell and supported by James Beveredge; 3rd

---

[1] Francis Brown Douglas, 1814-86, an Independent Liberal, had been elected lord provost the previous day. *Edinburgh Evening Courant*, 5 November 1859.
[2] This was evidently a meeting of the trades council, not an ad hoc meeting of trades as on 1 and 5 November.

resolution to be moved by George Lorimer, seconded by John Watson.[1] It was agreed that the following Gentlemen be written to requesting them to attend the meeting: Adam Black, M.P., Sir John Melvel,[2] Dr Guthre,[3] Dr Beg,[4] and Mr Chambers.[5] The Secretary was instructed to prepare a programe of proceedings at the Public Meeting for the Chairman.

PUBLIC MEETING

Queen Street Hall

11 November 1859

The Public Meeting called for the consideration of resolutions in reply to Mr Black's lecture on Wages, Trades Unions and strikes was held here, the Right Honourable The Lord Provost in the Chair.

The chairman opened the proceedings by a few interductory remarks of an entirely nuteral charracter, not committing himself to any side of the question, but stating that his object was to here both sides of the question stated. Mr Black had stated the one side and he expected to here the other tonight.

The first resolution, as follows, was Moved by John Iverach, seconded by John Sutherland: That in the opinion of this meeting the theory of Supply and demand as applied to the producers of labour by Mr Black is unsound in principle and opposed to the true interests both of Employed and Employer. Mr Barton, Painter, moved an Amendment which, not finding a seconder, fell to the ground and the resolution was carried by acclamation.[6] The Second Resolution was as follows: That this meeting is of opinion that the statements of Mr Black regarding Trades Unions are generaly inac-

[1] Robert Gunn and James Beveredge have not been identified; John Watson may have been the blacksmith who became a delegate to the trades council on 18 June 1867.
[2] Sir John Melville, 1802-60, lord provost of Edinburgh 1854-9.
[3] Rev. Dr Thomas Guthrie, 1803-73, a leader of the Free Church, apostle of ragged schools, temperance advocate, minister of St John's, Edinburgh, 1840-64.
[4] Rev. Dr James Begg, 1808-83, minister of Newington Free Church, Edinburgh, 1843-83, advocate of improved working class housing.
[5] William Chambers, 1800-83, publisher, lord provost of Edinburgh 1865-9.
[6] Barton's amendment was that trade unions were useless in face of the inexorable laws of supply and demand that regulated wages. Barton had evidently been an anti-unionist in Glasgow before he removed to Edinburgh. Scotsman, 12 November 1859.

curate and that they reflect very injouriously upon The Amalgimated Society of Engineers.[1] The resolution was moved by Mr Robert Gun, seconded by Mr William Newton, who was sent by the Amalgimated Society of Engineers from London.[2] On Mr Newton rising to address the meeting he was most enthusiasticaly received. In an address of great power and elequance he rebutted all Mr Black's charges against the Amalgimated Engineers, and mercilessly exposed the fallacy of his arguments upon the question of supply and demand as applied to labour. Mr Ramsay, Joiner, moved an amendment, which was seconded by Mr Barton, Painter. On the Vote being taken no hands were held up for the amendment.[3] The resolution was then carried by acclamation. The Third resolution, as follows, was moved by Mr George Lorimer, seconded by Mr John Watson: That this meeting, after having considered Mr Black's lecture, have no confidence in his views of social and Political economy. The resolution was unanimously adopted. A Vote of thanks was moved by Mr William Newton to the Lord Provost for his conduct in the chair. Carried by acclamation. Mr Alexander Frazer moved a hearty vote of thanks to Mr William Newton, for having, irrespective of truble and inconvenience, come from London to attend the meeting and for the able and elequent address he had delivered to them. The motion was most enthusiasticaly responded to. The Meeting, which was a large one – the hall being filled in every part – and very enthusiastic, then dispersed.

22 November 1859

The Vice President read the minutes of a special meeting of Delegates held on Saturday the 19th to the following effect: 1st, That it is the wish of the Amalgimated Trades that the addresses delivered at the Queen Street Hall meeting should be printed in the form of a small

[1] Black had described the powers of the executive committee of the A.S.E. as 'very great and very vague' and had alleged that 'every member is living under a spy system from the hour when he becomes a member, and a victim of this despotic organisation'. *Scotsman*, 24 October 1859.

[2] William Newton, 1822-76, a leading founder of the Amalgamated Society of Engineers who remained closely associated with it after he became a professional journalist in the mid-1850s. J. B. Jefferys, *The Story of the Engineers* (London, 1945), 45-8.

[2] It asked the meeting to 'repudiate the A.S.E.'.

pamphlet.[1] 2nd, That the Trades Delegates should take specal notice of the handsome manner in which the Amalgimated Society of Engineers have acted, especaly in sending Mr William Newton from London to represent their body. 3rd, Mr Read[2] is to give notice of a motion for the raising of funds to assist the Trades Delegates in carrying out any important object that they may take up. 4th, Mr Latimer to bring forward at nixt meeting a motion that a soriee of the Working Classes be got up by the Trades Delegates.

Mr William Troup moved the following resolution: That the Trades Delegates of Edinburgh take the earliest opportunity of recording their high apprecation of the handsom manner in which the Amalgimated Society of Engineers acted with refrence to the Public Meeting held in Edinburgh on the 11th inst., on Wages, Trades Unions and strikes, especaly in sending so able an advocate as Mr William Newton from London, who completly refuted Mr Black's lecture, and with great power and elequance defended the rights of labour. Seconded by James Reid and unanimously adopted. Likewise that the Secretary send a Copy of the same to the Council of the Amalgimated Society of Engineers.

Mr James Reid then brought forward the question with regard to which he had given notice, and moved as follows: That a circular be printed urging upon working men the necessity of supporting this assocation so as to enable us to carry out any important object that we may take up, and that the circular be distributed by the Delegates amongst the influincal members of their respective Trades Societys. The motion was seconded by Mr William Tait and agreed to. Mr Latimer's motion regarding the holding of a soriee was nixt considered. The Secretary was instructed to communicate with The Right Honourable W. E. Gladstone, Chancellor of the Exchequer, for the purpos of asirtaining whither he would attend a soriee.

6 December 1859

The Secretary read the following letter from the Chancellor of the Exchequer in reply to his of 30th November:

---

[1] Reprints of a newspaper report of Newton's speech were sent to branches by executive council of the A.S.E. *A.S.E. Monthly Report*, Dec. 1859.
[2] James Reid, glassmakers.

Downing Street

December 5, 1859

Sir,

I have had the honour to receive your letter of the 30th November written on behalf of the Trades Delegates Association of Edinburgh. My stay in Edinburgh will, from the pressure of other engagments, I fear be very limited,[1] but if it is desired by them who know the feelings of the working classes that I should attend one of their meetings, I will endeavour to make arrangements for the purpose. I have no doubt you will kindly excuse me if from the shortness of time I do not at once propose any particular time, but I will transmit your letter to my friend Dean Ramsay of Ainslie Place[2] whose guest I am to be and if you will communicate with him he will inform you whither within the time I am able to allow to my visit I can hope to bear the honour which you kindly propose. I remain, Sir,

Your very obedient servant,

W. E. Gladstone

William Troup and John Iverach was then appointed to wait upon Dean Ramsay with refrence to Mr Gladstone's letter, And if necessary upon the Lord Provost to asertain if he would take the chair in the event of the soriee taking place.

The nixt business taken up was the election of office bearers for the ensuing Six months. Mr William Troup was elected President on the Motion of Mr Alexander Frazer, seconded by George Latimer. Mr George Smith was Elected Vice President on the motion of John Iverach, seconded by William Thompson. Mr Tait was reelected Treasurer on the motion of George Latimer, seconded by John Miller. Previous to the election of Secretary it was resolved on the motion of William Troup, seconded by George Campbell, that he receive a minumum saleray of 30s. per annum. John Iverach was then Elected Secretary. A hearty Vote

---

[1] Gladstone visited Edinburgh on 12 December to preside as rector over a meeting of the university court. *Scotsman*, 13 December 1859.

[2] Edward Bannerman Ramsay, 1793-1872, dean of Edinburgh 1841-72, author of *Reminiscences of Scottish Life and Character*.

of thanks was awarded to Mr John Borrowman for his services in the chair.

20 December 1859

Vice President in the chair. In the absence of the secretary with the minutes there was no bussiness transacted and the meeting adjourned.

1860

17 January 1860

Delegates present: Brass Founders, Mr George Smith; Clock Makers, Mr George Latimer; French Polishers, Mr John Miller; Joiners, Mr William Tait; Machienest,[1] Mr George Campbell; Blacksmiths, Mr Alexander Frazer; Flint Glass Cutters, Messers John Beaton, Andrew Brown; Tailors, Messers William Troup, John Iverach. Mr George Smith, Vice President, in the Chair.[2]

The United Flint Glass Cutters having given in their adhesion to The United Trades Delegates Association, Mesers John Beaton and Andrew Brown appeared as the representatives of that body. It was Resolved on the Motion of Alexander Frazer That the Secretary be instructed to write to the Masons and Printers reminding them of their promase to assist in defraying the expences of the meeting held in the Queen Street Hall on 11 November 1859. On consideration of the services of Messers Bauld as Secretary and Tait as Treasurer for the Subscription in aid of the Lockouts in the Building Trades of London, it was resolved: That as there is a small balance of £1 1s. over they receive 10s. each, and that Mr Troup receive the remaining shilling as he had lost a good deal of time collecting during his working hours.

The nixt question taken into consideration was the propritey of requesting Dr Hodgson to deliver a lecture upon the 'Relations of Workmen and their Employers'.[3] The subject after a good deal of conversation was remitted to the President's Committee with power

---

[1] I.e., engineers. Delegates from the Amalgamated Society of Engineers are variously described in the minutes as engineers, machinists, or Amalgamated Trades.

[2] Troup, the president, was evidently present later.

[3] Dr William Ballantine Hodgson, 1815-80, educator and popular lecturer, an active Liberal, first professor of commercial and political economy and mercantile law at Edinburgh 1871-80.

to act according as they saw oppertunity to have an interview with him and report. Further consideration of the Soriee in honour of Lord Brogham and the Chancellar of the Exchequer was refferred to the Presedent's Committee.[1]

31 January 1860

Delegates present: Joiners, Messers William Tait, John Borrowman; Brass-Founders, Mr George Smith; Flint-Glass-Makers, James Reid; Clock Makers, George Latimer; Plumbers, J. G. Bauld; Flint Glass Cutters, Messers Andrew Brown, John Beaton; Black Smiths, Mr Alexander Frazer; French Pollishers, Mr John Miller; Tailors, Messers William Troup, John Iverach. Vice President in the Chair.[2]

The Secretary reported that he had written to the Secretarys of the Masons and Printers respectively with reference to their proportion of the expences of the Queen Street Hall meeting. He likewise reported having written to Lord Brougham and the Chancellor of the Exchequer regarding the Trades Delegates' demonstration in the event of their exceptance while in Edinburgh. Mr Latimer and the Secretary reported that they had heard Dr Hodgson's Lecture upon 'Popular Economic Fallacies', and from the general tenor of his views upon the subject they would not recomend the Trades Delegates to engage him to deliver a Lecture. Messers Bauld and Latimer were then appointed auditors to examin the Treasurer's Accounts.

Mr John Beaton read a paper upon the necessity of an aggregate union of the Associated Trades of the United Kingdom for the purpose of supporting one another when engaged in a struggle with Capitilists. He suggested a levy of 2d. per man per week during the continance of a strike or Lockout. A good deal of discussion took place upon the subject and it was ultimately referred for future consideration.

The Auditors reported that they had found the Accounts and Cash in the Treasurer's hand perfectly correct.

Mr Alexander Frazer then moved that the Secretary be instructed to write to the Secretary of the Associated Bulding Trades of London

[1] Lord Brougham was president of the Social Science Association and (1860-68) chancellor of the university of Edinburgh.
[2] Troup, the president, was evidently present later.

to enquire whither they were likely to send a Delegate again to Scotland, and in the event of their doing so to recomend that he be instructed to visit Edinburgh. Likewise that the Secretary be instructed to comunicate with the Glasgow Trades Council for the purpose of asertaining the means adopted by them to raise subscriptions for behoof of the Lockouts in London. Seconded by Mr John Miller.

14 February 1860

Delegates present: Joiners, Mr William Caw; Clock Makers, Mr George Latimer; Flint Glass Makers, Mr James Reid; Flint Glass Cutters, Messers John Beaton, Andrew Brown; French pollishers, Mr John Miller; Tailors, Messers William Troup, John Iverach.

The Secretary read correspondence from Lord Brougham, the Chancellor of the Exchequer, Mr Potter, Secretary to the London Building Trades,[1] and Mr Lawrence, Secretary to the Glasgow Trades Council.[2] The Secretary was then instructed to communicate with Dean Ramsay regarding the visit of Mr Gladstone and Lord Brougham to Edinburgh. Mr Caw then paid over to the Treasurer 10s., being the Joiners' contribution towards the expences of the Queen Street Hall Meeting. The Secretary paid over 5s. for the same object from Mr John Sutherland, Mason, being his own personal subscription. Mr John Beaton's paper upon the Amalgimation of Trades then came on for consideration. After long discussion it was ultimatly referred to a Select Committee to prepare for publication to which Messers Frazer, Beaton, and the Secretary were then appointed.

17 February 1860

Select Committee met to consider Mr John Beaton's paper on Amalgamation of Trades, and after having carefuly gone over it

---

[1] George Potter, 1832–93, a carpenter, first became prominent as a trade union leader in the London building trades strike in 1859; founded in October 1861 the *Beehive*, a weekly working class newspaper.
[2] Matthew Lawrence, a tailor, secretary of Glasgow trades council until January 1863, subsequently a leader of the London and English journeymen tailors' unions; a member 1866-8 of the general council of the International Working Men's Association. *Minutes of the General Council of the First International, 1866-8* (Moscow and London, 1964), 426; M. Stewart and L. Hunter, *The Needle is Threaded* (London, 1964), 54-5; *Glasgow Sentinel*, 10 January 1863.

made such amendments of its detales as appered necessary without making any alteration in the general principles. Agreed that Mr Beaton bring the amended copy forward at the nixt meeting of Delegates.

28 February 1860

Delegates present: Brass Founders, Mr George Smith; Joiners, Messers William Tait, William Thompson; Machienests, George Campbell; Clock Makers, Mr George Latimer; Flint Glass Cutters, Mr John Beaton; Tailors, Mr John Iverach. Vice President in the Chair.

The Secretary read a letter from the Secretary of the Glasgow Trades Council. The report of the select committee upon Mr Beaton's paper was then taken into consideration. The amendments were approved of and copys ordred to be sent to the Trades Confrence, London,[1] and the Trades Council, Glasgow, so as to get their opinions upon the subject.[2]

A deputation was then appointed to wate upon Dean Ramsay for the purpose of assertaining if he had got any information regarding the visit of the Chancellor of the Exchequer. Mr William Troup and the Secretary to form the deputation. Mr Latimer then gave notice of the following subject for consideration at the nixt meeting of Delegates, Viz.: That it is desirable that The Trades Delegates take up the question of Building Associations amoungst the Working Classes.

13 March 1860

Delegates present: Brass Founders, Mr George Smith; Flint Glass Cutters, Messrs John Beaton, Andrew Brown; Flint Glass Makers, Mr James Reid; Clock Makers, Mr George Latimer; French Polishers, Mr John Miller; Machienists, Mr George Campbell; Black Smiths, Mr Alexander Frazer; Tailors, Mr John Iverach. Vice President[3] in the Chair.

[1] The conference was formed by London trade unionists in the main building trades shortly before the 1859 lock-out. R. W. Postgate, *The Builders' History* (London, 1923), 168-76.
[2] If Beaton's paper was published as a pamphlet no copies of it are known to survive.
[3] George Smith, brassfounders.

The Secretary read a letter from Dean Ramsay with reference to the visit of Mr W. E. Gladston, in consequence of which the Deputation appointed at last meeting did not require to wait upon him.[1]

Mr George Latimer's Motion, of which he had given notice at the previous meeting, with regard to the propriety of forming Building Associations amoungst the working Classes, then came on for consideration. Information having been received to the effect that a meeting was being held at the present time in Mr Burden's for the purpose of forming A Building Association amoungst working men, it was deemed expedient not to proceed further in the matter untill such time as we had further information regarding their proceedings. Mr George Latimer and Mr George Campbell were then appointed to wait upon them and report. On their return they reported that a deputation from the Building Association would wait upon the Trades Delegates and give every information. Further consideration of the question was then suspended.

Mr George Latimer then intimated that he had been requisted by the Parlimentary Reform Association[2] to bring the question of Parlimentary Reform under the consideration of the Delegates, and to urge them to petition in favour of the present Goverment Bill, sugesting such amendments as they might think necessary.[3] Several members having given expression to their opinions on the subject, the question was ultimatly raised whither it was a subject that we could legitimatly consider under our constitution. The majority being of opinion that it was not, the subject droped.

The deputation from the Building Association was then received. They gave full details regarding the object they had in view and the organization of their association. Several questions having been asked and satisfactorily awnsered, the deputation received the thanks of the Delegates and withdrew. The Delegates having considered that the above association would fulfill the object Mr Latimer aimed

---

[1] Gladstone paid a brief visit to Edinburgh on 16 April 1860 as rector of the university.
[2] The Edinburgh committee of the Association had met on 5 March 1860 and had agreed to petition in favour of the Bill and to propose some modifications to it. *Edinburgh Evening Courant*, 6 March 1860.
[3] Bills to extend the franchise had been introduced by the Government on 1 March 1860 but were withdrawn in June.

at, it was not considered necessary to take any further proceedings in the matter.[1]

27 March 1860

Delegates present: Brass Founders, Mr George Smith; Joiners, Messers William Tait, David Henderson; Flint Glass Cutters, John Beaton, Andrew Brown; Plumbers, Mr J. G. Bauld; Tailors, Messers William Troup, John Iverach. Vice President in the Chair.

Correspondence read by the Secretary from the Secretary of the Glasgow Trades Council approving of the plan submitted to them by the Trades Delegates for A National League of the Working Classes. Mr Beaton likewise read a letter from the general Secretary of the Flint Glass Cutters' Association which expressed general approval of the scheme.

Mr David Henderson was then interduced as one of the representatives of the joiners in the room of Mr William Thompson, retired. Resolved on the motion of John Iverach, seconded by Andrew Brown, that Mr David Henderson's name be entered in the Minute book as one of the Joiners' representatives. It was then resolved that all the absent members be summond to attend the nixt meeting of Delegates for the purpose of considering the Rules of the Association preparrotry to printing new copys. Moved by John Beaton, Seconded by Andrew Brown. A deputation from the Working Classes Building Association was then received. They gave some general information regarding the progress they had made. The Delegates agreed to give them all the support in their power individualy and the Deputation withdrew.

10 April 1860

Delegates present: Brassfounders, Mr George Smith; Blacksmiths, Mr Alexander Frazer; Machienists, Mr George Campbell; Clock-Makers, Mr George Latimer; Joiners, Messers John Borrowman, William Caw, David Henderson; Flint Glass Makers, Mr James Reid; Flint Glass Cutters, Messers Andrew Brown, John Beaton; Tailors, John Iverach. Vice President in the Chair.

[1] No reference has been found in the press to this building association, but it may have been titled the Working Man's Building Association (see below, p. 32).

The Rules and Regulations then came on For consideration when it was moved by Alexander Frazer, Seconded by John Beaton, That the Association be named The Council of United Trades. William Caw Moved as an amendment, Seconded by John Borrowman, that the Association be called The Council of United Trades Delegates. After a good deal of discussion the amendment was carried by a small majority.

The Preamble was nixt considered and agreed too, with the alteration of the Name of the Association where it ocurrs and the substution of Council for Committee. First rule was agreed to without amendment. The second was agreed, with the substution of Council for Committee. The Third was agreed, with the omission of the Treasurer's Monthly statement. The Fourth was agreed without amendment. The Fifth rule was under consideration when a deputation from the Working Man's Building Association was interduced. They stated that the shareholders had agreed to advertize instead of calling a public meeting and that they had mentioned the name of the Trades Delegates as approving of the scheme in their advertizment. After some further conversation regarding the progress of the Building Association the deputation withdrew. It being now past 10 oclock it was moved and agreed to that the meeting stand adjourned till Tuesday the 24th inst.

24 April 1860

Delegates present: Flint Glass Cutters, Messers John Beaton, Andrew Brown; Flint Glass Makers, Mr James Reid; Plumbers, Mr J. G. Bauld; Brass founders, Mr George Smith; Tailors, Messers William Troup, John Iverach.

The Secretary read correspondence from Mr George Potter, London, and Mr Matthew Lawrence of the Glasgow Trades Council, with refrence to the proposal for an amalgamation of the Trades Unions of the United Kingdom. A lengthend discussion then ensued upon the following resolution forwarded by the Glasgow Trades Council, Viz., 'That this Council approve of the Scheme for a Working Man's Mutual Protection and Co-operative league and that we leave it to the Edinburgh Delegates to submit a plan for the carrying out of the same. But that this Council desire that it be limited to Scotland.' Mr Beaton was of opinion that as Glasgow was the great center of Scottish industery it would be better that the Trades Council there draw up a plan. At the same time he would have no hesitation in undertaking the responsibility along with others of drawing up a plan if it was considered necessary by the Delegates. Mr James Reid concurred in Mr Beaton's views regarding the desirability of the Glasgow Council taking the responsibility of drawing up a plan, especaly as the Council had a stronger organiza-tion and occupied a more prominent place before the Public than the Edinburgh Delegates. Mr Brown strongly urged the propriety of the League extending throughout the United Kingdom and re-greted exceedingly that the Trades Council should have thought of confining it to Scotland as it would exclude the Glass-Cutters and Glass Makers from participating in the benifits of the League. Mr Smith and other members present having given expression to their opinions upon the subject much to the same effect, it was ultimately agreed that Mr Beaton and the Secretary be instructed to prepare a reply to the resolution of the Glasgow Trades Council embodying the views of the Delegates upon the subject. The other business upon the programe, Viz., the election of a Treasurer, and the con-sideration of the rules not disposed of at last meeting, was agreed to be left to the nixt meeting as it was to late to dispose of them at the present time.

8 May 1860

Delegates present: Black Smiths, Mr Alexander Frazer; Brass Founders, Mr George Smith; Clock Makers, Mr George Latimer; Plumbers, Mr J. G. Bauld; Flint Glass Cutters, Mr Andrew Brown; Flint Glass Makers, Mr James Reid; Joiners, Mr William Caw; Tailors, Messers William Troup, John Iverach.

Consideration of Rules resumed at the point they were left by the Meeting of 10th April. Rule 5th agreed to as followes: That Officebearers shall be elected at the first Meeting of the Council in December of each year, and that they shall hold office for Twelve Months. The respective Trades are recomended to appoint their delegates for the above period. Rule 6th agreed to, with the substitu-tion of Council for Association. Rule 7th amended as follows: That the Council meet every alternate Tuesday or oftener if Necessary for the transaction of the general business of the Association. The

c

President to have the power of calling Special Meetings on the requisition of the Delegates of any trade in Connection with the Council. Five to form a quorum. Rule 8th Omitted. Rule 9th Amended as followes: That notice of all Motions be given at the Meeting previous to their coming on for discussion. Said Motions to have precedince of other business. Rules 10th, 11th and 12th agreed to with the substution of Council for Committee and Association where they occurr in said Rules. Rule 13th Omitted. The following byelaw was then agreed to: That the Chair be taken at a quarter past eight each night when the roll shall be called, and if their is not a quorum present the meeting stand adjourned for that night. And that no business be taken up after 10 oclock.

Mr James Reid then gave notice of the following motion for nixt meeting: That the Council resolve itself into Committee for the purpose of considering the best means for raising funds to carray out the general objects and business of the Council. The nixt business taken up was the election of Treasurer, When Messers Frazer and Caw were proposed. Mr Frazer declined to stand as, owing to other engagements, he could not attend to the dutys. Mr William Caw was then duly Elected. It was then agreed that A Sub Committee be appointed to make the nesscary enquiries preparatory to making arrangments for the Annual Trip. The following Committee was appointed, Viz., Messers Latimer, Caw, Beaton, Frazer, and Troup.

22 May 1860

Delegates present: Brass Founders, Mr George Smith; Flint Glass Makers, Mr James Reid; Flint Glass Cutters, Mr Andrew Brown; Black Smiths, Mr Alexander Frazer; Plumbers, Mr J. G. Bauld; Joiners, Messrs William Caw, David Henderson; Tailors, Messrs William Troup, John Iverach; Engineers, Mr George Campbell.

Correspondence was read from the North British and the Edinburgh, Perth and Dundee Railway Companys stating terms upon which they would give Excursion Trains to the Various places on their respective lines. Likewise a letter from P. H. Rathbone, Esq., one of the Secretaries to the Social Science Association,[1] requesting

---

[1] National Association for the Promotion of Social Science, founded 1857.

the Edinburgh Trades Delegates to forward information upon the subject of their enquiries, viz., The relationship of Employer and Employed and the particulars of strikes and lockouts.

The business on the program was then proceeded with. 1st The Excursion was considered and unanimously agreed that it should be to Glasgow. Messrs Caw and Frazer were appointed to go to Glasgow and make the necessary arrangments and obtain what priviledges they could for the Excursionists. The dates fixed upon for the Trip were the last Saturday in July or the first in August.

A long discussion took place upon the best means of meeting the views of the Social Science Association. It was ultimatly agreed that the Secretary be instructed to write requesting copys of Questions so as to suply all the Trades represented at the Council.

Mr James Reid's Motion with regard to the Ways and Means was posponed untill nixt meeting. Likewise the amended Copy of Rules was delayed untill such time as Mr Reid's motion was considered, the Council being of opinion that it should be embodied in them.

A report of A Meeting held in Glasgow for the purpose of raising a fund to Aid Garibaldi, which had been adressed to the Secretary of the Council, was then considered. It was ultimatly agreed that the subject was one that did not come within the Constitution of the Council and it was accordingly dismissed.

5 June 1860

Delegates present: Brassfounders, George Smith; Blacksmiths, Alexander Frazer; Engineers, George Campbell; Flint Glass Cutters, John Beaton, Andrew Brown; Plumbers, J. G. Bald; Joiners, David Henderson, William Caw, John Borrowman; Tailors, William Troup, John Iverach; Clockmakers, G. Latimer. Vice President in the Chair.[1]

Correspondence from various Parties was read and the subject of Trades Societies and the printed Queries issued by the National Association of Social Science. . . . On the motion of William Caw, seconded by George Latimer, it was unanimously agreed to send the various Circulars to the different trades represented at the Council and for them to have the answers sent here not later than next meeting.

[1] George Smith, brassfounders. Troup, the president, was evidently present later.

Annual Excursion: The report of the deputation to Glasgow was then given by William Caw. It was moved by George Campbell, seconded by G. Latimer, the Schedule of agreement be signed by the President and Secretary and transmitted to the Edinburgh and Glasgow Railways Company's office, Mr J. Borrowman dissenting. The Secretary then paid in to the Council the sum of Ten Shillings, being the Printers' Subscription in aid of the Public Meeting held in Queen Street Hall on 11th November 1859, on the Labour Question. The Council then considered the subject of the Painters of Glasgow.[1] After a long discussion it was unanimously agreed to call a Special meeting of the Council, along with Edinburgh Painters or their Committee, and after hearing both sides to act accordingly, said meeting to be held here on Friday evening the 8th current at 8 oclock p.m.

The draught of a Bill for Posting and circulation was read and approved and 250 large and 1000 small Bills was ordered to be printed and circulated.[2]

The Secretary, John Iverach, in pursuance of notice given 4 weeks ago, then resigned his office and Alexander Frazer was unanimously elected for the next 6 months. On the motion of the Secretary the usual gratuity of 15s. was given to the retiring Secretary and a unanimous vote of thanks for his effecient services during the last 6 months. The expenses of the deputation to Glasgow (£1) was ordered to be paid them.

19 June 1860

Delegates present: Brassfounders, George Smith; Blacksmiths, Alexander Frazer; Flint Glass Cutters, John Beaton, Andrew Brown; Plumbers, J. G. Bald; Joiners, William Caw, John Borrowman; Tailors, William Troup, John Iverach; Engineers, George Campbell. Vice President in the chair.[3]

The Council took up the subject of the Annual Excursion. They agreed to meet on Saturday the 23rd current for the dispatch of Business and Reporting the answers to the Queries sent by National Social Science Association. The Secretary then reported concerning

[1] They were in the eighth week of a strike against the refusal of their employers to continue existing wages and other conditions. *Glasgow Sentinel*, 9 and 21 June 1860.
[2] This seems to relate to the annual outing.
[3] Troup, the president, was evidently present later.

the Special Meeting with the Painters of Edinburgh and the Secretary was instructed to write to Secretary of the Glasgow Painters accordingly.

The motion of Mr Reid was then considered. After some discussion the following was agreed to as Rule XI: That this Council, in order to carry out the objects they have in view, recommend that all the Trades represented at this Board should make quarterly subscription among their members or vote a portion of their Funds to provide the necessary means for furthering the important objects specified in the above Rules. Seconded by W. Caw and unanimously agreed to. The Secretary then brought before the Council the subject of an Address to be printed and circulated among the Tradesmen of Edinburgh. After a long discussion the subject was referred till next regular fortnightly meeting.

3 July 1860

Delegates present: Brassfounders, George Smith; Blacksmiths, Alexander Frazer; Glasscutters, Andrew Brown; Plumbers, J. G. Bald; Tailors, William Troup; Joiners, William Caw, John Borrowman; Engineers, George Campbell.

A Letter designed to be sent to the Secretaries of the National Social Science Association was read and approved and answers to the printed Queries sent by said Association were read from the Joiners and Brassfounders. The Tailors reported that their answers were not ready but would be in the Secretary's hands before Saturday the 7th, when said letter and documents were to be dispatched to London. Rule XI was then read and approved and ordered to be added to the list of Rules.

A Paper from London on the Proposed Organization of Trades and General Trades Union Directory was read and the consideration of it deferred.[1] The proposed Address to the Tradesmen of Edinburgh was then considered and after some discussion was again deferred. There was nothing further to do about the Excursion to Glasgow except writing to some of the Places to be open to Excursionists, which the Secretary was instructed to do.

[1] The paper was presumably from London trades council, which was in the process of formation and published the *Directory* in 1861. G. Tate, *London Trades Council 1860-1950* (London, 1950), 5-9.

17 July 1860

Delegates present: Brassfounders, George Smith; Blacksmiths, Alexander Frazer; Engineers, George Campbell; Glassmakers, James Reid; Glass Cutters, Andrew Brown, James Beaton; Plumbers, J. G. Bald; Joiners, J. Borrowman, William Caw, D. Henderson; Tailors, William Troup; Clockmakers, G. Latimer.

Correspondence was read from London, and a verbal report was given by the President as regarding the answers given by the Tailors to the Printed Queries issued by the Congress of Social Science. Mr Caw then suggested that the Secretary be instructed to write to the Secretary of the [Glasgow] Trades Council to see if a meeting could be held with them on Saturday the 28th, the day of the Excursion to Glasgow, about 4 or 5 p.m., leaving them to arrange the details of said meeting.

The Secretary then brought before the Council for them to consider the propriety of sending a deputation to the National Congress of Social Science, whose next meeting is to be held in Glasgow on the 24th of September. Mr Campbell moved that the subject be delayed till this day fortnight, seconded by G. Smith. G. Latimer then moved as an Amendment that this Council pledge themselves to send two of a Deputation to that Congress, seconded by James Reid. The motion was carried by the casting vote of the Chairman.

G. Campbell intimated to the Council that at their next meeting he would bring before them the subject of a proposed Testimonial to Mr Newton, Engineer, London. Agreed to meet on Tuesday, Wednesday, Thursday and Friday next to further the Annual Excursion.

31 July 1860

Delegates present: Brassfounders, George Smith; Blacksmiths, Alexander Frazer; Joiners, William Caw, J. Borrowman, D. Henderson; Tailors, William Troup; Clockmakers, George Latimer; Bakers, John Scott.

The Council took up the subject of sending a Deputation of two of their number to attend the meeting of the National Congress of Social Science. It was proposed by William Troup, seconded by John Borrowman, that Messrs Frazer and Caw be sent to the National

Congress and farther that the Secretary be instructed to write to the General Secretary of said Congress intimating the same and requesting him to send the Council a Programme of the Business neccessary for the guidance of the deputation, and also authorizing the Treasurer to pay the Subscription if it should be required before the next meeting of this Council by the General Secretary of said Congress.

John Scott, a delegate from the trade of Bakers, appeared and was unanimously admitted a member of this Council.

The Council then considered Mr Campbell's motion. After some discussion and on account of Mr Campbell's absence it was agreed to defer this subject till next meeting. Mr Latimer gave notice of a motion for next meeting, Viz., That a request be sent to Lord Brougham to attend a Soiree to be given him in Edinburgh should he be present at the National Congress meeting in September next, time and place to be afterwards considered.

14 August 1860

Delegates present: Blacksmiths, Alexander Frazer; Engineers, George Campbell; Glassmakers, James Reid; Glass Cutters, James Beaton; Joiners, William Caw, J. Borrowman; Tailors, William Troup.

The subject of the deputation to the National Congress of Social Science was considered. The Council agreed that the sum of £3 be allowed the deputation for their expenses, being at the rate of 5s. per day. On the motion of G. Campbell, the Treasurer was authorized to pay the subscription to said Congress amounting to £1 1s.

The motion of G. Campbell relative to the proposed testimonial to Mr Newton was then considered, and G. Campbell moved: That this Council recommend to their respective trades to aid the Amalgamated Trades in this subscription. Seconded by James Reid and unanimously agreed to.[1] The motion of G. Latimer was then agreed to stand over, by reason of his absence, till next meeting, and the

[1] For 'the able manner in which he advocated the cause of the Amalgamated and all other Trade Societies', Newton was presented with a testimonial in 1860 in the form of a silver goblet, 300 sovereigns, and an address on vellum. J. B. Jefferys, *The Story of the Engineers* (London, 1945), 46 (quoting the minutes of the executive council of the Amalgamated Society of Engineers, 28 May 1860).

council decided that the principal business of the next meeting was to be the consideration of a Paper drawn up by the Secretary and designed to be sent to the General Secretary of the National Congress.

28 August 1860

Delegates present; Brassfounders, G. Smith, John Purdie; Blacksmiths, A. Frazer; Engineers, G. Campbell; Joiners, W. Caw, J. Borrowman, D. Henderson; Bakers, John Scott, Andrew Simpson; Clock makers, G. Latimer; Masons, J. Sutherland, George Herbert; Glass Cutters, Andrew Brown, J. Beaton; Glass Makers, J. Reid; Tailors, William Troup.

On the Minutes of the former meeting being read G. Campbell moved that an alteration be made to the following effect: That the allowance voted to the deputation who are to represent this Council at the meeting of National Congress on the 24 inst. form no precedent to the Council for future guidance in these matters. Seconded by J. Beaton. William Caw moved that the minutes remain as they are, seconded by J. Reid. 5 voted for G. Campbell's motion and 3 for William Caw. The alteration was then made and the minutes approved.

G. Latimer then brought forward his motion. It was seconded by G. Campbell. An amendment was made by J. Beaton that the subject be not gone into. 9 voted for the amendment and 2 for the motion. Correspondence was read from Glasgow relating to Social Congress; from the Operative Brassfounders of Edinburgh and Leith appointing two Delegates; and also from the operative masons of Edinburgh appointing two Delegates who were cordially received and their names added to the Roll. There was brought before the Council a statement which appeared in the *Glasgow Sentinel* of the 18th curt. reflecting on the doings of this Council in regard to the Painters on Strike there, and the Secretary was instructed to write to the Trades Council of Glasgow in regard to the same.[1] Papers designed to be sent to the Council of the National Congress were read by

[1] Above, p. 36. The *Sentinel* reported a statement at a meeting of Glasgow trades council on 15 August that the Edinburgh painters had never had any invitation from Edinburgh trades council to discuss the strike in Glasgow.

A. Frazer and William Caw. They met with general approval and were ordered to be transmitted to London before 1st September.

11 September 1860

Delegates present: Bakers, John Scott, Andrew Simpson; Brass-founders, G. Smith, J. Purdie; Blacksmiths, Alexander Frazer; Clockmakers, G. Latimer; Engineers, G. Campbell; Glass makers, J. Reid, J. Kelly; Glass Cutters, Andrew Brown; Joiners, William Caw, D. Henderson; Masons, G. Herbert; Tailors, William Troup.

Correspondence was read from the Secretary of the Trades Council of Glasgow in reply to a letter addressed to them which letter gave general satisfaction. A Letter was also read from the local Secretary of the Social Congress enclosing members' cards for the deputation, which was approved off. The subject of a gratuity to the Servants of the Hunterian Museum, Glasgow, [was raised] when G. Latimer moved that the sum of not less than 5s., nor more than 7s. 6d., be given to them. Seconded by Andrew Brown. G. Campbell moved as an amendment that a discretionary power be given to the deputation to grant a sum to the servants of said Museum, the sum not to exceed 15s. Seconded by W. Caw. There voted for the amendment 9, for the motion 2.

The Rules of the Council were then read and the following addition was made to Rule 5: And it shall be the duty of said Delegates to report the past proceedings of the Council at the meeting of their trade preceeding their re-election or the election of others. 250 copies of Rules were ordered to be printed before next meeting. The subject of Ways and Means was then taken up and after considering it each Delegate was enjoined to bring the subject before their respective trades at their first meeting.

25 September 1860

Delegates present: Plumbers, J. G. Bald; Glass Cutters, J. Beaton; Brassfounders, G. Smith; Clockmakers, G. Latimer; Masons, J. Sutherland; Tailors, William Troup.

A letter from the Right Honourable the Earl of Caithness [was received][1] and some papers Lodged by Mr Sutherland respecting

[1] James Sinclair, fourteenth earl of Caithness, 1821-81, inventor, lecturer on scientific subjects, and representative peer of Scotland 1859-66.

the nine hours movement intended by the operative Masons in the spring of 1861. A Newspaper was handed in from the Delegates at present in Glasgow. The conversation turning upon the Social Science Congress meeting, other business was deferred until the next meeting of the Council.

9 October 1860

Delegates present: Bakers, John Scott, Andrew Simpson; Blacksmiths, Alexander Frazer; Brassfounders, George Smith; Clockmakers, G. Latimer; Glass makers, James Reid; Glass Cutters, Andrew Brown; Joiners, William Caw, D. Henderson, J. Borrowman; Masons, J. Sutherland; Tailors, William Troup.

Correspondence was read from the operative Masons anent the 9 hours per day movement. After it was stated that the operative Joiners intend holding a meeting in reference to above object, The Council recommend to the various trades represented at the Council to bring it before their respective trades and report at next meeting.

The Council then took up the subject of the Letter to the Trades Council of Glasgow anent the operative Painters there. It was the unanimous wish of the Council that the names of the Parties connected with the Painters here should not be sent to Glasgow as it might operate injuriously against them, and the Secretary was instructed to write the same.

Messrs Latimer, Reid and Brown were appointed a deputation to wait on operative Printers at their meeting on Saturday the 13th, the same to be intimated to their Secretary Mr J. Wilkie. A verbal communication was then made regarding a course of Lectures on Physiology by Dr Hogdson.[1] The Council agreed to co-operate in the same as individuals. The Report of the Delegates of the Council to the Social Science Congress was then given and cordially received. On the motion of Mr Sutherland, seconded by G. Smith, a unanimous vote of thanks was given to the Delegates for their services and their extra expenses authorized to be paid them.

23 October 1860

Delegates present: Brassfounders, G. Smith, J. Purdie; Blacksmiths, Alexander Frazer; Glass Makers, J. Reid, J. Kelly; Glass Cutters,

[1] Dr W. B. Hodgson; see above, p. 26, n. 3.

J. Beaton; Joiners, W. Caw; Masons, J. Sutherland, G. Herbert; Tailors, William Troup. The Vice President in the Chair.[1]

Reports anent operative Masons' 9 hours per day movement, showing the present position of it among the members of trade in Scotland, was read by Mr Sutherland and various reports, generally favourable, from the different members of the Board were then given. The Secretary then reported that he had written to the Secretary of the trades Council of Glasgow and to that there had been no answer. A verbal report was given in by the deputation regarding their interview with the operative Printers, who promised to consider the subject the deputation brought before them.

Reports were also given regarding the Subscription in aid of Trades Council funds. It was agreed to print 200 Subscription Sheets, to be issued among the various trades of this city. The subject of the Delegates' extra expenses for attending the Social Congress, amounting to £1 4s. 4d., was then considered and that sum was ordered to be paid them. The Council then considered the subject of Free Libraries for the Working Classes, but as none of the members of this board could positively state whether the Free Libraries Act extended to Scotland, it was deferred till next meeting.

6 November 1860

Delegates present: Brassfounders, G. Smith, J. Purdie; Blacksmiths, Alexander Frazer; Glassmakers, J. Reid; Clockmakers, G. Latimer; Joiners, William Caw, J. Borrowman; Tailors, William Troup.

Report given anent the Subscription Sheets and the following were given out: Mr Troup, 4 Sheets – 8, 9, 11, 12; Mr Reid – 1, 2, 6; Mr Smith – 4, 5; Mr Purdie – 3; Mr Latimer – 10; Mr Caw – 1 to 20. The Secretary reported that the Free Libraries Act does not extend to Scotland, and the subject dropped.[2] A long conversation then took place regarding a course of Lectures this winter. It was agreed that until the Subscription sheets be returned said lectures be

---

[1] George Smith, brassfounders. Troup, the president, was evidently present later.
[2] The Act of 1855, which permitted certain local authorities to levy a rate of up to 1d. to establish buildings for public libraries and museums, applied to England only. But the Public Libraries (Scotland) Act, 1854, allowed any burgh adopting the Act to levy a rate of up to 1d. to provide buildings and books, maps, and specimens. J. Minto, *A History of the Public Library Movement* (London, 1932), 94, 99.

not entered into. Note: Mr Reid got *Parliamentary Report on Councils of Conciliation*.

20 November 1860

Delegates present: Brassfounders, G. Smith, J. Purdie; Bakers, James Inglis; Blacksmiths, Alexander Frazer; Engineers, George Campbell; Joiners, William Caw, J. Borrowman; Plumbers, J. G. Bald; Masons, G. Herbert, D. Lockerbie, William Glen. The vice President in the Chair.

D. Lockerbie and William Glen were received as Delegates from the operative Masons in addition to G. Herbert; and James Inglis was received as a Delegate from the operative Bakers. Verbal reports were given in regarding the Subscription Sheets: the sheets were in circulation, but no report could be given in till next meeting. The Council were then engaged in drawing up a course of Lectures for the benefit of the working classes of this City.

4 December 1860

Delegates present: Brassfounders, G. Smith, J. Purdie; Blacksmiths, Alexander Frazer; Clockmakers, George Latimer; Glassmakers, James Reid; Glass Cutters, Andrew Brown, James Beaton; Joiners, William Caw, J. Borrowman; Tailors, William Troup; Masons, G. Herbert, D. Lockerbie, William Glen.

Reports were given in regarding the Subscription Sheets, when there was reported from the Joiners' Sheet, No. 2, per D. Bain, 2s. 3d.; from the Brassfounders', per G. Smith, 3s. 3d.; from the Blacksmiths', per A. Frazer, £1 5s. 1d. – total £1 10s. 7d. A Letter was read from the Secretary of the Edinburgh Branch of the Amalgamated Society of Engineers stating that they had re-elected G. Campbell as their Delegate for the next 12 months.

The Council then considered the Programme of the course of Lectures. The subject was deferred till next meeting. J. Borrowman gave notice that at the next meeting of the Council he would bring before them the following motion: The propriety of a Public meeting for the purpose of furthering the nine hours amongst the working classes of this City. The Secretary was instructed to communicate with the Trades Council of Glasgow anent the above subject and also on the proposed course of Lectures. The Council then proceeded to the election of Office Bearers for 1861. [William Troup was elected President by 8 votes to 3 for James Beaton; G. Herbert Vice President by 8 votes to 2 for G. Smith; and Alexander Frazer and William Caw were unanimously elected Secretary and Treasurer respectively.] Messrs Smith and Beaton were appointed Auditors to Audit the Books and report at next meeting, the President Convener. The Council authorized the payment of the half yearly salary of the Secretary of 15s., and a gratuity to the Treasurer of 10s.

18 December 1860

Delegates present: Brassfounders, G. Smith, J. Purdie; Blacksmiths, Alexander Frazer; Glass Makers, James Reid, James Kelly; Glass Cutters, Andrew Brown; Joiners, William Caw; Tailors, William Troup, J. McWhinnie; Masons, G. Herbert, D. Lockerbie, William Glen. The Vice President and afterwards the President in the Chair.

Correspondence was read from the Secretary of the Trades Council of Glasgow. Reports were then given in regarding the Subscription Sheets and there was received from the Masons, per D. Lockerbie, £2; from the Glass Cutters, per Andrew Brown, 6s. 4d.; from the Glass Makers, per James Reid, 7s. 2d. – total £2 13s. 6d. The Council then took up the proposed Lectures and after some Alterations it was remitted to the President's Committee with full powers, said committee to meet on Friday the 21st at 8 p.m.

A Deputation from the United Corkcutters of Edinburgh and Leith here entered and having stated the reason why they were out on Strike, and after some questions had been put and answered, the Council came to the following Decision, viz., That as the United Corkcutters of Edinburgh and Leith are not represented by Delegates at this Board, the Council cannot take up their case but do hereby express their Sympathy with them in their present struggle for their just rights and recommend them to bring their question before the different trades represented at this Board.[1]

---

[1] No reference to the corkcutters' strike has been found in the press.

The Council then considered the motion of J. Borrowman for a Public meeting of the Working Classes of this City in regard to the nine hours per Day movement. It was moved by William Caw, seconded by D. Lockerbie, and unanimously agreed to that a Public meeting be held, and the following were appointed a Committee to carry the same into effect, viz., Messrs Borrowman, Lockerbie, Glen, Reid, Beaton, Smith, J. Borrowman Convener. Said Committee to meet here on Friday first at 8 p.m.

1861

29 January 1861

Delegates present: Brassfounders, G. Smith, J. Purdie; Blacksmiths, A. Frazer; Glassmakers, J. Reid, J. Kelly; Glasscutters, A. Brown, J. Beaton; Joiners, W. Caw, J. Borrowman; Masons, D. Lockerbie, G. Herbert; Tailors, W. Troup; Clockmakers, G. Latimer. The Vice President and afterwards the President in the chair.

Subscriptions were received from the Glassmakers, per James Reid, 3s.; from the Clockmakers, per George Latimer, 2s. 6d.; and from the Joiners, per William Caw, £2 4d. 3d. – total £2 9s. 9d.

Report was then given in by the Committee appointed to secure a Chairman for the proposed Public Meeting, regarding their interview with the Lord Provost.[1] He declined presiding at the meeting on account of the office he holds. Baillie G. C. Russell also declined because he did not approve of the 9 hours movement.[2] The Council then considered the Public Meeting on the above subject and a Letter was read from George Potter, secretary to the United Kingdom Association for shortening the Hours of Labour, intimating his willingness to come and to deliver a Lecture or address on this subject.[3] Some discussion then took place whether the admission should be free to the meeting or whether 1d. or 2d. should be charged. D. Lockerbie moved, seconded by George Herbert, that the price of admission be 1d. each. An amendment was moved by James Reid, seconded by J. Kelly, that it be 2d. each. There voted for

[1] Francis Brown Douglas.
[2] Bailie George Eliza Russell, a merchant, and an Independent Liberal.
[3] The Association had been formed earlier that month at a conference at Derby of building trade union representatives. Its object was to put the nine hours movement on a national basis. G. Howell, *Labour Legislation, Labour Movements and Labour Leaders* (London, 1905 edn.), 134.

the amendment 5, for the motion 7. The Secretary was instructed to write to the Trades Council of Glasgow asking them to co-operate with this Council in getting Mr Potter to deliver an address in Glasgow. Agreed to have a Special meeting of the Council on Tuesday, 5 February. Note: February 5. Mr Brown got the *Parliamentary Report*.[1]

12 February 1861

Delegates present: Brassfounders, G. Smith, J. Purdie; Blacksmiths, A. Frazer; Glassmakers, J. Reid, J. Kelly; Glasscutters, A. Brown, J. Beaton; Masons, D. Lockerbie, William Glen; Leith Bakers, James Farquhar, Alexander Potter, William Kerr; Joiners, William Caw, J. Borrowman; Tailors, William Troup, John Gardner; Clockmakers, G. Latimer; Plumbers, J. G. Bald; Leith and Edinburgh Coopers, Daniel Campbell, William Mason, Thomas Dalgleish.

Contributions from the Leith Bakers, per James Farquhar, to the amount of 7s. 6d. was received. Correspondence was read from the Society of the Bakers of Leith, appointing James Farquhar, Alexander Potter, and William Kerr to represent them at this Board; also from the Leith and Edinburgh Coopers' Society, appointing Daniel Campbell, William Mason and Thomas Dalgleish to represent them at this Board. These gentlemen were then unanimously received as Members of this Council.

A Letter was read from George Potter, Esq., London, enclosing a copy of the Resolution he wished to speak to at the public meeting on the 20th curt. A discussion then followed on said Resolution. The Secretary was instructed to write to Mr Potter to call his attention to the identity of the first Resolution and the one he sent and requesting him if convenient to meet the Council on Tuesday the 19th. The President was appointed to wait on Mr Potter on his arrival in Edinburgh. The Secretary then reported anent securing Brighton Street Chapel for the 20th, also regarding the Bills calling the meeting, proofs of which were shown and 250 large ordered to be printed and posted, and 500 small for circulation. Agreed to meet on Tuesday the 19th.

[1] Presumably that on councils of conciliation.

PUBLIC MEETING

Brighton Street Chapel
20 February 1861

A public meeting of the working Classes of Edinburgh, convened by the Trades Council, was held this evening. The chapel was crowded, with upwards of 2,000 persons present. On the motion of Mr Troup, President, Captain Ramsay[1] was called to the chair and the following Resolutions were unanimously agreed to: 1st, That this meeting considers the Nine Hours Movement a great and important means of improving the Physical, Moral, Social, and Intellectual condition of the working classes. Therefore pledges itself to use all legal means to establish the Nine hours as a day's work instead of Ten as at present. Proposed by Mr George Lorimer, Builder,[2] seconded by William Caw, Joiner. 2nd, That a reduction in the hours of labour is necessary through the introduction of Machinery and increased Skill of the workman. That the operatives in conjunction with Machinery are enabled to produce sufficient for the requirements of Society by working Nine hours a day, and to prevent all grounds of complaint on the part of employers the workmen are willing to accept nine hours' pay for nine hours' work. Proposed by Mr George Potter from London, seconded by J. Beaton, Glass Cutter. 3rd, That this meeting recommends all classes of working men who have not as yet taken any part in the Nine hours Movement to come forward at once and do so, that they may become participators in the benefits arising from shortening the hours of labour, and this meeting pledges itself to prosecute the Nine Hours untill it is adopted by the Employers. Proposed by John Borrowman, Joiner, seconded by J. Gardner, Tailor.

A vote of thanks to Mr Potter by George Troup, Esq., Editor of *Witness* and unanimously agreed to;[3] also a vote of thanks to

[1] Captain W. H. Ramsay, lieutenant of No. 12 company (freemasons'), city of Edinburgh Rifle Volunteers.

[2] George Lorimer, 1812-65, a master builder, dean of guild at the time of his death in January 1865 when attempting to save a workman from the fire that destroyed the Theatre Royal. *Scotsman*, 14 January 1865.

[3] George Troup, 1811-79, editor of several Liberal and Free Church newspapers in Scotland, including the *North British Daily Mail* (1847-51); he became editor of the

Captain Ramsay by A. Frazer, Secretary to the Trades Council, unanimously agreed. The large meeting then broke up.

26 February 1861

Delegates present: Bakers, J. Inglis; Brassfounders, G. Smith, J. Purdie; Blacksmiths, Alexander Frazer; Corkcutters, Thomas Rawett, John Alston; Leith and Edinburgh Coopers, Daniel Campbell, William Mason, Thomas Dalgleish; Leith Bakers, James Farquhar, Alexander Potter, William Kerr; Glass Makers, James Reid, John Kelly; Glass Cutters, Andrew Brown, James Beaton; Joiners, William Caw, John Borrowman; Masons, William Kelly; Plumbers, J. G. Bald; Tailors, William Troup, John Gardner.

An account of the money drawn at the Public meeting: received in Silver £1 9s. 9d., in Copper £5 9s. 5d. – total £6 19s. 2d. A Letter was read from Mr George Potter, London, thanking the Council for their kindness to him on his late visit to Edinburgh; also from the Edinburgh and Leith operative Corkcutters, appointing Thomas Rawett and John Alston delegates to represent them at this Board, and these were unanimously received as such. Verbal reports were then given regarding the Nine Hours movement by William Caw, for the operative Joiners, and William Kelly for the Masons.

The Secretary then brought before the Council the propriety of inviting Sir A. Alison to redeliver in Edinburgh his Lecture on Trades Union.[1] The subject was agreed to lie over till next regular meeting. A verbal report was given by the Corkcutters regarding Cooperation in their trade; as regards there present Struggle with their Employers there was no difference [in the position]. There was received as Subscriptions from the Brass Founders, per J. Purdie,

---

Witness c. December 1859, and from September 1861 until early in 1863 was editor of the *Beehive*. *Essays in Labour History in memory of G. D. H. Cole,* ed. A. Briggs and J. Saville (London, 1960), 186-7, 201; R. M. W. Cowan, *The Newspaper in Scotland* (Glasgow, 1946), 288-9; W. Norrie, *Edinburgh Newspapers Past and Present* (Earlston, 1891), 44.

[1] Sir Archibald Alison, 1792-1867, Tory, historian and sheriff of Lanarkshire. He had argued in a lecture to a meeting of workmen organised by Glasgow trades council in December 1860 that unions and strikes were unavoidable, but that strikes should be used only in favourable conditions. Sir A. Alison, *Some Account of my Life and Writings* (Edinburgh, 1883), ii, 296-300.

10s. 4d.; from the Leith Coopers, per Daniel Campbell 10s. The delegate from the Edinburgh Bakers also intimated they would subscribe 10s. per quarter. The council then agreed to hold a Special meeting on Tuesday the 5th March to hear reports anent the Nine Hours movement.

12 March 1861

Delegates present: Amalgamated Trades,[1] George Campbell; Leith Bakers, James Farquhar, Alexander Potter; Brassfounders, George Smith, J. Purdie; Blacksmiths, Alexander Frazer; Clockmakers, George Latimer; Glass Makers, J. Kelly; Glass Cutters, Andrew Brown, James Beaton; Joiners, William Caw, John Borrowman; Masons, G. Herbert, David Lockerbie; Plumbers, J. G. Bald; Tailors, William Troup, John Gardner; Leith and Edinburgh Coopers, Daniel Campbell, Thomas Dalgleish.

There was paid into the funds £1, per Mr Gardner, being subscription from the Society of operative Tailors. A Deputation from the Horseshoers were then heard requesting the assistance of this Council in securing to that Body the Saturday Half Holiday. According to the Rules of this Council, the Horseshoers not being an organized body the Council could not assist them directly, but recommended them to organize and send Delegates to this Board and in the meantime the Council would assist them Indirectly.

The Secretary then reported anent Special meetings which had previously been held anent the Public Meeting. After some slight alterations on the Resolutions the final arrangements were made for the Public Meeting on the 13th current. The Secretary was instructed to write to Sir A. Alison to request him to redeliver in Edinburgh his Lecture on Trades Societies, Strikes, Lock-Outs, Etc., date and place to be afterwards fixed.

PUBLIC MEETING

Brighton Street Chapel
13 March 1861

A Public Meeting of the working Classes of Edinburgh, called by Advertisement, was held this evening for the purpose of hearing

---

[1] Engineers.

Statements from the operative Masons and Joiners now on Lock-out on account of the 9 Hours Movement, and to submit Resolutions to the Meeting on their behalf.

The Church was crowded, about 2,000 persons being present. On the motion of Mr Troup, Captain Ramsay was called to the chair and shortly addressed the meeting. A statement was then made by William Caw regarding the present position of the Joiners and by D. Lockerbie regarding the Masons. Mr George Lorimer, master Builder, then moved the first Resolution: That this meeting is of opinion that the request made to their Employers by the operative Masons and Joiners of this City to reduce the hours of Labour from 10 to 9 hours per Day, or 51 hours per Week, is moderate and reasonable, and this meeting is also of opinion that the Refusal of the Employers is unnecessary and uncalled for and subjects the Public to much Inconvenience. Seconded by D. Lockerbie and unanimously agreed to. 2nd Resolution, moved by John Beaton, Glass Cutter: That this meeting is of opinion, seeing that the request of the operative Masons and Joiners has been refused by many of the Employers, it is the duty of all Tradesmen to support them to the best of their ability while this struggle lasts, and this meeting pledges itself to use all lawful means for this object. Seconded by J. Purdie, Brassfounder, and unanimously agreed to. 3rd Resolution, moved by Alexander Frazer, Blacksmith: That this meeting hereby calls upon all Tradesmen whether organized or not to come forward and assist the Masons and Joiners so that the Rights of Labour may not be overpowered by the weight of Capital. Seconded by J. Borrowman, Joiner, and unanimously agreed to.

On the motion of Mr Reid[1] of the *Scottish Press* newspaper[2] a cordial vote of thanks was then given to Captain Ramsay for his conduct in the Chair. The meeting then broke up. Drawn at Public Meeting £4 7s.

Hugh Gilzean Reid, 1836-1911, professional journalist, said to have played a leading part in the foundation of the Edinburgh Co-operative Building Company in 1861 (below, p. 54); a founder and first president 1888-90 of the Institute of Journalists; Liberal M.P. for Aston Manor 1885-6; knighted 1893; see also below, p. 165 and n. 1.
[2] The *Scottish Press*, 1847-63, independent Liberal, founded to support the United Presbyterian Church but changed ownership in 1862; published in Edinburgh twice or thrice weekly. Norrie, op. cit., 38.

26 March 1861

Delegates present: Bakers, Alexander Potter, William Kerr; Brass-founders, George Smith, J. Purdie; Blacksmiths, Alexander Frazer; Clockmakers, George Latimer; Glass Makers, James Reid; Glass Cutters, John Beaton; Masons, D. Lockerbie; Joiners, William Caw, John Borrowman; Plumbers, J. G. Bald; Tailors, William Troup, John Gardner; Leith and Edinburgh Coopers, William Mason.

A Letter was read by the Secretary from Sir A. Alison stating that on account of his official duties he had not time to re-deliver his Lecture, but intimated his willingness to send a corrected news-paper report of the same for the Council to publish it in a cheap form. The Council having considered this proposal are of opinion that Sir Archibald should deliver his Lecture and they are willing to wait his convenience. The Secretary was instructed to communicate the same.

A Letter was read from Captain Ramsay, Edinburgh Rifle Volunteers, wishing 12 or 15 men to complete No. 12 Company. The Council agreed to circulate the same amongst the different Trades. Mr Beaton then brought before the Council the subject of a General Trades League throughout the Country and was heard in support of the above. It was agreed to let the matter lie over till next meeting.

The Secretary brought before the Council the propriety of the Council purchasing a Copy of the Report by the Committee appointed by the National Association of Social Science on Trades Societies, price 7s. 6d.[1] It was then moved by William Caw, seconded by D. Lockerbie, that a Copy of the same be ordered for the Council. Agreed to. The Secretary was instructed to write to the Secretary of the operative Plasterers requesting a meeting with them with the view of them sending Delegates to this Council, Messrs Lockerbie and Beaton to be the Deputation.

---

[1] *Trades Societies and Strikes. Report of the Committee on Trades Societies appointed by the National Association for the Promotion of Social Science at the Annual Meeting of the Association in Glasgow, 1860* (London, 1860).

PUBLIC MEETING

Brighton Street Chapel
9 April 1861

A Public Meeting of the working Classes of Edinburgh was held,
George Lorimer, Esq., in the chair. The Chapel was entirely filled.
The Chairman shortly addressed the meeting on the present position
of the Operative Masons' Lockout for the 9 hours movement.

Mr Campbell, operative mason, then moved the first resolution,
viz., That this meeting regrets that the joiners, although acting in
the circumstances as they only could, had to depart from the position
they assumed, in consequence of the want of funds, arising from
their not having any union. They would deduce from that the
necessity for trades unions effeciently organized. Seconded by Mr
Borrowman, Joiner, and unanimously agreed to.[1] Mr McQueenie,[2]
operative tailor, moved the second resolution: Seeing the Masons at
present on Lock-Out have sought every legitimate means to effect
an amicable settlement of the present dispute, this meeting regrets
that the employers have not seen it their duty or interest to accede
to the terms proposed; and while expressing their sympathy with
the workmen, pledges itself to support them until their reasonable
and necessary proposal is granted. Seconded by Mr Henry, joiner,
and unanimously agreed too. George Troup, Esq., late Editor of the
Witness, moved the third Resolution: That this meeting, while
regretting the efforts made have failed in effecting a settlement of
the present dispute, rejoices to learn that a co-operative society is
being organized by the operative Masons, and would recommend
this principle to other classes of workmen, and the support and
sympathy of the Community. Seconded by Mr Bruce, joiner, and
unanimously agreed to.[3]

[1] The joiners had evidently returned to work because of 'want of unanimity among
themselves' as well as lack of funds. *Edinburgh Evening Courant,* 10 April 1861, quoting
John Borrowman.
[2] Probably an error for McWhinnie.
[3] The Edinburgh Co-operative Building Company Ltd was instituted on 25 May 1861,
and the seven masons who were the original subscribers included James Collins. He
and two other delegates to the trades council, George Herbert and David Lockerbie,
were among the directors of the company in its first year. *Articles of Association*
(Edinburgh, 1861), 3, 6.

On the motion of Mr William Troup a vote of thanks to the Chairman, and by Mr A. Frazer a vote of thanks to George Troup, Esq., were then cordially given and the meeting sepereated. Note: there was drawn at the door the sum of £3 16s. 3½d.

16 April 1861

Delegates present: Bakers, Alexander Potter; Blacksmiths, Alexander Frazer; Clockmakers, George Latimer; Glass Cutters, John Beaton; Joiners, William Caw, Henry Bruce; Tailors, William Troup; Leith and Edinburgh Coopers, William Mason.

Mr Beaton's motion was taken up. It was agreed to consider it along with the Proposal of the Glasgow Trades Council for a Federation of the Trades in Scotland. A Letter was read from the Secretary of the National Association of Social Science containing several queries on the subject of Apprenticeships. The Secretary was instructed to write to London for more Copies. The subject of a Public meeting with reference to the operative Bakers was then considered. The Delegate from that trade stated that in the meantime they wished the proposed meeting delayed. Note: There was paid into the funds £1, being subscription from the operative Bakers on 5 April per Alexander Potter and William Kerr.

23 April 1861

Delegates present: Bakers (Leith), Alexander Potter; Bakers (Edinburgh), John Scott; Blacksmiths, Alexander Frazer; Clockmakers, George Latimer; Glass Cutters, Andrew Brown; Leith and Edinburgh Coopers, Daniel Campbell, William Mason; Joiners, William Caw, William Henry; Tailors, William Troup.

A Conversation took place on the subject of Apprenticeships to trades. The Federation of the Trades was then considered. It was agreed to defer further consideration till it was known how it had been decided in Glasgow. A long discussion took place upon a Subject brought up by the delegate from the Leith Bakers, but no decision was come to by the Council.

7 May 1861

Delegates present: Bakers, Leith, Alexander Potter, William Kerr; Blacksmiths, Alexander Frazer; Brassfounders, George Smith;

Clockmakers, George Latimer; Glass Cutters, John Beaton, Andrew Brown; Glass Makers, James Kelly; Leith and Edinburgh Coopers, Thomas Dalgleish, D. Campbell, William Mason; Joiners, William Caw; Tailors, William Troup; Masons, David Lockerbie.

The subject of Apprenticeships was considered, and as there was only one copy of the queries issued by the Social Congress it was agreed the subject should be deferred till more copies should be procured from London. The subject of the Federation of the Trades as proposed by the Trades Council of Glasgow was then considered. It was agreed in the meantime to defer the subject. In Answer to a question by the President, the Treasurer stated that the sum at present in his hands was £3 14s.

The Annual Excursion was then considered and on the motion of William Caw, seconded by Andrew Brown, unanimously agreed that the Excursion be to Glasgow. The following were appointed to make the necessary enquiries along with the President's Committee: Messrs Beaton, Brown and Mason. To report at next meeting. The Secretary then gave intimation that on this day month he would resign the office. Mr Brown got report of the *Transactions of the Congress of Social Science* and Mr Kerr, *Report of the Committee of the House of Commons on Councils of Conciliation.*

21 May 1861

Delegates present: Leith Bakers, Alexander Potter, William Kerr; Blacksmiths, Alexander Frazer; Brassfounders, George Smith, J. Purdie; Clockmakers, George Latimer; Glass Makers, James Reid, J. Kelly; Glass Cutters, J. Beaton, Andrew Brown; Leith and Edinburgh Coopers, Thomas Dalgleish, D. Campbell, William Mason; Joiners, William Caw, H. Bruce; Masons, D. Lockerbie; Tailors, William Troup.

There was paid into the funds the sum of 7s. 6d., being quarter's subscription from the Leith Bakers, per Alexander Potter and William Kerr. The Annual Excursion to Glasgow was then considered and it was agreed to take place on Saturday 27th July. Mr Caw was unanimously appointed one of the Deputation and Alexander Frazer proposed George Smith as his Colleague, seconded by J. Kelly. Andrew Brown was then proposed by G. Latimer, seconded by James Reid. There voted for George Smith 5, for Andrew Brown 7.

The usual sum of £1 was allowed them for their expenses. Mr Lockerbie got the report of the *Transactions of Social Science Congress,* and the *Report of the Committee of the House of Commons* was put into the Box.

4 June 1861

Delegates present: Smiths, Mr Fraser; Edinburgh Coopers, Mr Mason; Clockmakers, Mr Latimer; Glassmakers, Messrs Reid, Kelly; Masons, Mr Lockerbie, Mr Collins; Edinburgh Bakers, John Scott; Leith Bakers, Mr Kerr; Joiners, Messrs Bruce and Caw; Brass-founders, Messrs Smith, Purdie; Glasscutters, Messrs Brown, Beaton; Tailors, Mr Troup.

The Council proceeded to the election of a secretary, when John Beaton was proposed by J. Purdie, seconded by William Kerr. John Beaton was then elected secretary for the ensuing six months, Mr Fraser retiring. Mr Latimer spoke highly in favour of the conduct and abilities of the retiring secretary and moved a vote of thanks which was unanimously accorded. Mr Caw, treasurer, presented the secretary with the salary allowed by the Council. Mr Fraser then brought before the Council's notice the book on the report of the committee of trades societies which was laid upon the table. Mr Purdie accepted of it, to be brought back in two weeks. The queries on the Conditions of Labour Enquiry was distributed among the Council, some being for the operatives to answer, others for employers of Labour, to be brought back at the end of a month with the replies or answers.

Mr Caw than stated that owing to a mistake he made in the date of the month he had thought it would be proper to defer for another week his and Mr Brown's trip to Glasgow for the final settlement with the manager of the Edinburgh and Glasgow railway of the delegates' annual excursion. Some discussion then took place relating to the *Black Prince* War ship being opened for the excursionists, it was finally left in the hands of Messrs Brown and Caw to try what could be done in that matter, the parties to proceed on the first Friday of June and report the next Tuesday night.

Mr Fraser then proposed that the old course of Lectures as formerly proposed[1] be again taken up, the Lectures to commence in Novem-

---

[1] Presumably refers to above, p. 45.

ber; and that the secretary be authorized to write to the different gentlemen to obtain their consent and time, and to report the result at some future meeting. Mr Lockerbie seconded the proposition, when the council gave their consent.

Mr Smith gave over to the treasurer, Mr Caw, the sum of 5s. as the Brassfounders' subscription to the trades Council. Some discussion then took place on the advisability of making out a six months' Balance sheet of the Income and expenditure of the Council through their treasurer. The majority approved of the same being done.

11 June 1861

Delegates present: Tailors, Mr Troup, John Gardner; Edinburgh Coopers, Mr Mason; Leith Bakers, Mr Kerr; Joiners, Mr Bruce, Caw; Blacksmiths, Mr Fraser; Clockmakers, Mr Latimer; Glasscutters, Messrs Brown, Beaton; Brassfounders, Mr Smith.

The Council of united trades met to hear the report from the deputation sent to Glasgow on behalf of the July excursion. It was agreed that we print full particulars: Posters 250, Handbills 1,000. Mr Cannon, Bill Printer, Thistle Street, to Print them and have Proof sheet ready on tuesday night, 18 June, for approval or otherwise. Orders were then given to the secretary to write to the Provost of Glasgow to use his influence to obtain permission for the excursionists to visit the Botanical Gardens on payment of the usual fee of 1d. and show ticket. Also to write Mr Grainger of the Govan Iron works for permission to view his works.[1] Also to write Mr G. Potter of London to send to the delegates 24 Copies of his pamphlet on the reduction of the hours of labour in the Building trades.[2]

11 June 1861[3]

Delegates present: Smiths, Mr Fraser; Bakers, Messrs Scott, Kerr; Masons, Mr Collins; Joiners, Messrs Bruce, Henry, Caw; Coopers, Mr Mason; Glassmakers, Messrs Reid, Kelly; Glasscutters, Messrs

---

[1] Robert Granger, manager.
[2] *The Labour Question: an address to the Capitalists and Employers of the Building Trades . . . being a few reasons in behalf of a reduction of the hours of labour, etc.*, by George Potter (London, 1861).
[3] The date should presumably read 18 June 1861.

Brown, Beaton; Clockmakers, Mr Latimer; Tailors, Messrs Troup, Gardner; Cabinet Makers, Mr Sheddin; Brassfounders, Messrs Smith, Purdie.

The treasurer's book and accounts having been overhauled previously to the assembling of the delegates by the Auditors appointed at former meeting, it was found that the treasurer's book was quite correct, and the same was submitted to the meeting. Mr Sheddin, as representative of the Cabinet and Chair makers, was on production of his Credentials admitted as a member of the Council. Mr Potter's appeal on behalf of the Lockouts was then read over. A long and general discussion followed, the result being that Mr Fraser proposed that appeal be remitted to the various trades for their support, Seconded by Mr Collins.

Mr George Potter's Pamphlet on the Labour question was then distributed to the various delegates present. The annual excursion bill was submitted and, with one or two insertions and one alteration, was approved of. The members taking tickets for the excursion for the various shops received their quantity. Mr Purdie having delivered up the report on the Social science transactions Mr Fraser accepted of the same, to be brought back in a fortnight.

2 July 1861

Delegates present: Joiners, Mr Caw; Smiths, Mr Fraser; Masons, Mr Herbert; Brassfounders, Mr Purdie; Glasscutters, Messrs Brown, Beaton; Tailors, Messrs Troup, Gardner; Coopers, Mr Mason; Bakers, Mr Potter; Slaters, Messrs Rattray, Munro.

Another long discussion ensued on the hour system of payments relating to the building trades, the Scotch building trades apparently approving of the hour payment systems with no apparent evils resulting from the same. At the same time the London builders are partly approving of the system and the others striking against it. The Council not being in possession of all the objections of the London builders to the hour payment system, the secretary was authorized to write to Mr George Potter for fuller information. The appeal at present for support of the London Lockouts of the Building trades was not approved of and fell to the ground. It was then ascertained that the various trades would take in all 300

Copies of Mr Potter's pamphlet on the Labour Question, at the same time to desire Mr Potter to let us have them as soon as possible.

Mr Fraser gave up the book on the social science report, Mr Brown accepting of the same to be brought back at the next meeting of Council. The Slaters were then admitted members of the Council on production of credentials. Proposed by Mr Caw. Seconded by Mr Herbert.

14 July 1861[1]

The Correspondence was read bearing on our winter evening lectures, some gentlemen being willing to lecture, others not, from various reasons. Mr Potter's Communication was then discussed at full length, as well as the opinions of the Press bearing on the same. Mr Fraser proposed the following resolution: That the trades Council of Edinburgh, having considered the present dispute of the London operatives in all its Bearings, decline for the present to support them. Seconded by Mr Herbert, and carried. Mr Caw gave notice of his resignation as treasurer for this day fortnight. The Council agreed to meet the following tuesday to ascertain the result of the sale of tickets for the annual trip on 27 July.

23 July 1861

It was proved that the sale of the excursion tickets was about 350, almost covering our guarantee of 400, and on finally meeting on the friday following to ascertain the result it was proved that all the disposable tickets were sold, amounting to 957. The Council hen settled with the railway company, and received a receipt for the same. The delegates present then agreed to meet on the following tuesday. Paid Railway Company £144 6s.

30 July 1861

Delegates present: Tailors, Messrs Troup, J. Gardner; Masons, Messrs Lockerby, J. Collins; Brassfounders, Messrs Smith, Purdie; Cabinetmakers, Mr Sheddin; Glasscutters, Messrs Brown, J. Beaton; Clockmakers, Mr Latimer; Coopers, Mr Mason; Slaters, Mr Munro; Joiners, Mr Caw; Smiths, Mr Fraser; Bakers, Mr Potter.

Professor Aytoun's secretary's reply was read, stating that the Professor was not at home, but as soon as he arrived our letter to

---

[1] The date should be 16 July 1861; the 14th was a Sunday.

him would be laid before him.[1] Professor McAdam's reply was then read, stating his willingness to lecture but requesting an interview.[2] The Council appointed Messrs Troup and Beaton to wait on him.

The treasurer gave notice of his final decision to resign office, When Mr Latimer proposed Mr Fraser, Seconded by Mr Collins. Mr Fraser, declining office, proposed Mr Collins, seconded by Mr Smith, and Mr Collins was then duly elected to be treasurer to the Council in room of Mr Caw, who retires altogether from the Council with the regrets of all the Members. Mr Fraser and other members then spoke very favourably of the conduct of Mr Caw during the number of years he has been a member of Council, and it is to be hoped that if he succeeds above his most sanguine expectations, he will not forget the days of old. Mr Munro, Latimer, Collins were then appointed to audit and square the treasurer's book this day fortnight. Mr Fraser proposed and Mr Brown seconded, that the treasurer's salary of 10s. be paid to him on his retirement from office.

Mr Troup then reported to Council the proceedings at the meeting of the Edinburgh and Glasgow delegates at Glasgow, the meeting separating with mutual expressions of good will. Mr Fraser explained the smallness of attendance of Glasgow delegates, and the workings of co-operation, as seen in Glasgow.

A discussion then ensued on the necessity or otherwise of having reporters present at our meeting, when Messrs Caw and Lockerby spoke decidedly against, other members also not approving of it. Mr Fraser opened up the question on the *Beehive* newspaper, to see if the Council or trades were going to do anything in the way of taking out numbers in order to support it, when nothing definite being elicited the matter dropt.[3] Mr Sheddin and Munro took up the pamphlets on federation for perusal.

---

[1] William Edmonstoune Aytoun, 1813-65, professor of rhetoric and belles-lettres at Edinburgh 1845-65.
[2] Stevenson Macadam, PH.D., lecturer in chemistry at Surgeon's Hall and afterwards in the School of Medicine at Edinburgh 1855-1901, and at the School of Arts 1856-87.
[3] The *Beehive*, a weekly founded by George Potter in October 1861, 'in the interests of the working classes'. It was the organ at one time or another of the London trades council, the First International, and the Trades Union Congress. Renamed the *Industrial Review* in 1876, it ceased publication in 1878. *Essays in Labour History in memory of G. D. H. Cole*, ed. A. Briggs and J. Saville (London, 1960), 174.

13 August 1861

Delegates present: Bakers, Messrs Kerr, Potter; Tailors, Messrs Troup, Gardner; Coopers, Mr Mason; Masons, Messrs Collins, Herbert; Slaters, Mr Munro; Brassfounders, Messrs Smith, Purdie; Cabinetmakers and Chairmakers, Mr Sheddin; Joiners, Messrs Bruce, Caw; Glasscutters, Mr Beaton.

Professor Aytoun's reply was read, stating from various reasons his inability to comply with our request to form one of a course of Lectures. Messrs Troup and Beaton then detailed the interview they had with Professor McAdam, no final decision being elicited, McAdam only promising to write in a few days.

Messrs Collins and Munro then stated that they had audited the books and found everything correct, when the treasurer's book was taken possession of by the Treasurer, Mr Collins. Another discussion then ensued on the *Bee Hive* newspaper through Mr George Potter requesting the Council to take up and further the object he has in view. The Council object to move in the matter, principally on the grounds that there will be no Edinburgh news in it.

Some young man then requested the Council to sanction the raising of subscriptions under the pretence that the money so raised would be devoted to the training of an instrumental band, to be called the United trades delegates band. The Council requested this person to call again in one hour's time. In the interval the Council discussed the request, and having arrived at no favourable opinion of the parties, it was determined not to give them the liberty asked, and at the same time to cry the scheme down in the Public Press. This was fully intimated to them when they called again.

Mr Bruce took the book on Social science congress, to be brought back in a fortnight. Mr Gardner gave up pamphlet on Scottish federation, which was left to remain with the secretary. Mr Troup distributed the Glasgow trades delegates' pamphlet, on the proposed Basis for a federation of the various United Trades of Scotland. Mr Herbert laid a Poster bill before the Council the purport of which was a presentation to Mr Lorimer, with an intimation that the Council were to be admitted on the same terms as the public.[1]

---

[1] No press report of the presentation has been found; it seems to concern a journeyman mason of that name, not George Lorimer the master builder.

Mr Caw then spoke for some time before finally leaving the Council, detailing the origination of the Council in the saturday afternoon holiday movement, and subsequent emergement into the United trades Council. Mr Herbert then moved a vote of thanks to Mr Caw which was cordially given.[1]

A deputation of shoemakers were introduced to the Council, requesting the patronage of the United trades in favour of their annual Ball, to be held on the first week of January. They were told to send their request in writing to the secretary, when it would be laid before the Council in proper form.

27 August 1861

Delegates present: Tailors, Messrs Troup, Gardner; Masons, Mr Collins; Clockmakers, Mr Latimer; Glasscutters, Mr Beaton; Smiths, Mr Fraser; Glassmakers, Messrs Reid, Kelly; Joiners, Mr Bruce; Brassfounders, Mr Smith; Cabinetmakers, Mr Sheddin.

A deputation of unemployed Printers were introduced to the Council, their object being to solicit pecuniary assistance from the United trades. The interview ended in the trades Council promising to lay their case before the various united trades. A letter from the boot and shoemakers stated that they had withdrawn asking the various trades for their patronage in favour of their annual ball. A letter from Potter was read asking for payment for 300 Pamphlets, which was ordered to be paid. The lecture question was then gone into. It was shown that 5 gentlemen had complied with the request, 3 declined, 2 had returned no answer, 1 uncertain.

A discussion then ensued on the Lorimer presentation Owing to the delegates not being invited on other terms than the public. It was shown that as we had taken the matter in hand at the first we might have been invited to a gratioustous ticket at the wind up. Mr Reid took the loan of the Book on social science transactions, Mr Troup the report on trades societies, to be brought back in a fortnight. A little discussion then ensued on Trades federation, ultimately ending in Mr Sheddin moving for a general discussion this day fortnight, Mr Collins seconding.

[1] For a few biographical details of Caw see above, p. xxiii.

10 September 1861

Delegates present: Brassfounders, Mr Purdie; Glassmakers, Mr Reid; Cabinetmakers, Messrs Young, Wilkes; Smiths, Mr Fraser; Slaters, Mr Munro; Joiners, Messrs Grant, Henry, Bruce; Coopers, Mr Mason; Glasscutters, Messrs Brown, Beaton; Tailors, Messrs Gardner, Troup.

The minutes of last meeting on being put to the meeting for approval, Mr Fraser made a remark that he thought there was a misstatement in so far as regards the laying of the unemployed Printers' appeal before the Various united trades. It was proven that although no actual vote took place on the subject yet there was no actual dissentient voice on the matter and the Chairman also stated that before the Printers closed the interview with the council he gave them an assurance that we would endeavour to bring their case before the various trades represented here at this board.

A letter was read from Mr G. Potter stating that he had received a remittance for the 300 pamphlets and soliciting the Council to endeavour to dispose of the remainer. After the discussion the matter was allowed to drop, no delegate being prepared to give an order.

Mr Thomas Young and John Wilkes were then introduced to the Council as representatives, along with Mr Sheddin, from the Cabinet and chairmakers' society. They produced their credentials. Mr Francis Grant was introduced by Mr Henry, joiner, as a representative from that body.

On the Lecture question the chairman stated that he had waited on Professor McAdam for his final answer but had found that he had gone to the country. He would endeavour to get an interview as soon as possible.

The secretary then stated in regard to Lorimer's presentation that he had seen that evening one of the committee appointed by the masons and in answer to enquiries the committee man replied that the delegates' free ticket was spoken of by one or two parties but was not brought forward and put in a formal manner as a motion. But when mentioned the masons' committee man objected on the grounds of the improbability of the realized profits being able to bear the expence. The chairman then stated that he had been told quite the contrary and beleived he was right when he said that the masons were the cheif obstacles to any courtesy being shown to the delegates for the trouble and expence we as a council had put ourselves too on their behalf. A remark was then made that it was hoped this matter would be entirely droped.

Mr Troup brought forward the book on trades societies and strikes for a two weeks' perusal to any member wishing the same. Mr Henry, joiner, accepted. Mr Reid stated that he had forgot to bring his book.

The evening was then devoted to the question of Federation as put forth in a printed paper sent to us by the Glasgow United Trades Council. The secretary stated that he beleived his trade[1] could not take the matter in hand as designed in its present form; but, if embracing the United kingdom, he beleived his trade would willingly take up the scheme and form as a trade one of the federative body. He stated as a reason that the non-society men bore so small a percentage to the society men they could not be considered an obstacle. He adduced other reasons for the necessity of an established form of federation, but he beleived at the same time, owing to the present state of trades unions in general, that the Loan system was the only form of federation that could be made workable. Mr Reid stated that he could not see how the scheme could work at all owing to the immense developement of mind that would be necessary to carry on the machinery in a correct working state. Mr Fraser then stated his opinion that the time had not arrived when such a scheme could be taken up without a dread of failure. The proportion of non-society men to society men in the most of trades were as 3 to 1, and until the present proportion of non-unionists to unionists was reversed he did not think it would be prudent of the unionists of the various trades to attempt to carry out the scheme. But when such would be the case then it would have to be considered if the apple so much desired was not ripe and within reach for plucking. Mr Gardner then stated that the unionists in his trade in Edinburgh bore the proportion of one fourth, and did not think his trade could enter into the scheme. Mr Young stated his opinion that the scheme could not be carried out owing to the immense expence that would

---

[1] Glasscutters.

E

in all likelihood be incurred. Mr Wilkes said that we ought to look on such a scheme in as favourable a light as possible and endeavour to bring it to a working state, and at the same time he expressed himself as differing from some of Mr Fraser's opinions in a decided manner. Other delegates having joined in the discussion, Mr Fraser proposed as a motion in answer to the united trades council of Glasgow: That the Council of United trades of Edinburgh, after having discussed and reviewed the federation of trades in all its bearings as set forth in a Glasgow pamphlet, we as a council think that the trades are not as yet ripe for such a scheme, hoping at the same time that the day is not far distant when the scheme will be workable. After a little discussion on the motion it was agreed that the secretary should draw up a reply and submit the same to the council for approval at its next sitting before sending it away.

23 September 1861[1]

Delegates present: Smiths, Mr Fraser; Masons, Mr Collins; Coopers, Mr Mason; Tailors, Messrs Troup, Gardner; Cabinetmakers, Messrs Sheddin, Wilkes, Young; Brassfounders, Mr Smith; Glassmakers, Messrs Kelly, Reid; Glasscutters, Mr Beaton.

Owing to a rather thin attendance of the various delegates, the meeting was opened in a very unusual manner by going into the Business of the present meeting before the minutes of last meeting were read. A great deal of time was lost by the procedure and it is hoped it will not be attempted to be repeated. I do not say this from any spirit of dictation, my only motive being regularity.

A reply was read from Professor Blackie stating his inability to comply with our request owing to his academical duties.[2] The secretary was authorized to write to Mr Archer, Industrial Museum, to endeavour to obtain his compliance to give a lecture, and if necessary to wait on him.[3] The secretary read a draft of a letter he was authorized to draw up and submit to council for their approval or otherwise in reply on Federation discussion. The same was approved of. A motion was then approved of, for a Printed abstract

[1] The date ought probably to read 24 September 1861.
[2] John Stuart Blackie, 1809-95, professor of Greek at Edinburgh 1852-82.
[3] Thomas Croxen Archer, d. 1885, director 1860-85 of the Industrial Museum of Scotland. The Royal Scottish Museum 1854-1954 (Edinburgh, 1954), 3, 10.

of all monies received and disbursed by the Council to be drawn up every six months. Last Balance sheet made out on the 4th June.

A question was asked if any delegate was prepared to give an order for nine hours' pamphlet. The secretary was authorized to write for 200 for 12s. Per offer. Mr Smith paid 2s. 6d. for 30, and Mr Troup 10d. for 10 nine hours' pamphlets. The book on Social Science was taken for a two weeks' perusal by Mr Gardner. Mr Bruce not being present, the book on trades societies was consequently retained by him.

Mr Fraser then made a motion to the effect that the Council reconsider their former verdict on the appeal of the London building operatives, as the strike was still going on.[1] Seconded by Mr Reid. The secretary was ordered to write to Mr George Potter for full information regarding the unions and rates of levy of the London Building trades.

8 October 1861

Delegates present: Tailors, Messrs Troup, Gardner; Masons, Mr Collins; Coopers, Mr Mason; Slaters, Mr Munro; Joiners, Messrs Bruce, Grant; Cabinetmakers, Messrs Young, Wilkes; Glassmakers, Messrs Reid, Kelly; Clockmakers, Mr Latimer; Glasscutters, Messrs Brown, Beaton.

The Chairman stated that he had an interview with Mr Archer and McAdam on the lecture question, Mr Archer declining but McAdam quite willing and thinks saturday evening, commencing at six O'clock, very good. A discussion ensued on the most proper person to open the Lectures and the most proper place to hold them, Mr Gardner moving Brighton St Chapel and Sir David Brewster giving the opening Lecture,[2] seconded by Mr Bruce. The Chairman's committee were then left with full power to wait on the Lecturers and arrange with them and also to ascertain the Prices of different Halls.

The secretary stated that he had sent the reply on federation to Glasgow trades council. Mr Collins, Treasurer, read a draft sheet of the income and expenditure. He also stated that Mr Bald, Plumber,

[1] Above, p. 60.
[2] Sir David Brewster, 1781–1868, principal 1859–68 and vice-chancellor 1860–8 of the university of Edinburgh; elder brother of the Chartist Rev. Patrick Brewster.

owed the Council 13s. for excursion tickets. The secretary was authorized to write Mr Bald for payment.

Mr Fraser not being present to open the discussion on the present position of the London Builders, his seconder, Mr Reid, took the first position and stated that he thought it would be a good plan to bring Mr Potter and a London Mason to Edinbro to awake the scottish trades to the necessity of giving pecuniary assistance to the London Building operatives. A discussion took place on the merits of the strike. Mr Young objected to the pay hour system as the masters' wish, but approved of the men's desire for a certain number of hours as the maximum of a day's labour. The secretary then read a Printed document, setting forth in a number of Clauses, and very explicity, the true grounds that make the London Builders' strike just and equitable. Mr Collins spoke to some length on the hour system as worked in Scotland, contending that the London Building operatives were striking work for the very reverse and that the scottish trades as paid by the hour were quite as respectable as any other class of tradesman. Other delegates also spoke on the subject but the hour getting late Mr Latimer moved that the debate be adjourned, Mr Collins seconding. Mr Gardner returned the book on social science, Mr Wilkes takes it.

21 October 1861[1]

Delegates present: Tailors, Mr Troup; Smiths, Mr Fraser; Joiners, Mr Bruce; Slaters, Mr Munro; Brassfounders, Messrs Purdie, Smith; Cabinetmakers, Messrs Sheddin, Young; Glasscutters, Mr Beaton.

The chairman stated no arrangement with regard to the Lectures had been come to as yet. He had made enquiries as to the Price of Queen St Hall and was told that the whole charge would be £3 5s. The secretary stated that he had made enquiries about Brighton St Chapel: the charge for that Place would be 35s. for saturday night. A letter was read from Professor Balfour declining to lecture.[2] A discussion ensued, resulting in the chairman's committee being authorized to endeavour to get an interview with Sir David Brewster, arrange with him to give the opening lecture, and ascertain the subject he would lecture on, as well as the rest of the Lecturers

---

[1] The date ought probably to read 22 October 1861.
[2] John Hutton Balfour, 1808-84, professor of botany at Edinburgh 1845-79.

A letter was read from George Potter acknowledgeing the receipt of Postal Order for 200 *Labour Questions*. The secretary stated that he had written to Mr Bald, Plumber, to make up his account for the sale of the excursion tickets, but had received no answer. It was agreed that he be cited to appear at next meeting of Council.

The discussion on the London Building operatives' strike was resumed. According to the most reliable accounts, there were 250 masons on the strike roll and the strike was mainly confined to the mason body, the rest of the Building trades supporting. The following delegates took part in the discussion: Fraser, Bruce, Sheddin, Munro, Beaton, Young. As the discussion bore all the features of former discussions it is needless to recapitulate them all here, a few observations being all that is necessary. Messrs Bruce and Munro, as Building operatives, stated the practices ruling in their trades in regard to time working at jobbing, which practices certainly seemed to bear very distant relationship to one another. Mr Young spoke in very depreciatory terms of operatives who would desire to work more than a certain number of hours, say nine or ten, for a day's labour. He had a kind of arithmetical argument in support of some of his views which it might be as well to notice, that as 1 and 3 made 4 so 3 and 1 makes four, and that what you cannot get at one time he can see no harm in making it up again when you can get it. It is the equalization of this arithmetical argument that the London Builders are now and have been striving for. The conclusion of the Discussion was that according to the Present state of trade it was considered injudicious to Bring George Potter and a London Mason to Edinburgh as the realizations might not cover the expence.

5 November 1861

Delegates present: Tailors, Mr Troup; Masons, Mr Collins; Glassmakers, Mr Kelly; Cabinetmakers, Messrs Sheddin, Young; Clockmakers, Mr Latimer; Brassfounders, Messrs Smith, Purdie; Glasscutters, Messrs Beaton, Brown.

The Chairman reported the progress made in the lecture movement, which gave general satisfaction. A letter from Sir David Brewster was read declining to take any part in the Lectures.

A Note was read from Patrick Dove, the essence of which was neither one thing nor the other.[1] A letter from Mr Bald, Plumber, was read stating he would pay all demands in a few weeks. A letter from Glasgow trades council was then read urging us to take up the question of Reform. As a trades council we decline. It was agreed to meet again on saturday evening and report progress.

9 November 1861

Delegates present: Mr Troup, Mr Young, Mr Sheddin, Mr Collins, Mr Brown, Mr Beaton.

According to Previous arrangements the delegates who found it convenient met here this evening to hear the progress made in the lecture business. It was stated by Mr Troup that the first lecture on the hours of labour would be delivered next Saturday, the 16th inst., by Professor Miller in Brighton St Chapel.[2] Doors open at 6 O'clock. The Lord Provost[3] to take the chair. Full power was given to the lecture committee to advertise and order bills but the expence in getting up the opening lecture by giving full sway to advertiseing was considered very great.

PUBLIC MEETING

Brighton St Chapel
Half past 6 O'clock p.m.
16 November 1861

1st Lecture. Stormy Night. Attendance about 306. Professor Miller's opening Lecture took Place this evening, the Lord Provost in the chair. Subject: the Hours of labour. The Provost opened the meeting with some remarks on the cotton trade and the general slackness of trade. Professor Miller's remarks went to prove the necessity of an equal division of day in 3 parts. He was frequently applauded. Mr Young, cabinetmaker, proposed a vote of thanks to the able lecturer. Mr Herbert, mason, proposed a vote of thanks to the Honourable chairman. The meeting then broke up. Collection 25s.

[1] Patrick Edward Dove, 1815-73, philosophic writer, inventor of rifled cannon, advocate of Scottish nationalism.
[2] James Miller, 1812-64, professor of surgery at Edinburgh 1842-64.
[3] Francis Brown Douglas.

19 November 1861

Delegates present: Engineers, Messrs Campbell, Turnbull; Tailors, Messrs Troup, Gardner; Masons, Mr Collins; Joiners, Messrs Bruce, Grant; Coopers, Mr Mason; Cabinetmakers, Messrs Sheddin, Young, Wilkes; Glassmakers, Mr Kelly; Glasscutters, Messrs Brown, Beaton; Brassfounders, Messrs Purdie, Smith.

The secretary asked the council what course should be taken with the Reform programme issued by the Glasgow council of United trades.[1] Mr Collins spoke in terms showing that it was contrary to the laws and constitution of the council to engage in Politics, and that he thought we should not do so. Messrs Turnbull and Gardner concurred. Mr Campbell spoke in favourable terms and moved that he sees no reason why we should not go into the reform movement, and also that we should take the earliest opportunity to communicate with the reforms committees existing. Agreed to. The secretary was authorized to write to each of the reform committees and send a copy of the Glasgow programme.

The lecture question was then discussed. Regretful remarks were made that the attendance at the opening lecture was so small, some remarks being made that the advertisements were insufficient. Mr Brown moved that a man should be employed on the saturday to walk the bridges with a board. Mr Bruce seconded; and intimated that a slip of paper with 'Tonight' should be pasted across the board. Agreed to. Mr Campbell moved that the words 'Council of united trades' should be printed at the top of the placard and also that the bills should announce the lecture to commence at seven O'clock, Mr Brown seconding. Agreed to. The secretary then stated the interview he had with Mr Archer of the Industrial Museum. Mr Archer would be agreeable to give a lecture relating to the fifteen different trades represented at the Council, on the condition that we print 800 copies for sale or distribution. After some remarks about our ability to carry out the conditions, Mr Wilkes moved that we should comply, Mr Kelly seconding. The Council then distributed the lecture bills and agreed to meet again at Brighton St Chapel on saturday evening.

[1] First read by George Newton, the president, at Glasgow trades council on 23 October, adopted, and issued as an *Address to the Working Men of the United Kingdom*. *Glasgow Sentinel*, 2 November 1861.

Brighton St Chapel
23 November 1861

Second lecture. Clear night. Attendance about 450. Professor
MacAdam's lecture took place this evening, Mr Archer of the Industrial Museum in the chair. The lecture, the Chemistry of common food, was beautifully, cleverly and wondrously exemplified,
and called forth the repeated applause of the audience. Mr Wilkes at
the conclusion of the lecture moved a vote of thanks to the lecturer
which was unanimously responded to and repeated. Mr Troup
moved a vote of thanks to Mr Archer, chairman, which was
responded too. Collections 37s.

Brighton St Chapel
30 November 1861

3rd lecture. The evening was fine. Attendance about 249. Captain
Gorrie's lecture on 'Diggings into the city records' came off this
evening.[1] Bailie Mossman[2] in the chair. The lecture was highly
amusing throughout, and well delivered, intersperced now and
again with a few serious episodes. Mr Troup moved a vote of thanks
to the lecturer, John Beaton to the chairman.

3 December 1861

Delegates present: Cabinetmakers, Messrs Wilkes, Young, Sheddin;
Engineers, Messrs Turnbull, Campbell; Brassfounders, Messrs
Purdie, Smith; Blacksmiths, Mr Fraser; Clockmakers, Mr Latimer;
Tailors, Messrs Troup, Gardner; Coopers, Mr Mason; Glassmakers,
Mr Kelly; Masons, Mr Collins; Glasscutters, Messrs Brown, Beaton.

On the Glasgow Political programme the secretary stated that he
had written to the middle classes' and workman's reform committees. Had received no answer from the middle class reform club.

---

[1] John Gorrie, 1829-92, advocate, captain in the Edinburgh Rifle Volunteers, a colonial
judge from 1870, knighted 1882, suspended 1892 on the report of a commission of
investigation into his methods of administering justice.
[2] Adam Mossman, a Liberal, head of a firm of jewellers and watchmakers.

Had been called upon by Mr Laing, chairman of workman's reform club, who handed over a paper with committee's name upon it.[1] After asking what course should be taken in the matter, the secretary was authorized to return the document with explanation.

A little discussion then ensued on the lecture business, the delegates expressing themselves well pleased with the amount of advertisements. The secretary stated that he had made enquiries regarding the rates of bill printing and had found out that the expences for same could be reduced less than one half. Power was given to the chairman's committee to carry this out. The lower part of Brighton St Chapel could be had on saturday evenings for 25s. Agreed to take it. The secretary then asked what steps should be taken with regard to the lecture on co-operation. It was agreed that in the event of Chambers[2] not complying, that if the co-operative bodies in Edinburgh would pay Campbell's expences the delegates would endeavour to meet the rest.[3] The secretary was requested to manage this matter with the Co-operative bodies if agreeable.

The Treasurer than gave a full and detailed account of Income and expenditure. On the intimation being given that this was the proper evening for electing new office bearers, it was agreed to meet the next tuesday for that purpose. Moved by Mr Latimer, Seconded by Mr Brown.

PUBLIC MEETING

Brighton St Chapel
7 December 1861

4th Lecture; evening fine; attendance less than 300. The Lecturer this evening was Mr William Lees, on 'The life and character of Sir Isaac Newton', with Illustrations.[4] The lecturer did ample justice to his subject, the audience giving repeated testimony to the

[1] Laing has not been identified, and no information has been discovered about the workmen's reform club.
[2] William Chambers, publisher.
[3] Presumably Alexander Campbell, 1796-1870, the former Owenite missionary who helped to refound Glasgow trades council in 1858, reported its meetings for the *Glasgow Sentinel*, and was a leader of the Master and Servant Act agitation from 1864. W. H. Marwick, *Life of Alexander Campbell* (Glasgow, n.d.), 17.
[4] William Lees, lecturer 1856-1902 in mechanical philosophy at the School of Arts (latterly Heriot-Watt College).

same. Bailie Blackadder in the chair.[1] Mr Troup moved a vote of thanks to the lecturer, Mr Sheddin to the chairman, both of which were responded to. The delegates present, on account of the small collection, agreed to put off the special meeting formerly agreed to and meet again the regular night.

PUBLIC MEETING

Brighton St Chapel
14 December 1861

5th Lecture; evening very fine; attendance about 336. The lecturer this evening was Dr Bedford,[2] subject – 'The Gorilla'. The lecturer did his best to prove the existence of an animal that great numbers of people consider to be altogether a Hoax, and even insinuated that he had his doubts about the gentleman. The audience seemed very well pleased, by the reception they gave the lecturer. Bailie Boyd in the chair,[3] on account of the unavoidable absence of Bailie John-ston.[4] Mr Campbell moved a vote of thanks to the lecturer, J. Beaton to the chairman.

17 December 1861

Delegates present: Engineers, Messrs Campbell, Turnbull; Brass-founders, Messrs Purdie, Smith; Cabinetmakers, Messrs Sheddin, Wilkes, Young; Glassmakers, Mr Kelly; Glasscutters, Messrs Brown, Beaton; Smiths, Messrs Fraser, Dewar, Fleetham; Tailors, Messrs Troup, McCormick, Grindley; Masons, Mr Collins; Coopers, Messrs Mason, Campbell; Slaters, Mr Munro; Joiners, Mr Grant.

In regard to the reform question the secretary had had no com-munication further on the subject. In regard to the lecture on co-operation he had come to no definite understanding yet with the co-operative store societies. Mr Campbell asked why the special

---

[1] Bailie James Blackadder, an Independent Liberal.
[2] Frederick William Bedford, LL.D., D.C.L,, 1824-80, headmaster of George Heriot's Hospital, Edinburgh, 1854-80. C. B. Gunn, *George Heriot's Hospital* (Edinburgh, 1902), 177.
[3] Sir John Boyd of Maxpoffle, K.T., 1826-93, house agent, lord provost of Edinburgh 1888-91; boycotted the ceremony in 1889 at which Parnell was given the freedom of the city.
[4] Bailie Robert Johnston, an Independent Liberal.

meeting had been deferred till the 17th when it was agreed to meet on the 10th. After explanations were given, he expressed himself as averse to such doings, and hoped one section of the Council would not undo what had formerly been agreed to by the body. The subject then droped.

The lecture question was then gone into. It was agreed that Dr Struthers' lecture on saturday the 21st inst. be the last this season,[1] and that they be resumed again on saturday the 18th January 1862, by Professor Archer opening the second course. Professor Archer's letter on this lecture was then read. Mr William Chamber's letter was then read declining to lecture on co-operation as he had published a tract on the subject already.[2] Some discussion then ensued on our ability, considering the expence, of Publishing Mr Archer's lecture. The conclusion arrived at was that as we had given our assent to do so we could not well go back and that it should just go on. It was agreed to meet again on saturday the 28 inst., at half past 7 p.m.

Mr Troup then presented the delegates' credentials from the united operative tailors including, along with himself, Messrs D. McCormick and John Grindley. Mr Fraser, Smith, intimated that this was his last evening at the council, and in his stead his trade had elected Messrs Andrew Dewar and William Fleetham. He then addressed those present for a few minutes on the occasion of his retirement, which was replied to by the secretary. A letter was then read from the National association for the promotion of social science, informing us of the necessity of forwarding one guinea to insure the delivery of one volume. It was agreed not to take it.

Mr Sheddin, on behalf of the chair and Cabinet makers' society, tendered 15s. as their subscriptions towards the funds of the council, the secretary reading and giving a receipt. Mr Fraser was requested to give a vote of thanks to Dr Struthers for the lecture on the hand, on saturday evening the 21 December. He agreed to do so. Mr

---

[1] John William Struthers, M.D., 1823-99, lecturer in anatomy at Surgeons' Hall and surgeon at the Royal Infirmary, Edinburgh; professor of anatomy at Aberdeen, 1863-89; president of the Royal College of Surgeons, Edinburgh, 1895-7; knighted 1898.
[2] *Co-operation in its Different Branches. No. 1 of Chambers's Social Science Tracts (Manuals for the working-classes)*, by William Chambers (London, 1860).

Mason, cooper, said that his trade had lately been making attempts to obtain the saturday half holiday, but had been only partially successful. After a little discussion on the subject, Mr Mason gave a list of employers to the chairman of compliers and non-compliers, he the chairman promising to get the same inserted in several of the newspapers.

The election of office bearers then took place. Mr Turnbull moved that Mr Troup be re-elected as chairman, Mr Kelly seconding. Unanimously agreed to. Mr Young moved that the present secretary be re-elected, Mr Mason seconding. Agreed to. Mr Kelly moved that Mr Collins be re-elected as treasurer, Mr Brown seconding. Agreed to. Mr Collins moved that Mr Sheddin be re-elected as Vice President, Mr Smith seconding. Unanimously agreed to. Auditors were then appointed to audit the books and report – Messers Campbell, Engineer, and Young appointed. Mr Fraser proposed that the secretary's salary be paid, seconded by Mr Mason. Messrs Wilkes and McCormick then gave notice of a motion, and passed some remark thereanent on the necessity of showing an account sheet of the attendance of the various delegates from the different bodies during the half year.

PUBLIC MEETING

Brighton St Chapel
21 December 1861

Evening fine; about 230 present; drawing 19s. 4d. The lecture this evening was given by Dr Struthers, subject 'The hand'. Bailie Johnston in the chair. Mr Fraser moved a vote of thanks to the able lecturer, Mr Troup to Bailie Johnston.

Saturday evening, 28 December 1861

Delegates present: Tailors, Messrs Troup, McCormick, Grindley; Engineers, Messrs Turnbull, Campbell; Cabinetmakers, Messrs Sheddin, Young; Coopers, Mr Mason; Masons, Mr Collins; Slaters, Mr Munro; Brassfounders, Messrs Purdie, Smith; Glassmakers, Mr Reid; Glasscutters, Messrs Brown, Beaton; Joiners, Messrs Bruce, Grant.

At 10 minutes to 8 Mr Collins proposed, in the absence of President and Vice President, that Mr Campbell, engineer, take the chair, Mr Reid seconding. Agreed to.[1] The only notice of motion that was on the table being the balance sheet of delegates' attendance, it was accordingly discussed. The conclusion arrived at was that it ought to be drawn up and printed, and the secretary furnished with the address of the secretarys of the various trades in order to deliver officially the document into his hands to be read over at his trade meeting. The treasurer passed some remarks on our ability to do so considering we had no funds whatever.

Mr Troup intimated that he had got the coopers' business inserted in four different newspapers. Archer's lecture was then taken up. After various remarks from different parties it was finally agreed that if Professor Archer was ready to lecture on the subject he had chosen on the 18th January '62, that the lecture accordingly go on. If not, the chairman's committee were left either to delay or get another.

The treasurer then read over as drawn up by the auditors the balance sheet of income and expenditure. Mr Young made some remarks on dates and incidentals. The treasurer stated that he would give dates for all transactions, and accounts definitely for all items of expenditure, so that a balance sheet might go before the public without a fear of challenge. Mr Reid proposed that the same three auditors go over the accounts and arrange them. Mr Collins made an amendment that the secretary be added to the auditors, seconded by Mr Turnbull. Agreed to. The secretary was then authorized to call on Mr Bald for his arrears and if not produced to threaten extreme measures. After some remarks about the lowness of funds it was agreed that all the trades who had given no sub-scriptions latterly, should be requested by their delegates to advance a recognition. It was finally agreed to meet again on the 14 of January.

The secretary read a letter from a person signing himself James Liddle,[2] requesting the delegates to endeavour to establish a co-operative store after the principles he had advanced in the Public Press. His scheme was then read over. The secretary then called for

[1] The president, William Troup, and the vice-president, John Sheddin, were evidently present later.
[2] Not identified.

the *Edinburgh News* of today[1] in which a person signing himself F.B. had given him an answer. The same was read. A stormy and general discussion ensued, in the midst of which the meeting broke up.

[1] The *Edinburgh News*, 1808-63, from 1858 to 1860 the organ of the Independent Liberals supporting Duncan McLaren. In 1860 it again changed hands and became largely a reprint of the *Scottish Press* under the editorship of H. G. Reid. W. Norrie, *Edinburgh Newspapers Past and Present* (Earlston, 1891), 21-2.

1862

Delegates present: Engineers, Messrs Turnbull, Campbell; Glass-makers, Messrs Kelly, Reid; Glasscutters, Mr Beaton; Slaters, Mr Munro; Brassfounders, Mr Smith; Cabinetmakers, Messrs Sheddin, Young, Wilkes; Joiners, Messrs Bruce, Grant; Masons, Mr Collins; Coopers, Mr Mason; Smiths, Mr Dewar; Tailors, Messrs Troup, McCormick, Grindley.

The Minutes of last meeting were read and approved of, except an omission relating to new members of Council being served with a copy of the laws. Mr Munro, delegate from the United operative Slaters, tendered a subscription of 10s. from that body to the funds of the Council. Mr Munro moved that the law relating to trades subscriptions be carried out as far as possible in a systematic manner, at the same time to avoid making it burdensome. Mr Grindley seconded. Mr Reid urged the necessity of carrying this motion out. Unanimously agreed to.

On the lecture question the President gave a statement of the progress made. A letter was read from Professor Archer craving delay as he had been unwell. The professor stated he would not be able to lecture till the 1st February. The President then stated that he had seen Archer that day and that he had promised to lecture on the 25th and that he had hopes of providing a chairman in the person of the Lord Advocate.[1] Some discussion then ensued on the payment at the door; it was finally agreed to make it optional. The Lecture – 'Subjects of thought for artizans'.

[1] James Moncrieff, first Baron Moncrieff of Tulliebole, 1811-95, Liberal M.P. for Leith Burghs 1851-9, Edinburgh 1859-68, and Glasgow and Aberdeen Universities 1868-9; lord advocate 1851-2, 1852-8, 1859-66 and 1868-9; lord justice clerk 1869-88.

Mr Young then stated he and the treasurer had met according to appointment, but that the secretary and Mr Campbell did not make their appearance. Both parties explained the reason why. It was finally agreed that the secretary be convener of the meeting and that we meet on saturday first, the 18th, at five o'clock. The secretary then stated that he had called Mr Bald for the Balance of his account but had no hopes of getting it at present. Immediately after, Mr Bald sent in for the secretary and tendered the debt of 13s. The same was handed to the treasurer.

The secretary then requested what answer he should return to Mr James Liddle regarding his desire for the trades delegates to advocate his scheme on the co-operative Provision store. It was agreed that the secretary return him an answer to the effect that it was quite out of our line of business to enter upon anything of the kind.

The secretary then read a note from Duncan McLaren, Esqr., regarding an enclosed note on a London conference on the reform question, hinting that if we were subscribing for that object he would be very willing to subscribe for the same. It was agreed to send the note to Mr Laing, chairman of the workingman's reform association, and also to acknowledge Duncan McLaren's note, with the remark that as a body of trades delegates we do not meddle with politics.

The President then urged the necessity of the various trades handing in a list of their expenditure for meetings, in order to arrive at a conclusive estimate regarding the extent in price that the United trades might go to in order to erect a convenient Hall for meetings with committee rooms attached. Mr Collins, mason, made the remark that he did not think it could be done under £3,000. The meeting broke up at a late hour, unable to arrive at any conclusion on the subject.

PUBLIC MEETING

Brighton St Chapel
25 January 1862

Professor Thomas Archer of the Industrial Museum delivered a lecture to the United trades – subject: 'Thoughts for Artisans'.

James Richardson, Esquire, Chairman to the board of commerce, in the chair.[1] Collection 19s. 9½d.

28 January 1862

Delegates present: Amalgamated Engineers, Messrs Campbell, Turnbull, Tod, Sheddin; Brassfounders, Messrs Purdie, Smith; Glassmakers, Mr Reid; Glasscutters, Messrs Brown, Beaton; Cabinetmakers, Messrs Sheddin, Wilkes, Young; Tailors, Messrs Troup, Grindley, McCormick; Joiners, Messrs Grant, Bruce; Coopers, Mr Mason; Slaters, Mr Munro; Masons, Mr Collins; Blacksmiths, Mr Dewar.

The minutes of last meeting were read and approved of, except an omission regarding a subscription from the Brassfounders to the amount of 4s. On the motion regarding the subscriptions for the Council, the joiners' and masons' delegates, expressed themselves as unable to effect anything that way without the aid of subscription sheets. It was generally agreed to provide a number for the use of those trades that might need them. The treasurer then read over his report showing the amount of funds he had received and expended and the amount in hand.

A discussion then ensued regarding the number of Archer's lecture pamphlets that we should publish. Mr Collins made a motion that we should publish 800 copies, seconded by Mr Dewar. Mr Grant made a counter-motion that we should publish 1,000, Mr Sheddin second-ing. On being put to the vote, 5 were for Mr Collins' motion, which was lost, the majority being in favour of Mr Grant's. A letter from James Richardson, Esqr., was then read expressing himself as willing to act as chairman on the occasion of Proffessor Archer's lecture. The secretary then gave the chief contents of the Lord Advocate's letter declining to act as chairman on account of a previous engage-ment. Mr Grindley moved that the lectures be discontinued, a general assent being given.

Mr Troup then took a detailed statement of the expenditure of the various trades for meetings, amounting in all to about £35. Mr Troup gave notice for the subject to be discussed at next meeting

[1] James Richardson, an Independent Liberal, president of the Chamber of Commerce 1861-3. J. B. Mackie, *Life of Duncan McLaren* (London, 1888), ii, 40; *Souvenir of the Edinburgh Chamber of Commerce 1785-1945* (Edinburgh, 1945), 80.

F

and that the secretary read over the former minutes on the same subject. Mr Smith returned the Book on social science, Mr Dewar accepting the Loan of it.

11 February 1862

Delegates present: Engineers, Messrs Campbell, Tod; Glasscutters, Messrs Brown, Beaton; Glassmakers, Mr Kelly; Brassfounders, Mr Smith; Cabinetmakers, Messrs Sheddin, Young; Masons, Mr Collins; Coopers, Mr Mason; Tailors, Messrs Troup, Grindley; Joiners, Messrs Grant, Bruce; Smiths, Mr Dewar; Slaters, Mr Munro.

The secretary made a remark that he had reason to beleive that some of the delegates intended to withdraw on account of the trade not supporting them. He hoped that no delegate would consider himself under the necessity to do so, as he had no doubt that all trades would see the utility to do so before long. The subscription sheets were then distributed to the various trades requiring them and numbered by the secretary. Archer's lecture pamphlet was then distributed for sale by the secretary to the various delegates. The Chairman made some remarks on the necessity of sending a copy to the various gentlemen who are kindly disposed towards the council. Mr Campbell made a motion to that effect, Seconded by Mr Dewar. This matter was left for the chairman's committee to carry out. Mr Dewar returned the Book on *social science transactions*, Mr Campbell accepting of the same.

Mr Troup's motion on a hall for the United trades next came on for discussion. Mr Troup spoke at some length on the advantages and necessities, and centralising influence such a hall would have upon the working classes. He also gave a description of what like the construction of it should be, according to his ideas and the requirements of the various trades that would use it. Also the manner in which subscriptions might be raised to defray the interest on any debt that might be incurred in the raising of it. Mr Campbell argued that if the working men of Edinburgh would give a day's wage the Hall might be raised at once. Mr Collins thought a day's wage too much to ask, but in his opinion if the various trades would devote a year's money that they expend on meetings, along with the money that might be raised for letting the Hall, sufficient would be raised to defray the bank interest on advance. The motion was left open for further information to be obtained on the question.

Mr Young then read over the treasurer's account as made out by the committee appointed for that purpose. The same was considered quite correct. Mr Campbell moved that the delegates indeavour to ascertain that as the law stands at present could trades unions be registered the same as friendly societies. Some remarks were made in the negative sense.

25 February 1862

Delegates present: Clockmakers, Mr Latimer; Cabinetmakers, Messrs Young, Wilkes; Glassmakers, Messrs Kelly, Reid; Brassfounders, Messrs Purdie, Smith; Engineers, Mr Turnbull; Glasscutters, Mr Beaton; Slaters, Mr Munro; Joiners, Mr Bruce; Tailors, Messrs Grindley, Troup; Moulders, Messrs Baxter, Johnston.

The secretary stated that in accordance with the minutes a few copies of Archer's pamphlet had been delivered to Balies Mossman and Grieve.[1] The secretary read a notice from the United Scottish Moulders that they had sent Messrs John Baxter, Robert Johnston, Robert Robertson[2] as representatives from that body to this council. They were accordingly approved of. The President then asked the moulders what amount of outlay they were for meeting. A satisfactory answer was returned.

Mr Campbell's motion on the registration of trades unions next came on. In the absence of Mr Campbell, Mr Turnbull took up the question, producing the laws relating to friendly societies. In the 32 Article, Page 23, he argued that as the laws stand at present trades societies could not be registered. A general assent seemed to prevail that such was the case. The subject then dropped. Mr Turnbull gave notice of a motion of federation for trades Councils.

Mr Troup spoke on the threatened strike of the bakers of Edinburgh for the reduction of the hours of labour, arguing that in his opinion that they were acting in a very precipitate manner and in

[1] Ex-bailie R. S. Grieve, head of a firm of furnishers, an Independent Liberal.
[2] Robertson is not shown present.

doing so are acting without advice or counsel from this board. Several more of the delegates concurred.[1]

11 March 1862

Delegates present: Engineers, Messrs Campbell, Turnbull, Sheddin; Glassmakers, Mr Reid; Glasscutters, Messrs Brown, Beaton; Brass-founders, Mr Purdie; Cabinetmakers, Messrs Sheddin, Young; Moulders, Mr Baxter; Masons, Mr Collins; Slaters, Mr Munro; Joiners, Messrs Grant, Bruce; Tailors, Messrs Grindley, Troup.

Mr Troup, on the Trades Hall, intimated that he had received accounts amounting to about £50 of the expenditure of various trades for meetings or room rent. This with other monies that would come in would go a long way to pay the percentage on the advance. Mr Bruce said it would be as well to have a circular drawn up bearing on the subject and issued to the various trades for their approval and support or otherwise. This course seemed to obtain general support.

The secretary intimated his interview with Professor Archer by desire of the latter; the subject of the interview being the desire of an Australian Gent. to give a lecture on that country, offering £2 towards liquidating the expence. The chairman's committee did not think it proper to carry this object out. The other part of the interview related to workingmen about to proceed towards the Industrial Exhibition, the Professor being desirous to obtain a reduction in the price of fares for workmen who would take tickets through his committee.[2] The secretary was desired to write the Professor for further details.

Mr Troup intimated that the society of Tailors would in all probability be dissolved as the expenditure was equal to the income. A general discussion then ensued on the relative merits of the different trades unions, clearly showing the advantages of a national amalgamation of any given trade, and also the great similarity of means used to make them efficient.

The treasurer read his account of income and expenditure, and asked for auditors to be elected to square his accounts. Messrs

[1] A meeting of the bakers had resolved on 15 February to enquire how many of their trade would support a strike for shorter hours and limitation of apprentices. Any strike called was to begin about 1 March. *Scotsman*, 17 February 1862.
[2] The International Industrial Exhibition opened in London on 1 May 1862.

Campbell and Young, the former auditors, were then requested to audit the books again, a little remuneration being allowed for the same. Several subscription sheets were handed in, which will be duly accounted for. Mr Sheddin returned the book on social science transactions, Mr Munro accepting of the same.

25 March 1862

Delegates present: Coopers, Messrs Gunn, Begg, Mason; Engineers, Messrs Campbell, Turnbull; Tailors, Mr Troup; Corkcutters, Messrs Alston, John Clark; Glassmakers, Mr Reid; Glasscutters, Mr Beaton; Brassfounders, Messrs Purdie, Smith; Moulders, Mr Baxter; Masons, Messrs Collins, Lockerbie; Cabinetmakers, Messrs Young, Wilkes; Slaters; Mr Munro; Joiners, Mr Henry; Blacksmiths, Mr Dewar.

On the proposed trades Hall, further additional items of trades expenditure for meetings was given in, making the total amount known at present to reach £60. This would pay for a Loan of £1,200 at the rate of 5 per cent. The secretary stated that he had not made a circular out on the above scheme, knowing the treasurer to be tight with funds.

The President and secretary stated the kindness of Professor Archer of the Industrial Museum in inviting them at the opening converzationie, and his communications regarding admitting working men. The secretary read a letter of thanks to Professor Archer which he had drawn up for the considerations of the trades delegates, the same if approved of to be sent to Press. It was agreed to try the press to insert it with proposed alterations. The secretary then read a Printed letter from the Social Science Association requesting us to send our annual subscription of one guinea. Our former resolution on this point was agreed to, viz., to decline to give it.

Treasurer's account as drawn up by the auditors was read over, and considered satisfactory as regarded correctness. It was considered necessary that the year's income and expenditure be entered in the minute book and that in future all trades be furnished with a Quarterly balance sheet of income and expenditure.

Mr Lockerbie stated that Mr Gorrie, Advocate, has kindly offered his services to endeavour to get any petition from this body carried into the house of commons. Mr Reid stated that he had noticed that the trades council of Glasgow were indeavouring to do away with the Law on Arrestment of wages and as he considered it a very pernicious one, he thought the sympathy of this council ought to be given to help them on.[1] It was ultimately agreed that the secretary be authorized to convey our opinions and sympathy to the Glasgow trades council. Subscriptions from the masons, £1 10s. 6d.; from the Coopers, 10s.

Report of the Monetary transactions from 4 December 1860 to 4 December 1861 of the Council of United trades delegates

INCOME	£	s	d
Balance on hand 4 December 1860	3	14	4½
Contributions from: Blacksmiths	1	5	1
Joiners	2	6	6
Brassfounders		18	7
Masons	2	0	0
Feb. and Mar. Collections of 3 Meetings in Brighton Street Chapel on short time movement, aggregate	15	12	6
Contributions from: Glassmakers		10	2
Glasscutters		6	4
Leith Coopers		10	0
Edinburgh Bakers	1	0	0
Leith Bakers		14	6
Tailors	1	0	0
Clockmakers		2	6
5 Nov. Excursion to Glasgow: gross gain	11	0	9
From tracts on Labour Question	1	10	0
Per Mr Troupe for prise Essays	1		1½
Collections from Lectures, delivered by Professor Miller, Dr McAdam and Mr Gorrie	4	10	6½
Total Income	£47	2	11½
Expenditure[2]	46	6	1
Balance in hand	£0	16	10½

[1] Below, p. 289.
[2] According to the sums itemised the expenditure should total £45 10s. 4d. Presumably the difference is due to an omission by the secretary of an item or items in copying the accounts into the minute book.

EXPENDITURE	£	s	d
Incidental Expenses connected with the short time (masons and Joiners) movement	1	14	9
Feb. and Mar. For advertising the above meetings	2	1	6
Rent of Brighton Street Chapel for 3 meetings on the above movement	4	17	6
For printed Sheets (Opinions of Press)	1	1	0
Cab fares in connection with the above movement		6	6
By time for 2 Members of Council in connection with the above movement		14	6
Cost of Bringing Mr Potter from London	7	0	0
Mr Canon's (Bill Poster's) account (aggregate)	4	11	0
4 June. Secretary's Salary for 12 months	1	10	0
7 June. Allowance to 2 members of Council for arranging trip to Glasgow	1	0	0
19 June. Mr Canon's Bill account for above trip	2	8	0
To D. Hardie, Bill poster		10	0
26 June. Book of Social Science Report, Glasgow		8	0
26 July. Returning treat to trades Council of Glasgow	1	7	0
29 Aug. To Mr Potter for tracts on Labour Question	1	2	9
8 Oct. Pamphlets and their carriage from London		14	6
9 Nov. Lost time on account of winter Lectures		10	6
30 Nov. To Mr Canon for printing bills for the above	1	19	0
To D. Hardie, Bill Poster		2	6
For advertising the above 3 Lectures		19	6
Rent of Brighton Street Chapel for 1st 3 Lectures	5	5	0
3 Dec. For Bill Boards		4	0
Room rent for 46 Council and committee meetings	2	6	0
Half year's salary to secretary, Mr Beaton		15	0
To previous treasurer, Mr Caw, for 9 months	1	0	6
3 Months' Salary to Mr Collins, Treasurer for 4th Quarter		5	0
Stationary and Postage stamps		16	4
Total expenditure	£46	6	1
Balance on hand		16	$10\frac{1}{2}$
	£47	2	$11\frac{1}{2}$

We have examined the vouchers in the hands of the treasurer and find the summations correct. Signed, Thomas Young, Auditor; George Campbell, Auditor.

7 April 1862[1]

Delegates present: Coopers, Messrs Mason, Begg, Gunn; Moulders, Messrs Baxter, Johnston; Engineers, Messrs Campbell, Turnbull, Cunningham, Sheddin; Corkcutters, Messrs Alston, Clark; Glasscutters, Messrs Brown, Beaton; Slaters, Mr Munro; Brassfounders, Messrs Purdie, Smith; Cabinetmakers, Messrs Sheddin, Young; Joiners, Mr Bruce; Masons, Messrs Collins, Lockerbie; Smiths, Mr Dewar; Glassmakers, Mr James Reid. Vice President in the Chair.

The secretary intimated that by request of Professor Thomas Archer a meeting took Place the result of which was that the Industrial Classes were to hold a converzationie, under the auspices of the trades delegates, in the Museum on saturday evening, the 26th Inst. from 6 till 8 O'clock. Admission by ticket, six hundred ultimately agreed to be printed for issue.

The secretary intimated that he had received a small book from the National Science Association, containing a list of Names of members. After some discussion it was agreed to adhere to our former resolution of making no contribution. In support of the foregone decision Mr Campbell proposed a motion to this effect, viz., That we as a Trades Council, representing sixteen different Trades, feel ourselves much aggreived on account of the short space allowed in the book on social Science in support of opinions bearing on the good effects of and necessity for trades Unions, while on the opposite side full allowance is given. Seconded by Mr Munro, and unanimously agreed to.

Mr Johnston, Moulders, intimated that the employers of Falkirk were making united efforts to reduce the wages of the workmen 20 per cent, but as yet no active steps had been taken in the matter. If anything decisive occurred he would let us know.

Mr Smith intimated he understood that the President was due three days' pay for time lost during the saturday evening lecture movement. It was agreed that he be paid the same when he ten-

---

[1] The date ought probably to read 8 April 1862.

dered his account. The secretary then intimated that he had sold a large number of the lecture pamphlets, and that those parties that had got a number on hand had better bring them at next meeting. Mr Bruce returned 34 same evening. Mr Johnston, moulder, Paid 2s. for pamphlets, and tendered 3s. 2d. as a subscription.

22 April 1862

Delegates present: Moulders, Messrs Baxter, Robertson; Engineers, Messrs Campbell, Turnbull, Sheddin; Smiths, Mr Dewar; Clockmakers, Mr Latimer; Glassmakers, Mr Kelly; Joiners, Messrs Bruce, Grant; Masons, Mr Collins; Cabinetmakers, Messrs Sheddin, Wilkes, Young; Glasscutters, Messrs Brown, Beaton; Coopers, Messrs Mason, Gunn, Begg; Slaters, Mr Munro; Tailors, Mr Troup; Brassfounders, Messrs Purdie, Smith. Vice President in the Chair.[1]

Regarding Mr Campbell's motion on social Science, the secretary stated that, having doubts about being authorized to transmit that motion to London, he had not as yet done so. The secretary was authorized to do so.

The secretary stated that he had given the greater part of the tickets for the Converzatione in Industrial Museum to the delegates in as fair a proportion as he thought proper. The remainder were then divided. Some considerable discussion then ensued regarding the line of conduct to be pursued on that evening; full information was elicited. The subject of a Gratuitious Gift to the Museum was given over to the chairman's committee to manage as they thought proper. Mr Troup, President, was then called upon to give a vote of thanks to Prof. Archer, the secretary to second same.

The Iron Moulders had no report to give of any active offencesive or defensive measures being resorted to in Falkirk. The Masons said their was no extra news of the Dundee nine hours movement to give, the fight still continuing.[2] A small pamphlet, headed *Contract for establishing The Association of Employers in the building Trades of Dundee* was tabled. This again shows what has long been considered criminal in working men is being rapidly imitated by the employers,

[1] John Sheddin, cabinetmakers. Troup, the president, was evidently present later.
[2] The Dundee masons had begun a strike on 1 March to secure the nine hours day. *Scotsman*, 4 March 1862.

through virtue of necessity. Mr Troup made the remark that a meeting of his trade, the Tailors, had been convened to ascertain if there should be a union or not. He was happy to say that the result had been very gratifying.

Mr Campbell, engineer, then called for an account bearing on the distribution of the tickets. The same was drawn up and handed to him, the majority if not all of the delegates Present being quite satisfied. Subscriptions: Clockmakers 2s. 3d.; Engineers 11s.; Glassmakers for Pamphlets 3s. 7d., returned 32; Moulders 1s. pamphlet; Engineers returned 12; Blacksmiths returned 12. The President was then Paid 3 days for lost time during the lecture movement at the rate of 5s. per day.

6 May 1862

Delegates present: Glassmakers, Messrs Kelly, Reid; Glasscutters, Messrs Brown, Beaton; Slaters, Mr Munro; Engineers, Messrs Turnbull, Sheddin, Cunninghame; Moulders, Messrs Robertson, Baxter; Brassfounders, Messrs Purdie, Smith; Cabinetmakers, Messrs Young, Sheddin; Clockmakers, Mr Latimer; Masons, Messrs Herbert, Collins; Coopers, Mr Begg; Tailors, Mr Troup. In absence of the President Mr Young, Cabinetmaker, called to the chair.[1]

The secretary stated that in accordance with former instructions he had dispatched the resolutions bearing on the social science committee to that board, and had received a reply. In the discussion which followed the reading of the reply, some proposed that we should throw off all recognition of that committee, others argued that we should hold a remote connexion. Ultimately Mr Turnbull moved that we do not get the social Science Book for 1861, Seconded by Mr Collins. Mr Brown moved a counter-motion that we do get the Social Science book for 1861 and that the secretary be authorized to write to that effect. Seconded by Mr Young, who had just previously vacated the chair on the arrival of the President. 2 only voted for the motion, the majority for the counter-motion. Some questions were then asked if we had any copies of or the original Papers, that Frazer and Caw read on Trades Unions at the social Science gathering at Glasgow. A reply was made in the negative.

---

[1] Sheddin, the vice-president, and Troup, the president, were present later.

The secretary was ordered to write these parties to see if they could furnish the Council with their manuscripts.[1]

Gratuitious gift to Museum: The president intimated that Professor Archer would not hear of anything of the kind being done, and also reported that everything had gone off well. Mr Young made some remarks that the numbers were excessive, making the premises very crowded.

The Iron Moulders reported all quiet at Falkirk. Mr Herbert, Mason, gave a long and minute account of the struggle of the Dundee Nine hours movement, ending in soliciting the trades for any pecuniary sympathy they might feel inclined to bestow. A memorial was tabled from the Nottingham Framework knitters, embodying an account of their greivances and soliciting support from the trades.[2]

Mr Collins proposed it was now time for us to take into consideration the propriety of holding our annual trip to Glasgow. It was left to the Chairman's committee to make enquiry concerning the same and to report at next meeting. A discussion having arisen about apprenticeships, the secretary said this was a subject he should like to have discussed as there were many different notions held. The hour however being late the council broke up. Mr Smith Paid for pamphlets 4s., returned 3.

20 May 1862

Delegates present: Engineers, Messrs Cunninghame, Turnbull, Campbell; Tailors, Mr Troup; Glasscutters, Messrs Beaton, Brown; Glassmakers, Mr Kelly; Slaters, Messrs Clark, Robertson; Moulders, Mr Robertson; Brassfounders, Messrs Smith, Purdie; Cabinetmakers, Mr Young; Clockmakers, Mr Latimer; Masons, Messrs Collins, Herbert; Coopers, Messrs Gunn, Mason.

The new representatives from the United Slaters presented their

---

[1] A summary of the paper read by William Caw on 'Trade Unions and their Objects', and by Alexander Fraser on 'Trade Unions not injurious to the welfare of the Community', is included in the *Transactions of the National Association for the Promotion of Social Science, 1860* (London, 1861), 877-8.

[2] Their specific grievances have not been ascertained but presumably arose from the 'state of prostration' of their trade from March 1862 to January 1865. E Renals, 'Arbitration in the hosiery trades of the Midland counties', *Journal of the Royal Statistical Society*, 30 (1867), 548-66.

credentials to the Council in the place of Mr Munro, who had been withdrawn. They were accordingly approved of.

The secretary read a reply from Mr Caw, Joiner, stating that he could not furnish the delegates with a copy or the original paper read by him at the Glasgow social Science meeting. Mr Fraser, Blacksmith, also sent the same reply. Some remarks of a depreciatory nature regarding these papers were made, but the President and others strongly advocated there value. The subject then dropped.

After a little discussion on the Glasgow trip Mr Smith moved that 26th July be the day for the annual trip, Seconded by Mr Latimer, and agreed to. It was then agreed that Messrs Troup and Brown be the parties to go to Glasgow and make final arrangements with the manager of the railway company and also with the owners of the various factories and places visited by the excursionists, and to report at next meeting; also to endeavour to get 1,500 tickets for sale. Mr Collins then moved that in order to get as many committee tickets as possible that the secretary be authorized to furnish the railway deputation with a List sheet of members, seconded by Mr Latimer. Some remarks were then made to endeavour to impress upon the railway manager the desirability of imposing a sixpence extra on those parties wishing to stop till monday. Agreed to. The subject then dropped. One Pound sterling allowed for wages and travelling expences.

The Slaters intimated that a strike of that trade had taken place in Glasgow, by a non-compliance of the employers to a request of the operatives for an improved method of dividing the day. It was intimated that above four hundred were thus thrown out of employment. Mr Herbert stated that the numbers of Masons on funds[1] were about the same as last fortnight; also that the country had been beaten up for subscriptions, good promises being the result, but that they had hopes of a speedy settlement.

A letter was then read from a person signing himself A. Kennedy, w.s., bearing upon a pamphlet he had written on the high price of food, hinting that he was wishful that the trades delegates should assist him to make it more public.[2] It was proposed by Mr Collins

[1] At Dundee.
[2] Alexander Kennedy, w.s., 1802-68, author of *The High Price of food, butcher-meat, meal, and bread-stuffs, etc., stated and illustrated; with reference to what was expected*

that the President should read it and report his opinion on same at next meeting. Mr Brown then proposed, Seconded by Mr Herbert, that the secretary acknowledge the receipt of the letter and pamphlet.

3 June 1862

Delegates present: Engineers, Messrs Campbell, Turnbull; Glass-cutters, Messrs Beaton, Brown; Glassmakers, Mr Reid; Slaters, Messrs Clark, Robertson; Moulders, Messrs Baxter, Robertson, Johnston; Brassfounders, Messrs Smith, Purdie; Cabinetmakers, Messrs Sheddin, Young; Clockmakers, Mr Latimer; Masons, Messrs Collins, Herbert; Coopers, Messrs Mason, Begg; Tailors, Mr Troup; Joiners, Messrs Bruce, Grant. The Vice President in the chair.[1]

The secretary read the agreement with the Edinburgh and Glasgow Railway which was approved of and signed by President and secretary. Mr Brown gave in his report stating the different places to be open for the excursionists, also that the committee were allowed 38 tickets and that about 12 of the committee might be allowed to remain till Monday. 1,200 tickets to be given for the first instalments. 1,000 Small bills were then agreed upon and 250 Posters. On some discussion arising about the drawing up of the bill Mr Campbell, engineer, moved: That the committee be empowered to draw it up as in former years. Seconded by Mr Reid and agreed to. On a Refreshment bill brought before the council being digested, the secretary was authorized to write to Glasgow to make arrangements for the convenience of the excursionists.

Mr Baxter took the book on social science, Mr Herbert spoke for the next loan. A Letter from the operative Skinners of Scotland was then read stating that they had agreed to send delegates to the council. This produced an agreable impression and the secretary was authorized to write them giving the information they desired. Mr Collins returned 15 of Professor Archer's lecture pamphlets, Mr Dewar[2] 10, and Mr Johnston paid 1s. 2d. for 14 sold.

The Slaters intimated that the strike still continued in Glasgow

---

under Free Trade as expected in 1847 . . . , by a Writer to the Signet [A.K.] (Edinburgh, 1860).
[1] Troup, the president, was evidently present later.
[2] He is not included in the list of delegates present.

and that a considerable number of men were still out of employment. A bill, however, was shown stating the names of 22 employers
who had acceded to the just request of the men. Mr Herbert,
Mason, intimated that the strike still continued in Dundee. In the
course of his remarks he seemed to dwell on the necessity and urgency
of the council endeavouring to raise subscriptions. Considerable
discussion arose on this question, merging ultimately on the necessity
of the United Trades forming a federation by paying a sixpence per
member per Quarter to a central fund and when on strike or lock-
out receiving 2s. 6d. per week. Some remarks were made that this
might well be discussed among the various trades in meeting and
their opinions taken on same. If 500,000 workmen joined this league,
the fund remaining untouched for 12 months would amount to
£108,333 6s. 8d., exclusive of interest.[1] This, disbursed at the rate of
2s. 6d. per week per member, would support for 12 months 8,000
men, including the interest of the money.

Auditors were then chosen to add the books up on saturday evening, Messrs Baxter and Young being the parties chosen. The secretary's and treasurer's salary was then ordered to be paid.

17 June 1862

Delegates present: Engineers, Messrs Turnbull, Cunninghame;
Tailors, Mr Troup; Glasscutters, Messrs Beaton, Brown; Glass-
makers, Messrs Reid, Kelly; Slaters, Messrs Clark, Robertson;
Moulders, Messrs Baxter, Robertson; Brassfounders, Messrs
Purdie, Smith; Cabinetmakers, Messrs Sheddin, Young; Clock-
makers, Mr Latimer; Masons, Messrs Collins, Herbert; Coopers,
Messrs Mason, Begg; Skinners, Messrs J. Curle, Fleming; Joiners,
Mr Bruce.

The minutes of last meeting were read and on being put to the
meeting Mr Herbert, Mason, objected to that part of them bearing
reference to his having dwelt in his remarks at the former meeting
on the necessity of the council endeavouring to raise subscriptions
for the Dundee masons. The secretary intimated that he might have
misunderstood Mr Herbert, and had thereby conceived a wrong
impression. Mr Collins then proposed that the minutes be adopted,

---

[1] This does not make sense.

Seconded by Mr Sheddin, who made a remark that in his opinion the secretary in making out his minutes ought to confine himself strictly to business and not insert any remarks of his own.

It was intimated that we had chosen the wrong day for the Annual Glasgow trip as the cavalry races were to take place on 1 August, After some discussion it was agreed by a majority of votes that we hold to 26th July.

An appeal from the Glasgow slaters, at present on strike, was read, backed out by a letter from the Glasgow trades Council. This subject brought the discussion of federation, in which Messrs Young, Robertson, and Turnbull and others took part, when Mr Robertson, moulder, made a motion that at next meeting of council the delegates discuss the subject of Federation, seconded by Mr Turnbull. Agreed to. Mr Turnbull then moved that federation be remitted to the trades in order to ascertain their opinion on same. Seconded by Mr Herbert. The secretary intimated that his trade were already taking votes on the subject. Mr Young then made the remark that parties discussing this question should bring their remarks on paper. The secretary was ordered to reply to these letters of appeal.

The secretary read Mr Alexander Kennedy's letter bearing on the pamphlet he had written on dear food. The secretary was ordered to acknowledge the receipt of the letter and give explanations. Mr Young read the Quarter's Balance sheet. Mr Robertson, Moulder, moved the approval of the same, seconded by Mr Smith. The secretary was authorized to ascertain what would be the cost of printing a number of copies. Mr Brown then proposed that we meet weekly till the trip day on account of pressure of business, Seconded by Mr Kelly. Mr Collins moved an amendment that we meet once a fortnight, Seconded by Mr Herbert. For Mr Brown's motion 6 voted, For Mr Collins' amendment 9 Voted.

1 July 1862

Delegates present: Engineers, Messrs Turnbull, Sheddin, Campbell; Glassmakers, Messrs Kelly, Reid; Glasscutters, Messrs Brown, Beaton; Cabinetmakers, Messrs Young, Wilkes, Sheddin; Smiths, Mr Dewar; Joiners, Messrs Grant, Bruce; Slaters, Messrs Clark, Robertson; Masons, Messrs Herbert, Collins; Moulders, Messrs Baxter, Robertson, Johnston; Brassfounders, Mr Smith; Clockmakers, Mr Latimer; Coopers, Mr Mason; Skinners, Mr Fleming; Tailors, Messrs Troup, Grindley.

On the Glasgow slaters' strike the secretary intimated to the Council the reason why the committee of his trade[1] felt themselves unable at present to grant any aid. The secretary read two letters from Mr Kennedy, w.s., and gave a little information, as also the President did, regarding the matter contained in the Pamphlet On Dear Food, and also an account of the interview he had with the gentleman.

The secretary then read the report of the delegates, to be adopted or otherwise. A remark being made that the clause referring to the Joiners might prove damaging, drew out an opposite opinion not only from the Joiners themselves, but particularly from Messrs Campbell, Fleming and others. Mr Campbell moved a suggestion, Seconded by Mr Turnbull, that two other clauses might be inserted in the report bearing on the necessity of other united trades sending delegates to this Council, and also referring to the good that might accrue to disunited trades by unity. This was agreed. On the Printing of 100 Copies of the report the secretary said he had been informed that the cost would be above a £1 sterling. The Chairman's Committee was ordered to look after the cost of printing various numbers.

Mr Wilkes took the Book on *Transactions of social science*. Glasgow Excursion tickets were delivered out to the number of 1,120. The Brassfounders tendered a subscription of 4s. The hour now being late the motion for debating the subject of federation was postponed, the Council agreeing to meet on the tuesday of the next week.

8 July 1862

Delegates present: Engineers, Messrs Sheddin, Campbell; Glass-cutters, Messrs Brown, Beaton; Brassfounders, Messrs Smith, Purdie; Coopers, Messrs Begg, Mason; Tailors, Messrs Grindley, Troup; Masons, Messrs Herbert, Collins; Smiths, Mr Dewar; Clockmakers, Mr Latimer; Cabinetmakers, Messrs Sheddin, Young; Joiners, Mr Bruce; Moulders, Messrs Baxter, Robertson.

Mr Collins, treasurer, read over the ticket list which was found

---

[1] Glasscutters.

to be correct, as certified by the replies of the different holders. Mr Latimer intimated that a case on instant dismissial had been decided in the Sherrif court adverse to the pursuer, a working joiner. He considered this case of great importance to the trades of Edinburgh and working men generally. Mr Bruce, joiner, gave explanations on the case, stating that Sheriff Jamieson sided with the employer because he had previously Posted a bill in a workshop stating that no notice would be given or taken. Mr Troup stated that he did not think a recognized trade law would in a Sheriff's opinion override a Private shop law. Mr Collins thought if an employer paid a week's wage he was bound to give a week's notice, and any shorter practice was contrary to public recognized law.[1] Mr Sheddin stated a case of the same nature were an employer, a Cabinetmaker, got an adverse decision. Mr Robertson, moulder, stated that in his trade it was instant notice. After some further discussion Mr Herbert stated a case werein he was a witness, and to the best of his recollection he beleived there was an act of parliament particularly bearing on the point at issue, and requiring the bill to be of a certain size and letters also. He then moved that we, either through a committee or other means as may seem best, endeavour to ascertain the exact bearings of the law on the subject. Seconded by Mr Sheddin, Engineer. Messrs Bruce and Herbert were then appointed along with the Chairman's committee to meet on thursday night to meet Mr Buchanan, lawyer,[2] and obtain his opinion, and endeavour to get the act of Parliament. The subject then droped.

Mr Robertson, Moulder's, Motion on Federation then came on for discussion. Mr Robertson stated that it was necessary in his opinion for the easy and successful working of this scheme that all trade levies should be equal. Mr Collins did not see any necessity for all trade levies to be alike, so long as they always paid their proportionate share to this scheme. The secretary then stated his opinion, contending that the scheme could be worked as easily as a trades union if the trades would embrace it. Mr Baxter, moulder, thought

[1] The *Scotsman*, 28 June 1862, reported that the joiner had sued his employer for 18s. 7d. of wages due, as he had been dismissed without notice. The sheriff held the employer was entitled to alter the custom of the trade by making it a rule that no notice be given on either side. Andrew Jameson was a sheriff-substitute of Midlothian 1845-65 and sheriff of Aberdeen 1865-70.

[2] Presumably James Buchanan, solicitor, 37 George Street, but not further identified.

G

the easiest way would be to divide the countries into districts, appoint a local committee to manage the income and expenditure, and send a balance sheet to headquarters. Messrs Mason, Dewar, Smith, and Brown thought the best plan would be to endeavour to form a local federation first. Other members joined in the discussion but the hour being late the Council broke up, arranging to meet on tuesday the 15th Instant. Mr Bruce paid 1s. 4d. on account per Archer's lecture.

15 July 1862

Delegates present: Engineers, Messrs Turnbull, Sheddin, McDonald, Campbell; Tailors, Mr Troup; Clockmakers, Mr Latimer; Glass-makers, Mr Reid; Glasscutters, Messrs Brown, Beaton; Brass-founders, Messrs Smith, Purdie; Cabinetmakers, Messrs Young, Sheddin, Wilkes; Coopers, Messrs Mason, Begg, Gunn; Smiths, Mr Dewar; Moulders, Messrs Baxter, Robertson; Joiners, Messrs Bruce, Grant; Slaters, Mr Robertson; Skinners, Mr Fleming; Masons, Mr Collins.

While the President was engaged taking the numbers of excursion tickets sold, the secretary gave an account of his interview with the lawyer, Buchanan, regarding the instant dismissal of a joiner from his employment.

The Slaters' delegate gave in a report regarding the strike in that trade in Glasgow, the men on strike being in a precarious position from the want of funds, the masters at the same time from a know-ledge of their position assuming a domineering tone. Mr Fleming, Skinners, gave a report of a strike in his trade in Glasgow, the men on strike being non unionists, but supported by voluntary contribu-tions from Union Skinners. The Masters in this instance seek to reduce the men 10 per Cent. A number of questions having been asked of the delegates of these two trades, the Chairman was handed the Engineers' Magazine or report Book and read a speech delivered by Mr Lee to the London society of amalgamated Carpenters and joiners, showing the necessity for and benifits of systematic trades Unions.[1] Mr Collins then intimated the result of the Dundee Masons' strike for the nine hours to be a failure and that the Lodges

---

[1] Lee has not been identified and his speech was not published in the journal of the Amalgamated Society of Engineers.

had declared that it be brought to an end. The Roll stood as follows: working 9 hours – 47 men; working 10 hours – 183 men; men still on strike – 48.

Mr Fleming gave the treasurer 1s., the Price of one Dozen of Archer's Lectures, and took other 2 Doz. The Council agreed to meet next tuesday evening to ascertain the result of the sale of excursion tickets.

22 July 1862

The delegates met here this evening for the purpose of ascertaining the result of the sale of the tickets for the annual excursion. The result of the sale amounted to a few above 300.

The Slaters' delegate intimated to the council the state of the men on strike in that trade in Glasgow and read a copy of printed regulations issued by the employers holding out against the men, for the workman's signatures before being allowed to start work. The same was ordered to be copied into the minute book.

The secretary was also ordered to write a note to the Glasgow secretary of trades council and insert a Trip bill. On Wednesday night the sale of the tickets as given in amounted to 400. On Thursday night to 600 and on friday night to 1,028.

Rules of the Glasgow Association of Master Slaters

All Journeymen, Labourers, and Apprentices, presently employed, and to be hereafter employed, are and shall be engaged subject to the following Rules, viz.: 1. Wages to first Class journeyman to be at the rate of 5d. per hour. 2. Labourers and Apprentices to be paid per arrangement or agreement. 3. The Wages of journeyman Slaters, Labourers, and Apprentices in all cases to be paid fortnightly. 4. The Masters reserve liberty, in all cases, to employ Journeyman, whether members of any society or union or not, as they please. 5. No rule heretofore made or to be hereafter made by any society or union of Journeyman operatives to be binding in any way on the employers. 6. Journeyman not desirious of Joining any society or Union shall not be compelled to do so, nor shall they be interfered with in any manner of way. 7. The Employers not to be restricted in any way as to the number or proportion of Apprentices which they may have engaged or may at any time hereafter engage. 8. The Employers are to be the judges of the kind of work at which labourers are to be employed. 9. No alterations to be made on the above rules without three months' previous notice being given.

29 July 1862

Delegates present: Engineers, Messrs Turnbull, Campbell; Glassmakers, Mr Reid; Glasscutters, Mr Beaton; Brassfounders, Messrs Smith, Purdie; Tailors, Mr Troup; Joiners, Messrs Bruce, Grant; Cabinetmakers, Messrs Sheddin, Young; Skinners, Mr Fleming; Slaters, Mr Robertson; Masons, Mr Collins; Moulders, Mr Robertson; Coopers, Mr Mason.

On the report of trades, Mr Robertson, Slater, said that the strike in his trade was settled as the men had no funds to maintain the struggle longer. Several members expressed themselves that with a proper systematic Union this would not have happened, but hoped that this defeat would pave the road to success the next time. Mr Fleming, Skinner, said he had no report to give in concerning the strike of non-Unionists in his trade in Glasgow.

The Secretary read a letter from the social science committee in reply to one he had sent some time previously regarding the price of the *social science transactions of 1861*. Mr Young expressed sentiments adverse to entering into a discussion regarding the acceptance of the social science committee's offer, it being in his opinion of a secondary nature; and moved that we settle up the accounts with the trip, and ascertain what profit we had. Mr Collins stated that he paid £159 6s. to the Railway Manager, but had got no receipt yet. The President and the treasurer then agreed to go to the Railway manager and get it. They returned unsuccessful.

During the absence of the President the vice President took the chair, and while discussing the after-mentioned paper, a committee entered and asked the Delegates' permission to allow them to bring a petition before their notice for the opening of the Botanical Gardens on sundays after church hours. The committee read the Petition and made a few remarks, a number of the delegates expressing themselves favourably inclined in support of the Petition and promising to do all in their power to get signatures. The committee then withdrew. The secretary then drew again the attention of the delegates to a notice he had drawn up of the decisions of

Sheriffs Jamieson and Hallard[1] in the recent dismissal cases.[2] The delegates expressed themselves pleased with the document, and hoped the *Edinburgh News* would insert it.

Mr Troup intimated that a mishap occurred to him – the momentary loss of his excursion tickets, which occasioned him to purchase 5 others. These tickets having been recovered, he hoped the delegates would consider his position favourably. The delegates expressed themselves that in the meantime he had better try and settle the account with the Railway Manager.

12 August 1862

Delegates present: Engineers, Messrs Turnbull, McDonald; Glasscutters, Mr Beaton; Cabinetmakers, Messrs Young, Sheddin; Clockmakers, Mr Latimer; Moulders, Mr Baxter; Coopers, Mr Mason; Brassfounders, Messrs Smith, Purdie, McDonald; Slaters, Mr Robertson; Tailors, Messrs Troup, Grindley; Skinners, Mr Fleming; Masons, Mr Collins; Smiths, Mr Dewar.

The treasurer said he wished the delegates to understand that he had got a receipt from the Railway Manager, but that the President had an account to settle with the delegates. The President then intimated that he had been successful in getting forwarded to him the price of the 5 tickets he had momentary lost, and handed over the sum of 15s. to the treasurer. The Treasurer intimated that the total outlay for managing the Annual trip was £4 3s. 7d. The total profit £5 2s. 2d., exclusive of the price of 24 tickets the delegates had made over to themselves. The profit was considered satisfactory. Tickets 1,200. Returned 100. Sold 1,038. Delegates 62.

The credentials of Mr McDonald, Brassfounder, as an extra delegate from that body was read and received with approbation. Mr Fleming, Skinner, intimated that the strike of the non-unionists was over, one half giving in after a week's cessation from labour, the

[1] Frederick Hallard, a sheriff-substitute of Midlothian 1852-82, died 1882. *Edinburgh Evening Courant*, 13 January 1882.
[2] The case decided by Hallard on 25 July concerned some forty masons' labourers who had struck work without notice after refusal of their demand for increased wages. Their employer brought the action as a test case. The sheriff held that the men were bound to complete their day's work and found in favour of the employer, with costs. *Scotsman*, 26 July 1862.

other half gaining after a four weeks' struggle and becoming members of the union.

The committee for the opening of the Botanical Gardens then requested an audience and were welcomed. A conversation ensued, eliciting much information of a favourable nature, success being almost certain, The signatures being well up for 10,000.

Mr Collins intimated that having occasion to be at the printer he asked his opinion regarding the price of printing the report, received an answer that in all probability 15s. would cover it. Mr Young moved that the secretary be authorized to write for the *Social Science Transactions of 1861* and that the treasurer remit the amount. Agreed to.

Mr Young intimated that he had condensed the last two Quarters' monetary transactions into one report to econimise the funds of council. He also wished a slight remark to be made in the secretary's report on the reason for only giving a six months' report, and he also requested that, in addition to the Chairman's augmented committee, the auditors, or at least one of them, should be present to preside over their work, and if necessary give explanation. It was ultimately agreed that one of them should be present. Chairman's Committee comprises the following persons: Troup, Beaton, Collins, Sheddin, Bruce; presiding auditor – Mr Young. Mr Young hoped the subject of federation would be resumed next meeting.

26 August 1862

Delegates present: Engineers, Mr Turnbull; Brassfounders, Messrs Smith, Purdie; Moulders, Messrs Baxter, Robertson; Glassmakers, Messrs Reid, Kelly; Glasscutters, Messrs Beaton, Brown; Masons, Mr Collins; Coopers, Messrs Begg, Gunn, Mason; Joiners, Mr Bruce; Cabinetmakers, Messrs Young, Wilkes; Tailors, Messrs Troup, Grindley; Smiths, Mr Dewar; Slaters, Mr Robertson.

The secretary intimated that the first annual report was printed and ready for delivery, Price £1 1s. Sterling. It was then agreed that 6 Copies be the first delivery to each trade, and a few to be handed into other bodies not represented. Mr Turnbull, engineer, intimated that he was under the impression that according to the revised act now passed relating to Industrial & Provident Societies, that trades unions could be registered. It was agreed that the treasurer purchase the act and report.[1]

Mr Young then expressed himself that the delegates in his opinion ought to discuss Watt's *Bane and Antidote* and endeavour to form conclusive opinions regarding it either favourable or otherwise, and wished that the same be discussed next meeting. It was agreed that the subject be discussed.[2] A deputation from the united Printers of Edinburgh then requested permission to ask a few questions of the delegates. He was allowed, and every information given him regarding our constitution and objects, when he withdrew.

Some discussion ensued on the irregular manner in which the chair was addressed. Mr Dewar moved that all persons wishing to speak, rise and address the chair. Seconded by Mr Baxter and agreed to.

9 September 1862

Delegates present: Engineers, Messrs Turnbull, Dewar[3]; Glass-makers, Mr Reid; Glasscutters, Messrs Beaton, Brown; Cabinet-makers, Messrs Young, Sheddin; Smiths, Mr Dewar; Masons, Messrs Hart, Storm, Collins; Slaters, Mr Clark; Brassfounders, Messrs Smith, McDonald; Coopers, Messrs Mason, Gunn; Skinners, Mr Fleming; Tailors, Mr Troup.

The Credentials of Messrs Hart and Storm were read and accepted as delegates from the Masons' Union.[4] The Joiners intimated that they had been withdrawn from the council and retired. The Amended act relating to Industrial and Provident Societies was read; nothing relating to the registration of trades Unions was found in them. Mr Dewar then moved that the treasurer be empowered to purchase the act relating to friendly societies, as he thought it bore reference to the registration of trades unions. Agreed to, Seconded by Mr Turnbull.

[1] Industrial and Provident Societies Act, 25-26 Victoria, c. 87.
[2] John Watts, PH. D., *The Workman's bane and antidote: comprising the essay on strikes read at the British Association, etc.* (London, 1864). The *Report* of the British Association meeting in 1861 includes an abstract of a paper by Watts 'On Strikes' (London, 1862), 249-50.
[3] This seems to be a confusion with Dewar, blacksmiths. If another engineer was present he was probably Sheddin or Campbell.
[4] For a few biographical details of Hart see above, pp. xxv-vi.

A few remarks were then made about the Clockmakers having no Union and if so it was contrary to the constitution of the Council to allow any of that trade to take a part in the business of the meeting. Mr Turnbull then moved that the secretary write Mr Latimer for his credentials, seconded by Mr Collins.

According to the Minutes of former meeting, Watt's *Bane and Antidote* came on for reading and discussion. Mr Young made some opening remarks on Federation, in the end expressing himself that according to his ideas Dr Watt's pamphlet bears some remarks on same, and wished the President to read the first part of said book. This was done. The discussion took a wide range, a few of the members expressing themselves as concurring in a great measure in Dr Watt's Views, while the marjority seemed to be of opinion that his reasoning was untenable and might be in a great measure refuted. Mr Brown took the book of *social Science transactions for 1861.*

23 September 1862

Delegates present: Masons, Messrs Hart, Storm, Collins; Glasscutters, Mr Beaton; Engineers, Messrs Turnbull, Sheddin; Brassfounders, Messrs Purdie, McDonald; Tailors, Mr Troup; Smiths, Mr Dewar; Cabinetmakers, Mr Young; Glassmakers, Mr Kelly; Slaters, Messrs Clark, Robertson; Skinners, Mr Fleming.

The treasurer produced the amended act to consolidate the laws relating to Friendly societies. The secretary by request was about to read the 9th clause relating to the practical purposes of a Friendly society, when Mr Turnbull moved that the Act be read individually, before being discussed, the reading in council and discussion to take place this night four weeks.[1] Seconded by Mr Young and agreed to. A note was then read in reply to the Council's request for credentials of Mr Latimer, Clockmaker. The Council authorized the secretary to endeavour to obtain the secretary's address of the United Clockmakers and request credentials to be forwarded to the Council authorizing Mr Latimer to appear as a delegate from that body. The above was motioned by Mr Turnbull, Seconded by Mr McDonald.

The further reading and discussion of Watt's *Bane and Antidote*

---

[1] 23-24 Victoria, c. 58, amended the Act of 1855 (18-19 Victoria, c. 63) whose ninth clause dealt with the purposes of a friendly society.

next took place. When the President had done reading, Mr Young spoke at some length on the views as embodied by Dr Watt on the subject of strikes, contending that the Dr's grounds for argument were fallacious, his views one-sided, and the general tenor of his expressions showing him to be entirely ignorant of the laws and operations of trades Unions; ending in totally condeming the Dr's arguments. A great discussion followed, numerous points in Trades Union history being commented on, the general tone of same backing out Mr Young's speech.

The President then intimated to the Council that the society of United Tailors of Edinburgh, of which he was a member, had voted the sum of twenty shillings in aid of the funds of Council, and handed over the same to the treasurer, Mr Collins. Mr Dewar took the New Book on *social Science transactions*. Mr Young then proceeded to read the Quarterly Balance sheet, was interrupted, but after the passage of a few words was allowed to proceed. The account was considered satisfactory.

7 October 1862

Delegates present: Engineers, Mr Turnbull; Masons, Messrs Hart, Storm, Collins; Glassmakers, Mr Reid; Glasscutters, Mr Beaton; Brassfounders, Mr McDonald; Cabinetmakers, Messrs Young, Sheddin; Coopers, Messrs Mason, Gunn; Smiths, Mr Dewar; Tailors, Mr Troup; Skinners, Mr Fleming.

The secretary stated that after reading the amended act to consolidate friendly societies, he thought it would be useless to endeavour to carry out Mr Turnbull's, engineer, motion, as it was his opinion that the act only related to Benifit and friendly societies, and that only those portions of the laws of a Trades Union would be registered if embodied separately relating expecially to aiding a member out of employment, in sickness or death, or any other benifit the Union may agree upon, and that members might be pursued for arrears of subscriptions and defalcations. A general discussion then took place regarding sick and funeral societies, summonses against these societies, and the general coincidence of the Sheriffs with the pursuer, though really having no law sanctioning the exercise of authority in these matters. Mr McDonald made some remark cheifly bearing out the above, citing a case where the sheriff practically bore out the above remark by refusal to hear a case. Mr Dewar made some remarks, contending that under this act trades unions could be registered, as the Smiths' society was already so. Some remarks were made about the probable softness of the Smiths' laws, but was instantly checked. Mr Collins and Hart then related the late case of the Masons' society being pursued for funeral money and the defeat of the pursuer, though judgement in a similar case had been given some-time previous for the pursuer. The discussion then dropt.

The Secretary read the reply of Mr Latimer, Clockmaker, stating in the meantime the suspension of all intercourse between the Council and that Union. Mr Turnbull, Engineer, than gave notice of motion that the apprentice Law be discussed this night 4 weeks. Seconded by Mr McDonald and assented to.

Mr Turnbull, after hearing that portion of the Minutes re-read referring to the remarks passed at former meeting on Watt's *Bane and Antidote*, contended that Mr Young's remarks did not fully bear out the Council's opinion. The mover and seconder of the minutes, however, contended that the minutes were correct. During the discussion, some irratating remarks were passed, when the President reprehended the parties, stating that we met for higher purposes than cavilling and that our language ought to partake of politeness. Mr Young then made motion: That the secretary be authorized by the Council to embody in writing their opinions fully on Dr Watt's work either with or without help. Seconded by Mr Fleming. Mr Hart moved an amendment: That the Council, as many as please, prepare themselves with written papers on that subject, to aid in carrying out Mr Young's motion. 3 voted for Mr Young's motion, 6 for the amendment, and 4 remained neutral.

Mr Turnbull and others then intimated that the Council were accused of being the instigators for opening the Botanical Gardens on Sunday after divine service, and that he wished the secretary to contradict the statement in the public press. Mr Reid made a motion that no notice be taken of same till we be publicly accused, seconded by Mr Collins, Mason, and agreed to.

21 October 1862

Delegates present: Engineers, Messrs Turnbull, Sheddin; Masons, Messrs Collins, Hart; Brassfounders, Messrs McDonald, Purdie,

Smith; Skinners, Mr Fleming; Coopers, Messrs Mason, Gunn;
Slaters, Mr Robertson; Tailors, Mr Troup; Glasscutters, Mr Beaton;
Smiths, Mr Dewar; Cabinetmakers, Mr Young.

The mover for the discussion of the Friendly societies act intimated
that he had not prepared himself with written or verbal matter for
this discussion; the seconder also was not present. However, the
discussion was entered upon, the remarks being chiefly a repetition
of views as expressed at former meetings on the same subject. The
prevailing idea on the obstacle to the registration of Trades Unions
seemed to rest on the laws of the regulation of the number of
apprentices and the strike system. To ascertain the opinion of the
Council on the necessity or inutility of registering Trades Unions,
two Motions were made and votes taken. Mr Dewar, seconded by
Mr Gunn, recommends all trades Unions to endeavour to get
registered. 4 voted for this motion. Mr Collins made a Counter
Motion, expressing himself on the inutility of the registration of
trades unions seeing no good practical results are likely to flow from
it. Seconded by Mr McDonald. 8 voted for this motion.

Mr Hart, Mason, then read a paper, prepared by himself, giving
his opinion on Dr Watt's *Bane and Antidote*, which was attentively
listened to and applauded. This was the only paper read on this
subject. Mr Young brought back the Book on *social science transactions*.

Mr Hart's, Mason, Summary on Dr Watt's
Bane & Antidote

After a careful perusal of *The workman's Bane & Antidote* by Dr
John Watts of Manchester, I have arrived at the following con-
clusions: 1st, That the reasons alleged by him as being the occasion
of Strikes is erroneus and shows clearly that his wishes were Father
to the thoughts that gave birth to his fallacious and one-sided
arguments. 2nd, That the cure proposed by him is utterly inadequate
to effect the purpose he has in view, and not at all practicable in the
present state of trades unions.

But while admitting with Dr Watt that strikes are an evil, I
beleive that they are necessary evils but by a little prudence properly
exercised there occurrence would be less frequent, and the Hard-

ship endured on account of them would be greatly mitigated. I humbly suggest the following precautions on the part of those who have too good reason to resist the tyranny and aviricous selfishness of their employers: 1st, When a strike is in contemplation, three fourths of the number of those who are likely to be directly affected by it should be unanimous as to its necessity. 2nd, When a dispute arises between employer and employed offers should be made by the employees for arbitration. 3rd, The means at the disposal of the employers for prolonging the struggle should be ascertained as far as possible. 4th, The state and prospect of the trade and the position of the labour market. 5th, The funds at the disposal of the society and the probable sums likely to be obtained from other sympathising trades unions and the toiling millions generally.

In conclusion I beleive were these suggestions or others embodying the same sentiments but minute in detail faithfully carried out in practise, the number of strikes would be reduced and those that are absolutely necessary would stand a better chance of being crowned with success, thus raising the moral tone of Trades Unions in the opinions of those whose good opinions and cooperations are really worth having.

J. Hart

4 November 1862

Delegates present: Glasscutters, Messrs Beaton, Brown; Masons, Messrs Hart, Collins; Brassfounders, Mr McDonald; Cabinetmakers, Messrs Sheddin, Young; Smiths, Mr Dewar; Glassmakers, Messrs Reid, Kelly; Skinners, Mr Fleming; Tailors, Mr Troup.

The minutes of last meeting were read, and Mr Dewar said he objected to that part wherein it states that he wished trades unions to be registered, as he had said he only wished them to be certified as according to common Law. Mr Hart then moved the adoption of the minutes with this correction, Seconded by Mr Dewar.

The Secretary then read a note of appeal on behalf of the Cotton Operatives at present out of employment through the rebellion of the southron States. In considering this appeal, a great and varied discussion, principally of a political nature, took place, the government generally receiving blame for not having more than one market for raw materials for our home manufacturers. Mr Collins was of opinion that the secretary should be authorized to acknowledge the reception of the note. This was agreed to. Mr Hart, Mason, then proposed as a motion, That we do not entertain this appeal as it does not properly form a part of our duties at this board. Seconded by Mr Collins. 2 voted for this motion. Mr Reid then made an Amendment: Considering that the Richer Classes were to hold a meeting on the 11th,[1] that we postpone taking any further steps in the cause till our next meeting. Seconded by Mr Brown. For Mr Reid's Amendment 7 voted. Carried accordingly.

Mr Fleming Suggested that the secretary endeavour to ascertain if the Trades Delegates association could get insertion in Oliver & Boyd's *Almanac*.[2] Seconded by Mr Young and agreed to. Mr Collins then proposed that as an inducement for papers to be brought forward to confute Dr Watt's *Workman's Bane and Antidote*, one guinea be given as a prize for the best production. Seconded by Mr Reid and agreed to. Mr Fleming brought back the Book, *Social Science Transactions*, Mr Kelly accepting a loan of same.

18 November 1862

Delegates present: Engineers, Messrs Turnbull, Sheddin; Glassmakers, Messrs Kelly, Reid; Glasscutters, Messrs Beaton, Brown; Blacksmiths, Messrs Dewar, Fraser; Masons, Messrs Collins, Hart; Brassfounders, Messrs Purdie, McDonald; Slaters, Mr Robertson; Tailors, Mr Troup; Coopers, Messrs Mason, Gunn; Cabinetmakers, Mr Young; Skinners, Mr Fleming.

The secretary intimated that he had written to Oliver & Boyd's as authorized last meeting but had received no reply. A letter was then read from Padiham, East Lancashire, giving explanations as to their position on the relief fund. Mr Fraser, Smith, requested leave to offer explanations and pass remarks on this case and was allowed to do so. He dwelt heavily on the extreme urgency of the case, and

---

[1] The meeting was held on 12 November.
[2] Sir James Y. Simpson once declared that the two books he 'most used and valued as a Scotsman' were the Bible and Oliver and Boyd's *Almanac*. The *Almanac* was published from 1812 to 1932 as a continuation of almanacs issued by other publishers in Edinburgh from 1740. W. M. Parker, 'The House of Oliver and Boyd' (unpublished typescript in Edinburgh Public Library), 5, 10.

on the necessity of calling a public meeting of the working classes. Mr Young then remarked that in his opinion the working classes should cooperate with the influential committee and not seek to take any leading position. Mr Young then made a motion against holding a public meeting, Seconded by Mr Hart, and supported by Mr Collins. This motion was subsequently withdrawn. After some further discussion on the subject of relief, for and against the delegates taking any active steps in the matter, opinions were freely and generally spoken, merging into two motions, The first proposed by Mr Robertson, slater, That we as a body do not entertain the question at all but leaves the same as it is in the hands of the public. Seconded by Mr Mason. 6 voted for this motion. Mr McDonald proposed that the trades delegates call a public meeting in aid of the distressed cotton weavers of Lancashire, Seconded by Mr Reid. 8 voted for the counter motion – carried accordingly. The opposite party then declared that all the trouble of getting this meeting up would devolve on those supporting the counter motion. This party agreed to meet on the following thrusday to make arrangements.

The subject of Watt's *Bane and Antidote* was again brought forward. The remarks made were as to the best means to be adopted to get a proper argumentative refutation of Dr Watt's *Workman's Bane and antidote*. Mr Collins spoke as to the necessity of a argumentative refutation. He proposed that his original motion be still offered and adhered to. Mr McDonald supported the motion with this proviso, that it be extended to the public. Seconded by Mr Turnbull. Mr Dewar, blacksmith, proposed as a motion that we drop the *Bane and Antidote* subject and go into Federation. 2 voted for Mr Dewar's motion, 7 for Mr Collins'.

Mr Young then spoke on the necessity of something being done in the way of showing the trades by what best method they could better their condition and maintain their unions and extend their influence. Mr Fraser thought the best way to accomplish that end was to advise McKinnon to insert a clause in his bill for the registration of Trades unions. That subject, he was informed, had been already disposed of.[1]

---

[1] Above, p. 11.

20 November 1862

The committee for getting up a public meeting in aid of the distressed Lancashire operatives met this evening. Seven gentlemen were selected to be wrote to, to speak on the occasion. Mr Kelly and Reid to wait on the Lord Provost[1] and the Revd. J. Graham, Newhaven,[2] Messrs McDonald and Turnbull to wait on the Revd. Guthrie[3] and Tasker[4]. The meeting then adjourned till saturday evening to report.

22 November 1862

The result came to at this meeting was that McDonald be appointed to wait on the influential committee and answer any questions that may be asked, and make observations. In the meantime the secretary to write Sir William Johnston[5] acquainting him of the appointment of Mr McDonald; also to write Mr McDonald a note appointing him to wait on the influential committee. The result of all this was that, owing to the very vigourous and extensive measures about to be put in force by the influential committee, we did not see any utility at present in calling a public meeting.

31 December 1862

Delegates present: Glasscutters, Mr Beaton; Glassmakers, Messrs Reid, Kelly; Tailors, Messrs Troup, Dalzean; Masons, Messrs Collins, Storm; Cabinetmakers, Messrs Young, Sheddin; Brassfounders, Messrs Smith, McDonald; Skinners, Mr Fleming.

The President read the Credentials of Mr Dalzean as a co-delegate along with himself from the society of United tailors of Edinburgh. Some remarks then passed on the necessity of the delegates bringing Credentials at different periods. The general opinion was that such ought to be the practice.

The secretary read all the correspondence in relation to the appeal

[1] Charles Lawson of Borthwick Hall, seed merchant, lord provost of Edinburgh 1862-5, died 1874.
[2] Rev. William Graham, minister of Newhaven.
[3] Rev. Dr Thomas Guthrie.
[4] Rev. William Tasker, minister of West Port Free Church.
[5] Sir William Johnston, 1802-88, co-founder of W. and A. K. Johnston, publishers; lord provost of Edinburgh 1848-51.

from Padiham. He strongly supported the appeal, in order to render the power of the middle class impotent to ill use trades Unionists or co-operators, explaining the latter's position in relation to the Law. Mr Troup also commented on the system pursued to co-operators, relief being denied them so as to break up the system for the present. Messrs Young, Sheddin, Collins, Reid, and others, seemed to be of opinion that it would prove ultimately to be a great evil to these parties to aid them in setting up a relief committee in opposition to the middle class, various reasons being assigned in support of their opinions. The secretary was then ordered to acknowledge the receipt of the *Bee Hive* newspaper and send a reply stating the opinions of the majority of the Council on the appeal. Also to write the middle class committee of this city thanking them for their kindness in causing the complaints to be investigated.

Mr Troup, Tailor, then gave explanations on the Sweating system, showing the evils likely to be entailed on people who gave orders to shops carrying on such a system, the safest place for parties getting goods made up being the workshop where healthy men were only at work. He also called the attention of the trades to the dispute in the firm of Messrs Brown & Tregilgas, through the introduction of a machine, giving satisfactory explanations regarding the dispute.[1]

Mr Smith, on behalf of the United Brassfounders of Edinburgh, tendered to the treasurer a subscription of 6s., being a half-yearly subscription. The secretary having read a letter from the Committee of the Social Science Association requesting us to forward our Annual subscription of one guinea, it was decided as their next meeting would be held in Edinburgh that we forward the subscription.

[1] The premises of Brown and Tregilgas were at 56 North Bridge.

1863

13 January 1863

Delegates present: Tailors, Mr Troup; Glassmakers, Mr Reid; Glasscutters, Messrs Beaton, Brown; Brassfounders, Messrs Purdie, McDonald; Skinners, Messrs Fleming, Anderson; Cabinetmakers, Mr Young; Masons, Messrs C. Smith, Collins; Slaters, Mr Clark; Coopers, Messrs Mason, Begg; Smiths, Mr Dewar.

Credentials from Charles Smith, Mason, Peter Anderson, Skinner, and Thomas Young and Sheddin,[1] Cabinetmakers, were read and heartily approved of. A letter from Padiham was read urging the trades of Edinburgh to follow in the wake of several other Large towns in England in support of the workingman's Central relief fund. This brought on a general discussion on the prospects of the Cotton trade, ending in a general expressed opinon that the delegates did not see any solid grounds for altering their former decision; but that if good cases of wilful neglect of trades Unionists could be substaniated, their opinion might alter. The secretary was according requested to answer the note, and insert the opinions of the Council. In order to watch the grounds of any complaints, Mr McDonald moved that the delegates remit a Quarter's money to the manager of the *Bee Hive*, the paper to be sent to the secretary. This was agreed to.

Mr Troup, Tailor, then reported that the tailors Union were entirely done with the firm of Messrs Brown & Tregilgas, Union men having given up all connection with that firm for the Present.

In order to hold a membership with the social Science Association the secretary was instructed to transmit one guinea. Mr Young, Auditor, then read over the half yearly statement of Income and Expenditure. He also read papers on Labour, proving that a man

---

[1] Sheddin is not shown present.

H

man might be poor in pocket, but at the same time a noble genius, and that what he could not get willingly conceded to him as a fair day's pay for a fair day's work, he had every just right then to combine with his fellow workmen, in order to effect the desired object. He was frequently applauded while reading.

Election of office Bearers: President, Mr Troup; Vice President, Mr McDonald; Secretary, John Beaton; Treasurer, Mr Collins; Chairman's committee, Young and Fleming.

27 January 1863

Delegates present: Amalgamated Engineers, Messrs Campbell, Turnbull; Masons, Mr Hart; Glassmakers, Mr Kelly; Glasscutters, Mr Beaton; Cabinetmakers, Messrs Young, Sheddin; Brassfounders, Messrs Purdie, Smith, McDonald; Tailors, Mr Dalzean; Coopers, Messrs Mason, Gunn; Smiths, Messrs Dewar, McIvor; Skinners, Mr Fleming. In the absence of the President the vice President, Mr McDonald, was called to the chair.

The Credentials of Messrs Andrew Dewar and John McIvor were then read and approved of as delegates from the Edinburgh Branch of Scottish Blacksmiths. Messrs Campbell and Turnbull were also received as delegates from the Edinburgh branch of Amalgamated Engineers. The secretary read the receipt for one guinea from the secretary of the Social Science committee, and a reply from the East Lancashire workman's committee drawing a fearful picture of the distress in that unhappy county. After some remarks from the most of the delegates Mr McDonald requested leave to have Lord Derby's remarks read on the witholding of relief from Co-operators and Trade Unionists, Lord Derby in that article endeavouring to make a distinctive scale of allowance for various parties, but co-operators in spinning mills were not to be relieved on any account.[1] This caused a very general discussion, the remarks made being more favourable towards the co-operators than on former discussions, a great deal more of light being thrown on these societies. Mr Campbell then moved that the letter from Padiham be

[1] This may be a reference to Derby's statement at a meeting of the Lancashire relief fund committee on 19 January. He said that members of co-operative societies should be excepted from the rule that no relief funds be given to persons with property, and that mortgage of the applicant's co-operative shares should be the most demanded of him by local relief committees. *The Times*, 20 January 1863.

sent to the middle class committee of Edinburgh. Seconded by Mr Hart with this proviso, that we would rest content with this arrangement if carried out, that whatever sums the cooperators may receive as profit from any scheme they may be share holders in, that they receive also a weekly grant from the relief fund in order to place them on the same level with non-cooperators. This was agreed to. Should this arrangement not be carried out, the secretary was authorized to state that we would endeavour to stop the subscriptions altogether or divert into a different channel.

Mr Young then stated that at the last meeting he had given out various questions with a view to discuss what were the best means to be adopted and followed out for ameliorating and advanceing the condition of the working classes. This was replyed to as following, That all trades have one Union, one scale of wages for a certain amount of work performed where applicable; good, commodious and open dwellings, to insure good health, and also the entire disuse of intoxicating liquors, and a good general system of instructions to youths and also to grown-up persons. These remarks received a general assent.

Mr Fleming made some remarks upon the utility this Council might be turned to if it was more fully known and that we should endeavour by an appeal to the trades to get them to send delegates and support the Council. Mr McDonald then replied at some length that what Mr Fleming had advocated had been tried several times and failed. That we were well known when any class wanted anything from us but unknown at any other time.

10 February 1863

Delegates present: Glassmakers, Mr Reid; Glasscutters, Messrs Brown, Beaton; Masons, Messrs Hart, Collins, Smith; Cabinetmakers, Messrs Young, Sheddin; Skinners, Mr Anderson; Tailors, Mr Troup; Smiths, Messrs Dewar, McIvor; Brassfounders, Messrs Purdie, Smith, McDonald; Slaters, Mr Robertson.

The secretary read a copy of a letter he was formerly authorized to write to the middle class committee of this city. It was considered very satisfactory. An acknowledgement of the same was also read.

The Slaters[1] informed the Council they had been reelected to represent their trade.

The Secretary then informed the delegates that a public meeting would shortly be held in Edinburgh to express sympathy with President Lincoln of the United States and that the cooperation of the Council was requested to make it a thorough working man's meeting, and also that a deputation would wait upon the Council this evening to request the President to take the chair. This office the President declined. Mr Collins, Mason, passed a few remarks against the objects of the meeting, reading an article written by Lord John Russell in support of his views. A heavy discussion then took place on the merits of the question, a number siding with Mr Collins while a Larger number were averse to his opinion. The deputation then requested leave to say a few words and an audience was granted. Having stated their objects, they were informed that we had come to no settlement of the question, but the secretary would be authorized to write them a note of decision. Mr Hart moved: That this council do take a prominent part in furthering the objects of the meeting. Seconded by Dewar. Mr Collins moved an amendment, That we send a deputation to the emancipation committee from this board, but that we take no prominent part. Seconded by Mr McDonald. 8 voted for the motion, 6 for the amendment. Mr Collins made a motion that a special meeting of delegates be called if found requisite. It was further moved that a deputation of two be sent from this board, this was agreed to. Dewar and Beaton were then chosen.[2]

24 February 1863

Delegates present: Masons, Messrs Hart, Collins; Smiths, Messrs Dewar, McIvor; Brassfounders, Messrs McDonald, Purdie, Smith; Coopers, Mr Mason; Skinners, Messrs Fleming, Anderson; Tailors, Messrs Dalzean, Troup; Cabinetmakers, Messrs Sheddin, Young; Glassmakers, Mr Kelly; Glasscutters, Mr Beaton. In the absence of the President the vice President was called to the chair.[3]

[1] Only one is shown present.
[2] The meeting was held on 19 February in Brighton Street Chapel, with John Beaton, secretary of the trades council, in the chair. *Edinburgh Evening Courant*, 20 February 1863.
[3] John McDonald, brassfounders. Troup, the president, was present later.

The secretary informed the delegates that he had received a reply from the Edinburgh middle class committee to his letter. He gave an account of its contents. Some remarks then passed on the necessity of informing the public of this city by placard or otherwise of the withholding of relief from certain parties. After various remarks had been made, Mr Hart made the following resolution: That this committee publish by placard, not in a detailed but in a concise form, the steps we have taken anent the distribution of this money and the total denial of cooperators as not entitled. Mr Troup made an amendment that the question be shelved. On being put to the vote the amendment was carried.

The secretary then read a letter and draft prayer of a petition for the opening of the Botanical Gardens on sunday. After considerable discussion Mr Dewar made the following resulution, Seconded by Mr Hart: that this subject be deferred for a fortnight till the opinions of the trades are ascertained. 6 voted. Mr Sheddin moved: That the opening or closing of the Botanical gardens on sunday is not a competent subject for this board to entertain. 5 voted. Mr Mason Seconded. Mr Troup made an amendment, viz., That this board, on account of the various opinions held by our constituents, decline to appear to take any lead in the movement. Seconded by Mr Anderson. 7 voted, carried accordingly. The secretary was authorized to transmit the result of the debate to the committee for opening the Botanical Gardens on Sunday. It was also agreed that as the Prince of Wales' marriage would be celebrated on the forenoon of the next meeting night, we pospone any business for a month, with powers given to call an earlier meeting if found necessary.

17 March 1863

Delegates present: Engineers, Mr Sheddin; Smiths, Messrs Dewar, McIvor; Brassfounders, Messrs McDonald, Purdie, Smith; Masons, Messrs Charles Smith, Collins; Cabinetmakers, Messrs Young, Sheddin; Skinners, Messrs Anderson, Fleming; Tailors, Mr Troup; Glassmakers, Mr Reid; Glasscutters, Messrs Beaton, Brown.

The secretary read a letter from Mr Fleming, Skinners' delegate, requesting the secretary to call an early meeting to consider the propriety of requesting Lord Palmerston to address the working classes of Edinburgh. The secretary stated that there was another party in the field anzious to read an address to Lord Palmerston on Poland. This caused a deal of discussion, but ultimately a motion was made by Mr McDonald: That this Association request Lord Palmerston to address the working classes of this city during his visit if found convenient.[1] Seconded by Mr Sheddin, Engineer. Charles Smith then proposed McDonald and Beaton wait upon the Provost[2] and request his favour to carry out our desires. Agreed to. Powers was granted to call a meeting if found requisite.

19 March 1863

Delegates present: Masons, Messrs Smith, Collins; Tailors, Mr Troup; Engineers, Mr Sheddin; Brassfounders, Messrs Smith, McDonald; Cabinetmakers, Messrs Young, Sheddin; Glassmakers, Mr Reid; Glasscutters, Messrs Brown, Beaton; Skinners, Mr Anderson; Smiths, Messrs Dewar, McIvor.

The deputation gave in their report and produced a draft of a requisition to Lord Palmerston for acceptance or otherwise. Several found fault with this, when the President drew up one which was agreed to. The secretary also submitted a paper, for insertion in the press, contradicting a statement that had been pubicly made of our proceeding, bearing a special reference to Poland. The contradiction was ordered to be inserted.[3] The same deputation was authorized to submit the requisition to the lord Provost.

24 March 1863

Delegates present: Brassfounders, Messrs Smith, McDonald, Purdie; Coopers, Messrs W. Peddie, D. Henderson; Masons, Messrs Collins, C. Smith; Smiths, Mr McIvor; Slaters, Mr Robertson; Cabinetmakers, Messrs Sheddin, Young; Engineers, Mr Sheddin; Glasscutters, Messrs Brown, Beaton; Tailors, Messrs Troup, Dalzean; Skinners, Mr Fleming.

As a part of the minutes, the President made some remarks on the actions of the operatives in Lancashire in consequence of being

---

[1] Palmerston visited Edinburgh from 1 to 4 April 1863.
[2] Charles Lawson.
[3] No reference has been found in the press to any statement concerning the trades council and Poland.

kept in a state of Partial starvation. Some more remarks were made, when the subject droped. The deputation to the Lord Provost then gave in their report anent Lord Palmerston. Mr Sheddin moved a vote of thanks to the deputation, Seconded by C. Smith and responded to. A desultory discussion then ensued, in case Lord Palmerston should consent to address the working classes, as to the best means for carrying out the arrangements. This part was confided to the office bearers and chairman's committee, with this previso, not to exceed 2,000 tickets. Powers was also given to the secretary if he thought requisite to cry down an advertisement that would likely appear, calling upon secretaries of trades Unions and trades delegates to attend a meeting at a given place for the purpose of addressing Lord Palmerston on Poland. The Quarter's report was then read by Auditor Young and explanations asked were answered.

7 April 1863

Delegates present: Masons, Messrs Collins, Hart; Glassmakers, Messrs Kelly, Reid; Glasscutters, Mr Beaton; Coopers, Messrs Mason, D. Henderson; Brassfounders, Messrs Smith, Purdie, McDonald; Cabinetmakers, Messrs Young, Sheddin; Smiths, Mr McIvor; Engineers, Mr Sheddin; Tailors, Mr Troup.

The secretary stated that he had received no reply to the requisition forwarded by the Provost to Lord Palmerston. Remarks were passed that it was very discourteous not to send any reply. Mr McIvor moved that the secretary be authorized to write the Lord Provost requesting information why no reply was returned to the requisition, seconded by James Reid and agreed to.

The secretary had received a letter from Mr Potter, manager of the *Bee Hive* newspaper, that he had sent ten newspapers for distribution among the heads of the trades. The same were then distributed.

The secretary then stated that he had received a letter from a Mr Mathieson of Lanark, regarding a roguish peice of business attempted to be practiced on a number of weavers by an agent. The case had been in the law courts for nearly five years. The weavers, owing to the depressed state of trade, were unable without outside assistance to carry on the case. They therefore appeal to the trades to enable them to do so. Mr Hart moved That in his opinion the petition is a proper subject for this board to entertain and recommend the same to their various trades. Seconded by James Reid and agreed to. Bills received bearing on the case were then distributed for the information of the trades.

The secretary stated that the Glasscutters' executive had taken out a warrant against a branch secretary for embezzelment. The case was being heard in the Law courts; the result of the trial would prove whether uncertificated societies could sue or be sued. He promised to give the Council all information at the next meeting.[1] Mr Hart stated that the masons were endeavouring to establish a literary institute and had a very fair prospect of accomplishing their purpose. He also gave further information on the scheme.

21 April 1863

Delegates present: Tailors, Mr Troup; Glassmakers, Mr Reid; Glasscutters, Messrs Brown, Beaton; Brassfounders, Messrs McDonald, Smith, Purdie; Coopers, Messrs Mason, Henderson; Slaters, Mr Robertson; Skinners, Mr Fleming; Cabinetmakers, Mr Young; Masons, Mr Collins. Vice President in the chair.[2]

The Lord Provost's reply to the enquiry relating to the non-acknowledgement of the requisition forwarded to Lord Palmerston was read. Mr Potter's notice of the expiry of Quarter's remittance for the *Bee Hive* was also read. A little information on the appeal of the Lanark weavers was elicited, but as yet nothing of a very hopeful character was reported. The Glasscutters then related the case of embezzlement by a branch secretary, the delinquent escaping in the meantime, through the evident connivance of a magistrate who was an anti-trade unionist. Another case was reported of swindling society funds. This case was brought to the bar but the defender acknowledged the debt and consented to pay it.

Mr Reid proposed that the secretary have note paper supplied with a heading to show the official authority of the communications, seconded by Mr Brown. It was postponed till next meeting. The secretary read the reply from the manager of the North British

---

[1] No report of this case has been found.
[2] John McDonald, brassfounders. Troup, the president, was evidently present later.

Station relating to the conditions he would grant a trip to Newcastle and back upon. The same was considered very satisfactory. The chairman's committee was requested to wait upon the manager for further particulars. Mr Collins moved that this meeting discusses at next meeting the propriety of drawing up a subject or subjects to be read at the social science meeting to be held in Edinburgh. Seconded by Mr Fleming and supported by Mr Young.

5 May 1863

Delegates present: Brassfounders, Messrs McDonald, Smith; Glass-cutters, Messrs Brown, Beaton; Coopers, Messrs Mason, Henderson, Peddie; Glassmakers, Messrs Reid, Kelly; Tailors, Mr Troup; Masons, Mr Collins; Cabinetmakers, Messrs Sheddin, Young; Engineers, Mr Campbell; Skinners, Mr Anderson. Vice President in the chair.[1]

Mr Brown moved that the secretary be supplied with note paper having a stamped designation to be agreed upon. This was seconded by J. Reid. Mr McDonald gave full information as to the prices. It was ultimately agreed to order 100. The secretary then intimated that he had received a note from Mr Mathieson, Lanark weavers' secretary, to the effect that he would be in waiting to give the Council full information regarding the Law suit carried on by the weavers against Mr Row, Cloth agent, for the recovery of monies due for work illegally withheld. On Mr Mathieson being introduced he gave a general statement of the case, also of the weavers' union and their amount of subscriptions weekly and their organization under a code of laws. The remarks appeared to give great satisfaction as being concise and to the point, ending in urging upon the council to bring the weavers' case before their respective trades that means might be got to fight Might and establish Right. He was applauded. Several members spoke in support. The gentleman then withdrew.

Mr Mason tendered a subscription of 10s. to the treasurer from the United Coopers of Edinburgh and Leith. The secretary intimated that he had written to the Manager of the North British Railway for grants for the committee similar to those allowed by the Edinburgh and Glasgow Railway, but promised to call on saturday

---

[1] Troup, the president, was evidently present later.

evening. Having done so he found the manager had gone to the country. The President then stated that he had promised to call but had forgot to do so. He, however, agreed to carry out his original promise. A discussion then ensued as to whether we should undertake a trip to Newcastle and give up the Glasgow trip. Mr Reid proposed that we have a trip to Newcastle on the second week of August, seconded by Mr Brown. No opposition being offered it was agreed to, as also that we have the annual Glasgow trip. The hour now being late Mr Collins' motion on the propriety of submitting topics to be read at the social Science meeting to be held in Edinburgh had to be deferred till next meeting.

19 May 1863

Delegates present: Glasscutters, Messrs Beaton, Brown; Masons, Messrs Collins, Smith; Slaters, Messrs Clark, Robertson; Brassfounders, Messrs Smith, Purdie, McDonald; Skinners, Messrs Fleming, Anderson; Cabinetmakers, Mr Young; Tailors, Mr Troup; Coopers, Mr Henderson.

Mr McDonald stated that the official note paper had cost 5s. per hundred owing to an additional line. The President then gave an account of the steps taken in reference to the Newcastle trip. A unanimous expression of opinion prevailed to the effect that the trip must take place on a friday, returning on saturday night or monday morning, power being given to the Preses and secretary to carry out arrangements only on these terms.

Mr Collins brought forward his motion on social science topics. After passing a few remarks on the utility of reading a subject at the forthcoming Social Science Congress to be held in Edinburgh, Mr Collins moved that we do appoint a member to attend the meeting, Seconded by Mr Smith. After considerable discussion on trades unions and other topics, considerable attention was drawn to the Reductions of the Hours of Labour, the subject being much approved of. Mr Collins' motion was then approved of with this previso, that at some future meeting one or two delegates would be appointed.

The treasurer received the sum of 8s. from Mr Fleming, Skinner, as a subscription from his trade society. Mr McDonald gave notice of motion that at next meeting, he would move that the trip to Glasgow be held on the Musselburgh Race Saturday.

2 June 1863

Delegates present: Cabinetmakers, Messrs Sheddin, Young; Glass-makers, Messrs Reid, Kelly; Glasscutters, Messrs Brown, Beaton; Masons, Mr Smith; Coopers, Messrs Mason, Henderson, Peddie; Brassfounders, Mr McDonald; Skinners, Mr Fleming; Tailors, Mr Troup; Slaters, Messrs Clark, Robertson.

Information was given anent the Newcastle proposed trip that no arrangement had been come to as yet on account of the seeming inability of the company to carry us on the friday. This scheme was ordered to be left in obeyance for a week but that the committee call again before next meeting. Collins' Social Science motion, on account of the mover's absence, was ordered to lie over. Mr McDonald brought forward his motion on the Glasgow trip. He proposed that the arrangements be entered into at once. This was agreed to. The secretary was requested to accompany Mr Troup. Full power was given to endeavour to obtain a full share of favours.

A letter was read from Mr Mathieson, Lanark, on the weavers' case, requesting to know if anything was being done on their behalf. The secretary was requested to see the gentleman and state that the weavers' case was under consideration by the trades.

16 June 1863

Delegates present: Tailors: Mr Troup; Cabinetmakers, Messrs Sheddin, Young; Glassmakers, Messrs Kelly, Reid; Glasscutters, Messrs Beaton, Brown; Brassfounders, Messrs Purdie, Smith; Coopers, Messrs Mason, Henderson; Slaters, Mr Robertson; Skinners, Mr Fleming; Masons, Mr Collins.

The secretary informed the meeting that he had written to the manager of the North British Railway that unless the company could comply with our request the projected excursion to Newcastle would fall to the ground. He had received a letter in reply, stating the inability of the company to comply with our request, hoping however that some other days would be equally convenient. Mr Purdie moved that the former minute be sustained, seconded by

Mr Reid and agreed. The secretary was ordered to write the manager that the project was ended.

Considerable discussion took place on the subject of Collins' motion on Social Science. Some urged that the subject should be left to choice, while others urged that the subjects should be agreed upon by the Council and the honor of attending the social science congress be competed for. It was however ultimately moved by Mr Brown that parties desirous to compete should write articles of their own choice and bring them here for examination and approval or otherwise not later than two months hence. Mr Collins seconded this, which was agreed to.

Information was given anent the success of the committee who were appointed to make arrangements for the Glasgow trip. The fare would be 3s. 3d. for adults, half fare for children under 12 years of age, and 38 Tickets to members of committee. About a Dozen or so to be endorsed for return on the monday. The train would leave the Waverley Bridge Station at 20 minutes to six A.M., returning from Glasgow at 8.30 P.M. Number of tickets 1,200. The Chairman and secretary was requested in the name of the Council to sign the contract and carry out arrangements. The treasurer requested that he be empowered to purchase a dozen books for members who took tickets for sale, as a security to them and the Council. This was agreed to.

The secretary then intimated that Professor Archer had requested him to call upon him. At the interview the Professor stated that during the social science congress to be held in this city the committee were anxious to call a monster meeting of the working classes under the Presidency of Lord Brougham. To check a crush, they at present were proposing to admit by ticket, price sixpence. Afterwards the trades delegates were to have a supper of Monte Video Beef to test its qualities as an article likely to be consumed in this country. Several explanations were asked and given, when the Council requested the secretary to state to the Professor that they would do all in their power to make the meeting a success, but at the same time they desired that the price of admission should be as low as possible. As for the supper if it suited their palate they would do ample justice to it, when and wherever required, and give a verdict accordingly.

The secretary had received a letter from Mr Mathieson praying that the Council urge upon their various trades to support the weavers' law suit, as their lawyer was pressing them for money, and they had none to give. If no money was coming the case would have to be abandoned, and Might would again Triumph over Justice and Poverty. The secretary was authorized to return for answer that the delegates had urged the matter before their various trades and for the present could do no more. The secretary was paid his half yearly salary.

30 June 1863

Delegates present: Tailors, Mr Troup; Glassmakers, Messrs Reid, Kelly; Glasscutters, Mr Beaton; Cabinetmakers, Messrs Young, Sheddin; Brassfounders, Messrs Smith, Purdie; Coopers, Mr Mason; Masons, Messrs Collins, Smith; Slaters, Mr Robertson; Skinners, Messrs Fleming, Anderson.

The secretary stated that he and the President waited on Professor Archer, but not being able to see him wrote him our opinion on his Social Science propositions. On account of the omission of two parties' names from the excursion bill for tickets sellers, some dissatisfaction was expressed. Apologies were made. The Brassfounders gave a subscription of six shillings. The treasurer's Quarterly Balance sheet was read over by Auditor, Mr Young. Distribution of excursion tickets took place.

14 July 1863

Delegates present: Glassmakers, Mr Kelly; Glasscutters, Messrs Beaton, Brown; Masons, Messrs Collins, Smith; Tailors, Mr Troup; Brassfounders, Messrs Purdie, McDonald; Cabinetmakers, Messrs Young, Sheddin; Slaters, Messrs Robertson, Clark; Coopers, Messrs Mason, Henderson; Skinners, Mr Fleming.

Mr Collins intimated that there were two new Books in the market he beleived well worthy the attention of working men: *Better days for working men*, by Blackie, minister, Edinburgh;[1]

---

[1] *Better Days for Working People* (London, 1863), by Rev. William Garden Blaikie, 1820–99, minister of Pilrig Free Church, Edinburgh, 1844–68, professor of apologetics and pastoral theology at Edinburgh 1868–97, temperance reformer, advocate of improved working class housing.

Workingmen and their Earnings, by Samuel Smiles.[1] Mr Collins proposed that we purchase these works, Seconded by Mr Young. After a little discussion by the delegates the purchasing of the works was postponed.

28 July 1863

Delegates present: Tailors, Mr Troup; Cabinetmakers, Messrs Young, Sheddin; Brassfounders, Messrs Smith, Purdie, McDonald; Masons, Mr Collins; Skinners, Mr Fleming; Glassmakers, Mr Reid; Smiths, Mr Dewar; Coopers, Messrs Mason, Henderson; Glasscutters, Mr Beaton.

Mr Collins brought forward his motion for the purchase of two new works written respecting working men. Mr Sheddin seconded the motion. Mr Young made some suppositionary remarks regarding their subject matter not at all in favour nor particularly against the purchasing of the works. This was followed by the general body of the delegates taking part in the discussion. It was ultimately agreed that we get the works and power was given to the treasurer to purchase them.

On the Report so far as drawn up and read at a former meeting by the secretary much dissatisfaction was expressed. He was ultimately advised to endeavour to draw up another of a general nature having no pointed references. On the Glasgow Excursion the Treasurer stated that he was unable to balance as yet the profit and loss of that enterprise.

12 August 1863[2]

Delegates present: Tailors, Mr Troup; Masons, Mr Collins; Cabinetmakers, Mr Young; Coopers, Messrs Mason, Henderson; Brassfounders, Messrs Purdie, Smith, McDonald; Blacksmiths, Mr Dewar; Skinners, Mr Fleming; Glasscutters, Mr Beaton.

The Treasurer stated that he had purchased Blackie's *Better Days for working men*. He gave a slight resumé of its contents and bearing, the same being generally approved of. The treasurer than gave an account of the amount of outlay in getting up the Glasgow excursion, together with the gross and nett profits. Some remarks were

[1] *Workmen's Earnings, Strikes, and Savings* (London, 1861), by Samuel Smiles; reprinted from the *Quarterly Review*.
[2] The date should probably read 11 August 1863.

then passed on a delegate's deficiency when it was agreed that he be exempt from payment. The Chairman also got a ticket price returned him, as a slight token of esteem. The secretary read his report so far as drawn up. It seemed to meet with general approval, but the part referring to Federation brought on a lengthy discussion, but it was agreed to retain it in the report. The chairman's committee were empowered to criticise it when finished.

26 August 1863[1]

Delegates present: Tailors, Mr Troup; Cabinetmakers, Mr Young; Skinners, Messrs Fleming, Anderson; Brassfounders, Messrs Smith, Purdie, McDonald; Glasscutters, Mr Beaton; Smiths, Mr Dewar; Masons, Mr Collins.

The secretary having to attend a meeting elsewhere, Mr Fleming was appointed acting secretary for the night. Some remarks were made regarding minutes of President's committee meeting not being entered on the minute book. As the secretary was absent the subject was droped. The President then read the annual report of the Council, when after some observations by the delegates it was agreed to.

A letter was read from George Newton, secretary of the Council of United trades, Glasgow,[2] calling the attention of the Council to an enclosed printed circular issued by the Glasgow Council to the trades Councils and societies of Great Britain and Ireland. The circular was entitled 'Justice to the labourer'. It pointed out the unequal state of the Law in regard to breach of contract between employed and employer and enumerated the many greivances which workingmen was subject to under the working of the Masters and Workmens acts. No fewer than 10,393 cases were heard in England and Wales in 1861, and these figures alone justify the enquiry, What law was broken, Who broke the law, Who were the judges as to whether the law had been violated? After stating the objections they had to the law, they submitted the following propositions for consideration or amendment, and when agreed

---

[1] The date should probably read 25 August 1863.
[2] George Newton, 1830-67, a potter, secretary of Glasgow trades council 1863-7, of the Glasgow Reform Union, and of the Executive Committee for reform of the Master and Servant laws. *Democracy and the Labour Movement*, ed. John Saville (London, 1954), essay by Daphne Simon on 'Master and Servant', 173-4.

upon would be submitted to Parliament: 1st, To transfer the power of determining in complaints between masters and servants from the justices of Peace to the Judges of County Courts and in Scotland to the Sherrif. 2nd, That instead of being arrested offenders be summoned into Court, in accordance with the practices of the Courts named – the pursuer to name a sum as compensation for the broken contract, to be sued for as a debt. 3rd, That in the event of judgement going for the pursuer, the defender shall only be sent to prison in default of payment – the term not to exceed three calender months; and in cases where only a notice was not given, the term of imprisonment not to exceed the term of notice required. 4th, That no rules be admitted as proof in such cases, except such as have been duly certified as being in accordance with the law of the country by some legal functionary in the pay and service of the State.

After reading the propositions for amending the Law a good deal of discussion took place on the necessity of condensing the third clause. It was ultimately moved by Mr Collins and seconded by Mr Smith, That the circular be remitted to the President's committee and report at next meeting. This was agreed to. The secretary was requested to acknowledge the letter and ask for more papers. The President then read the first programme of the social Science Congress meeting in Edinburgh which elicited various remarks from the Delegates.

8 September 1863

Delegates present: Glasscutters, Mr Beaton; Brassfounders, Messrs Smith, Purdie, McDonald; Cabinetmakers, Messrs Young, Sheddin; Skinners, Mr Fleming; Coopers, Messrs Mason, Henderson; Slaters, Mr Robertson; Tailors, Mr Troup.

The President intimated that a packet of circulars had been left at his house for distributions among the trades. He handed a circular to all the delegates Present. On being read the same caused a great sensation not at all favourable to the party who had issued the circulars, namely the Central Cooperative Committee.[1] An immense

---

[1] No copy of this circular has been found. The Edinburgh Central Co-operative Committee or Association had been formed among local societies in June as a whole-sale buying agency. It arranged, in connection with the gathering of the Social Science Congress, a public meeting on 9 October 1863 for discussion of co-operation. *First*

amount of talking took place, principally bearing on the idea that the Coops had stole a march on the trades to supersede them. A few offered explanations, but their remarks would not be tolerated. Several motions were proposed but one made by Mr Sheddin had the greatest support: That we issue circulars of our own concerning and relating to the monster meeting of the working classes to be held under the Presidency of Lord Brougham and that the chairman's committee be empowered to draw up the circulars and issue them for an early meeting. Also that the chairman return the circulars to the party who issued them. Mr Fleming Seconded. Supported by the majority. The chairman's committee agreed to meet the following evening.

9 September 1863

The Chairman's committee met this evening in pursuance of Mr Sheddin's motion. The Chairman stated that he had taken the circulars back enclosing a note bearing on our opinions as expressed the evening before. Beaton and McDonald stated that they had received explanations relating to the circular. On consideration of these statements Mr Young thought it would not be advisable to proceed any further in the matter and proposed that three should be chosen to attend the meeting. The secretary in the meantime drew up a draft of a circular but could not get it submitted on account of the opposite opinions expressed. Ultimately it was proposed Young and Beaton should go direct and call upon Professor Archer for explanations. Having done so they returned stating that they had been unable to see him. The hour being ten o'clock the secretary declined waiting any longer or to attend another meeting unless for strictly business purposes.

15 September 1863

Delegates present: Cabinetmakers, Messrs Young, Sheddin; Masons, Messrs Hart, Collins; Brassfounders, Messrs McDonald, Purdie, Smith; Glassmakers, Mr Reid; Glasscutters, Messrs Beaton, Brown; Tailors, Mr Troup; Smiths, Messrs Dewar, Fraser; Coopers, Messrs Mason, Henderson.

Fifty Years of St Cuthbert's Co-operative Association, Ltd, 1859-1909, ed. W. Maxwell (Edinburgh, 1909), 40-2.

I

The business of the meeting being particularly on the preliminary meeting to be held on the 17 Inst., a great deal of discussion took place as to what should be done at that meeting. Eventually two resulutions were framed, one to be put to the meeting pledgeing themselves to assist in making the great meeting on the 9th october a success; the second resulution, embracing the idea of the necessary steps for carrying out the meeting, being left to the delegates and was only to be put if necessary.

Drummond St Hall
17 September 1863

The Office Bearers of six and twenty different United trades and seven Cooperative associations met here this evening, Professor Archer in the chair. The Professor called on the secretary to state what he had done. Professor Archer then entered at some length in explanations, reading also a letter from Isa Craig.[1] Mr Fraser proposed the resulution hinted at in the former minute, which was unanimously carried. The meeting proposed that speeches be made on the following subjects: Cooperation, Trades Unions, Sanitary Reform, Temperance, The Late Short time movement, The establishment of evening classes in connection with the University, The application of machinery to labour, and how the working classes should conduct themselves under the changes that are taking place, The laws of health in relation to the position and occupations of the working classes. Professor Archer then made a speech on Monte Video and the Great dinner to be given to the trades officers, after which the meeting gave a vote of thanks to the chairman. The meeting empowered the delegates to carry out the details.

22 September 1863

Delegates present: Slaters, Messrs Clark, Robertson; Brassfounders, Messrs McDonald, Smith, Purdie; Cabinetmakers, Messrs Young, Sheddin; Glassmakers, Mr Reid; Masons, Mr Collins; Smiths, Messrs Dewar, Frazier; Moulders, Messrs Johnston, Rutherfurd; Skinners, Mr Fleming; Engineers, Mr Campbell; Glasscutters, Mr Beaton; Tailors, Mr Troup. Vice President in the Chair.[2]

[1] Assistant secretary, Social Science Association.
[2] John McDonald, brassfounders. Troup, the president, was evidently present later.

Mr Young produced and read his paper on 'Claims advanced in favour of the working Classes'. Mr Fleming read a brief unfinished paper on 'The Necessity of shortening the Hours of labour of the Industrial Classes'. The discussion on Mr Young's Paper resulted in a prevalence of opinion that, owing to the generalities taken up but not efficiently dealt with, intermingled also with Politics and religion, it was not a fit paper to go from this board to be read at the Social Science Meeting; and furthermore it was moved by Mr Collins that Mr Young reconsiders his paper and if possible reconstruct the reading, and at some future date, if willing, may read it before the Council. Seconded by Mr Sheddin and agreed to. On Mr Fleming's Paper some approving remarks were made owing to the style in which he had handled his subject. The Council expressed themselves anxious to hear it more fully and hoped Mr Fleming would finish it. The secretary read a draft of a letter to Mr Hastings, secretary of Social Science Association,[1] urging on his notice the desire of the Council that some gentlemen favourable to Trades Unions should speak on that subject. It was agreed that it should be sent and that the local secretary should be informed of it. Information was asked about the distribution of the tickets for the 9th October. Full information was given on the subject.[2]

29 September 1863

Delegates present: Tailors, Mr Troup; Masons, Mr Collins; Skinners, Mr Fleming; Engineers, Mr Turnbull; Moulders, Messrs Johnston, Rutherfurd; Smiths, Messrs Frazier, Dewar; Cabinetmakers, Messrs Young, Sheddin; Glassmakers, Messrs Reid, Anderson; Brassfounders, Messrs Smith, Purdie, McDonald.

A Special Meeting. In the Absence of the secretary Mr J. Fleming was appointed acting secretary for the meeting. The minutes of last meeting were read and it was moved by Mr McDonald,

[1] George Woodyatt Hastings, general secretary, Social Science Association 1857-70, president 1870-83; Liberal (latterly Liberal Unionist) M.P. for Worcestershire East 1883-92. See also below, p. 139.
[2] The great meeting of working men was held on that date in the Circus, Nicolson St. The vote of thanks to Brougham was moved by Alexander Frazer and John Beaton. Some 250 working men later ate a dinner of Monte Video beef at the Calton Convening Room. *Scotsman*, 10 October 1863.

Seconded by Mr Sheddin, that the secretary revise them and that they be read at next meeting for approval.

A letter was then read from Mr John Crawfurd, secretary to the Paisley Emigration Society, in which he expressed himself desirous to read a pamphlet to a public meeting in this city on the above question, sometime during the sitting of the social Science Congress, but under the auspices of the United trades Council. The President moved the following resulution: That the Council highly approve of the intentions of the writer, But that at present we could not enter into arrangements for calling a public meeting, owing to having so much business on hand; however, that we would be glad to hear it on some future occasion. The secretary was instructed to write him in accordance with this resulution. Mr Frazier's former suggestion that the Council hold a Soirie on the evening of the Social Science Congress dinner was now taken up. Mr Reid moved that the Council shall hold a Sorrie on the night of the Social Science Congress Dinner, and that the tickets be one Shilling each; also that the President's committee make such arrangements as will appear advisable. Seconded by Mr Purdie and carried unanimously. The representatives to the Social Science Congress were next chosen. On the number of admissions allowed to each ticket some alterations had been made since the meeting in Glasgow, one guinea ticket now only admitting one person, a two-guinea ticket admitting three. In consideration of this Mr Sheddin moved that the President, Mr Troup, be sent as one representative to the congress, Seconded by Mr Purdie and unanimously agreed to.

6 October 1863

Delegates present: Tailors, Mr Troup; Masons, Messrs Collins, Smith, Hart; Engineers, Mr Campbell; Smiths, Messrs Dewar, Frazier; Coopers, Messrs Mason, Henderson; Skinners, Mr Fleming; Corkcutters, Mr Ancrum; Glassmakers, Messrs Reid, Anderson; Glasscutters, Messrs Brown, Beaton; Brassfounders, Messrs McDonald, Purdie, Smith; Slaters, Messrs Clark, Robertson; Cabinetmakers, Messrs Young, Sheddin; Moulders, Messrs Johnston, Rutherfurd. Vice President Mr McDonald in the Chair.

Mr Campbell made some remarks on the illegality of the election of Mr Troup as a representative to the Social Science Congress.

Explanations were given of a satisfactory nature. A deal of discussion then took place on the revision of the former minutes or that part of them making a reference to the treatment of the 'Claims advanced in favour of the working class'. The secretary contended that the minutes were correct. This subject was agreed to be left over till next meeting. The secretary gave in his report on the interview he had with Miss Isa Craig, in reference to the desires of the Council that a gentleman should speak in favour of trades Unions at the workingmen's meeting.

Mr Troup gave explanations why no further action had been taken in reference to the sorrie. Some hints having been droped that the Cooperators would take part with us in getting up a sorrie, it was proposed that we cooperate with the Cooperators but subsequently withdrawn. Also that we make no advances to them. This was also withdrawn in favour of full power being given to the chairman's committee to advance or withdraw from the enterprise as circumstances may guide them. After discussion about the payment of last year's ticket, and the inaplicability of it to this year's meeting, together with the advantages at present conferred by taking a two guinea ticket, Mr Fleming moved: That this Council shall be enrolled as an associate body in the Social Science Association. Seconded by Mr Henderson and agreed to. Mr Sheddin then proposed that we send two members, Mr Collins and Mr Troup. Mr Hart said he could occasionally give a look up: his services were accepted. Mr Troup intimated that he had got the tickets for the delegates from Professor Archer's Janitor and that he was requested to pay them before lifting them, and did so accordingly.

Mr Hart intimated that his trade had subscribed the sum of £2 4s. 2d. to the funds of Council and handed the same over to the Treasurer, for which a receipt was given. The Corkcutters' delegates[1] handed over their credentials with a subscription of ten shillings, a receipt being given for the latter.

20 October 1863

Delegates present: Tailors, Mr Troup; Glasscutters, Mr Beaton; Smiths, Messrs Dewar, Fraser; Masons, Mr Collins; Brassfounders, Messrs McDonald, Smith; Corkcutters, Mr Ancrum; Moulders, Mr

[1] Only one is shown present.

Rutherfurd; Cabinetmakers, Mr Young; Coopers, Mr Henderson; Engineers, Mr Campbell; Skinners, Mr Fleming.

The Secretary stated that he made a slight alteration of the minutes referring to the meeting held on the evening of the 22 September and explained the same.[1] After considerable discussion, Mr Young begged to dissent from the opinions of the delegates as expressed in the minutes. Mr Collins proposed that we move the previous Question. Seconded by Mr Young and agreed to.

The President gave an account of the Soiree of the Associated bodies held in Mr McLaren's Temperance Hotel, St Andrew St, on the 13th Instant.[2] Some remarks were made regarding parties not having received notice. The Secretary gave explanations regarding the amount of labour he performed in endeavouring to make the meeting a successful one. The President also intimated that he had waited personally on a number, but the result proved anything [but] satisfactory. Several letters were read from different Parties excusing themselves from attending the soiree on account of business. A letter was also read from Miss Isa Craig regarding the guinea paid in the early part of the year. She expressed herself sorry, at the same time hoping we had got the mistake rectified, but these matters did not relate to her department. The President and Treasurer stated what steps they had taken to recover the guinea, but were unsuccessful. Some proposed that the secretary write Mr Hastings for explanations, but this was ultimately abandoned.

The Secretary read the letter formerly received from Mr John Crawfurd, Esq., of 24 Abbey St, Paisley, relating to a lecture he wished to deliver on Emigration to Canada in this city under the Auspices of the United Trades Council. Mr Collins and Mr Troup gave some information of a pecuniary nature elicited from the gentleman in conversation. The majority of the delegates objected to the gentleman's Ideas. Mr Collins moved that the secretary be empowered to write the gentleman that we will render all the assistance in our power to make the meeting a successful one but that Mr John Crawfurd must defray all expences. Seconded by Mr Campbell and agreed to.

---

[1] There is no sign of any alteration in the MS., except that the word 'interlined' on page 131, line 6, has been altered to 'intermingled'.
[2] No report of the soirée has been found in the press.

Mr Campbell gave notice of motion that at next board meeting he would move that the delegates meet once a month for ordinary business. The Secretary read a letter from the Revd. Henry Solly of London requesting an interview with him in the Parliament House on workmen's Clubs and Institutes.[1] The Secretary then related what passed in relation to this subject. A letter was also read from Mr John Russell,[2] on behalf of the Rev. Mr Solly, requesting the attendance at his House of the Secretary. The Secretary related what had taken place during the interview, and the offer of Miss Catherine Sinclair[3] to pay one year's rental of any premises occupied by any body of working men forming a Club after the model of other workmen's Clubs. Papers were then distributed on this subject.

The secretary read the proposed amended law on master and servant as drawn up by the Council of United Trades of Glasgow and submitted to all the Trades Councils in the Kingdom for their approval or amendment. He also read an amendment to their propositions as drawn up by himself, which seemed to meet with approval.

2 November 1863[4]

Delegates present: Brassfounders, Messrs McDonald, Smith, Purdie; Masons, Messrs Collins, Hart; Cabinetmakers, Mr Young; Skinners Mr Fleming; Smiths, Messrs Dewar, Fraser; Tailors, Mr Troup; Engineers, Mr Campbell; Moulders, Messrs Johnston, Rutherfurd; Corkcutters, Mr Ancrum; Glasscutters, Mr Beaton. Vice President, Mr McDonald, in the chair.[5]

Messrs Troup, Collins, and Hart gave a report of the proceedings of the Social Science Congress. Mr Fraser concurred in the accuracy of their statements. Some few remarks were made by the delegates on House building, but as the subject did not properly belong to the board it was droped. Mr Fleming proposed: That the Council pass

---

[1] Rev. Henry Solly, promoter of the working men's clubs movement; he was joint editor with George Potter of the *Beehive* in 1870. G. D. H. Cole, *A Short History of the British Working Class Movement* (London, 1948), 165; Royden Harrison, *Before the Socialists* (London, 1965), 226.

[2] Not identified.

[3] Catherine Sinclair, 1800-64, novelist, philanthropist, daughter of Sir John Sinclair of Ulbster.

[4] The date should probably read 3 November 1863.

[5] Troup, the president, was evidently present later.

a vote of thanks to the delegates appointed by this board for their services at the congress and that their report be approved of. Seconded by Mr Smith and unanimously agreed to. As the Hour was ten o'clock Mr Campbell withdrew his motion for the night, but to be the first business taken up next meeting. Agreed to.

The Secretary submitted an amended draft to the Circular 'Justice to the Labourer' as issued to the Trades Councils of the United Kingdom by the Glasgow Trades Council. The following is the amended draft as agreed to with reasons for same and as sent to the Glasgow Trades Council: Mr Newton. Sir, In answer to your Circular 'Justice to the Labourer', I have been instructed to say that with the first Clause we entirely agree. Reason: Because it removes the pursued as far as possible from the influential shadow of the employer. 2nd Clause, 2nd Part – the pursuer to name a sum not exceeding half a week's wage as compensation for the broken contract, to be sued for only as a debt. Reason for same: We consider that if a man has left his work for a week he is a loser thereby, and that if an employer wishes him to refund to him the employer what he has lost by the man's neglect, that fifty per cent on the man's wages is full compensation, the employer only to be allowed the priviledge of suing for the same as a debt. 3rd Clause – We object totally to the party being sent to prison, only admitting the priviledge of suing for debt. Reason: Is an honest working man because he may choose to take a week's play or even change his employer, to be sent to prison for not more than three months because he is disinclined or unable to pay the employer's terms of compensation? The idea appears and is monstrous at first sight. The total loss to the employer might not exceed ten shillings and yet the man might be liable to be sent to prison for ninety-three days. A common thief would not get more for the same sum if his third offence, and must an honest working man be sent to herd with felons because he happened to take a week's play? With the fourth Clause we entirely agree. We give no reasons, convinced they are not necessary. In prosecuting the amendment of the law we sincerely hope you may be successful. Should you need any pecuniary assistance I have not the slightest doubt that if an appeal be made it would be liberally responded to. Trusting that you may be successful, I am, sir, yours respectfully, John Beaton, Secy.

17 November 1863

Delegates present: Brassfounders, Messrs McDonald, Smith, Purdie; Masons, Mr Collins; Glasscutters, Messrs Brown, Beaton; Cabinetmakers, Mr Young; Smiths, Mr Dewar; Engineers, Mr Campbell; Corkcutters, Mr Ancrum; Moulders, Messrs Rutherfurd, Johnston. Vice President in the Chair.

Mr Campbell's motion for monthly meetings was submitted to the Council but not meeting with a seconder it fell to the ground. A letter was read from the trades council of Glasgow soliciting us to follow the advice given in the letter. Power was given to the secretary to answer the note, referring them to our amendment on the circular. The above was moved by Mr Campbell, seconded by Mr Johnston.

On the subject of Clubs and Institutes, the secretary gave every information and the reason why he had brought it before the notice of the Council. Mr Campbell moved that this business be dismissed, Seconded by Mr Collins. Mr Dewar spoke in support of Clubs and Institutes and made an amendment accordingly, Seconded by Mr Brown. Mr McDonald also spoke in support of them. Mr Ancrum made an amendment, that the subject be remitted to the trades, seconded by Mr Johnston. After some more discussion it was agreed to let the subject lie over for another fortnight so as to obtain the minds of the trades as far as possible.

1 December 1863

Delegates present: Tailors, Mr Troup; Masons, Mr Collins; Brassfounders, Messrs Purdie, McDonald, Smith; Corkcutters, Mr Ancrum; Glasscutters, Mr John Beaton; Smiths, Mr Fraser.

Mr Collins made the following motion: That it be recommended to the trades from this Council to ascertain as far as possible whether they have been retrograding or progressing during this last twenty years; if machinery has been introduced how they have been affected by it; if the Principle of Free Trade has affected them in any way and What way; if the hours of labour have been shortened how has it affected the Trade, wages, labour and Capital considered; if the number of Hands have increased or vice versa; if female labour is superseding male labour and what likelihood of it continuing to do so; if the morality and sobriety of the Trade has decreased or increased and what reasons can be adduced for either. The motion was seconded by Mr Purdie and agreed to.

Mr Rutherfurd, Moulder, tendered a subscription of six shillings and sixpence from that body to the funds of the United Trades Council.[1] A letter was read from the secretary of the Glasgow Trades Council[2] relative to the receipt of the amended law clauses in workman's bill as agreed to by the Edinburgh Council of United Trades Delegates, disagreeing with our amendments generally, on personal opinion, the letter being unauthorized.

In the matter of Workmen's Institutes nothing further had been done, except getting a few signatures. Mr Fraser spoke of the difficulty of organising an Institute composed of workmen and in his opinion considered it would not be very effective. Several more of the delegates gave their opinions, bearing favourably on the subject. This business was still left for the trades to organize. Mr Collins moved that the Auditors meet on saturday night first at six o'clock to audit the books for the half year. Seconded by Mr Smith and agreed to.

15 December 1863

Delegates present: Tailors, Mr Troup; Masons, Mr Collins; Skinners, Messrs Fleming, Gilien; Cabinetmakers, Messrs Young, Sheddin, Austin; Smiths, Messrs Dewar, Fraser; Corkcutters, Mr Ancrum; Brassfounders, Messrs Smith, McDonald; Glassmakers, Mr James Reid; Glasscutters, Mr John Beaton.

A note was received and read from the Secretary of the Cabinet and Chairmakers' Union certifying the Election and appointment of Mr John Austine and the reelection of Messrs John Shedden and Thomas Young to act as representatives from said Society. A note was also received and read from the secretary of the Scottish Association of United Skinners Certifying the Election and appointment of Mr Peter Gilion to act as representative from said society. A Subscription to the funds of the Council of ten shillings was tendered to the treasurer by Mr James Reid, Glassmaker, stating at the same time his inability to attend regular but if any business of great importance came before the delegates he would endeavour to attend if forewarned.

---

[1] Rutherford is not listed among the delegates present.   [2] George Newton.

Some observations were passed on Mr Collins' motion of Enquiry
into the condition of the Trades. Mr Dewar moved, Seconded by
Mr Sheddin, that the secretary give a Copy of Motion to all the
Trades. This was agreed to. The Subject of a Workman's Institute
caused considerable debate, but any public expression of opinion
was posponed by Mr Collins moving That this subject be brought
up this day month, 12 January, and takes precedence of all other
business. This was agreed to.

The Secretary read a note from F. W. Carter,[1] manager of the
Scottish Friendly Life Assurance Coy., 5 St Andrew Square, requesting the distribution of tracts among the trades and intimating
that if desired a lecture could be given on the advantages of life
Assurance to the families of workmen. The secretary was empowered
to correspond with the manager, intimating acquiescence in his
views, and that we would do all in our power to make the meeting
a success. Mr Young read the Income and expenditure of the Council
for the Half year. Mr Smith moved its adoption, Seconded by Mr
Ancrum. Mr Fleming took the Loan of the *Social Science Transactions of 1861*. Mr Fraser then proposed that the secretary be empowered to write Duncan McLaren, Esqr., of Newington House,
thanking him in the name of the Council for the service he has
rendered to the community by the exposure of the doings of the
Social Science Committee and that he have power given him to
make what use of our letter he thinks proper. Seconded by Mr
Collins and agreed to.[2]

[1] Frederick Haynes Carter, C.A. He was also secretary of the Blind Asylum.
[2] McLaren had criticised the alleged behaviour of G. W. Hastings who was said to
have posed as honorary secretary of the Social Science Association while receiving a
considerable sum per annum for editing its *Transactions*. *Edinburgh Evening Courant*,
3, 7, and 9 December 1863.

1864-1868

Interiors of Holyrood Glassworks in the 1860s

1864

12 January 1864

Delegates present: Tailors, Mr Troup; Corkcutters, Mr Ancrum; Smiths, Messrs Dewar, Fraser; Cabinetmakers, Messrs Young, Sheddin; Brassfounders, Messrs Smith, Purdie; Skinners, Mr Peter Gillion; Glasscutters, Mr Beaton.

In consequence of the absence of the mover and seconder of the motion on Workman's Institute, this subject was deferred till next meeting, retaining its condition of precedence of all other business. The Credentials of Messrs Troup and Renton as delegates from the society of United Tailors of Edinburgh were read and approved of.[1] A great deal of discussion took place concerning the matter contained in the book *Self Help*, some asserting one thing and some another.[2] Leave was given to the treasurer to purchase it, but a discretionary power as to time was granted as hopes were held out that it might be produced at next meeting when the book would disclose its contents.

26 January 1864

Delegates present: Blacksmiths, Messrs Dewar, Frazer; Brassfounders, Messrs McDonald, Purdie; Cabinet Makers, Messrs Shedden, Young, Austine; Glass Cutters, Mr Beaton; Masons, Messrs Collins, Hart; Tailors, Mr Troup.

Some discussion took place on Smiles' *Self Help*, on the Book being handed round. The general opinion of the Council was that it was of no advantage to them and there was no need to purchase it. It was then suggested that the *History of the middle and working*

---

[1] Renton seems never to have attended any meeting of the trades council.
[2] *Self Help* (London, 1859), by Samuel Smiles.

Classes, by John Wade, People's Edition,[1] was a work which would be useful for the Council to have, and the Treasurer was authourized to purchase the same, also the *Report of the Committee of the house of Commons on Combinations of Workmen*[2] – application to be made to Lord Advocate[3] for it. The subject of Workmen's Institutes was deferred till next meeting.

The next business was the election of Office Bearers for 1864. Alexander Frazer proposed Mr Troup should be re-elected to the office of President, seconded by Mr Purdie, and unanimously agreed to. For vice President Mr Young – proposed by Mr Hart, seconded by Mr McDonald and elected. Secretary – A. Frazer was proposed by Mr Shedden, seconded by Mr Hart. Mr Purdie was proposed by A. Frazer for the same office but declined, and A. Frazer was elected. Treasurer – Mr Collins was proposed for Re-election by Mr Shedden. Carried by acclamation. Auditor – Mr Shedden was proposed by Mr Hart, seconded by Mr Young and unanimously agreed to. Votes of thanks were unanimously awarded to the retiring office Bearers and replied to. The Secretary gave some explanations on the forthcoming lecture on Life Assurance, when Mr Hart proposed that A. Frazer propose a vote of thanks to the Lecturer, F. H. Carter, Esq., CA.

9 February 1864

Delegates present: Blacksmiths, Messrs Dewar, Frazer; Brassfounders, Messrs McDonald, Purdie, Smith; Cabinet Makers, Messrs Shedden, Young, Austine; Masons, Messrs Collins, Hart; Corkcutters, Mr Ancrum; Skinners, Mr Gillon. Vice President in the chair.

Some conversation took place on the Lecture on Life Assurance delivered in the Pheonix Hall on 28 January last, when it was unanimously agreed to award a vote of thanks to Mr Carter for his able Lecture, but the Council declined taking any further steps in this subject. A letter was read from Mr Adams, Secretary to the Lord Advocate, stating that his Lordship would endeavour to procure the Reports we desired on Combination of Workmen. The

---

[1] Presumably the fourth edition, published in Edinburgh in 1842 by W. and R. Chambers.

[2] *Report of Select Committee on Combinations of Workmen* (1838).

[3] James Moncreiff.

Secretary then produced two Reports which he had received from his Lordship, when it was unanimously agreed to award a special vote of thanks to him for his kindness and prompt attention to our request. The Treasurer here intimated that he had purchased Burton's *Political Economy*[1] instead of Wade's *History* but that it could be exchanged. Credentials of Messrs Dewar and Frazer from the Blacksmiths [were read].

The Council then took up the subject of Workmen's Institutes. It was moved by Mr Ancrum: That this subject be left an open question, but in the event of any philanthropic gentlemen desirous of instituting the same this Council shall then take it up. Seconded by Mr Dewar. Mr Collins then moved as an amendment The previous question, seconded by Mr Hart. There voted for the amendment 7, for the motion 4. The next business was the queries addressed to trades, but as several of the members had not received copies of the same the Secretary intimated that copies could be had here on Saturday first. The treasurer was instructed to purchase a Copy of Wade's *History*, and as the Council were of opinion that Burton's *Political Economy* was a Book which would be useful it was agreed to keep it. Mr Sheddin here returned the *Social Science transactions for 1861*.

23 February 1864

Delegates present: Blacksmiths, Messrs Dewar, Frazer; Brass-founders, Messrs Smith, Purdie; Cabinetmakers, Messrs Young, Austine; Tailors, Mr Troup; Skinners, Mr Fleming.

Answers to Queries from the Blacksmiths were laid on the table when it was agreed to defer the consideration of the queries untill all the Trades represented here send in their returns. There was paid in by Mr Dewar the sum of one pound sterling, being contribution to the funds from the Edinburgh Branch of the Scottish Blacksmiths Society for 1864, and a receipt was given for the same.

The Secretary then Brought before the Council the subject of Free Libraries and the propriety of this board aiding and supporting the same, when a Deputation from the operative Type Founders here entered and addressed the council, stating the reasons why they were out on Strike, on account of the exorbitant and uncalled for

[1] *Political and Social Economy: its practical applications* (Edinburgh, 1849), by John Hill Burton.

K

reduction of wages by the firm of Messrs Millar and Richard of this City. After a good deal of conversation with the deputation a vote of thanks was unanimously awarded to them, the council recommending them to their respective trades, as the Type Founders not being represented here we cannot take up their dispute. The deputation then withdrew. It being now to late to resume the discussion on the question of Free Libraries it was unanimously agreed to defer this subject till next meeting. Mr Young returned *Social Science Transactions for 1860*, Mr Purdie returned *Report on Combinations, Part 1st*; Mr Smith returned *Better Days for Working People*.

8 March 1864

Delegates present: Blacksmiths, Messrs Dewar, Frazer; Cabinet Makers, Messrs Shedden, Young; Masons, Mr Collins; Skinners, Mr Fleming; Tailors, Mr Troup.

There was no answers to queries given in but the delegate from the Skinners stated that in all probability the answers from his trade would not be given in till the month of May as they intended embraceing the Trade in Scotland in their inquiries. Mr Shedden paid over to treasurer the sum of fifteen shillings, contributions from the operative Cabinet Makers, and a Receipt was given for the same.

The Council then resumed the consideration of the subject of Free Libraries upon which a long discussion took place. The Council generally approved of the object, but were not to be held committed in the offer of their services to any or every method the promoters of this Free Library might adopt, and the Secretary was instructed to write in terms of the above. The President then brought up the subject of making a carriage drive of the Middle walk of the Meadows, but there was no time for to consider it.[1] Mr Fleming returned *Report on Conciliation*, and *Better Days for Working Men*, Mr Frazer *Social Science Transactions for 1860*.

22 March 1864

Delegates present: Blacksmiths, Messrs Dewar, Frazer; Brassfounders, Messrs Smith, Purdie, McDonald; Cabinetmakers, Mr

[1] A public meeting to protest against the town council's proposal had been held on 7 March. *Edinburgh Evening Courant*, 8 March 1864.

Young; Masons, Messrs Collins, Hart; Skinners, Messrs Fleming, Gillon; Tailors, Mr Troup.

The President brought before the Council the subject of the Middle walk of the Meadows. It was moved by Mr Purdie that the subject be deferred. Mr Hart then moved: That each Delegate bring this subject before their respective trades and report progress. Seconded by Mr Dewar. Mr Purdie withdrew his motion and Mr Hart's was unanimously agreed to. The Secretary intimated to the council that as he had not been able to obtain the address of the Secretary of the Free Library Committee he had not sent the letter as formerly instructed. He was empowered, if the said Secretary's address could not be obtained, to communicate the same to the Lord Provost.[1] A short conversation took place on the subject of a Trades Hall but it was agreed to defer it till next meeting. The Secretary then intimated there was to be a meeting of the committee on Working men's Clubs on Thursday first, the 24th currt., to which meeting the Council are invited.[2] Mr Hart returned Burton's *Political Economy*, Mr Young returned *Report on Combinations of Workmen, Part 1st*.

5 April 1864

Delegates present: Blacksmiths, Messrs Dewar, Frazer; Brassfounders, Messrs Smith, McDonald; Cabinet Makers, Messrs Young, Shedden, Austine; Glass Cutters, Messrs Brown, Jeffries; Corkcutters, Mr Ancrum; Masons, Mr Collins; Skinners, Mr Fleming; Tailors, Mr Troup.

The President gave a verbal report of the committee meeting on Working Men's Clubs and Institutes, which was agreed to. Certificates were read from the Flint Glass Cutters, appointing Messrs John Jeffries and Norman Pringle as delegates for the Year 1864; and from the Corkcutters, appointing Messrs John Ancrum and John Alston for the same period.[3]

The President brought before the Council the subject of a Trades Hall and was heard in support of the same. Discussion then took

[1] Charles Lawson.
[2] A Working Men's Club and Institute was opened on 5 November 1864 in Writer's Court, High Street, Edinburgh. *Scotsman*, 5 November 1864.
[3] Pringle seems never to have attended any meeting of the trades council, and Alston none until 23 July 1867.

place, but at this stage of the business a Deputation from a meeting of working men, relative to a demonstration in honour of General Garibaldi, entered. Mr Mitchell, Mr Iverach and Mr Brown, members of the deputation,[1] addressed the Council in support of this demonstration, after which several of the Council having stated their views on the subject The Secretary moved: That this Council cordially unite with the deputation in carrying the same into effect. Seconded by Mr Ancrum and unanimously agreed to. The deputation having expressed a wish that some of the members of this council should accompany them to the Lord Provost on the following day, the Secretary and Mr Young were appointed, and Mr Fleming moved that their lost time be paid them. Agreed too. The discussion on Trades Hall was then resumed for a time. Mr Dewar returned Burton's *Political Economy* and Mr Fleming got the same.

19 April 1864

Delegates present: Blacksmiths, Messrs Dewar, Frazer; Brassfounders, Messrs Smith, Purdie; Cabinetmakers, Mr Young; Corkcutters, Mr Ancrum; Glasscutters, Mr Jeffries; Masons, Messrs Collins, Hart; Skinners, Messrs Fleming, Gillon; Tailors, Mr Troup.

The subject of a Trades Hall was again considered, and after a long discussion upon the question whether the necessary funds should be raised by subscription or by a Joint Stock company, the Secretary moved: That it be remitted to the President's committee to draw up a prospectus recommending a Trades Hall to be built by a joint stock company or by subscription to be submitted to the council and if approved to be sent to the different trades. Seconded by Mr Fleming and unanimously agreed to.

The subject of Breach of contract by Workmen, in reference to the trial of some of Mr Tennant's workmen before the justice of peace court, was then considered by the Council, and after hearing different members of the council express their opinions on the subject, it was moved by Mr Hart and unanimously agreed to: That the Secretary be instructed to write to Mr Gifford sympathysing with the men in Messrs Tennant's and indicating that the Trades

[1] Mitchell and Brown have not been identified. Iverach was presumably John Iverach, tailors.

Council were willing to co-operate with them to get the Law altered or repealed.[1] The following Books were then returned: Burton's *Political Economy* – Mr Fleming; *Report on Councils of Conciliation* and *Better Days* – Mr Frazer.

3 May 1864

Delegates present: Blacksmiths, Messrs Dewar, Frazer; Brass-founders, Messrs McDonald, Purdie; Cabinet-makers, Mr Young; Glass-cutters, Mr Jeffries; Masons, Messrs Collins, Hart; Skinners, Messrs Fleming, Gillon; Tailors, Mr Troup.

The Secretary intimated that in accordance with the minute of last meeting he had written to Mr Gifford and had a verbal communication from him approving of the conduct of the Trades Council. A long and earnest discussion then took place on the subject of Breach of contract by workmen, when Mr Collins moved: That the Secretary be instructed to write to the Trades Council of Glasgow asking them for information as to what they are doing and expressing our desire to co-operate with them in endeavouring to get said Law altered or repealed. Seconded by Mr Hart and unamiously agreed to.

Mr McDonald paid to the Treasurer the sum of 3s., being the quarterly payment from the Brassfounders and a receipt was given for the same. Mr Collins then moved: That as there is no likelihood of General Garibaldi visiting Edinburgh at the present time, this Council withdraw from the working men's Committee. Seconded by the Secretary and unanimously agreed to. The subject of a Trades Hall was then brought up and the President's committee were appointed to consider the Prospectus for the same and to lay it before the Council at their next meeting, said committee to meet here on Saturday first. The Secretary then introduced the subject of the Council starting a newspaper to advocate the rights of Labour. After several of the members had expressed their opinion it was

[1] Eight engine fitters employed by Tennant and Co., Bowershall Iron Works, Leith, who had gone on strike for an increase of wages, were sentenced on 16 April to eight days' imprisonment with hard labour for leaving their employment without due notice. The men did not, however, serve the sentence as they agreed immediately after conviction to return to work to complete the fortnight's notice the firm claimed was due. Gifford was probably James Gifford of the A.S.E., a delegate to the trades council in 1871.

agreed to lie over till next meeting. Mr Young returned *Social Science transactions for 1860*.

17 May 1864

Delegates present: Blacksmiths, Messrs Dewar, Frazer; Brass-founders, Messrs Smith, McDonald; Cabinetmakers, Messrs Young, Austine; Glass-cutters, Mr Jeffries; Masons, Messrs Collins, Hart; Skinners, Mr Gillon; Tailors, Mr Troup.

The Secretary read the correspondence from Glasgow in reference to the Breach of Contract of Masters and Workman's Act, along with 500 Copies of Statement and Appeal which have been distributed among the operatives in Edinburgh. After considering the subject Mr Hart moved: That the Secretary be instructed to write to Glasgow that we will receive the deputation on Friday the 20th and suggest to them that they should leave Glasgow by the first train. Messrs Hart and McDonald were appointed a deputation to receive the gentlemen from Glasgow on their arrival and assist them as far as they could. The Council then fixed that the meeting of the Representatives of the various trades be held here on Friday the 20th, at 8 o'clock evening. The Secretary was instructed to write to the following M.P.s, soliciting an interview with them, viz., the Lord Advocate[1] and Mr Adam Black, members for this City, Mr Dunlop, M.P. for Greenock,[2] Mr Miller, M.P. for Leith[3]; also to write to all the trades having Societies but who are not represented at this Council. Mr Hart produced a Sketch of a Plan for a Trades Hall but as it was late it was to lie over till next night of meeting. Mr Gillon returned Burton's *Political Economy*.

31 May 1864

Delegates present: Blacksmiths, Messrs Dewar, Frazer; Brass-founders, Mr Smith; Cabinetmakers, Messrs Young, Austine; Corkcutters, Mr Ancrum; Glasscutters, Mr Jeffrey; Masons, Messrs Collins, Smith; Tailors, Mr Troup.

---

[1] James Moncreiff.
[2] Alexander Colquhoun-Stirling-Murray-Dunlop, 1798-1870, a legal adviser to the Free Church of Scotland, Liberal M.P. for Greenock 1852-68.
[3] William Miller of Manderston, Radical M.P. for Leith 1859-68, and for Berwickshire 1873-4.

The Secretary read the report of the meeting of the representatives of different trades as it appeared in *The Glasgow Times*, which was received by the Council.[1] A long conversation took place on the Law of Breach of Contract and the best means we could adopt here for the purpose of getting the alterations on this Law carried into effect. It was recommended that each Delegate should bring the subject of ways and means before their respective trades.

The Secretary read a prospectus of a Plan for building a Trades Hall in Edinburgh. Some discussion took place on the merits of the two plans before the Council, but as some of the details were awanting it was agreed it should lie over till next meeting of the Council. Mr Smith then brought before the Council the subject of the annual excursion to Glasgow, when the President was instructed to call upon Mr Stewart, the Superintendant, and report at the meeting on 7 June. Mr Jeffrey returned *Social Science transactions for 1860*, Mr Young Blackie's *Better days*.

14 June 1864

Delegates present: Amalgamated Trades, Mr Turnbull; Blacksmiths, Messrs Dewar, Frazer; Brassfounders, Messrs Smith, Purdie, McDonald; Cabinetmakers, Messrs Young, Austine; Corkcutters, Mr Ancrum; Masons, Messrs Collins, Hart; Slaters, Mr Carmichael; Tailors, Mr Troup; Skinners, Mr Fleming.

The Secretary reported the result of the meeting of the representatives of different trades, Respectfully soliciting the advance of £1 to them to carry on the agitation for an alteration of the Law of Breach of Contract upon condition of repaying all the past expenses the Trades Council had been at in the agitation of this matter. Mr Hart moved: That the Council authorize the same. Seconded by Mr Collins and unanimously agreed to, Mr Young dissenting.

The Council then took up the subject of the Annual Excursion to Glasgow. The President gave a verbal report of what he had done in this matter and two letters were read from the Superintendent of the Edinburgh and Glasgow Railway stating the terms (3s. per

[1] *Glasgow Times and Western Counties' Chronicle*, 1855-69, Liberal in opinion. None of the three issues that survive in Scottish libraries covers the date of the meeting referred to, and no other press report of it has been found. J. P. S. Ferguson, *Scottish Newspapers in Scottish Libraries* (Edinburgh, 1956), 29.

ticket) that they would give an excursion to Glasgow on 30 July.
Mr Fleming moved: That the deputation be instructed to enquire
upon what terms the Port of Leith excursion are going to Glasgow,
and if they find that is at the same rate the Edinburgh and Glasgow
Railway Company have offered to the Council, they are to proceed
no farther in the matter. Seconded by Mr Hart and agreed to.
Messrs Troup and Fleming were appointed a deputation.

There was paid to the Treasurer the sum of £1 from the operative
Corkcutters, per Mr Ancrum; and from the operative Slaters 10s.,
per Mr Carmichael. The subject of a Trades Hall was ordered to lie
over till next meeting for want of an Architect's estimate.

Mr Hart then read an Appeal to the Working Classes of Edinburgh
to support by their subscriptions the agitation for the alteration of
the Law of Breach of Contract. A long and very irregular discussion
followed after which it was put to the vote, when it was agreed that
it should be printed. It was moved by Mr Fleming: That it be
printed as it is. Seconded by Mr Collins. The Secretary then moved
as an amendment: That it be printed with a different heading and
that the words 'and committee' be added after Trades Council.
Seconded by Mr Turnbull. The motion was carried by a majority
of one. Mr Collins returned Burton's *Political Economy*.

28 June 1864

Delegates present: Amalgamated Trades, Mr Turnbull; Blacksmiths,
Mr Frazer; Brassfounders, Mr Smith; Cabinetmakers, Messrs
Young, Shedden, Austine; Corkcutters, Mr Ancrum; Masons,
Messrs Collins, Hart; Slaters, Mr Carmichael; Tailors, Mr Troup;
Skinners, Mr Fleming.

Mr Troup gave a verbal report of what the deputation had done
in regard to the Annual Excursion to Glasgow. He read a letter
from the Superintendant of the Edinburgh and Glasgow Railway
declining to give an excursion any cheaper than their former Statement. Mr Turnbull moved: That the negotiations with the Edinburgh and Glasgow Railway be abandoned. Seconded by Mr Collins.
An amendment was moved by Mr Ancrum: That the President
be empowered to write to Mr Thompson stating that the Trades
Council are willing to have an excursion to Glasgow at 3s. per
ticket if the Company will give 7½ per cent discount. Seconded by

Mr Fleming. On the vote being taken it was 5 for the motion and 5 for the amendment; the President gave his casting vote for the motion. The council then considered whether there was any other place they could have an excursion to, when Mr Collins moved: That there be no excursion this year. Seconded by Mr Hart and unanimously agreed to.

Mr Fleming brought before the council the new Act of Parliament relating to stamped certificates, and the treasurer was instructed to procure a copy of the Act,[1] price not to exceed 1s., and the subject to be considered at a future meeting. Mr Collins brought up the subject of the working men's address to General Garibaldi, and the share the representatives of the Council had in it.[2] It was agreed that the representatives of the Council defer voting any money untill the Ballance sheet is produced to the delegates.

12 July 1864

Delegates present: Blacksmiths, Messrs Dewar, Frazer; Brassfounders, Mr Smith; Masons, Messrs Collins, Hart; Cabinetmakers, Messrs Young, Shedden; Skinners, Mr Fleming; Tailors, Mr Troup.

Mr Collins gave a verbal report regarding the act of Parliament on stamped Certificates for delegates; and Mr Troup of the proceedings of the Committee relating to the address of the working men of Edinburgh to General Garibaldi, which on the motion of Mr Hart was unanimously agreed to.

A letter was read from the Secretary of the operative Brassfounders Society, appointing Messrs Smith, Thorburn, and Lawrie as delegates for the next 12 months. Mr Collins then called the attention of the Council to the fact that it was time that the Books should be Audited, and it was agreed that the Auditors should meet here on Saturday first at 7 o'clock evening for that purpose.

Mr Hart then produced a Plan of a Trades Hall drawn out by Mr Sutherland,[3] price, not including Seating, £4,750. The details was examined by the members of the Council. A long discussion then followed, mainly upon the point whether the Council with the aid of other parties were able to raise the sum of £10,000 by

[1] Presumably 27-28 Victoria, c. 18.
[2] The address has not been found in the press.
[3] Possibly J. Sutherland, mason, a former delegate to the council.

subscription. But no decision was come to. The Secretary gave notice that at the next meeting of the Council he would bring before them the propriety of establishing a Newspaper in Edinburgh specially devoted to the interests of the industrial classes.

26 July 1864

Delegates present; Amalgamated Trades, Mr Turnbull; Blacksmiths, Mr Frazer; Brassfounders, Messrs Smith, Thorburn, Lawrie; Cabinet Makers, Messrs Young, Shedden, Austine; Masons, Mr Collins; Skinners, Mr Fleming. Vice President in the chair.

The financial report by the Auditors of the past half-year was read by Mr Fleming, and after a slight alteration its adoption was moved by Mr Collins, seconded by Mr Turnbull, and unanimously agreed to. The Secretary was instructed to have a draft of the Annual Report ready for this day fortnight. The further consideration of a Trades Hall was deferred on account of the absence of Messrs Troup and Hart. Mr Fleming produced the Act of Parliament regarding stamped certificates for delegates. After considering the Act the Council were of opinion that it did not refer to them and dismissed the subject.

Mr Fleming paid to the Treasurer the sum of 10s., being subscription from the operative Skinners for 1864-1865, and a receipt was given for the same. The Secretary then brought before the Council the subject of a Newspaper and was heard in support of the same. Several of the delegates expressed their approval. Further consideration of it was deferred till next meeting and the Secretary was instructed to write Mr Campbell of the *Glasgow Sentinel*, Mr Potter of the London *Bee Hive* and Mr Reid of Peterhead[1] for information on the subject. Mr Collins returned the *Social Science Transactions* for 1863, and Mr Fleming for 1860.

9 August 1864

Delegates present: Blacksmiths, Mr Frazer; Brassfounders, Messrs Smith, Lawrie; Cabinetmakers, Mr Young; Corkcutters, Mr Ancrum; Masons, Mr Collins; Tailors, Mr Troup; Skinners, Mr Fleming.

[1] Hugh Gilzean Reid, see above, p. 52, n. 1.

The Secretary read a draft of the annual report for the past year. Some additions were suggested and the Secretary was instructed to have them embodied in the report, said report to be read next night of meeting. The further consideration of a Trades Hall was again deferred. The Law of Breach of Contract was then considered and a letter was read from Mr Alexander Campbell, Glasgow, stating that a Bill for the alteration of said Law had been introduced into the House of Commons on 21 July.[1] The Council agreed to defer the public agitation of this question till their first meeting in September.

The subject of Newspaper was then taken up, but as the Council were not in posession of sufficient information it was to lie over till next meeting. There was paid to the Treasurer the sum of 3s., being quarterly Subscription from the Brassfounders, per Mr Smith, and a receipt given for the Same. Mr Fleming returned *Social Science Transactions for 1863*, Mr Young Burton's *Political Economy*.

23 August 1864

Delegates present: Amalgamated Trades, Mr Turnbull; Blacksmiths, Mr Frazer; Brassfounders, Mr Smith; Cabinetmakers, Mr Young; Cork-cutters, Mr Ancrum; Masons, Mr Collins; Skinners, Mr Fleming; Tailors, Mr Troup.

The Draft of the Annual Report was read and approved. Some conversation followed, cheifly on the Auditing of the financial parts, and the printing of the Report was deferred for some time. A Letter was read from Major F. Hamilton, M.P., intimating that he would receive a Deputation of the Council in a few days, and Messrs Troup, Hart and Frazer were appointed to wait on the honourable M.P.[2] A Letter was also read from Mr George Potter, London, in regard to the subject of a Newspaper. This gave rise to a considerable discussion, after which the Secretary was instructed to write to Mr Potter thanking him for his communication. The Secretary was also instructed to draw up a Prospectus of a Newspaper to be ready for the next meeting of the Council.

There was paid to the Treasurer in behalf of alteration of the Law

---

[1] By J. M. Cobbett, Radical M.P. for Oldham.
[2] Walter Ferrier Hamilton, younger, of Westport, Conservative M.P. for Linlithgowshire 1859-65.

of Breach of Contract the following sums: from Mr Fleming 3s. 2d., from Mr Dewar from Edinburgh Blacksmiths 3s. 2d., from Mr Pettie from Leith Blacksmiths 2s. 11d. – total 9s. 3d.

6 September 1864

Delegates present: Amalgamated Trades, Mr Turnbull; Blacksmiths, Mr Frazer; Brassfounders, Messrs Smith, Lawrie; Masons, Mr Collins; Tailors, Mr Troup.

The Prospectus of a Newspaper was read and the Secretary was instructed to extend it and have it ready by next night of meeting. The Law of Breach of Contract was then considered. It was agreed to have a preliminary meeting on this subject, to be called by advertisement in the Newspapers. The Secretary was authorized to make the necessary arrangements and to report at next meeting. There was paid to the Treasurer on behalf of alteration of the Law of Breach of Contract from Engineers, per Mr Turnbull, the sum of 10s. 3d., and from Brassfounders, per Mr Smith 1s. 9d.; receipts given for the same.

20 September 1864

Delegates present: Blacksmiths, Mr Frazer; Brassfounders, Messrs Smith, Thorburn; Cabinet Makers, Mr Young; Tailors, Mr Troup; Slaters, Mr Munro.

A Letter was read from Mr Reid of the *Buchan Observer* highly approving of a Newspaper for working men. The Prospectus of the Newspaper as amended was then read and after some discussion it was agreed to defer it till next meeting. The subject of the Law of Breach of Contract was considered, cheifly with reference to the holding of the preliminary meeting. It was agreed to defer the matter till next meeting. Mr Troup gave a verbal report imparting some information regarding a Trades Hall. Mr Young returned *Social Science Transactions for 1863*, Mr Frazer Burton's *Political Economy*.

4 October 1864

Delegates present: Blacksmiths, Mr Frazer; Brassfounders, Mr Smith; Corkcutters, Mr Ancrum; Cabinetmakers, Mr Young; Masons, Mr Collins; Skinners, Mr Fleming; Tailors, Mr Troup.

There was paid in by Mr Munro from the Edinburgh operative Slaters the sum of 2s. 6d., on behalf of the funds for altering the Law of Breach of Contract, and receipt given for the same. There was also paid into the funds of the Trades Council by Mr Smith the sum of 3s., being quarterly subscription from the Edinburgh operative Brassfounders and a receipt given for the same.

The Council considered the Prospectus of the Newspaper. It was agreed before printing it to call a special meeting of the Council on Tuesday 18th currt., and each delegate was recommended in the interval to procure all the information he can on this subject. The Law of Breach of Contract was then taken up, after which the Council agreed to defer till next meeting, it being a special one, the holding of the preliminary meeting and the other details of this part of the business.

18 October 1864

Delegates present: Amalgamated Trades, Mr Turnbull; Blacksmiths, Messrs Dewar, Frazer; Brassfounders, Mr Smith; Glassmakers, Mr Reid; Glasscutters, Mr Jeffrey; Cabinetmakers, Messrs Young, Shedden; Masons, Messrs Collins, Hart; Tailors, Mr Troup; Skinners, Mr Fleming.

The attention of the Council was called to the papers sent by the National Association for the promotion of Social Science by mistake to Buchanan's Temperance Hotel and had been kept by him since 22nd July.[1] The President and Secretary was instructed to wait on Mr Buchanan and thereafter to write to Mr Hastings, London.

Mr Fleming read an appeal from the Edinburgh operative Skinners now out on Strike and Lock out.[2] The Council recommended their case to the different trades represented at this Board. The subject of a Newspaper was then taken up. Mr Bishop[3] gave some very useful information and kindly offered to prepare a statement for the next meeting of the Council, which offer was accepted. A unamious vote of thanks was given to Mr Bishop. The Law of Breach of Contract was the next business. After a long discussion,

[1] Buchanan's Temperance Hotel was almost directly across the High Street from Burden's Coffee House, the trades council's meeting place until 1867.
[2] The skinners were reported to be out 'for an increase in wages and alteration of hours'. *Scotsman*, 18 November 1864.
[3] Not identified.

cheifly in reference to holding a preliminary meeting, Mr Hart moved: That before this meeting be held the Secretary be instructed to write to Glasgow for them to inform us what they are at present doing in this matter. Seconded by Mr Dewar. The Secretary moved as an amendment: That we go on with the preliminary meeting. Seconded by Mr Reid. There voted for the amendment 4, for the motion 5.

1 November 1864

Delegates present: Amalgamated Trades, Mr Walker; Blacksmiths, Messrs Dewar, Frazer; Brassfounders, Mr Smith; Cabinetmakers, Messrs Young, Shedden; Glassmakers, Mr Reid; Glasscutters, Mr Jeffrey; Masons, Messrs Collins, Hart; Skinners, Mr Fleming. Vice President in the chair.

Mr Bishop read a Statement in reference to the proposed Newspaper, giving some very important information. A long conversation then took place, cheifly in reference to the carrying out the details, after which a unanimous vote of thanks was awarded to Mr Bishop for his services. A long discussion took place on the Prospectus and Financial [statement] being blended together and being printed, but no decision was come to.

There was paid into the fund on behalf of Alteration of the Law of Breach of Contract from the Leith operative Masons the sum of 13s. 4d., and a receipt given for the same. A Letter from Mr Newton, Secretary to the Glasgow Trades Council, inquiring what we were doing in Edinburgh on the above subject, but nothing was said on the matter.

The following then volunteered to visit the different trades in the course of the ensuing fortnight about the Newspaper and to report at the next meeting: Amalgamated Trades, Messrs Smith, Frazer; Joiners, Messrs Hart and Jeffrey; Masons, Mr Hart; Smiths, Mr Dewar; Plasterers, Messrs Collins and Frazer.

15 November 1864

Delegates present: Blacksmiths, Messrs Dewar, Frazer; Brassfounders, Mr Smith; Cabinetmakers, Mr Young; Glasscutters, Mr Jeffrey; Plasterers, Messrs Laing, Lyons, Aitchison; Masons, Mr Collins; Skinners, Mr Fleming; Tailors, Mr Troup.

The Secretary introduced Messrs Laing, Lyons and Aitchison as delegates from the United operative Plasterers of Edinburgh, who were cordially received as members of the Council and their names added to the list. Reports were given by the deputations visiting the trades about the Newspaper. The Amalgamated trades could not receive the deputation on account of a press of Business that night; The Masons very favourable; the Joiners' committee favourable and said they would bring it before the next trade meeting; The Plasterers very favourable; Blacksmiths – it was not brought before them, but would be at their next meeting. The following were appointed to visit other trades during the fortnight and to report at next meeting: Messrs Troup and Frazer, the Amalgamated Branch and the Printers; Messrs Troup and Jeffrey, the Bricklayers and Bakers; Mr Dewar, the Ironfounders; Messrs Hart and Young, the Bookbinders.

The council then considered the subject of a preliminary public meeting in reference to the Law of Breach of Contract, after which it was agreed to call the public meeting by placard. Mr Fleming moved that the meeting be held on the first Saturday of December, seconded by Mr Collins and unanimously agreed to.[1] 100 copies of the Statement on this question was given to the Plasterers. Mr Jeffrey got out Burton's *Political Economy*.

29 November 1864

Delegates present: Blacksmiths, Messrs Dewar, Frazer; Brassfounders, Mr Smith; Cabinetmakers, Messrs Young, Shedden; Masons, Mr Collins; Plasterers, Messrs Laing, Lyons, Aitchison; Skinners, Mr Fleming; Slaters, Mr Munro; Tailors, Mr Troup.

Reports were given by the Delegates of the different Trades visited during the past fortnight. Edinburgh Branch of the Amalgamated Trades (Messrs Troup and Frazer) very favourable; Printers – no report; Bakers and Bricklayers (Messrs Troup and Jeffrey) favourable; Bookbinders (Messrs Young and Frazer) favourable; Blacksmiths (Mr Frazer) favourable. A message from the society of the Joiners was here received intimating that they would receive a deputation from the Council on Friday first at

---

[1] No report of this meeting has been found in the press.

½ past 9 o'clock evening. Messrs Troup and Frazer were appointed to visit them. Also from the Glassmakers to meet them on Saturday.

The Council took up the subject of the preliminary public meeting on the Law of Breach of Contract, when the Placard calling the meeting was read and approved and 700 ordered to be printed and posted at twice.[1] The following were appointed to take part in the meeting: Messrs Troup, Frazer, Hart and Fleming. Mr Fleming made a short statement regarding the position of the Skinners now out on strike.

The President stated he had been authorized to ask if any member of the Council married and having a family would be willing to give evidence before the Royal Commission now sitting on the subject of National Education for Scotland.[2] Mr Young intimated his willingness to go. Mr Fleming moved that the Council accept Mr Young's offer and pay his lost time, but it fell to ground their being no seconder. Mr Young got out *Social Science Transactions for 1861* and Mr Shedden *Social Science Transactions for 1863*.

13 December 1864

Delegates present: Blacksmiths, Mr Frazer; Brassfounders, Mr Smith; Cabinetmakers, Mr Young; Masons, Mr Collins; Plasterers, Messrs Laing, Lyons, Aitchison; Skinners, Mr Fleming; Slaters, Mr Munro; Tailors, Mr Troup.

Messrs Troup and Frazer gave in reports of the different Trades they had visited during the past fortnight: operative Joiners very favourable; Glassmakers – no report; Tailors very favourable, and the Committee of the Printers the same. The sum of 5s. was paid in by the operative Marble Cutters on behalf of the proposed alteration on the Law of Breach of contract and a receipt given for the same; also the sum of 3s., being quarterly subscription to the funds of the Council, and 3s. for the Law of Breach of Contract, per Mr Smith,[3] and receipts given for these sums.

The proposed Newspaper was then considered. Mr Fleming moved that the Prospectus, with an additional clause, be printed,

[1] Error for 'at once'.
[2] The royal commission to enquire into schools in Scotland had been appointed in August, with the duke of Argyll as chairman. Its reports were issued in 1865-7.
[3] Brassfounders.

seconded by Mr Aitchison and agreed to. The council then considered what name the paper should have. It was moved by Mr Jeffrey,[1] seconded by Mr Young, that the name be the *Workman's Advocate*. Mr Frazer moved the Newspaper be called the *Scottish Workman and Social Reformer*. There voted for the amendment 8, for the motion 3. The Council then authorized the President and the Secretary, along with Mr Bishop, to have the prospectus printed for next night.

The report was given in regarding the meeting of the committee on 8 December in reference to the Law of Breach of Contract. It was stated that on account of the absence of the office bearers of this Council there was nothing done. Several remarks were then made upon the absence of these parties; after explanations had been given the subject dropped.

Mr Fleming then gave notice of the following motion: That a Committee be appointed to consider the best means of making the Trades Council have more influence in the Trades of Edinburgh and to revise the present Laws. The council then authorized the President's committee, along with the Auditors, to meet on Saturday the 24th for dispatch of business.

27 December 1864

Delegates present: Blacksmiths, Messrs Dewar, Frazer; Cabinetmakers, Messrs Young, Shedden; Masons, Messrs Collins, Hart, Campbell; Plasterers, Messrs Laing, Lyons, Aitchison; Tailors, Mr Troup.

Mr Troup gave in a report of the trades visited during the past fortnight: Glasscutters – no report; the committee of the Curriers said they would bring it before their Body and send a report in a few Days. The Law of Breach of contract of service was then considered by the Council and it was agreed to hold a Public Meeting of the inhabitants of Edinburgh on Friday, 20th January 1865, in Brighton St Chapel, to petition Parliament in favour of an alteration or amendment of the present Law. Resolutions to be proposed at the Public meeting were then submitted and after some slight alteration were agreed to. Movers and seconders were also appointed.

---

[1] Glasscutters; he is not shown in the list of delegates present.

L

Estimates for printing the Prospectus were read from Messrs Schenk and Macfarlane, £2 12s. 6d.; Messrs Ballantyne & Co., £2 9s. 6d. It was remitted to President's Committee with full powers and to endeavour to have the Prospectus with the names of all the Delegates printed on it by next night of meeting. On Account of Mr Fleming's absence, the motion he had given notice of was allowed to stand over till next night of meeting. The Secretary was impowered to send circulars to all the Delegates absent summoning them to the next meeting which it was agreed to hold as a special meeting.

1865

Delegates present: Blacksmiths, Messrs Dewar, Frazer; Brass-founders, Mr Smith; Corkcutters, Mr Ancrum; Masons, Messrs Collins, Hart, Campbell; Plasterers, Messrs Laing, Lyons, Aitchison; Cabinetmakers, Mr Young; Slaters, Mr Munro; Tailors, Mr Troup. Mr Hart in the chair.[1]

A corrected proof copy of the prospectus for the newspaper was submitted to the council. After some slight alterations and additions Mr Collins moved: That the proof be adopted and sent to the Printers, Messrs Shenck and Macfarlane, and that 2,000 be printed. Seconded by Mr Campbell and agreed to. The Secretary moved that a committee of the council meet here on Friday first, the 13th curt., at 8 o'clock evening, for the purpose of distributing the prospectus, etc. Seconded by Mr Campbell and agreed to. The following agreed to form the committee: Messrs Troup, Campbell, Hart, Collins, Dewar.

A Bill for calling the Public Meeting was then submitted to the Council and unanimously approved and 500 large Bills were ordered to be printed and posted in Edinburgh and Leith. The Chairman's Committee were appointed with full powers to arrange all the details for making the meeting effective.[2]

A Letter was read from Mr Alston, Secretary of the operative Corkcutters, appointing Mr John Ancrum as their Delegate for the present year.[3] The Council then proceeded to the Election of Office-Bearers. President – Mr Troup, proposed by Mr Collins, seconded by Mr Aitchison. Vice President – Mr Young, proposed by Mr Dewar, seconded by Mr Munro; Mr Hart, proposed by Mr Lyons,

[1] Both Troup, president, and Young, vice-president, were evidently present later.
[2] George Newton, secretary of Glasgow trades council, was the principal speaker at he meeting. *Scotsman*, 21 January 1865.
[3] Ancrum seems not to have attended any subsequent meeting of the council.

seconded by Mr Laing; for Mr Hart 6, for Mr Young 3. Secretary –
The Secretary intimated his resignation. Mr Young, proposed by
Mr Lyon, seconded by Mr Dewar; Mr Frazer, proposed by Mr
Campbell, seconded by Mr Collins. For Mr Young 3, for Mr Frazer
7. Treasurer – Mr Collins, proposed by Mr Laing, seconded by Mr
Smith. Auditor – Mr Young, proposed by Mr Collins, seconded by
Mr Campbell.

24 January 1865

Delegates present: Blacksmiths, Messrs Dewar, Frazer; Brass-
founders, Mr Smith; Cabinetmakers, Mr Young; Masons, Messrs
Collins, Hart, Campbell; Plasterers, Messrs Laing, Lyon, Aitchison;
Skinners, Mr Fleming; Slaters, Mr Munro; Tailors, Mr Troup.

Mr Laing, on behalf of the united operative Plasterers, paid the
sum of one Pound, being contribution by them in aid of altering
the Law of Breach of contract of service, and a receipt was given.
Accounts were presented from Mr Wright for printing 500 bills
for public meeting (16s. 6d.), and from Mr Hardy for posting the
same (10s.). The Treasurer was authorized to pay.

Arrangements were then made for the attendance on the Saturday
evenings for issuing prospectuses, and the President generously
volunteered to attend every Saturday evening as long as the committee should sit, two and two to attend in rotation.

The Council authorized Mr Hart to procure ruled paper for
5,000 names as signatures to the Petition, as agreed to, at the Public
meeting. The Secretary was instructed to write to Mr Newton,
Glasgow, for printed copies of the Petition. Mr Fleming was then
heard in support of the motion he had given notice of.[1] A long
discussion followed, after which A. Frazer moved the previous
question, which was seconded by Mr Campbell. But no division
took place, the motion being withdrawn. Note: The number of
Prospectuses issued to the above date is: Masons 100, Blacksmiths
50, Bricklayers 10, Tailors 50, Plasterers 50, Slaters 20, Brassfounders 50, Skinners 25, Total 355.

7 February 1865

Delegates present: Blacksmiths, Messrs Dewar, Frazer; Brassfounders, Mr Smith; Cabinetmakers, Mr Shedden; Masons, Messrs

[1] Above, p. 161.

Collins, Hart, Campbell; Plasterers, Messrs Laing, Lyons, Aitchison; Tailors, Mr Troup.

The Council considered the best way they could adopt for raising funds for carrying out the proposed alteration of the Law of Breach of Contract, as the fund collected for this object had been expended. The Treasurer was authorized to uplift the sum of £1 from the funds of the Council to carry the Petition to Parliament into effect. A number of Prospectuses was then given out and copies of the Petition for signatures. The committee was appointed to meet on Saturday first and Saturday week for general business. Additional Prospectuses issued during the past fortnight: Plasterers 50, Painters 60, Masons 9, Blacksmiths 12, Brassfounders 6, Joiners 50, Glass Blowers 50, Glass Cutters 50, Amalgamated Engineers 50, Printers 12, Cabinetmakers 50, Total 754.

21 February 1865

Delegates present: Blacksmiths, Messrs Dewar, Frazer; Brassfounders, Mr Smith; Cabinetmakers, Mr Shedden; Masons, Messrs Collins, Campbell; Plasterers, Messrs Lyons, Aitchison; Slaters, Mr Munro; Tailors, Mr Troup.

The only business this evening before the Council was the receiving of a number of sheets with signatures and giving out others to be filled up. It was suggested by the Treasurer that we should ascertain the number of shares in the *Scottish Workman* the delegates present would take. It was found that 27 was the number and the money value £6 15s. After sitting the usual time the committee agreed to meet on Saturday first and Saturday [week] for issuing prospectuses, etc.

7 March 1865

Delegates present: Blacksmiths, Messrs Dewar, Frazer; Brassfounders, Mr Smith; Cabinetmakers, Mr Young; Masons, Messrs Collins, Hart; Tailors, Mr Troup.

The Secretary intimated that he had received a letter from Mr H. G. Reid of the *Buchan Observer*[1] enquiring about the Newspaper

[1] An independent Liberal paper published at Peterhead 1863-75 and continued from 1875 to c. 1890 as the *East Aberdeenshire Observer*. J. P. S. Ferguson, *Scottish Newspapers in Scottish Libraries* (Edinburgh, 1956), 6.

and that he had forwarded to Mr Reid a copy of the prospectus with a letter. Also that he had written to Mr Alexander Campbell, Glasgow, enquiring when the Bill for the alteration of the Law of Breach of Contract would be introduced into parliament, but as yet had received no answer. The Secretary was also instructed to write to Glasgow in reference to a statement that appeared in some of the papers, viz., 'That the names of the President, Secretary and committee were enough for any Trade petition to Parliament', as it was fitted to mislead many. There was paid into the fund for alteration of said Law from workmen in the employment of Messrs J. & T. Scott, Cabinetmakers, the sum of 4s. 10d. and from workmen of Messrs Morison 1s. 10d., and receipts given for the same.

21 March 1865

As there was not sufficient members to form a quorum the minutes of the former meeting were not read. There was paid into the funds of the Council the sum of £1, being subscription from the operative Tailors, and a receipt given for the same.

4 April 1865

Delegates present: Brassfounders, Mr Smith; Cabinetmakers, Mr Young; Masons, Mr Collins; Plasterers, Messrs Laing, Lyons; Tailors, Mr Troup.

There was paid in to the funds of the Council the sum of 3s., being quarterly subscription from the operative Brassfounders, and receipts given for the same. 3s. 6d. for Breach of Contract. A Letter was read from Mr William Smith, secretary to the Edinburgh Cabinet and Chairmakers Society, intimating that Messrs John Shedden, Thomas Young, and John Liddell were elected delegates to this Council for the current year. The following books were returned: Burton's *Political Economy*; Burton's given out to Mr Collins.

18 April 1865

Delegates present: Blacksmiths, Mr Frazer; Brassfounders, Mr Smith; Masons, Messrs Collins, Hart; Slaters, Mr Monro; Cabinetmakers, Mr Young; Plasterers, Messrs Lyons, Aitchison; Tailors, Mr Troup.

A Letter was read from Mr Newton, Glasgow, intimating that the Council would require to elect two of their number as competent to give evidence as witnesses before a Committee of the House of Commons, 'should they be requested', on the Master and Workman's Act.[1] The following were nominated: Alexander Frazer, Thomas Young, James Collins. The Council agreed to transmit the names of the three individuals nominated, leaving it to the executive in Glasgow to select whom they thought best fitted. The Council agreed to have tables on the street on the following Friday and Saturday for the purpose of getting as many signatures as possible to the petition to Parliament anent the Master and Workman's Act. Mr Hart agreed to take charge of the same.

3 May 1865[2]

Delegates present: Blacksmiths, Messrs Dewar, Frazer; Brassfounders, Mr Smith; Cabinetmakers, Messrs Young, Shedden; Masons, Messrs Collins, Hart; Plasterers, Messrs Laing, Aitchison; Tailors, Mr Troup.

Mr Shedden paid to the Treasurer the sum of fifteen shillings, being annual subscription from the operative Cabinet and Chair makers' Society, and a receipt was given for the same. Mr Hart gave a verbal report of what had been done in regard to the petition to Parliament on the Master and Workman's Act, and the result was that 1,700 additional signatures had been added to the Petition. Mr Hart reported what the Newspaper committee had done in having an appeal printed and 200 copies of the same were laid before the Council. They agreed to distribute it among the trades.

The attention of the Council was then called to the fact that the time had now come when they should consider having the annual excursion to Glasgow. The Secretary was instructed to write to the Secretaries of the Edinburgh and Glasgow and Caledonian Railway Companies regarding the terms of an excursion.

[1] A Select Committee of the Commons was appointed in May 1865 and reappointed a year later with Lord Elcho, independent conservative M.P. for Haddingtonshire (East Lothian), as chairman. None of the Edinburgh trades council nominees were called on to give evidence.
[2] The date should probably be 2 May 1865.

16 May 1865

Delegates present: Blacksmiths, Messrs Dewar, Frazer; Brass-founders, Mr Smith; Cabinetmakers, Mr Young; Masons, Mr Collins; Plasterers, Messrs Lyons, Aitchison; Slaters, Messrs Munro, Duncan; Tailors, Mr Troup.

The Secretary read Letters from the Edinburgh and Glasgow and Caledonian Railway Companies regarding the Annual Excursion. The Council agreed to go by the Edinburgh and Glasgow Railway on the understanding that certain alterations should be made in the agreement, and Mr Troup was appointed to deal with Mr Stewart in Edinburgh for that purpose. Mr Smith and the President were appointed as Delegates to go to Glasgow and make the necessary arrangements.

There was paid into the funds of the Council the sum of 10s., being subscription from the operative Slaters, per Mr Munro. Mr Munro also introduced Mr Duncan as Delegate from the Slaters. An account was read from the *Glasgow Sentinel* newspaper giving some information regarding the progress of the Master and Work-men's Act in the House of Commons. The Council agreed to meet on Saturday first at 7 p.m. for the purpose of making up the Petition and sending it to the Lord Advocate[1] for presentation to Parliament.

30 May 1865

Delegates present: Blacksmiths, Messrs Dewar, Frazer; Cabinet-makers, Messrs Young, Liddell; Masons, Messrs Collins, Hart; Slaters, Messrs Munro, J. Duncan; Plasterers, Messrs Laing, Lyons. Vice President, Mr Hart, in the chair.

The Secretary gave a verbal report regarding the transmission of the Petition on Master and Workman's Act to the House of Commons signed by 3,126 persons; also regarding communications with the Edinburgh and Glasgow Railway anent the annual excursion. Both reports approved.

The Secretary called the attention of the Council to the state of the funds with special reference to fund raised for the purpose of amending the present Law of Master and Workman. Mr Collins moved: That the Secretary be instructed to write to Mr G. Newton,

[1] James Moncreiff.

Glasgow, informing him what had been done in this matter in Edinburgh but not to enter into any monetary statement. Carried unamiously. Some conversation then followed regarding the Auditing. Mr Dewar moved: That the Auditors meet here on the first Saturday of July to audit the Books for the past year. Seconded by Mr Lyons and unanimously agreed.

14 June 1865[1]

Delegates present: Blacksmiths, Messrs Dewar, Frazer; Cabinet-makers, Messrs Shedden, Young, Liddell; Brassfounders, Mr Smith; Plasterers, Messrs Laing, Lyons; Slaters, Messrs Munro, Duncan; Tailors, Mr Troup. In the absence of the President, Mr Dewar and afterwards the President in the Chair.

The Secretary reported regarding the presentation of the Petition from Edinburgh on the Master and Workman's Act, and read a letter from Mr Agnew[2] by order of the Lord Advocate anent the same. Some conversation ensued regarding the sending of a deputation from this council to the meeting of the Iron trades in Brighton St Chapel this evening for the purpose of establishing two successive holidays annually in Edinburgh. Messrs Dewar and Frazer were appointed to visit said meeting and to act according to circumstances.

The President and Mr Smith gave in report regarding their visit to Glasgow anent the annual excursion. The report was approved and the Treasurer authorized to pay their expences. Mr Dewar then reported what took place at the meeting in Brighton Street and what the deputation had done. Report approved. Mr Shedden gave in *Report on Social Science Transactions 1863*, Mr Lyon got out the same.

27 June 1865

Delegates present: Blacksmiths, Messrs Dewar, Frazer; Brass-founders, Mr Smith; Masons, Mr Campbell; Plasterers, Messrs Lyons, Aitchison; Tailors, Mr Troup.

The Secretary reported he had written to Glasgow and read an extract from the *Glasgow Sentinel* regarding said letter. There was paid into the funds of the council from the Edinburgh Branch of the Scottish operative Blacksmiths Society, per Mr Dewar, the

---

[1] The date should probably be 13 June 1865.   [2] Not identified.

annual subscription of one pound; also from the Edinburgh operative Brassfounders Society the quarterly subscription of three
shillings. The Business for this evening was to be arranging for the
distribution of the tickets for the excursion, but on account of the
absence of the Treasurer, who had the tickets, nothing was done.
The Secretary was instructed to write to him to be in attendance
tomorrow night for the purpose of giving out excursion tickets.

11 July 1865

Delegates present: Blacksmiths, Messrs Dewar, Frazer; Brassfounders, Mr Smith; Cabinetmakers, Messrs Shedden, Young,
Liddell; Masons, Mr Collins; Plasterers, Messrs Laing, Lyons;
Slaters, Messrs Munro, Duncan; Tailors, Mr Troup. Mr Shedden
and afterwards the President in the chair.

Explanations was given by the Treasurer regarding his absence
at the last meeting. The report from the Auditors was then called
for but not given, for which no very satisfactory reason was
given.[1] The Auditors were appointed to meet on Saturday the 15th
to Audit the Books and report at the next meeting of the Council.

The Treasurer reported regarding the distribution of tickets for
the excursion. Mr Collins returned Burton's *Political Economy*.

25 July 1865

Delegates present: Blacksmiths, Messrs Dewar, Frazer; Brassfoun-
ders, Mr Smith; Cabinetmakers, Messrs Young, Shedden, Liddell;
Masons, Messrs Collins, Campbell; Plasterers, Messrs Laing, Lyons,
Aitchison; Slaters, Messrs Munro, Duncan; Tailors, Mr Troup.

Minutes of the former meeting read and after some alteration
agreed to. On the report of the Auditors being called for, Mr Young
gave a verbal report stating that the transactions of the Treasurer
were all correct and that a written report would be submitted to
the Council soon. The Council were then for some time engaged in
the arranging and distribution of tickets for the excursion to Glasgow
on the 29th currt.

Messrs Laing and Aitchsion called the attention of the Council

---

[1] A subsequent insertion in the MS. says the absence of a report was 'in consequence of
the Auditors not being able to meet'.

to certain statements made by Mr Ross, representative of the operative Joiners of this City, at the Public meeting on the Nine hours Demonstration in the Queen's Park on Saturday the 22nd curt. seriously affecting the usefulness of the council in Edinburgh.[1] After considering this matter the Secretary was instructed to have a Letter written to be laid before the Council at their next meeting, calling the attention of the Joiners to the statements of Mr Ross. After agreeing to meet on Thursday and Friday first for excursion Business the Council then adjourned.

8 August 1865

Delegates present: Blacksmiths, Messrs Dewar, Frazer; Brassfounders, Mr Smith; Masons, Mr Collins; Slaters, Mr Munro; Tailors, Mr Troup. The President and afterwards Mr Collins in the chair.

The Secretary read a letter from Mr Newton, Glasgow, in reference to a further agitation on the Master and Workman's Act, and a number of copies of an address to workmen was then laid on the table and their distribution authorized by the Council. The Secretary was instructed to write to Mr Newton accordingly. Two letters were read from Mr Finlay Ross of the Edinburgh Branch of the Joiners' Society in reply to a letter from this Council, one letter exonerating the Joiners, the other an attempted answer to the letter of the Council. In regard to the first the Secretary was instructed to write a letter of thanks to the President of the Joiners; in regard to the second the Council thought in the meantime it was unworthy of further notice.

The Secretary was further instructed to write to Mr Watson, City Chamberlain of Glasgow, a letter of thanks for his kindness to the Excursionists from Edinburgh to Glasgow on 29th July last. On 18th July last there was paid into the funds of the council from the Edinburgh operative Society of Plasterers, per Mr Laing, the sum of one pound. This should have been in the former minute.

22 August 1865

Delegates present: Blacksmiths, Messrs Dewar, Frazer; Cabinetmakers, Messrs Young, Liddell; Masons, Mr Collins; Plasterers,

---

[1] Ross's remarks were not reported in the press.

Mr Aitchison. In the absence of the President Mr Collins in the chair.

A letter was read from Mr Purdie, Secretary to the operative Brassfounders' Society, intimating the withdrawal of their Delegates from this board. The council expressed their regret at this and the Secretary was instructed to communicate the same to that Society. The annual financial report of this council was read by Mr Young, after which the Council considered the best means of raising money on behalf of the Glasgow executive for carrying out the amendment of the Master and Workman's Act. It was agreed that those trades who had not contributed to this object should be waited upon for their subscription, and the following were appointed: for the Masons, Messrs Collins, Frazer; Joiners, Messrs Aitchison, Dewar; Tailors, Messrs Troup, Young. Mr Collins gave notice of a motion regarding the Newspaper and Mr Young regarding the Library. Mr Liddell got out Burton's *Political Economy*.

5 September 1865

Delegates present: Blacksmiths, Mr Frazer; Cabinetmakers, Mr Young; Masons, Mr Collins; Plasterers, Mr Aitchison; Slaters, Mr Munro; Tailors, Mr Troup.

The Secretary reported he had written to the Secretary of the operative Brassfounders society in terms of the former minute. Mr Collins not being present at this stage of the business, the motion he had given notice of was deferred till next night. Mr Aitchison gave a verbal report of his visit to the joiners, who promised favourably to consider the subject he had brought before them. Mr Troup stated that the present time was most unfavourable to visit the tailors, this being their dull season, but he would endeavour to bring the subject before them at their next quarterly meeting. Mr Collins gave a verbal report of what he had done in bringing this subject before the Masons and that there was a strong probability of a grant from their Society to the executive in Glasgow.

Mr Young then introduced the subject of the Library, which gave rise to a long and very irregular discussion. The Secretary called the attention of the delegates whose names had been sent to the executive in Glasgow as witnesses on the Master and Workmen's Act. Another irregular discussion took place, in the midst of which the President adjourned the Council.

19 September 1865

Delegates present: Blacksmiths, Messrs Dewar, Frazer; Cabinet Makers, Messrs Shedden, Young, Liddell; Masons, Mr Collins; Plasterers, Mr Laing; Slaters, Messrs Munro, Duncan; Tailors, Mr Troup.

Mr Troup reported that the subscription to the executive in Glasgow in support of an alteration of the Master and Workman's Act would come before the Tailors at their next quarterly meeting. Mr Collins brought forward the subject of the Newspaper and moved: That a meeting of the shareholders be called to be held here on 3 October and their money be returned to them in full. Seconded by Mr Laing. The Secretary moved that the last clause be omitted, seconded by Mr Shedden. For the amendment 3, for the motion 5.

Mr Young then brought up the subject of the Library. Mr Collins moved that 1d. of a fine be imposed upon all those who keep their Books longer than one fortnight and the same sum for every fortnight thereafter. Seconded by Mr Dewar. Mr Young moved that no fine be exacted, which was not seconded. Mr Dewar called the attention of the Council to the movement in the Iron trades for reducing the hours of Labour, but as the Iron Trades had made no application to this board, the Council could do nothing in the meantime.[1] Mr Young returned *Social Science transactions*, Mr Liddel Burton's *Political Economy*; Mr Young got out Burton's *Political Economy*, Mr Shedden Blackie's *Better Days*.

3 October 1865

Delegates present: Blacksmiths, Messrs Dewar, Frazer; Cabinet-makers, Messrs Young, Shedden; Masons, Mr Collins; Slaters, Mr Munro; Tailors, Mr Troup.

Mr Dewar communicated some information regarding the movement in the Iron trades for shortening the hours of Labour. The following shareholders received back the amount of Money they

[1] The iron trades were seeking a reduction of hours from sixty to fifty-seven a week. *Edinburgh Evening Courant*, 28 October 1865.

had previously paid for shares in the Newspaper: Mr Gardiner, Tailor, 5s; John Laurie, 2s; William Wight 2s; David Robertson 5s; William Willeson 5s; George Johnston 5s; George Duncan 4s; Charles Dyson 1s; William Thomson 1s; Adam Melrose 1s; Alexander Buchan 1s; Henry Cossar 1s. Mr Laing returned *Social Science transactions, 1863*,[1] Mr Shedden Blackie's *Better Days*, Mr Young Burton's *Political Economy*. Mr Collins got out *Social Science transactions 1863*, Mr Young Burton's *Political Economy*, Mr Shedden Blackie's *Better Days*.

17 October 1865

There was not a quorum present. The only business done was paying the rest of the shareholders of the newspaper their money, and thus winding up the newspaper proposal.

31 October 1865

Delegates present: Blacksmiths, Messrs Dewar, Frazer; Cabinet-makers, Messrs Young, Shedden; Masons, Mr Collins; Slaters, Messrs Munro, Duncan; Tailors, Mr Troup.

The Secretary read a Letter from Mr George Newton, Glasgow, requesting information if there were a case or cases of hardship in or near Edinburgh under the present Master and Workman's Act. The Secretary was instructed to write to the Secretaries of the different trades for information, also to visit the Newspaper offices to ascertain the judgement of the Court of Session on the case at Jedburgh and to report at next meeting.[2]

The Treasurer was authorized to pay the sum of 4s. 6d. due by the Council to Mr Knox, S.S.C., Hanover St, agent for the creditors of Mr Wright, Printer, Hunter Square. Mr Dewar gave a verbal report of the meeting of the Iron Trades in Queen St Hall a few days ago for the purpose of reducing the hours of Labour. The following Books were given in: Mr Shedden returned Blackie's *Better days*, Mr Collins *Social Science Transactions 1863*, Mr Young Burton's *Political Economy*; Mr Munro got out Blackie's *Better Days*, Mr Duncan *Social Science Transactions 1863*.

[1] Laing, plasterers, is not included in the list of delegates present.
[2] No report of such a case has been found in *Cases Decided in the Court of Session* (Edinburgh, 1864-6), third series, ii, iii, or iv, or in the press.

14 November 1865

Delegates present: Blacksmiths, Messrs Dewar, Frazer; Cabinet-makers, Mr Young; Slaters, Mr Munro; Masons, Mr Collins; Tailors, Mr Troup.

The Secretary reported that he had written to various Trade Societies Secretaries for information in terms of former minute. A letter was read from the Secretary of the Masons Edinburgh Lodge stating that no cases of a breach of the Law of Master and Workman had come under their knowledge but they would make further inquiries in the different lodges of their Society. The President gave in a similar report as regards the Tailors.

A Letter was read from Mr George Potter, London, requesting the names and addresses of the different Trade Societies Secretaries in Edinburgh and the Secretary was instructed to supply the same. The Secretary then called the attention of the Council to the subject of a Free Library for Edinburgh. The President and Secretary were appointed a deputation to wait on the Lord Provost[1] to call his attention to this matter. Mr Duncan returned *Social Science Transactions for 1863*,[2] Mr Munro Burton's *Political Economy*, Mr Dewar Blackie's *Better Days*.

28 November 1865

Delegates present: Blacksmiths, Mr Frazer; Cabinetmakers, Mr Young; Masons, Mr Collins; Slaters, Mr Munro; Tailors, Mr Troup.

The Secretary reported he had written to Mr G. Potter, London, and had received a communication from Mr Hartwell, London, regarding a Testimonial to Mr Potter which was read to the Council.[3] It was unanimously agreed to defer voting a sum of money till next night of meeting.

A Letter was read from Mr James Marshall, Secretary to the operative Joiners, Edinburgh Lodge, stating that [no] cases of prosecution under the Master and Workmen's Act had occurred in their trade as far as they knew. Mr Collins gave a verbal report,

[1] William Chambers, the publisher, had been elected lord provost on 10 November 1865.
[2] Duncan, slaters, is not listed among the delegates present.
[3] Robert Hartwell, b. 1812, a former Chartist, active in the working class movement, sub-editor 1861-3 and subsequently editor of the *Beehive*.

vice Fleming, in regard to the Case of the operative Skinner, stating that he Fleming had written to him about it and when he received his answer he would forward it to the council.[1] Mr Troup then reported why the deputation had not seen the Lord Provost in reference to the Free Library. The explanation was received and the deputation were re-appointed and to report at next meeting.

12 December 1865

Delegates present: Blacksmiths, Mr Frazer; Cabinetmakers, Mr Young; Masons, Mr Collins; Tailors Mr Troup. The deputation gave in a verbal report of their interview with the Lord Provost regarding a Free Library. His Lordship stated that he would consider what the deputation had laid before him. There not being a quorum of members present there was no business done this evening.

26 December 1865

Delegates present: Blacksmiths, Mr Frazer; Cabinetmakers, Mr Young; Masons, Mr Collins; Plasterers, Mr Laing; Tailors, Mr Troup.

The Secretary laid before the Council a Prospectus of a newspaper, the *Working Man*, published by Messrs Cassel, Petter and Gulpin, London.[2] There was some conversation on its merits but the opinion of the Council was not favourable to it. The next business was the voting of a sum of money to the testimonial to Mr George Potter, London. After hearing the opinions of the Delegates and by reason of the small number present it was agreed to defer this matter till next meeting. As the next meeting of the Council falls to be on the 9th January it was agreed to defer the meeting till the 23rd and to hold it a special meeting, the delegates not present to be written to for to attend, as the election of office-bearers would take place on that meeting. Auditors to meet an hour previous to the meeting of the Council to Audit the Treasurer's Book, etc.

[1] No information about such a case has been found.
[2] The paper, which was Liberal in principles, was established as a weekly on 6 January 1866.

1866

Delegates present: Blacksmiths, Messrs Dewar, Frazer; Cabinet-makers, Messrs Young, Shedden; Masons, Mr Collins; Plasterers, Mr Aitchison; Slaters, Messrs Monro, Duncan. In the absence of the President, Mr Young in the chair.

The Auditor's report was given in by Mr Young verbally that the Treasurer's Books, etc., were found to be correct. The Secretary read a letter from Mr Anderson, Joiner, in reference to Sabbath trains, Cabs, and the Short time movement, inviting the Council to attend a preliminary meeting on the above subjects to be held in Buchanan's Temperance Coffee House on Saturday 3rd February. Mr Aitchison moved: That the Council as such be represented at the above meeting, which was seconded by Mr Dewar. Mr Shedden moved as an amendment the previous question. The amendment, after some further explanation, was withdrawn and Mr Aitchison and Mr Shedden were appointed to represent the Council.

The proposed testimonial to Mr George Potter, London, was then considered, when it was found that as none of the trades represented here had taken up this matter the Council did not see it to be their duty to vote any money from their funds for this object and dismissed the same. The Council then proceeded to the Election of Office Bearers for 1866: President, Mr Troup, proposed by Mr Aitchison, Seconded by Mr Dewar. Secretary, Mr Frazer, proposed by Mr Collins, Seconded by Mr Dewar. Treasurer, Mr Collins, Proposed by Mr Frazer, Seconded by Mr Aitchison. Auditor, Mr Monro, Proposed by Mr Frazer, Seconded by Mr Dewar. These Office Bearers were unanimously elected.[1] Mr Collins got out *Social Science Transactions for 1863*.

[1] No vice-president appears to have been elected.

M

6 February 1866

Present: Messrs Frazer, Munro, Duncan. After waiting till 9 o'clock and not a quorum being present, the members present adjourned.

20 February 1866

Delegates present: Blacksmiths, Messrs Dewar, Frazer; Cabinetmakers, Mr Young; Masons, Mr Collins; Plasterers, Mr Aitchison. As there was not a quorum present till ½ past nine o'clock, there was not time to take up any business. A conversation took place on the subject of having two holidays together in the course of the year and it was agreed to consider this subject at the next meeting of the Council.

5 March 1866[1]

Present: Messrs Collins, Frazer, Duncan. After waiting till 9 o'clock and no others making their appearance, the members present adjourned.

20 March 1866

Delegates present: Blacksmiths, Mr A. Frazer; Cabinetmakers, Messrs Young, Shedden; Plasterers, Mr Aitchison; Masons, Mr Collins; Slaters, Mr Duncan; Tailors, Mr Troup.

The Secretary brought before the Council The propriety of having one or more holidays in the Summer season permanently fixed for the benefit of the working Classes of this City. After discussing this subject at some length, it was agreed that the delegates should bring this question before their respective trades and bring up a report next meeting.

A communication from their executive with a number of Printed Statements relative to the Lock Out of the File Trade in Sheffield was then laid before Council.[2] After considering their case and in the anticipation of a Lock Out of the operative Tailors here, the Council could do nothing further in the meantime than distribute

[1] The date should probably read 6 March 1866.
[2] The simultaneous strike and lockout of the Sheffield file trades had begun on 24 February over a wages dispute but developed into a conflict over the introduction of machinery. The strike collapsed after sixteen weeks. S. Pollard, *A History of Labour in Sheffield* (Liverpool, 1959), 140.

their Appeal among the different trades. They also instructed the Secretary to acknowledge the receipt of the communication.

3 April 1866

Delegates present: Blacksmiths, Messrs Dewar, Frazer; Cabinet-makers, Messrs Young, Shedden; Plasterers, Mr Aitchsion; Slaters, Mr Duncan; Tailors, Mr Troup.

Before proceeding to the business of the evening Mr McWhinnie, Secretary of the operative Tailors, made a statement regarding the points of dispute betwixt them and their employers which had resulted in the present Strike[1] and suggested the propriety of the Council issuing a recommendation to the different trades represented here to afford the tailors their moral and pecuniary support when they, the tailors, should call for it. The Council then tendered Mr McWhinnie a vote of thanks for the statement he had made to the Council.

The Secretary then reported that he had written to the Secretary of the File Smiths of Sheffield in terms of the former minute but had received no further communication. Reports were given in regarding the general Holiday in Summer: Plasterers, quite favourable; the Slaters had not considered it, ditto the Tailors; no reports from any other of the Trades. The recommendation as suggested by the Tailors was then drawn up and after considering it the Council agreed to have it inserted in the four daily newspapers of tomorrow or next day.

17 April 1866

Delegates present: Blacksmiths, Messrs Dewar, Frazer; Masons, Mr Collins; Plasterers, Mr Aitchison; Tailors, Mr Troup.

Mr Troup reported regarding the late strike of the operative tailors and how it had been settled by the adoption of both parties of the London time statement. The Secretary brought before the Council the present position and prospects of this Council as representing several of the Trades in Edinburgh. After several of the members had given their opinions it was agreed to consider this subject next night of meeting.

[1] The dispute was over wages and hours.

1 May 1866

Present: Messrs Troup, Frazer, Aitchison, Young, Dewar. As there was not a quorum present till ½ past 9 o'clock it was then to late to take up any business. After agreeing to hold the next meeting a special meeting by summoning the absent members, the members present adjourned.

15 May 1866

Delegates present: Blacksmiths, Mr Frazer; Cabinetmakers, Messrs Shedden, Young; Masons, Mr Collins; Plasterers, Mr Aitchison; Slaters, Mr Duncan; Tailors, Mr Troup.

The Secretary brought before the Council the present position they occupy as representing the Trades in this City. A long discussion then followed and the general opinion was that the Council should not dissolve but endeavour to extend itself through the various trades in the City not represented at this Board.

Mr Collins then moved that the President and Secretary be appointed a Deputation to wait on the Manager of the North British Railway Company regarding an excursion to Glasgow on 28 July and report at next meeting. There was paid to the Council the sum of ten shillings from the Edinburgh Branch of the Operative Slaters' Society, per Mr Duncan, being subscription from that Body.

29 May 1866

Delegates present: Blacksmiths, Messrs Dewar, Frazer; Cabinetmakers, Messrs Shedden, Young; Masons, Mr Collins; Plasterers, Mr Aitchison; Slaters, Mr Duncan; Tailors, Mr Troup.

Mr Troup gave in a verbal report regarding the arrangements the deputation had made for an excursion to Glasgow on 28th July next. After some consideration of the North British Railways Company's terms it was moved by Mr Duncan, seconded by Mr Aitchsion, that this Council agree to the Same. The Council then considered whether we should send a deputation to Glasgow or get the places of interest there opened by corresponding with them. It was moved by Mr Dewar, seconded by Mr Duncan, that we send a deputation, which was agreed to. Mr Troup and Mr Young were appointed and to report at next meeting. The Secretary read two communications from Sheffield, one in reference to the present

Lock out of the File Smiths there, and the other regarding a conference of Trades Delegates to meet there on 11th or 12th June.[1] A
long discussion followed on these two topics and the understanding
come to was that there would be no one sent from Edinburgh as
the time was so short.

12 June 1866

Delegates present: Blacksmiths, Messrs Dewar, Frazer; Cabinet-
makers, Messrs Shedden, Young; Masons, Mr Collins; Slaters, Mr
Duncan; Tailors, Mr Troup. Mr Shedden and afterwards the
President in the Chair.

The Deputation to Glasgow gave in the report of their visit and
the number of places of interest open to the Excursionists, which was
approved. The rest of the business was in arranging the details of
the excursion, getting bills printed and posted and appointing Delegates to get places for the sale of tickets, etc., and to report at next
meeting.

26 June 1866

Delegates present: Blacksmiths, Messrs Dewar, Frazer; Cabinetmakers, Mr Young; Masons, Mr Collins; Slaters, Messrs Munro,
Duncan; Plasterers, Mr Aitchison; Tailors, Mr Troup.

Minutes of the former meeting read. Mr Young objected to the
word Deputation in the former minutes, Mr Troup not being present
all the time when the report was given in. Mr Collins moved the
adoption of the minutes as they were read, Mr Aitchison seconded,
and unanimously agreed to.

Reports were given by the most of the Delegates regarding the
different shops, etc., for the Sale of Tickets, which was approved.
Mr Duncan intimated his resignation as one of the Delegates from
the Operative Slaters, which was accepted. He introduced Mr
Crichton as his successor in office. Agreed to.

The Delegates from the Slaters made a Statement of the Cause
of Dispute betwixt them and their employers which had resulted
in the present Strike of that Body.[2] The following Resolution was

---

[1] The conference was summoned as a result of the file trades dispute and actually met
on 17-21 July. Its outcome was the formation of a national organisation for resisting
lockouts: The United Kingdom Alliance of Organised Trades. A. E. Musson, *The
Congress of 1868* (London, 1955), 17-18.
[2] No report of this strike has been found.

then unanimously agreed to: The Trades Council, having heard the Statement made by the Delegates of the Slaters, approve of the means used by them for an advance of Wages and recommend them to the sympathy and support of the different trades represented at this Board. A Copy of the same signed by the President was then handed to the Slaters' Delegates for the use of the Society.

The Council then considered the advertising of the excursion by Bills, etc. It was moved by Mr Collins, seconded by Mr Aitchison, that it be remitted to the President's Committee to prepare a Bill and to get 250 large posted and 1,000 Small for circulation. After agreeing to hold a special meeting of the Council on Saturday the 30th at 7 o'clock evening, they adjourned.

30 June 1866

A Special meeting of the Council for the distribution of Excursion Tickets, etc. Mr Young got out Burton's *Political Economy*.

10 July 1866

Delegates present: Blacksmiths, Mr Frazer; Cabinetmakers, Messrs Shedden, Young; Masons, Mr Collins; Slaters, Mr Munro; Tailors, Mr Troup; Plasterers, Mr Aitchison.

The Cheif business this evening was in the distributing and arranging tickets for the Excursion on the 28th. The Council then considered the communication from Sheffield regarding the Conference to be held there on 17th July. It was agreed that the Secretary should prepare a Letter and submit the same to the Special meeting to be held here on the 14th currt. and if approved by them to transmit the same to Mr Dronfield, Secretary to the Sheffield Committee.[1]

14 July 1866

A Special meeting of the Council for General Business. The Letter to be transmitted to Sheffield was read and approved.

24 July 1866

Delegates present: Blacksmiths, Messrs Dewar, Frazer; Cabinet-makers, Messrs Shedden, Young; Masons, Mr Collins; Plasterers,

[1] William Dronfield, 1826-94, a compositor, secretary of Sheffield trades council 1858-67 and of the United Kingdom Alliance of Organised Trades. Musson, op. cit. 17-19; W. H. G. Armytage in *Notes and Queries*, cxciii (1948), 145-8.

Mr Aitchison; Slaters, Messrs Munro, Crichton; Tailors, Mr Troup.

The greatest portion of the evening was taken up in hearing reports and making arrangements to make the annual excursion as effective as possible. The Secretary intimated he would on the next night of meeting bring before the Council the resolutions formerly approved of by this [board] in reference to Trades progress but which had as yet [not] been carried into effect, with the view of having these queries printed and circulated among the different trades.[1]

SPECIAL MEETINGS

A Special meeting of the Council was held on Thursday and Friday the 26th and 27th for Excursion business only and a further special meeting was held on Tuesday the 31st for the purpose of settling up the Annual Excursion.

7 August 1866

Delegates present: Blacksmiths, Mr Frazer; Cabinetmakers, Mr Young; Slaters, Messrs Munro, Crichton; Masons, Mr Collins. In the absence of the President, Mr Munro in the chair.

The Secretary brought before the council the subject given notice of at last meeting relating to Queries on trades progress. They were of opinion that these queries should be printed to the number of 1,000 copies if the expense was not to exceed 10 shillings, but before doing so the Secretary was instructed to have a manuscript copy with an explanatory note written out and submit to the Council for their approval at next meeting.

21 August 1866

Delegates present: Blacksmiths, Mr Frazer; Cabinetmakers, Mr Young; Masons, Mr Collins; Plasterers, Mr Aitchison; Tailors, Mr Troup.

The Secretary read a manuscript copy of the queries with the preamble and explanatory note. The Council agreed to adopt it and authorized the same to be printed for distribution. The Secretary was instructed to send copies of the same by post to the Secretaries

[1] Above, p. 137.

of all organized trades in the City. A Copy of the *Glasgow Sentinel* of 18th August was laid on the table and an extract was read giving an account of the meeting of the executive committee relative to the Master and Workman's Act.[1] At this stage of the business a deputation from the Edinburgh branch of Joiners' Society appeared, asking information with the view of sending Delegates to represent said Branch at this Council, which being done the deputation retired. The subject of the above Act was then taken up and the Secretary was instructed to write to Glasgow to see if they could supply us with a copy of the evidence laid before Parliament before we could decide what we should do in the matter.

A Letter was read from Mr W. Thomson, 8 Gladstone Terrace, requesting payment for 4 Tickets = 10s., which he had to purchase in Glasgow on the Monday following the excursion, and threatening to summon the Delegates for the above sum. The Council agreed to take no notice of the Letter but if Mr Thomson should carry out his threat the Secretary was empowered to call a special meeting of the Delegates.

4 September 1866

Delegates present: Blacksmiths, Messrs Dewar, Frazer; Masons, Mr Collins; Plasterers, Mr Aitchison; Slaters, Messrs Munro, Crichton; Tailors, Mr Troup.

The Secretary reported that he had written to the Secretary of the Edinburgh Branch of the Joiners Society enclosing a copy of the Rules of the Council, but had received no answer. A Letter was read from G. Newton, Glasgow, recommending the Council to apply for a copy of the evidence on the Master and Workman's Act to D. McLaren, Esq., M.P. for the City, and the Secretary was instructed to apply accordingly. Copies of the printed Queries were laid on the Table and were distributed to the members of the Council, after which a conversation took place on the necessity of having a number of the Rules of the Council printed. It was agreed to defer the consideration of it till next meeting.

[1] The committee in Glasgow had on 15 August expressed dissatisfaction with the Report of the Select Committee of the Commons. The Report recommended retention in certain cases of imprisonment for workmen convicted under the laws, as well as punishment by fine. *Glasgow Sentinel*, 18 August 1866.

18 September 1866

Delegates present: Blacksmiths, Mr A. Frazer; Cabinetmakers, Mr Young; Masons, Mr Collins; Slaters, Mr Chrichton; Tailors, Mr Troup.

The Secretary reported he had written D. McLaren, M.P., and read Mr McLaren's answer in which he stated he had not received a copy of the *Report on the Master and Workman's Act*, but when he got it he would give the Council the loan of it. This gave rise to a conversation on the above Act, during which Mr Hart, as deputed by the Masons, made some enquiries regarding the printed queries, especially if these queries embraced anything political. Some of the members thought they did and others they did not, during which it was suggested that the council should make their next meeting a special one to consider this subject. Agreed to and the Secretary was instructed to write to all who were absent. The Secretary was directed to write to the Lord Advocate[1] asking his Lordship to procure for the Council a copy of the above *Report*.

A Letter was read from No. 6, or Edinburgh, Branch of the Scottish Blacksmiths' Society intimating, without any reason being given, the withdrawal of their delegates from this Council. Hereupon the Secretary, being a member of said Society, resigned his office but at the request of the Council agreed to discharge the duties until his successor was appointed. Mr Young returned Burton's *Political Economy* and got out *Social Science Transactions for 1860*.

2 October 1866

Delegates present: Cabinetmakers, Mr Young; Masons, Mr Collins; Plasterers, Mr Aitchison; Slaters, Messrs Munro, Chrichton; Tailors, Mr Troup.[2]

The Secretary read a letter from the Lord Advocate intimating that he had sent to London for a copy of the evidence laid before Parliament on the operation of the Master and Workman's Act for the use of the Council. A vote of thanks was unanimously awarded to his Lordship for his kindness. The subject of Parliamentary

[1] George Patton, Lord Glenalmond, 1803-69, Conservative M.P. for Bridgewater 1866, lord advocate 1866-7, lord justice clerk 1867-9, committed suicide.
[2] Alexander Frazer, the secretary, was also present but no longer as the official representative of the blacksmiths.

Reform was then considered. After a good deal of discussion it was agreed that the Council should by public advertisement in the News-papers call a preliminary meeting of all those favourable to this object, said meeting to be held in Buchanan's Temperance Hotel on Saturday first at 8 o'clock, on the understanding that the Council having taken the initiative the meeting then summoned was to carry on the agitation of this subject and the Council as such then ceased to do anything further.

16 October 1866

Delegates present: Cabinetmakers, Mr Young; Joiners, Messrs Thomson, Duncanson; Slaters, Messrs Monro, Crichton; Tailors, Mr Troup; [and A. Frazer].

The Secretary intimated that he had received a copy of the evid-ence laid before Parliament on the subject of Master and Workman, which he handed to the President. A Letter signed by the Secretary of the Edinburgh Branch of the Joiners Society was read intimating the appointment of three of their numbers as Delegates to the Trades Council. Two of them being present, Messrs Thomson and Duncan-son, were received as such. The subject of Parliamentary Reform was again considered, and after a verbal report had been given of what had been done at the meetings of the 6th and 13th it was agreed to call by public advertisement another preliminary meeting on the 20th and 24th currt.

30 October 1866

There was no business done and the meeting adjourned.

13 November 1866

There was no meeting this evening, the Council being all engaged in the Reform Demonstration to take place on the 17th.

27 November 1866

Delegates present: Cabinetmakers, Mr Young; Slaters, Messrs Monro, Crichton; Tailors, Mr Troup; [and A. Frazer]. It was past 9 o'clock before there was a quorum present.

The Secretary intimated that an application had been made for

the Trades Council to interest themselves and the working classes
of this City in support of an application to the Commissioners of
Works to have the Museum of Science and Art in this City completed. The Council instructed the Secretary to have a memorial
drawn up to be considered next night of meeting and, if approved,
to be signed and transmitted to the Board of Commissioners of
Works, London.[1]

11 December 1866

Delegates present: Joiners, Mr James Thomson; Slaters, Messrs
Monro, Chrichton; Tailors, Mr Troup; [and A. Frazer].

A number of copies of the Rules of the United Kingdom Alliance
of Organized Trades, sent from Sheffield, was distributed to the members of the Council.[2] The Secretary submitted to the Council a
draft copy of the memorial to the commissioners of works in favour
of an extension of the Museum of Science and Art which was after
some slight alterations agreed to. The Secretary was instructed to
have a corrected copy ready for next night of meeting. The Secretary
then brought before the Council the subject of a Working Men's
Association embracing the consideration of subjects both Social and
Political as far as they affect the interests of the Working Classes,
and was heard in support of the same. It was agreed to defer the
further consideration of it till next meeting.

25 December 1866

Delegates present: Cabinetmakers, Messrs Shedden, Young;
Joiners, Mr Duncanson; Slaters, Messrs Munro, Crichton; [and A.
Frazer]. In the absence of the President, Mr Shedden in the chair.

The memorial, as amended, to the Commissioners of works in
favour of an extension of the Museum of Science and Art was
submitted to the Council and, being approved, the Secretary was
instructed to have the same transmitted to London. The Council
then considered the subject of a Working Men's Association. A
long discussion followed and the general feeling was that it should

---

[1] The new building for the museum had been officially opened in May, but work on
the central block and main hall was not completed till some years later.
[2] Above, p. 181.

be delayed until the Working Men's Political Union was completed as it would interfere with its formation.[1]

The treasurer, Mr Collins, being absent through indisposition he sent a messenger, and the Secretary received his half year's salary 15s; for postages, stationery, etc. 2s; paid also for room rent 3s. The Council agreed not to meet till 22nd January 1867, which was to be held as a special meeting for the election of Office Bearers. The Secretary was instructed to summon by letter all those who were absent.

[1] The political union was presumably the Edinburgh branch of the Scottish National Reform League. The branch held its first annual meeting on 5 February 1868. William Troup, tailors, was president. *Scotsman*, 6 February 1868.

1867

22 January 1867

After waiting for some time and not a quorum being present, it was unanimously agreed to adjourn till 19th February and that that meeting should be a special one called by circular. Mr Young returned *Social Science Transactions for 1862*, which Mr Troup got out; also *report of Committee of House of Commons on Master and Workman*, which Mr Munro got out.

Buchanan's Temperance Hotel[1]
High Street
16 April 1867

Mr Troup in the chair. After stating the reasons why the meeting had been called, he read a Letter from Mr Paterson,[2] and also a document from the Royal Commission now investigating into the working of trades unions. He stated that there was no Secretary at present to take notes of the proceedings, and the meeting being asked to nominate one Mr Tarbet[3] moved, Mr Duncanson seconded, that Mr R. S. Laws[4] be appointed Interim Secretary, which was agreed too.

It was agreed that the Council furnish and transmit to the Secretary of the Royal Commission the names and addresses of trades Secretaries. A discussion then arose about the Night of meeting, when it was agreed that thursday first be the next night of meeting for the election of officebearers and reorganization of Council. Mr Duncanson was also elected Interim Treasurer, Messrs Troup, Young and Munro were appointed a deputation to wait upon the

---

[1] This minute was written by J. C. Burn, blacksmiths, who was formally appointed interim secretary at the following meeting.
[2] Presumably William Paterson, secretary of the joiners. See below, p. 193
[3] Not identified.   [4] Painters.

Late Secretary and Treasurer in order to receive the books and all other property belonging to the Council.

14 May 1867[1]

A meeting of members of various trades was held for the purpose of endeavouring to reorganize the trades council. Mr Troup in the chair. A Letter was read from Mr Laws, Interim Secretary, intimating that he was unable to officiate as Secretary. J. C. Burn was elected to act as Interim Secretary. A Letter was read from Mr Holmes, Treasurer to the trades Union Conference in London, which Mr Troup was to reply to.[2] A Circular was also read from Mr Proudfoot, Secretary to Master and Workman amendment act Committee,[3] requesting us to get up a petition in favour of the amendment on said act at present before parliament. It was considered that the council was not in a position to take up the subject.

It was then resolved that a circular be drawn up and printed and issued to the various trades in Edinburgh showing them the necessity for a trades council and requesting them to send representatives. Mr Wilson[4] submitted a draft of circular which he was to finish and hand over to Mr Duncanson to get printed, the same to be issued as soon as possible. Mr Troup stated that the remainder of the funds of the late council were at our disposal to meet the expenses incurred

[1] From this date until 6 August inclusive the minutes were re-written into volume ii of the MS. The few differences between the two versions are footnoted.

[2] The St Martin's Hall trade union conference, which was the immediate forerunner of the Trades Union Congress, had met in London on 5-8 March 1867. J. Holmes, West Yorkshire Miners, was the treasurer of the committee appointed by the conference to prepare the union case for the royal commission. The conference report described William Troup as the official delegate from Edinburgh trades council, but in fact he had been sent not by the council which at that time had been 'in a state of disorganisation', but by office-bearers of several Edinburgh unions. A. E. Musson, *The Congress of 1868* (London, 1955), 22-5; W. J. Davis, *The British Trades Union Congress* (London. 1910), i, 142; *Minutes of St Martin's Hall Trades' Conference Committee, 17 May – 7 August* (London, 1867), note to appendix.

[3] John Chambers Proudfoot, a joiner, secretary of the Glasgow joiners' union in 1854 and of the remodelled Glasgow and West of Scotland society until c. 1861; secretary of the committee appointed by the St Martin's Hall, London, trade union conference of March 1867; secretary of Glasgow trades council from January 1867. *Royal Commission on Trade Unions, 1867, Fourth Report*, 88, 96.

[4] Not identified.

in the work of reconstruction. It was agreed to meet every Tuesday night untill the end of June.[1]

28 May 1867

A meeting of those engaged in reconstructing the trades council was held, Mr Troup in the chair.

A Letter was read from James Ross, Glasgow, requesting our share of the expenses incurred by the Trades Union Committee in London.[2] There was also a parcel of appeals from Coopers' Secretary, Glasgow.[3] It was agreed that such Bussiness could not be taken up during the reorganising of the council. According to instructions received at previous meeting, appeals had been issued to all Trades Associations for which we had the addresses. Eleven trades had responded to it. Representatives from the following trades presented their credentials: George Brown and Robert Strachan, Bakers; Alexander Duncanson and James Kirkwood, Joiners.[4] Mr Troup, Tailor, presented his credentials some time ago.[5] Their were several other trades represented but had not been furnished with credentials. A Conversation then took place anent the Trades Delegates' Anual trip, when the meeting considered it premature and agreed to take no steps in the matter untill the reconstruction of the Council. Mr Munro returned *Report of Master and Workman Act*, the said Book given out to Mr Crighton.

11 June 1867

A meeting of those engaged in reorganising the trades council was held, Mr Troup in the chair. A Letter from Mr Proudfoot, Glasgow, was read makeing rash and false statements on the Edinburgh Trades.

---

[1] If weekly meetings were held they were not all minuted.

[2] This almost certainly refers to the St Martin's Hall conference committee; but it is possible that it refers instead to the expenses incurred by Proudfoot and Alexander McDonald in their Master and Servant Act lobbying. Ross, a joiner, was a delegate to Glasgow trades council and a member of the executive committee in Glasgow on the Master and Servant Act. *Glasgow Sentinel*, 9 March 1867.

[3] The Glasgow coopers had been on strike since January against a reduction of wages. *Glasgow Sentinel*, 2 February 1867.

[4] The version in volume ii of the MS. gives: Duncanson and James Thomson, joiners, and James Kirkwood, joiner, West Branch.

[5] The version in volume ii of the MS. gives Donald McAllan as a tailors' delegate, in addition to Troup.

The Secretary was instructed to reply. Alexander Munro and David Crighton, Slaters, presented their Credentials. Some discussion then took place about the anual excursion of the Trades Delegates, when it was agreed to leave it over till next meeting.

18 June 1867

A meeting of those engaged in reconstructing the Trades Council was held, Mr Troup in the chair. The following parties presented their credentials: John Gunn and R. S. Laws, Painters, and John Watson and John C. Burn, Blacksmiths. Refference being made by Mr Scott[1] to a Letter read at previous meeting from Mr Proudfoot, Glasgow, the Letter was again read, Likewise a copy of reply. After a few remarks the Subject dropt. A General Conversation then ensued regarding the future objects of the Trades Council and other trades matters.

2 July 1867

A meeting of those engaged in reconstructing the Trades Council was held, Mr Troup in the chair. Mr Troup intimated that a deputation from the Tailors would wait upon us to see what steps we intended to take in regard to the cases of prosecution of office bearers of Unions that had recently taken place, but before receiving said deputation it would be necessary to declare ourselves an organised Body. He therefore moved that we declare ourselves constituted The Trades Council of Edinburgh, which was agreed too.

Mr McWhinnie, deputy from Tailors, then stated that warrants had been issued against 5 of the office bearers of Tailors Society in London, not for any act of intimidation but merely because they had combined to endeavour to better their position. The warrant stated that they were attempting to impoverise the employers.[2] Considering also that two cases of the same description had transpired

---

[1] George Scott, glasscutters.

[2] The prosecution arose out of a strike during which employers' shops had been peacefully picketed. Baron Bramwell found the five men guilty of conspiracy and held that pickets, if acting in combination, were guilty of molestation even if they gave black looks only, or were merely present in large numbers. S. and B. Webb, *History of Trade Unionism* (London, 1901 edn.), 262-3.

in Scotland, viz., the Shoemakers in Hamilton,[1] and the Joiners in
Nairn,[2] he thought it necessary that the Trades of Edinburgh should
call a public meeting to give expression to their opinions on these
cases. He also stated that Mr Druitt from London[3] was to deliver
a Lecture in Glasgow on these cases and that if we decided on calling
a public meeting they would endeavour to secure his services, as
he was a very able speaker. He likewise stated that if the Trades
Council was not prepared to call a public meeting at the present
time that the Tailors of Edinburgh intended takeing advantage of
Mr Druitt being in Scotland by calling a general meeting of their
own trade and getting him to address it on these cases already alluded
too. Mr Paterson, Secretary of Joiners' Union,[4] stated that he had
conversed with a number of members of different Trades and that
they were all of one opinion that some steps should be taken in the
matter. Mr Sheddan[5] moved that a public meeting be held, which
was agreed too, the Tailors offering to furnish the money in the
meantime to defray the expenses incurred in carrying said meeting.
Said money to be returned as soon as possible by the Trades Council,
which was agreed too, on the motion of J. C. Burn, seconded by
Mr Duncanson.

Some discussion then ensued regarding the mode of supplying
the funds for the Trades Council. J. C. Burn moved that we adopt
the Glasgow System, viz., 10s. Entry Money for 300, and 5s. for
200 and under. Mr Kirkwood moved that the Entry Money be

[1] The president and secretary of the shoemakers' union at Hamilton had been convicted at the sheriff court there on 29 June of intimidating a union member who had
fallen into arrears with his dues. The men had been charged with threatening a strike
to bring about his dismissal from his employment unless he paid his arrears. Objection
by defence counsel to the relevancy of the charge on the ground that to threaten a
strike was not illegal was overruled by the sheriff, who sentenced each of the accused
to seven days' imprisonment. *Scotsman*, 1 July 1867.
[2] Arising from a strike against the continued employment of a non-unionist, two
carpenters were convicted at Nairn sheriff court on 8 August of unlawful combination
and sentenced to fourteen days' imprisonment. 'The sentence was heard with astonish-
ment by the working men who crowded the court.' *Scotsman*, 10 August 1867.
[3] George Druitt, president of the London Operative Tailors' Association, and one of
the members of the union prosecuted in London.
[4] William Paterson, 1843-1906, secretary of Edinburgh branch of the Associated
Carpenters and Joiners of Scotland, and from 1868-83 general secretary of the union.
For further biographical details see above, pp. xxiii-iv.
[5] Either cabinetmakers or engineers.

N

10s. 300 and upwards, 7s. 6d. for 200 and not 300, 5s. below 200. The motion was then withdrawn in favour of the amendment, which was agreed too. Mr Crighton returned *Report on Master and Workman*. The meeting then adjourned, agreeing to meet the following evening to take further steps in arrangeing for the public meeting.

3 July 1867

Mr Troup in the chair. No deffinate information haveing been received in regard to Mr Druit's coming to Edinburgh, but as he was expected to be here before we could have time to call a general meeting of the trades, the Council resolved to watch the course of events and if necessary call a general meeting of all the trades.[1]

9 July 1867

Mr Laws in the chair. A deputation from Printers' Union was heard, having been sent up by their trade to make enquiries as to what were the future objects of the Trades Council. These being stated, the deputation were requested to remain as we were just commencing to draw up a code of Laws for our guidance. The preamble was considered. Moved by J. C. Burn that we adopt the preamble of the late Trades Council and agreed too. Rule 1st was then taken up: moved by Mr Gunn, Seconded by Mr Strachan that each trade send two delegates. Mr Duncanson moved as an amendment, Seconded by Mr Thomson, that trades numbering 400 and upwards send 3 Delegates. Their voted for the amendment 5, for the motion 6.

Mr Donald Moore and Mr George Scott presented their Credentials as representatives of the United Flint Glass Cutters. Entry Money paid into the funds of the Council: Joiners, per Mr Duncanson, 10s; Joiners, West Branch, per Mr Kirkwood, 5s. The Council then agreed to meet every thuesday Evening untill the completion of the Rules, Bussiness to commence at 5 minutes past 8 and to adjourn at 5 minutes past 10 o'clock.

---

[1] Druitt addressed a meeting of trade unionists in Edinburgh on 5 July on 'Trade Prosecutions', and a resolution was carried unanimously condemning the prosecution of the tailors in London. *Scotsman*, 6 July 1867.

16 July 1867

Mr Troup in the chair. Mr Todd and Mr Munro presented their credentials as representatives of the Edinburgh Typographical Society; also Credentials from Mr Forrest and Mr Webster representing the Amalgamated Society of Engineers. The following trades paid their Entry Money: The Printers, per Mr Todd, 10s; The Painters, per Mr Laws, 10s; The Engineers, per Mr Forrest, 5s; The Blacksmiths, per Mr Watson, 5s.

The Council were waited on by two blind men, deputation from inmates of Blind Asylum. The Secretary read circular stating their case. Deputation then stated the position they were in. Two of their number for a triffling offence had been dismissed the asylum without warning of any description, and they had come up to ask the sympathy and support of the trades of Edinburgh in order that the case might be investigated and Justice properly administired. The deputation then withdrew.[1] It was agreed to take no steps in the matter untill next meetings. The Council devoted the remainder of the evening to the Rules. Rules 2nd, 3rd, 4th and 5th was agreed too.

23 July 1867

Mr Laws in the chair. Mr Donaldson and Mr McColl presented their Credentials as representatives of the Edinburgh Operative Masons. The following Trades paid their entry money: Cork Cutters, per Mr Alston, 5s; Glass Cutters, per Mr Moore, 5s; Bakers, per Mr Strachan, 5s; Tailors, per Mr McAllan, 10s; Masons, per Mr McColl, 10s.

The case of the Blind Men was taken up. After a Long discussion Mr Scott moved, Seconded by Mr Duncanson: That a Sub-Committee be appointed to communicate with the Blind Men or their agents to ascertain all the facts of the case and see in what manner we could assist them, said Committee to have the power to call a special meeting of Council if necessary to give in their report. Agreed too. Moved that Mr Laws, Mr Scott and Mr Moore form Sub-committee and agreed to.

---

[1] The two blind men had ostensibly been dismissed on the grounds of irregular attendance at the asylum chapel. They claimed they attended it more regularly than the chaplain himself. The real reason for their dismissal, they alleged, was their protest against a reduction of wages for some of the inmates. *Scotsman*, 6 August 1867.

The remainder of the evening was devoted to the Rules. Rules 6 and 7, anent Secretary and Assistant Secretaries' duties, was considered and agreed too. A Long discussion then ensued on Rule 8, anent raising a fund to defray the expenses of the Council. It was ultimately moved by Mr Donaldson, Seconded by Mr Duncanson, that the following be the rates of contributions: All trades numbering Less than 200 shall contribute five Shillings, and all trades numbering beyond 200 shall contribute two shillings and sixpence per hundred per annum, but if said sum be found inadequate to meet the expenses incurred by the Council it shall be contributed half-yearly instead of yearly.

30 July 1867

Mr Troup in the chair. The Blind Men's case was taken up, when the Sub-committee gave in their report. But as they had no deffinate information anent the public meeting to be called by Mr Lockyar[1] it was again remitted to them for further information. The remainder of the evening was devoted to the Rules when the whole were disposed off. The Secretary was instructed to have proof sheets by next meeting to place in the hands of members in order to give an opportunity for any alteration or improvement that may be considered necessary before getting them finally printed.

6 August 1867

Mr Todd in the chair. A Copy of Rules was handed to Each Member, including two inserted by the Secretary, viz., fifteenth and nineteenth. Some discussion ensued on rule 15, when it was agreed to with the following addition: after the word 'business' insert 'any member absenting himself for three successive meetings shall be reported to the trade which he represents'; and after the word 'Council' at end of Rule insert 'subject to first part of Rule 17'. Rule 19th was agreed too. Rule anent the election of Office-bearers was then taken into consideration. Mr Duncanson moved,

1 Edmond Beatty Lockyer, evidently an eccentric radical politician. He was sentenced at the High Court in March 1869 to twelve months' imprisonment for opening letters addressed to a lady for whom he was said to have had 'a passion for 30 years'. Lockyer claimed she was his wife. *Edinburgh Evening Courant*, 2 March 1869; *Scotsman*, 23 June and 4 July 1870.

seconded by Mr Webster, That officebearers be elected every six months. Mr A. Munro moved as an amendment, seconded by Mr Crighton, That 12 months be the period. Their voted for the amendment 4, for the motion 9. Moved and agreed too, That no officebearer shall be obliged to hold office longer than four periods. Rule on officebearers' salaries was then taken up, when the following was agreed to in the meantime: That the officebearers of the association receive such salary as may be agreed to from time to time.

The Sub-Committee gave in their report on the case of the blind men, stating the position they had taken in connection with public meeting, after their efforts had failed for want of time in calling a Special Meeting of Council.[1] Mr Scott stated that he had left work on Saturday for that purpose but had failed in calling together a sufficient number of delegates to decide on such important business. Moved by Mr Donaldson, and agreed too, that the Sub-Committee, along with other Members of Council who took part in Public Meeting, co-operate with the agents in this case in their endeavours to bring this matter to a successfull termination. It was also agreed to that Mr Scott's lost time and expenses be paid.

The Secretary was instructed to get all the Books necessary for conducting the Business of the Council, also to copy all Minutes of Meetings of this Council into new Minute Book. The Treasurer was instructed to pay all accounts and have the Books audited before next meeting. Mr Donaldson and Mr Watson were appointed auditors. Seeing business to be disposed of at next meeting was of so great importance it was considered necessary to summon every member, business being the Election of Officebearers and passing of Rules. The Secretary was therefore instructed to summons all members not present.

13 August 1867

Mr Kinlay and Mr Ritchie presented their credentials as representatives of the United Journeyman Bookbinders. Said trade also paid their entry money, 5s. Some discussion then ensued as to the

---

[1] A public meeting of working men on 5 August, with Lockyer in the chair, heard the statements of the blind men. Members of the trades council who were present moved motions that were approved demanding reinstatement of the men, immediate removal from office of the manager, and the placing of the asylum under the supervision of a government inspector. *Scotsman*, 6 August 1867.

admision of others than members. Mr Todd moved, seconded by Mr Watson, That as we had admitted others when sent up by their trade for information, that we make no exceptions but admit all who come on the same mission, which was agreed too.

The Council then proceeded to the election of officebearers. For the office of President, Mr Watson moved, Mr Todd seconded, James Donaldson. Mr Young[1] proposed, Mr Kinlay seconded, William Troup. Mr Troup haveing declined on account of his holding that office for a number of years in the late Council, Mr Donaldson was unanimously elected. For the office of Vice President Mr Watson proposed, Mr Duncanson seconded, Robert Webster. Unanimously agreed too. For the office of Treasurer Mr Burn proposed, Mr Donaldson seconded, George Scott. Unanimously agreed too. J. C. Burn was unanimously elected to the office of Secretary. William Todd was unanimously elected to the office of Assistant Secretary. Messrs Munro, Kirkwood and Moore were appointed Trustees. The auditors then submitted their report. Moved by Mr Todd that it be adopted. Mr Young took exception to the report as not containing any notice of any property other than money handed over by the late Trades Council. But as no reference was made in the Minutes to any other property Mr Young was appointed along with the Secretary to take notes of said property and have it duly minuted.

The Council then proceeded to consider the Rules as printed. The preamble was first taken up when Mr D. Munro stated that the whole were very faulty both as to composition and printing, and suggested that a committee be appointed to revise and lay them before the Council at next meeting. Mr Webster moved, seconded by Mr Strachan, that a committee be appointed, members to state in the meantime any alterations they thought necessary for the consideration of said committee, which was agreed too. Messrs Donaldson, Todd, D. Munro, and Ritchie, along with the Secretary, were appointed as committee. The remainder of the evening was taken up with the members stateing their opinions on the Rules. Mr Todd gave notice of the following motion: That this Trades Council consider the question of the institution of a free public Library in Edinburgh.

[1] Thomas Young, cabinetmakers.

20 August 1867

Letter was read from Secretary of Tinplate Workers stateing that they had appointed Mr Lawson to wait upon us for information regarding the constitution of the Council and report at their next meeting. The Slaters, per Mr Munro, paid their entry money, 5s. The Council then agreed to call the Roll each evening at 9 o'clock.

The Subcommittee submitted the Rules as revised by them for the consideration of the Council. They were agreed too with few slight alterations, the only important alterations being the election of office-bearers yearly and subject to re-election for two periods, instead of half-yearly and four periods; and regular meetings to take place on the second and fourth thursday of every month, instead of every alternate thursday. The Printers [delegates], Mr Munro and Mr Todd, were instructed to get 250 copies printed, with names of delegates present at the formation of the Council. Mr Todd's motion was deffered untill next meeting.

27 August 1867

Mr Young gave in Subcommittee's statement of money and property handed over by the late Trades Council, Council consisting at that time of Delegates from Tailors, Slaters, Cabinetmakers. The Joiners also had been represented for a short time. Inventor of property: £4 8s. 6½d. handed over on the 16th April. Also 1 vol. Blue Book *Report from the Select Committee on Master and Workman Equitable Councils of Conciliation*; 2 vol. Blue Book *Combination of Workman*; 1 vol. J. Hill Burton's *Political and Social economy*; 1 vol. Dr Blakie's *Better days for Working people*; 3 vol. *Reports of Social Science Meetings* of the years 1861-62-64, held in Glasgow, Dublin and Edinburgh; 2 vol. present and former of Treasurer's Account Books; 1 vol. Secretaries Minute Book, now completed, commenced in 1849.[1] Also a chest to hold these with letters and other documents. There had been formerly lost *Report of Social Science meeting* in London. There should also have been 2 copies of Acts of Parliment in the Box, which are not found. Mr Young also stated that a 1,000 copies of Professor Archer's Leture, delivered at the instance of the Council, had been printed by them, about a dozen of which were found in

---

[1] This should almost certainly read 1859.

the Box.[1] After a carefull investigation of the Treasurer it was found that only 736 were accounted for, leaveing 252 (21s. worth) either never supplied or appropriated by those who were the custodiers. Also amissing a Letter from Lord Brougham. It was thought that Alexander Frazer, Secretary to the late Trades Council, ought to be able to give an account of the missing property. Mr Young and Mr Burn were therefore appointed to wait upon Mr Frazer.

The Chairman then gave a short address on his appointment to that office. He moved that a vote of thanks be awarded to Mr Troup for the able manner in which he fulfilled the duties of that office, which was unanimously responded too. Payment of interim office-bearers: after several sugestions it was decided that the Secretary receive 10s. and payment for lost time, 6d. per hour. Mr Todd then submitted motion given notice of on the 13 August, viz., The institution of a free Public Library in Edinburgh. After giving a brief account of action he had taken on that subject previously, he moved that a subcommittee be appointed to consider the whole matter and report at next meeting, which was agreed too. The following members were appointed for said committee: Mr Todd, Mr Webster, Mr Donaldson, Mr Kirkwood, Mr Gunn, Mr A. Munro and Mr Burn. The following trades handed in a copy of their rules: Printers, Joiners, Bookbinders, Blacksmiths. The Secretary was instructed to issue a copy of Rules to all the Trades not represented, along with an appeal urging them to send up Delegates.

10 September 1867

A Letter from Alexander Frazer in answer to one from the Secretary anent missing property was read. The Secretary was instructed to reply. Also Letter from Sabbath Protection Association requesting a hearing for deputation on the Subject of the relation the Working Man bears to the Sabbath as a day of rest. On going to the vote it was decided to grant a hearing to said deputation. Printers Account of £1 8s. for printing Rules was then submitted to the meeting. The Treasurer was authorised to pay the same. A vote of thanks was then awarded to Mr D. Munro and others of the committee for the time and attention they had devoted in drawing up said rules. Free

[1] Above, pp. 80-81.

Library Committee then gave in there report. Its adoption was moved by Mr Duncanson and agreed too. Mr Todd stated that as Mr Bright was in Scotland it would be a great advantage to get him to deliver an address on the institution of Free Libraries.[1] The Committee were instructed to endeavour to Secure Mr Bright's Services for that purpose.

Mr Duncanson moved that a Sub-Committee be appointed to wait upon the Trades not represented to urge upon them the necessity of sending delegates to the Trades Council, which was agreed too. The following members were appointed: Mr Laws, Mr Watson, Mr Kinlay, Mr Ritchie, Mr McAllan. Mr Strachan gave notice of the following motion: That the Trades Council consider the case of Several Employers in the Baker trade employing young lads at hours in violation of the Law. Masons and Engineers handed in a copy of their rules.

24 September 1867

Letter from Mr Hartwell,[2] Secretary to Crystall Palace Banquet Committee, was read requesting the Trades Council to send a deputation to said Banquet.[3] Mr Watson moved, Mr Munro[4] seconded, that no delegates be sent, which was agreed too. Letter from Mr Fleming, Skinner, was then read bringing before the Council the desireability of haveing Mr Disraeli to address the Working Classes on his approaching visit to Edinburgh.[5] Letter from Mr Disraeli in answer to one from Free Library Committee was then read declining for want of time to address the Working classes of Edinburgh. But seeing that there was a probability of Mr Bright being in Edinburgh, the Committee was authorised to communicate with Mr Bright requesting him to address or take part in a Public Meeting Convened by the Trades Council for the advocacy of the institution of Free Public Libraries. But whether

[1] The *Saturday Review*, 28 September 1867, implies that Bright was salmon-fishing in Scotland at this time. No other evidence of his presence north of the border has been found.

[2] Robert Hartwell.

[3] To celebrate the passing of the Reform Bill the London Working Men's Association held a fête and banquet at Crystal Palace on 30 September over which George Potter presided. *Glasgow Sentinel*, 5 October 1867.

[4] Either Alexander Munro, slaters, or Daniel Munro, printers.

[5] Disraeli visited Edinburgh from 29 to 31 October 1867.

Mr Bright consented or not the Committee were instructed to endeavour to secure a number of the prominent speakers in Edinburgh and others who were favourable to the scheme.

The Secretary then gave in Statement from Mr Young, Cabinetmaker, stating that his Trade, on account of a press of business, had not appointed delegates to the Trades Council at their late meeting and requesting permission to attend the meetings of Council untill the next meeting of their Trade, which was granted. But to prevent the establishing of a bad precedent he was not to be allowed to vote. Deputation from Sabbath Protection Association was then heard on the relation the Working Man bears to the Sabbath as a day of rest. A vote of thanks was awarded to the deputation for the clear manner in which they had brought the Subject before the Council. Mr Watson moved that we delay consideration of said subject untill next meeting, which was agreed too.

Motion given notice of by Mr Strachan at previous meeting was then taken up, when Mr Todd moved that a Subcommittee be appointed to draw up a resolution embodying the opinions of the Council on that case, the same to be inserted in the newspapers. This was agreed too. The committee to consist of Mr Strachan, Mr Laws, Mr Troup, Mr Kinlay, Mr Todd. Received from Painters, per Mr Gunn, the sum of 7s. 6d., being their amount of contributions. Mr Munro handed in copy of Slaters Rules. Mr Watson gave notice of the following motion: That this Trades Council consider the expediency of Soliciting Ernest Jones to deliver an address to the working men of Edinburgh on the occassion of his visit to Glasgow to deliver one there.[1]

8 October 1867

Mr Laws in the chair.[2] Letter from Mr Gentle, Secretary to Printers Society, was read showing the manner in which Trades Unions inflicted injuries upon one another. Mr Gunn moved that consideration of said Letter Ly over till next meeting, which was agreed too.

---

[1] Ernest Charles Jones, 1819-69, Radical and former Chartist leader. Under the auspices of the Working Men's Political and Social Reform Association Jones had lectured in Glasgow on 10 October on 'Labour and Capital with reference to Trade Unions and Strikes'. *Scotsman* 11 October 1867.

[2] Donaldson, the president, was present later.

Several copies of printers circular was also handed in for distribution amongst the various Trades, also certificate from Bakers Union appointing James Crichton as Delegate in Room of George Brown.

Free Library Committee then gave in their report Stateing what progress they had made in secureing the Free Assembly hall for public meeting. Letter from John Bright was also read intimateing that there was no probability of his being in Edinburgh for some time and therefore could take no part in public meeting. Mr Todd stated that several gentleman that had been called upon advised the holding of a preliminary meeting for appointing of speakers for the various resolutions and to make all the necessary arrangements. On the motion of Mr Duncanson it was agreed that said meeting be held. The committee were also authorised to purchase act of parliment on Free Libraries. Mr Scott and Mr Strachan were added to committee.

Subcommittee on Bakers case then gave in there report stating that they had drawn up a resolution and had it inserted in the newspapers.[1] The Sabbath question as brought up by Sabbath protection association was then considered. After a long discussion, no definite conclusion being arrived at, the subject was allowed to drop. Mr Donaldson directed the attention of the delegates to a Letter that appeared in the *Scotsman* against the Masons Union and trades unions in general.[2] He then requested permission to use the name of the Council in answering said letter. It was agreed to appoint a subcommittee to act along with Mr Donaldson in answering said Letter. On the Council proceeding to nominate a Subcommittee he withdrew the motion, stateing the Masons would perhaps answer it themselves.

The following Trades paid there Share of Contributions into the funds of the Council: Corkcutters, per Mr Alston, 5s; Printers, per Mr Todd, 15s; Joiners, per Mr Duncanson, 15s; Engineers, per Mr Forrest, 5s. Motion given Notice of by Mr Watson anent Ernest

[1] The resolution drew attention to cases where the regulations of the Bakehouse Act had been violated by the employment of lads under eighteen between 9 p.m. and 4 a.m., and by failure to ensure cleanliness of bakehouses. *Scotsman*, 25 September 1867.
[2] The letter was from a journeyman mason whose adherence to the principle of 'free labour' and refusal to rejoin the union had precipitated a strike the week before. He urged the formation of an anti-union association. *Scotsman*, 7 October 1867.

Jones was then taken up. Mr Laws moved that a Letter be sent to that Gentleman requesting him to deliver an address in Edinburgh, which was agreed too.[1] Some conversation then ensued on the position of the funds of Trades Unions at the present time. Mr Todd suggested that as Mr Moncreff was about to address his constituents, questions should be put to that Gentleman regarding the course he would pursue in Legislating for Trades Unions. The Free Library committee were instructed to carry out Mr Todd's suggestion.[2]

23 October 1867[3]

Letters from the following parties was read: one from Mr Proudfoot, Glasgow, anent expenses incurred by Trades Union Conference in London; one from Mr Begg, Dundee, anent Free Library;[4] from Mr Turnbull, Secretary to Lithographers Society, stateing that they were unable at present to send Delegates to the Council; also certificate from Corkcutters appointing Mr John Alston as their Delegate at the Council. Mr Proudfoot's Letter was then taken up, when it was decided that as we had no connection with the conference and the position of our funds precluding us from giving any aid in defraying the expenses, the Secretary write to him accordingly.[5] Printers Letter anent Co-operation read at previous meeting was then taken up. Mr Todd moved that it Ly on the tabel untill they were able to bring it before the Council in a more practical form, which was agreed too.

Free Library Committee then gave in their report stateing that they had secured the Free Assembly Hall for public meeting, also

---

[1] Jones had already addressed a workmen's meeting in Edinburgh in January. He seems not to have returned to the city until 2 September 1868 when under the auspices of the Reform League he lectured on 'The Politics of the Day'. *Democracy Vindicated: Lecture by Ernest Jones in Edinburgh, 4 January 1867* (Edinburgh, n.d.); *Reformer*, 5 September 1868.

[2] Moncreiff declined on 11 October to give a categorical answer to a deputation from the trades council who asked 'whether he was in favour of amending the legislation in regard to trade unions and if so what restriction he thought should be put on that legislation'. *Scotsman*, 12 October 1867.

[3] The date should probably be 22 October 1867.

[4] Peter Begg, 1819-85, shoemaker, active Radical, leader of the free library campaign in Dundee.

[5] The conference was the one held in St Martin's Hall, London, on 5-8 March 1867. See above, pp. 190-1.

that the Lord Advocate, Gordon,[1] and Dean of Faculty, Moncrief,[2] had consented to take part in the proceedings. The Committee also gave in a report of the answers given by Mr Moncrief and Mr McLaren on the Legalising of Trades Unions. Mr Duncanson moved that a paragraph be inserted in the newspapers intimating That this Council record its entire approval of the clear and satisfactory manner in which Mr McLaren has explained his opinions on the Subject of Trades Unions and their legality, which was agreed too.[3] The Council then adjourned, agreeing to hold a Special Meeting on Tuesday the 29 of October for the purpose of appointing Speakers and makeing other arrangements for public meeting on Free Library question.

29 October 1867

A Special Meeting was held, the Business being the appointing of Speakers and makeing other arrangements for public meeting. It was agreed that the meeting take place on the 19th of November, the Secretary to read report of the action taken by the Trades Delegates on the subject. The Speakers from the Council to be Mr Todd and Mr Laws. The Committee were empowered to make all other necessary arrangements. The Treasurer presented account from Mr Wilson, Printer, for printing proof sheet of Rules (15s.) and was authorised to pay the same.

5 November 1867

Certificate from Joiners was read intimating that Mr Alexander Duncanson and Mr James Horn were appointed to represent their trade at the Council.[4] Mr Kirkwood directed the attention of the

[1] Edward Strathearn Gordon, Baron Gordon, 1814-79, lord advocate 1867-8 and 1874-6, Conservative M.P. for Thetford 1867-8 and for Glasgow and Aberdeen Universities 1869-76; lord of appeal 1876-9.
[2] James Moncreiff, M.P., dean of the faculty of advocates 1858-69.
[3] At a public meeting the previous evening McLaren had been asked by J. C. Burn, secretary of the trades council, if he would support a Bill to legalise trade unions. McLaren replied that unions ought to have legal protection for their funds and the right to prosecute defaulters and embezzlers. He believed these aims would be achieved not by a separate Bill to legalise unions but by an extension of the provident and friendly societies Acts to include unions prepared to submit their rules to the scrutiny of the registrar. *Scotsman*, 23 October 1867.
[4] They almost certainly represented the central branch.

Council to a Statement in the report of Trades Union Conference in London representing Edinburgh Trades Council to have contributed nothing towards defraying the expenses of said Conference and hoped that we would pay our share. The Secretary was instructed to write in conformity with previous minute on that subject. Free Library Committee then gave in there report. Letters were read from the Duke of Buccleuch[1] and Sir David Brewster[2] intimating their inability to preside at public meeting; from Lord Justice General Inglis consenting to preside;[3] 2 from Hugh Rose, Esquire,[4] anent said meeting. The Council then proceeded to make all other necessary arrangements for public meeting.[5]

26 November 1867

Mr Troup drew the attention of the Delegates to the part [in the Minutes of previous meeting] relating to the demand made on the Council for aid in defraying the Expenses incurred by the Trades Union Conference in London. After a long discussion the subject was allowed to drop. Certificate was read from Secretary of Brassfounders Union appointing Mr John McDonald and Mr John Lawrie to represent their Trade at the Trades Council. Said trade also paid there entry money (5s.). Free Library Committee then gave in there report of Public Meeting held in Free Assembly Hall and recommended that the city be canvassed for signatures in favour of said Library. Mr Burn moved, Mr Horn seconded, that we canvass the city and endevour to get as many signatures as possible, which was agreed too. Mr Forest then submitted a proposed act of Parliment relating to combinations and Trade Societies, for the consideration of the Council at next meeting.

---

[1] Walter Francis Scott, 1806-84, fifth duke of Buccleuch and seventh duke of Queensberry.
[2] Principal and vice-chancellor at Edinburgh university.
[3] John Inglis, Lord Glencorse, 1810-91, lord justice general 1867-91.
[4] Hugh Rose, 1806-91, founder of an oil and paint firm Craig and Rose; a leading supporter of Duncan McLaren; first lay president of the Baptist Church. *Scotsman*, 28 December 1891.
[5] Two of his judicial colleagues, Lords Ardmillan and Neaves, shared the platform with Lord Inglis at the meeting; E. S. Gordon, the lord advocate, sent apologies for absence. *Scotsman*, 20 November 1867.

10 December 1867

Letter was read from Mr Crighton, Delegate from Bakers Association, intimating his resignation on account of his time being fully taken up with his usual employment. The Slaters, per Mr Munro, paid 5s., being their share of contributions into the funds of the Council. The Delegates then proceeded to consider a proposed Act of Parliment relating to Combinations and Trade Societies drawn up by Several Trades in London.[1] After a thorough consideration of said bill the Council came to the unanimous decision that it was totaly inadequate to meet the requirements of a Trade Society and, seeing that some differences existed between the Laws of Scotland and England, this Council endeavour to get a Bill drawn up to meet the wants of Trade Societies in Scotland. The Secretary was instructed to write to London accordingly. Consideration of Bill for Scotland to be deffered till the next meeting. The Treasurer gave in report of income and expenditure and present state of funds. Mr Todd gave notice that he would bring up for consideration at next meeting the necessity of endeavouring to get all trades represented at the Council.

24 December 1867

Mr Duncanson in the Chair. The Free Library Committee stated that they intended to suspend operations untill the festive season was over. The motion tabled by Mr Todd at previous meeting was then taken up, viz., the necessity of getting all the Trades represented at the Council. Mr Todd stated that seeing that the committee formerly appointed to wait upon the Trades had never taken action he moved that a small committee be appointed for that purpose.[2] Seconded by Mr Gunn, and agreed too, the appointing of committee to be deffered till next meeting on account of the absence of a number of the members.

The Council then proceeded to consider the Legalising of Trades Societies. Mr Todd moved that a committee be appointed, with power to add to their numbers from there various Trades, in order

[1] The Bill had been drawn up by the Conference of Amalgamated Trades, with the help of Professor E. S. Beesly, Frederic Harrison and other middle class allies. The Conference had been formed in January 1867 and was in effect the 'Junta'. A. E. Musson, *The Congress of 1868* (London, 1955), 21, 27.
[2] Above, p. 201.

to define the various points wherein Trade Societies require Legal protection, prior to waiting upon the Lord Advocate[1] to Solicit him to draw up a bill for that purpose. Seconded by Mr Burn and agreed too. The following members were appointed to the committee: Messrs Donaldson, Strachan, Troup, Todd, Webster, Horn, Gunn, Kirkwood, Kinlay, Lawrie, Alston, Scott and Burn. Mr Todd gave notice of the following motion: That this Council consider the provisions of the factory act.

[1] E. S. Gordon.

1868

14 January 1868

Mr D. Munro in the chair. Letter was read from Secretary of Cabinet-makers stateing that at a general meeting of his trade it was decided not to send representatives to the Trades Council at present. Also certificate from Secretary of Bakers, appointing Mr James Wightman in Room of James Crighton, resigned. A committee was then appointed to wait upon the various trades not represented, viz., Mr McDonald, Mr Watson, Mr Todd, and Mr Kirkwood. Two auditors were appointed, viz., Mr Gunn and Mr Strachan, to audit the Books before next meeting. The Legalising of Trades Unions was then brought up, when the Secretary stated that owing to some missunderstanding in the committee as to there night of meeting nothing had been done in the matter. It was agreed to meet on Thuesday the 21st, the Secretary to summon all members not present.

Motion tabled by Mr Todd at Last Meeting was then taken up, viz., that the Council consider the provision of the factory act. Mr Todd moved, Mr Watson seconded, the following resolution . . . to be inserted in the newspapers;[1] also that a deputation be appointed to wait upon the Lord Advocate to make enquiries as to the carrying out of the act. Mr Strachan, Mr McDonald, and Mr Burn were appointed deputys. The Blacksmiths, per Mr Watson, paid 5s., being their amount of contribution into the funds of the Council.

28 January 1868

The Subcommittee appointed to wait upon the Trades not represented stated that they had not had any opportunity to wait upon any of these Trades but were endeavouring to find out their nights

---

[1] Not found in the press.

o

of meeting. Mr Gunn and Mr Strachan, Auditors, then gave in their report, stateing that they had examined the Books and Vouchers and found them correct, but suggested that the Secretary keep a check of all monies received and paid by the Council, which was agreed too. The committee appointed to consider the Legalising of Trades Unions stated that the Committee had met and after considering the question had appointed a deputation to wait upon the Lord Advocate to confer with him upon that subject. The members of deputation were Messrs Todd, Troup, Dewar,[1] Kirkwood, McDonald, Lawrie, and Burn.

The deputation to his Lordship on the Factory Act stated that they had met with a very courteous reception and that his Lordship stated that all the provisions of the Act would be carried out. Some conversation ensued on the position of the Bakers. They having a special act for themselves[2] did not come under the Workshop Act. Mr Strachan and Mr Wightman stated several greiveances in their trade and that Legislation was necessary to have these greiveances removed. Mr Todd moved that a Subcommittee be appointed to confer with the Bakers to see if nothing could be done in the matter, which was agreed too. Messrs Todd, Donaldson and Duncanson were appointed a committee.

11 February 1868

Mr Duncanson in the Chair. Certificate was read from tinplate workers association certifying that Mr John Smith and Mr Peter Lawson were appointed to represent their trade at this Council. Also certificate from Plumbers Association certifying the appointment of Mr William Angus and Mr Thomas Gilles to represent their trade at this Council. Mr McDonald, Convener of Agitation Committee, reported that the Iron Moulders and Tinplate workers had been waited upon and that the deputations were favourably received by both Trades. Mr Scott then asked the Council to receive a representative from the Glasscutters who wished some information in regard to the payment of delegates. Permission having been granted the gentleman stated that a general conference of his trade had been held and the question he had come upon was the remunera-

---

[1] Andrew Dewar, blacksmiths.
[2] Bakehouse Regulation Act, 1863.

tion of Delegates. He would feel indebted to the Council if the delegates would state what their trades allowed to members when delegated upon Society business. Several members haveing stated the remuneration allowed by their Societies it was agreed that any other who could give information on that subject was to leave it with Mr Buchanan[1] and it would be called for.

Deputation to the Lord Advocate on the Legalising of Trades Unions then gave in their report stateing the various points they had gone over with his Lordship, viz., the protection of the funds, the right to sue and be sued, the Separation of the Trade and provident funds, and other minor points. The remarks of his Lordship seemed to be very favourable. He also thanked the deputation for the information he had derived during the conference. Committee appointed to act with the Bakers stated that they had met with the Bakers and had drawn up a number of questions to be issued through the various Bakehouses to elicit the necessary information to lay before the Lord Advocate in order to have their greiveances redressed. Mr Todd directed the attention of the Council to a meeting of the Royal Society of arts, where a paper by Mr David Smith on Trades Union was read, also to the remarks by members of said Society.[2] After some consideration the Secretary was instructed to draw up a resolution embodying the opinion of the meeting and have it inserted in the newspapers.

25 February 1868

Mr Duncanson in the chair. An appeal from the Conference of the Amalgamated Trades in London in Support of their proposed Act of Parliment on Trades Societies was read.[3] It was agreed that the Secretary correspond with the various Trades Councils throughout the Country to get there opinion on that subject. Circular from the Manchester and Salford Trades Council anent a proposed Congress of Trades Councils was then read.[4] Mr Todd moved that it Ly on the table for future consideration, which was agreed too. Mr Gray, Glass Maker, then stated that he had been appointed to represent

---

[1] Proprietor of Buchanan's Hotel.
[2] No published version or report of the paper has been found.
[3] See above, p. 207 and n. 1.
[4] When it met in June the Congress became the first Trades Union Congress.

his trade at the Council untill the district meeting of the Trade when he expected regular representatives would be sent. Agitation Committee stated that they had waited upon the plasterers and that they seemed to be favourable [to sending representatives to the Council].

Free Library Committee then stated that they intended to resume action on that subject and asked full power to carry the subject to a final issue, which was agreed too. Certificate from the Moulders' Association was read appointing Mr Thomas McFarlane and Mr Robert Watson to represent their trade on the Council. The present Lockout of the Moulders was then taken into consideration.[1] Messrs Watson and McFarlane stated the particulars. After several members expressing there opinions on this case it was agreed to call a special meeting when the Moulders would furnish all the necessary documents, said meeting to be held on Thursday the 27th.

27 February 1868

A special meeting was held for the purpose of considering the present Lockout of the Iron Moulders. Deputation from the Moulders attended and gave a detailed account of the Lockout. After a thorough consideration of the case it was agreed to insert a paragraph in the newspapers recommending the various Trades to assist the Moulders in their present emergency. Also that a Public Meeting be held to Lay there case before the Public. A committee was then appointed to carry out the above resolutions consisting of President, Vice President, Treasurer, Secretary, Assistant Secretary, Mr Watson[2] and Mr Forest. A vote of thanks was then awarded to the deputation for the clear and satisfactory manner in which they had Laid their case before the meeting.

3 March 1868

A Special Meeting was held for the purpose of makeing arrangements for Public Meeting. Mr Duncanson in the chair. The

[1] The lockout had begun on 1 February throughout Scotland when the union, whose members had already had their wages reduced 2s a week, refused to agree to remove restrictions on overtime and on the ratio of apprentices to journeymen. *Scotsman*, 3 February and 12 March 1868.
[2] Probably Robert Watson, moulders, but could be John Watson, blacksmiths.

Secretary read the Minutes of previous meeting also report from Committee appointed at Special Meeting stateing that a paragraph had been drawn up and inserted in the newspapers, copies of which had been printed by the Moulders and handed to the Delegates. Also that they recommend the Public Meeting to be held in Queens Street hall or Princess's Theatre. Also that there were not sufficient funds in the Council to carry out said meeting. It was agreed that a Levy be made upon the Trades according to Rule and that the meeting be held in Queens Street Hall on Wednesday the 11th inst. The meeting then suggested various Speakers. It was remitted to the committee to make all the necessary arrangements. Messrs Kirkwood, Kinlay and Gilles were added to the Committee.

10 March 1868

Mr Duncanson in the chair. The Minutes of regular and two Summoned meetings were read. After takeing notice of some remarks at previous meeting and the omission of a motion by Mr Todd,[1] Mr Moore moved there adoption, seconded by Mr Gray and agreed too. The following contributions were paid into the funds of the Council: Plumbers, first contributions, 5s; Moulders, Entry Money and Contributions, 15s; Joiners, Second Contributions, 15s; Joiners, West Branch, Second Contributions, 5s; Corkcutters, Second Contributions, 5s; Engineers, Second Contributions, 5s; Brassfounders, 5s; Bakers, Second Contributions, 5s; Painters, Second Contributions, 7s. 6d.

An appeal from British Plate, Spoon and Fork Filers Society [Sheffield] was then read. Mr McDonald moved that the Secretary write stateing our circumstances and that we were not in a position to give any aid in the meantime. Circular from Manchester and Salford Trades Council anent Conference remitted from previous meeting was again remitted for future consideration.

The Moulders case was then taken up. Mr Duncanson stated that the Edinburgh Branch of Joiners Association had unanimously recommended their Society to grant £300[2] to aid of the Moulders. Mr Strachan stated that £7 had been given by the Leith Branch

---

[1] This seems to refer to Todd's motion on 25 February about the circular from Manchester and Salford Trades Council.
[2] Possibly this is an error for £30.

of Bakers Association, Mr Alston that the Corkcutters had given £5 and £5 on Loan, and several others stated that their trades were makeing regular weekly subscriptions. The committee then stated that resolutions were drawn up for Public Meeting, the first resolution to be moved by Mr McWhinnie,[1] seconded by Mr Wilson,[2] the second moved by Mr Gray, seconded by Mr Dewar.[3] No speakers being appointed for the third, Mr McDonald agreed to move and Mr Lawson to second it. The President being absent and not being sure of his presence at Public Meeting there was some difficulty in getting a chairman. Ultimately the Secretary Agreed to take the chair in the event of no other being found but to write to Mr Donaldson stateing that the Council were depending upon him takeing the chair. The Treasurer stated that seeing that we were calling upon the Trades for a Second Contribution and that the Masons and tailors had not paid their first they ought to be called upon for the same. The Secretary was instructed to write accordingly.

PUBLIC MEETING

Queens Street Hall
11 March 1868

A Public Meeting convened by the United Trades Delegates was held. Resolutions were submitted and carried unanimously condemnatory of the course pursued by the employers in the Iron Moulders case and maintaining the right of workmen to combine. The meeting also pledged its support to the Iron Moulders in their present struggle. It was also agreed to transmit the principal documents in this case to the Lord Advocate and other prominent members of the house of Commons by way of illustrating the latest development of the Trades Unions of Capitalists. A Letter from Edmond B. Lockyer, Esq., was also read expressing his sympathy with the Moulders, also kindly sent five pounds in aid of the cause. A vote of thanks was heartily awarded for his generosity. A vote of thanks was also awarded to Mr Skimming, Secretary of Moulders Association, for the clear and satisfactory [manner] in which he

[1] John McWhinnie, tailors.
[2] William Wilson, engineers.
[3] Andrew Dewar, blacksmiths.

had stated their case.[1] A vote of thanks having been awarded to the chairman the meeting then adjourned.

24 March 1868

Mr Duncanson in the chair. Certificates was read from United Operative Bricklayers of Edinburgh appointing Mr James Park and Mr John . . .;[2] also from the United Operative Plasterers appointing Mr David Laing and Mr George Thain, and from Painters Association appointing Mr Alexander Smillie to represent their respective Trades at the Council Board. The following Contributions were paid into the funds of the Council: From Plasterers, per Mr Laing, 7s. 6d. Entry Money and 7s. 6d. Contributions; Plumbers, per Mr Gillies, first and Second Contributions, 10s; from Bookbinders, per Mr Kinlay, Second Contributions, 5s; from Tinplate Workers, per Mr Lawson, 5s. Circular from Manchester anent Conference remitted from previous meeting was then read. After a thorough consideration of our financial position it was agreed on the motion of Mr Gray, seconded by Mr Gunn, that the Secretary be instructed to write to Manchester stateing that though highly approveing of the object they had in view we were not in a position to take part in said conference.

The Moulders case was then taken up. Mr Watson stated that the Moulders in Dundee had resumed work. A number had gone in on the employers' terms but the remainder had been allowed to resume work without signing the agreement. All the other members were still holding out. Glassmakers stated that they had resolved to assess themselves 2d. per week, also that they had submitted a motion to their society for a grant of £5. Plumbers stated that they had agreed to assess themselves 2d. per week. Bookbinders had subscribed £3 6s. 6d. Printers had granted £5 from their funds and were making weekly subscriptions. Tinplate workers and Painters were makeing voluntary subscriptions. Engineers and Bricklayers had motions before their societies for aid to the Moulders. The Secretary was instructed to get the principal documents in connection with

[1] Robert Skimming, general secretary of the Scottish Iron Moulders' Union 1867-9; died 1869 or 1870. H. J. Fyrth and H. Collins, *The Foundry Workers* (Manchester, 1959), 48.
[2] His surname is not given in subsequent minutes either.

this case before next meeting for the purpose of sending copies to the Lord Advocate and others. Mr Gray gave notice that he would bring before the Council at next meeting the necessity of a National Association of all the Trades Unions.

14 April 1868

The Vice President[1] in the chair. Certificates were read from Flint Glass Makers appointing Mr Robert Gray and Mr Joseph Hall, also from Leith Branch of Journeyman Bakers Association appointing Mr James Wright and Mr William Kerr, to represent their respective Trades at the Council Board. Glassmakers, per Mr Gray, paid 5s. Entry Money and 5s. Contributions; Leith Bakers, per Mr Wright, paid 5s. Entry Money and 5s. Contributions into the fund of the Council. The Secretary read Copy of Letter sent to Manchester anent Conference. Mr Todd then stated that he had communicated with Mr Redgrave, H.M. Inspector under the Factories Extension Act,[2] and had received several copies of said Act which were distributed to the members of Council. He also read a Letter from Mr . . .[3] stateing that he would be happy to give us every information in his power. Mr Todd was instructed to reply thanking that Gentleman for his Kindness.

Committee on Bakers case then gave in their report. Having taken the opinion of the trade on the various greiveances a report had been drawn up summary of which was read by Mr Todd. A hearty vote of thanks was then awarded to the committee for the clear and able manner in which they had drawn up said report, after which it was left in the hands of the committee to lay before the Lord Advocate.[4] Motion given notice of by Mr Gray was then taken up, viz., the necessity of a National Association of all trades unions. Mr Gray in a long speech pointed out the position of the workmen and the strong necessity for thorough unity. It was agreed on the motion of Mr McDonald, seconded by Mr Gray, that a special meeting be called to consider said question, meeting to be held on

---

[1] Robert Webster, engineers.
[2] Alexander (later Sir Alexander) Redgrave, inspector of factories 1847-91 (chief inspector from 1878).
[3] Redgrave, no doubt.
[4] Above, p. 211. The lord advocate was E. S. Gordon.

Tuesday evening 21st inst. The Moulders case was then taken up when the principal documents in connection with this case were remitted to the Bakers committee, with the addition of Mr Gray, to lay before the Lord Advocate.

21 April 1868

A special meeting for the purpose of considering the subject of a national association of all trades unions for trade purposes. After a thorough consideration of the subject it was the opinion of the meeting that the workmen were not sufficiently combined in their respective trades to render such a movement successfull at present and that a committee be appointed to advocate the cause of unionism in the various trades. The appointing of committee was delayed till next meeting.

28 April 1868

The Council proceeded to appoint a committee for advocating the cause of unionism amongst the trades, as agreed upon at Special Meeting. A committee was appointed consisting of Messrs McDonald, Gray, Todd, Laing and Burn. A Letter was then read from Mr Colston,[1] Honorary Secretary to the acting committee of the Royal Medical Infirmary Building fund, anent raising subscriptions among the working classes. Mr Todd moved, seconded by Mr Gray, that a special meeting be called to meet with a deputation from acting committee to confer with them upon the subject, which was agreed too. It was also agreed to hold said meeting on Saturday 2nd May. Mr Gunn gave notice that he would bring up the subject of the admission of labourers into the Trade Council. Mr Todd gave notice of motion that the Council consider the question of Foreign Labour. Mr Todd moved that the various Delegates report the particular diseases to which the members of their respective trades were subject too, which was agreed.

2 May 1868

A Special Meeting was held, object being to confer with a deputation from the acting Committee of the Royal Infirmary building fund.

[1] James Colston, 1830-97, an Independent Liberal town councillor 1865-82.

Deputations attended and gave a detailed statement of the movement and the support it had elicitied from the wealthier classes, and
strongly recommended the object to the attention of the Council.
The deputation, after receiving the thanks of the Council, retired.
The Council then proceeded to consider the question, when it was
agreed that the Council form itself into committee to raise subscriptions among the working classes and that a subcommittee be
appointed to make all preliminary arrangements, the subcommittee
being Messrs Wright, Kinlay, McDonald, Ramsay,[1] Gunn, Gray,
Lawrie, Donaldson, and Burn. On the motion of Mr Webster it
was recommended to the committee to get subscription books
instead of sheet as being more suitable for handing about through
large workshops.

12 May 1868

Bakers Committee gave in their report. Mr Strachan read letters
for[2] J. S. Mill, M.P.,[3] H. Fawcett, M.P.,[4] and Jacob Bright, M.P.,[5]
also a Letter from Bakers National Association. Assistant Secretary
read letter from Mr Skimming, also letter from Mr McLaren, M.P.
The Secretary was instructed to write to Mr Skimming for additional
information regarding the termination of Moulders dispute. Mr
Gunn then brought up the question of the admission of Labourers
to the Trades Council. It was agreed on the Motion of Mr Todd
that it be remitted to the agitation committee to invite the Labourers
to send Delegates to the Council.

Report on Diseases of Trades was then taken up. It was agreed that
the subject ly on the table. Mr Todd brought forward the question
of Forign Labour. It was resolved that a Special Committee be
appointed to confer with forign Consuls on the subject. The
Committee to consist of Messrs McDonald, Forrest and Thain.
Mr Forrest then gave notice of motion anent annual holidays.

---

[1] Not identified.
[2] Should probably read 'letters from'.
[3] John Stuart Mill, 1806-73, philosopher and economist, Radical M.P. for Westminster
1865-8.
[4] Henry Fawcett, 1833-84, the blind professor of political economy at Cambridge
1863-84; Radical M.P. for Brighton 1865-74 and for Hackney 1874-84.
[5] Jacob Bright, 1821-99, Radical M.P. for Manchester 1867-74 and 1876-85 and for
Manchester South 1886-95; brother of John Bright.

16 May 1868

A Special Meeting was held for the purpose of distributing subscription books and makeing other arrangements in connection the
Royal Infirmary Building fund. Mr Gunn presided. Two letters
from Mr Colston accompanying 3,031 Books was read. Some
discussion ensued on the time to commence agitation in Leith. It
was decided to delay calling a public meeting for 1 month. Books
were then distributed to a number of the members.

29 May 1868[1]

The Vice President[2] in the chair. Certificate from Slaters Association
was read appointing Mr Walter Clark, in room of Mr A. Munro, to
represent there trade at the Council. 2 Letters were read from Glasgow Workman Association,[3] 1 anent proper Trades Society Bill,
the other asking if we had any connection with the Elcho Banquet
Committee. Also a Letter from Mr Proudfoot, Secretary of Committee on the Masters and Servants Amendment act. Also a copy of
address to be presented to Lord Elcho. After a long discussion it was
agreed that said letters be answered and that a protest be put in the
newspapers against the Elcho Committee assuming the name of the
workmen of the United Kingdom in presenting the address to that
gentleman.[4]

Mr Forrest brought forward motion given notice of at last meeting anent the establishing of annual holidays. On the motion of Mr
Todd, seconded by Mr Wightman, it was agreed to delay discussion

[1] The date should probably read 26 May 1868.
[2] Robert Webster, engineers.
[3] The Glasgow Working Men's Association for Political and Social Reform had been
formed on 14 August 1867 as 'a means of promoting further political reform and
especially aid in obtaining those great social reforms for which an extension of the
franchise had been chiefly sought'. Its general council was composed of delegates from
local unions, which subscribed to its funds on a voluntary basis only. The Association,
and its allied body the Conference of United Trades Delegates formed in March
1868, seem to have carried on most of the work of the trades council, which was
'dormant' from 1867 to 1871. *Reformer*, 19 December 1868 (quoting the first annual
report of the Association), and 11 March 1871.
[4] Lord Elcho, 1818-1914, Conservative M.P. for East Gloucestershire 1841-6 and
independent conservative M.P. for Haddingtonshire (East Lothian) 1847-83. As chairman of the Select Committee on the Master and Servant laws, 1866, he was entertained to a banquet in Glasgow on 5 June and presented with an address by the Executive Committee of which Proudfoot was secretary. *Glasgow Sentinel*, 6 June 1868.

of said subject till next meeting. Several members then gave in their report of progress in circulating the subscriptions books for the Royal Infirmary throughout the various workshops.

9 June 1868

Copies of letters sent to Glasgow anent the Elcho Banquet were read, also reply from Mr Proudfoot. The question of the establishing of annual holidays was then brought up for consideration. It was decided not to take any steps in the matter. Deputation from Labourers' Association were then admitted. Agitation Committee stated that they had waited upon the Labourers and that they had agreed to send up a deputation to the first meeting. The deputation then stated that they had come up to ascertain the constitution and objects of the Trades Council so that they might report at their next meeting. These having been stated and copies of the rules handed to the deputation they intimated that their next meeting took place on the first Tuesday of July and that they would be happy to receive a deputation from the Council on that evening.

Mr Gray stated that according to former statement £5 had been handed to the Iron Moulders by the Glassmakers' Association. Infirmary business was taken up. After several members had given in their reports it was agreed to call a special meeting on Tuesday the 16 inst. to hear reports and make other arrangements. A vote of thanks was then awarded to the Deputation from the Labourers.

16 June 1868

A Special Meeting was held, Mr Gunn in the chair. Business: to hear reports and make other arrangements on the Infirmary business. Subcomite gave in report of their meeting with the Acting Comite. Application had been made to the acting comitte for subscription book. But they had given none as the matter was entirely in the hands of the Trades Delegates and we were expected to extend our operations to all under the designation of employees, with a few exceptions in the higher orders; also to give our work every publicity. The members then gave in report of progress made. Some discussion ensued on the using of Books in more than one shop. It was ultimately left to the discretion of the members. Public Meeting in Leith was then taken up, when it was remited to Mr Wright and Mr Kerr, Delegates from Leith, with power to add to their number, to make enquiries about a place of meeting and arrange about speakers and report at next meeting. Mr Todd then read Letter for insertion in the papers. Mr Todd was instructed to insert the same. The Secretary was instructed to summon delegates whose report had not been given in.

23 June 1868[1]

Mr Kirkwood presiding. A Letter was read from Mr Marshall soliciting the assistance of the Council in the working out of the arrangements of an Association for Improving the Condition of the Poor.[2] Mr Marshall stated that what was wanted was the personal co-operation of the constituents of the Council. The letter was ordered to lie on the Table.

The Leith delegates, Messrs Wright and Kerr, reported result of interview with Provost[3] and other influential gentlemen in Leith who seemed anxious to assist the movement to the best of their ability. It was moved that the meeting on the Rebuilding of the Medical Hospital be held in Leith on July 2, and that the other arrangements be left in the hands of the Infirmary Committee with the necessary powers. It was moved, seconded, and agreed to that the following Delegates second the resolutions at Meeting in Leith: Messrs Gray, Lawson, and Todd. Mr Gillies reported progress in connexion with Infirmary business for the Plumber trade, Mr Strachan made a statement concerning the Bakers' subscription. Mr Forrest, Engineer, returned nine books. It was moved by Mr Gunn and seconded by Mr Todd that considering the position of the Infirmary collection at Meadowbank that a courteous letter be sent to the Manager of the works soliciting his assistance with one hundred subscription books. A deputation from Emigration

---

[1] The minutes from this date until 14 July inclusive were written by William Todd, assistant secretary.

[2] The Association was formed as a result of the collapse of a tenement in the High Street in 1861 when thirty-five people were killed. Its objects included 'discouraging mendicancy, idleness and dissipation'. Marshall was presumably T. R. Marshall who became the Association's treasurer in 1881. Rev. Thomas Brown, *Alexander Wood* (Edinburgh 1886), 145; Oliver and Boyd's *Almanac*, 1870.

[3] James Watt, provost of Leith 1866-74.

Association waited upon the Council and were courteously received. The Treasurer was authorized to prepare financial abstract.

4 July 1868

A special meeting was held for the purpose of considering the Appointment of two Acting Secretaries to gather in and agitate subscriptions from working-classes. Mr Gray was called to the chair. Mr Gray explained the wish of Mr Boyd[1] in this matter, and suggested that a nomination should take place. It was resolved that the following delegates duly nominated be voted for at next meeting of Council: Messrs Lawson, Gray, Ritchie and Todd.

7 July 1868

A Special Adjourned Meeting was held, Mr Kinlay in the Chair. Business: the election of Secretaries to act on Infirmary business for working-class subscription. There voted for Mr Gray, 10, Mr Ritchie 3, Mr Lawson 0, Mr Todd 17. Messrs Gray and Todd were declared elected. The letter from Mr Marshall mentioned in minute of June 23 was again read, when it was ultimately agreed to allow it to lie on the table for the consideration of an ordinary meeting.

It was agreed that the consideration of the financial abstract with the position of trades not having paid their proper subscriptions be taken into serious consideration. It was likewise agreed that in the event of any delegate not being able to overtake his Infirmary subscription books that the secretaries be informed and relieve the delegate of the burden. A certificate was handed in and read appointing Mr John Bennet, in lieu of Mr James Wightman, resigned, to represent the Edinburgh Branch of the Operative Bakers National Association.

14 July 1868

Mr Kinlay in the Chair. The letter from Mr Marshall was read and after consideration it was agreed, after a division, that it be intimated to Mr Marshall that the Council cannot as a Council enter into it.

[1] Thomas Jamieson Boyd, K.T., 1818-1902, lord provost of Edinburgh 1877-82, partner in Oliver and Boyd, the publishers, convener of acting committee for rebuilding the Infirmary.

Mr Scott asked what was to be done with the annual accounts. It was agreed that the Secretary write the various trade secretaries intimating their obligation to the Council. A Committee consisting of Messrs Ritchie, Kinlay and Treasurer [was appointed]. It was stated that the acting Committee[1] wished minute of appointment of secretaries and what would be the wage per week. On the motion of Mr Burn it was agreed that the wage should be at the rate of 30s per week, and that they should keep an account of their expenses.

Mr Todd gave in Free Library Report which caused a considerable amount of discussion first in relation to the statement in the report that the opposition had been caused to a considerable degree by persons designated 'Independent Liberal shopkeepers'. It was moved that that statement be expunged from the report and that the committee be disolved, which was carried by a considerable majority. It was stated that the Agitation Committee had waited upon various trades for the purpose of helping them in their attempts to reorganize their unions. Likewise that the Joiners had given in a statement of the diseases peculiar to that trade. A letter was read from Trades Union Commission Secretary. Reply ordered to same. It was likewise agreed to take up the election of office bearers first on the roll of business.

25 July 1868[2]

Mr Kinlay in the chair. On the yearly financial abstract being read it was resolved that the Glassmakers and Leith Bakers be exempt from first Half yearly subscription on account of the Date of their Entry. It was moved, seconded and agreed to that the sum of £3 be Given to Mr Burn in recognition of his Service as Secretary during the Past Year, also that the sum of 10s be given to Mr Scott, Treasurer, on the same consideration. The following Gentlemen were duly elected officials of the Council: President, Mr William Kinlay, Bookbinder; Vice-President, Mr White;[3] Secretary, Mr Robert Gray, Glassmaker; Treasurer, Mr George Scott, Glasscutter; Assistant Secretary, Mr Horn. On the question of the annual statment

---

[1] For the Infirmary rebuilding fund.
[2] The date should probably read 28 July 1868.
[3] William White, joiners, central branch.

being taken up it was agreed that Messrs Burn, Ritchie, Gray, Scott and Todd form a Committee to draw up the same.

4 August 1868

A Special Meeting was held to consider Business connected with the Rebuilding of the Medical Hospital Royal Infirmary. After reports had been given by Messrs Todd and Gray, it was moved by Mr Gunn, seconded by Mr Lawson, that a report of all moneys paid by delegates be given in at next meeting. Agreed to. A complaint was then made by Mr Lawson regarding the treatment he had recieved from Mr Hall, High Constable,[1] after which it was moved and seconded that a deputation from the Council go along with Mr Lawson to see Mr Jamieson[2] regarding the same. Deputies: Mr Bennet, Baker, and Mr Lawson. Messrs Todd and Gray then requested the Council to elect a Finiancial Committee to aduit thier Books when it was agreed that Mr Horn and Mr White should form said committee. It was also agreed that Messrs Todd and Gray should advertise thier appointment by the Council as superintendents of contributions among the Trades.

11 August 1868

Letters were read by the Secratery from Mr Blanchard, Leith High Constables,[3] Mr Neilson, secretary Amalgamated Engineers, Leith, and Mr Donaldson, Mason's Delegate. A motion tabled by Mr Gunn was taken up. After a short discussion it was unanimously agreed that all business connected with Rebuilding the Medical Hospital be done at special meetings called for that purpose. Certificates were then read from the Bookbinders' Society appointing Mr William Kinlay and Mr George Hills Delegates to Trades Council for the next year. A certificate was also read from the Associated Carpenters and Joiners Society appointing Mr David Croall Delegate in room of Mr James Kirkwood, who is out of town. Certificates were also read from the Painters Society appointing Mr John Gunn and Mr James Kennedy Delegates to the Council for next 12 months.

---

[1] Thomas Hall, junior, secretary of Edinburgh high constables 1868 and president 1871-2.   [2] Not identified.
[3] George Blanshard, wholesale druggist and manufacturing chemist, moderator of Leith high constables 1868-9.

A circular was then read from the Conference of Amalgamated Trades on the Bill now being introduced into the House of Commons by Sir Thomas Fowell Buxton on Trades Unions.[1] After an animated Debate a Resolution to the following effect was unanimously agreed to, viz., That the act introduced by Mr Buxton on the Legality of Trades Unions is inefficient in Principle and Defective in the Means Proposed for the Legalising of Trades Societies. A conversation then took place regarding the Representation of the City in Parliament when it was agreed that a committee should be formed to draw up a series of questions on Trades Subjects, to be submitted to Candidates at the first opportunity. The following members were then elected: Mr Burn, Mr Scott, Mr Smith, Mr Strachan, Mr Bennet, Mr Gunn, Mr Horn, Mr Todd, Mr White, Mr Kinlay, Mr Gray. Mr Kinlay paid over the sum of 5s as subscription for second year to Council fund.

18 August 1868

A Special Meeting was held. A report was given in by the various Delegates relative to the present position of the various trades subscriptions towards rebuilding the Medical Hospital of the Royal Infirmary. It was then moved and seconded that if any member of Council extend his labour beyond Edinburgh on that business he shall report the same at first meeting of Council. Agreed to. A report was then given in by Mr Bennet of the Deputation that waited on Mr Jameson. Mr Wright's motion[2] was then taken up when it was unanimously agreed to that all money collected by the various delegates should be brought to the Council meetings and paid over to the appointed Secrateries, Messrs Todd and Gray, they having to attend each meeting at $\frac{1}{2}$ past seven oclock to recieve the same.

25 August 1868

A Certificate was read from the Edinburgh Branch of Operative Bakers appointing Mr Peter McEwan as Delegate in room of

[1] Sir Thomas Fowell Buxton, 1837-1915, Liberal M.P. for King's Lynn 1865-8. He introduced the Bill, which had been drawn up by the 'Junta' and their allies, on 7 July 1868. See above, pp. 207, 211.
[2] Not previously mentioned.

P

Robert Strachan, resigned. A Report was then given in by Mr Gray of the meeting of Bakers held in Leith, a deputation from the agitating committee having addressed the same on the utility of Trades Councils. A unanimous vote of thanks was awarded to the deputation. Mr Gray introduced the question of Legalising Trades Unions, also refering to the obnoxious state of the Combination Laws. After a very animated and Lenthy Debate it was moved by Mr Bennet, seconded by Mr Gunn, that a meeting should be called consisting of office bearers of every Trade Society, to consider the best means of bringing the whole subject before the Public. It was also agreed that the circular calling such meeting should be printed. A disscussion also took place regarding the drawing up of the annual report when it was moved and seconded and agreed to that Mr Burn should be communicated with regard to the same.

8 September 1868

A long debate took place regarding the postponment of the meeting on the Combination Laws, after which the subject dropt. It was then moved by Mr Munro, seconded by Mr White, that a copy of the Combination Laws should be purchased by the Council. Agreed to. It was moved and seconded that a Special Meeting be held to consider the Combination Laws and discuss the same on Tuesday first. The question of the annual report was then taken up. It was moved by Mr Bennet, seconded by Mr McEwan, that a note should be sent to Mr Burn to ask him if he will draw up the Report and when. Certificates were given in and read from the Edinburgh and Leith Branch of Amalgamated Slaters of Scotland appointing Mr Alexander Shankie delegate to represent them at this Council.

A motion was then tabled by Mr Hills on infirmary business: That Mr Todd and Mr Gray give in a report of moneys uplifted by them from week to week since there appointment as collectors and handed over to the Acting Committee, exclusive altogether of monies paid over to them by Delegates of Trades Council, also the expenses attending the same and that the said report be submitted to a Special Meeting of Council called for that purpose as early as possible. It was moved and seconded that a special meeting should be held on Thursday week to consider the same. Agreed to.

15 September 1868

A Special Meeting was held. An agreement had been come to Between Mr Burn, Mr Kinlay, Mr Scott, and Mr Gray to draw up the annual Report on any night that will be convenient for them, to be left to themselves to Settle. The Combination Laws were then Produced and Read by the secratery, after which a Lenthened and animated Debate took Place regarding thier effect on Trade Unions Generally. It was moved by Mr Burn, Seconded by Mr Bennet, that the Debate be ajourned until the next ordinary meeting. Agreed to. Mr Todd then suggested that someone should Prepare a Paper on the subject. Mr Todd agreed to Prepare the same.

17 September 1868

A Special Meeting was held. The motion of Mr Hills was taken up. Mr Gray stated that although the terms of the motion were not that a report was to be given in that night yet Mr Todd and himself had Prepared one. It was to the effect that since the appointment of Mr Todd and himself as Superintendents of Subscriptions amongst the Working Classes they had collected upwards of four Hundred Pounds, about three Hundred and fifty of which had been Paid into the Acting Committee and the remainder was to be Paid on next Day when they gave in their report for that week. The Expenses connected with the same were up to the 12th inst. thirty three Pounds one shilling. He also stated that they had recieved about thirty five Pounds of the sum which was Handed to the Acting Committee from the Delegates at Council Meetings, also that they had about 3 Hundred Books out in Edinburgh and Leith and 67 in the Country. The Council then approved of the report Given in. Mr Burn mentioned that a copy of the accounts ought to be Kept for the council, which was agreed to. The Motion not being Pressed, The Subject Dropt.

22 September 1868

Mr White, vice President, in the Chair. Mr Todd Gave in a report of the Deputation sent to the Horseshoers' Meeting, which was approved off. The Secretary stated that a Deputation from the Coopers had waited on him requesting a Deputation from the

Council to come and address a General Meeting of thier Trade in the Phenox Hall on Thursday Night, October 1st. Messrs Tod, Watson[1] and Gray agreed to form said Deputation. Mr Tod then read a very able Paper on the Combination Laws, which was warmly recieved. An animated Discussion took Place on the Same. It was moved by Mr Watson, Seconded by Mr Burn, That it is the opinion of this Council The Present Combination Laws are unjust, one-sided and acts very injuriously to Trade Unionists; Therefore ought to be swept of the Statue Book of the Country. Agreed to.

13 October 1868

Mr White, Vice President, in the Chair. There was also Present a Large representation of the office Bearers Connected with Trades represented at Council. A Deputation from the Labourers' Society waited on the Council requesting a Deputation to address a Public Meeting of thier Body in St Giles's Hall on the 3rd November. The request was complied with and Left over to the agitation Committee to arrainge Matters. It was stated by a representative of the Joiners that Mr John Bright, M.P. for Birmingham, was coming to Edinburgh to recieve the freedom of the City and thought some measures should be taken by the Council to Welcome him. It was agreed upon to Hold a special Meeting on Friday night, October 16, to consider the same, The Office Bearers to communicate the Same to Councillor Grieg[2] and make the nessesary arraingments. The Questions Drawn up by the Committee to be submitted to candidates for Members of Parliament were then gone into and after a Protracted Conversation agreed to.[3]

16 October 1868

A Special Meeting was Held. Mr White, Vice President, in the Chair. A Deputation consisting of Councillor Grieg, Mr Murray[4] and Mr Tunny[5] waited on the Council. Councillor Grieg gave a

---

[1] Both references to Watson in this minute may be to either Robert Watson, moulders, or John Watson, blacksmiths.
[2] John Greig, junior, an Independent Liberal and head of the printing firm mentioned below, p. 311.
[3] Above, p. 225.   [4] Not identified.
[5] J. G. Tunny, a photographer and calotypist.

minute account of the arraingments which had been made regarding
Mr Bright's visit, and urgently invited the Council to co-operate
with the independent Liberal Committee in making his reception as
Cordial as Possible. It was moved by Mr Burn, seconded by Mr
Gray, that this Council Draw up an address to be Presented to Mr
Bright at the Meeting in the Corn Exchange. Unanimously agreed
to. A Committee was then appointed to draw up said adress consisting of the following members: Mr Tod, Mr Burn, Mr Gunn,
Mr White, Mr Monro, Mr Kinlay, Mr Scott and Mr Gray. It was
also agreed to that a Special Meeting be held on Friday, 23 October,
to hear the report of the address committee.

Mr Burn then called the attention of the Council to the efforts
now being made by the London Trades to carry the Trade Union
Bill. It was arrainged that all members not on the address committee
should meet on Tuesday first to consider the same.

23 October 1868

A Special meeting was held. Mr White, vice President, in the Chair.
Mr Burn gave in a report of the action the committee had taken on
the Trade Union Bill and also read the Correspondence he had
regarding the same. The report having been unanimously aproved
of a vote of thanks was awarded to the committee, who were
requested to continue.

Councillor Grieg then waited on the Council and gave a further
Report of the arraingments he had made for the Meeting in honour
of Mr Bright in the Corn Exchange. Regarding the allocation of the
Tickets Mr Grieg Promised to Give the Council about one half of
the Tickets at his Disposal. A vote of thanks was awarded to Mr
Greig after which he Retired. Mr Todd then read the address drawn
up by the Committee to be Presented to Mr Bright. An objection was
raised by Mr Scott to that Part of it refering to the Benifits that free
Trade had confered on the Working Classes. After a Lenthened
Debate it was moved by Mr Scott, seconded by Mr Lawson, that
that Clause be ommitted. On the motion being Put it was Lost,
only two (mover and seconder) voting for it. It was then moved
by Mr Horn, seconded by Mr Bennet, that the thanks of the
Council be awarded to the address committee for thier Labours.
Awarded. A Conversation took place as to who should read

the address. It was settled that it was the Secretary's Duty to read the same.

27 October 1868

Mr White, Vice President, in the Chair. The Secretary gave in a report of his interview with Mr Grieg stating also that he had recieved 1,200 Tickets for Mr Bright's Meeting. The report being approved of the Tickets were allocated to the represented trades at the ratio of 26 Per Cent, the allocation to take Place according to the contribution Roll. It was then agreed that the Council meet on Tuesday night, 3rd November, and that the Secretary write to Mr Grieg regarding the Tickets of addmission for Members of Council.

3 November 1868

A Special Meeting was held. The Secretary read the correspondence he had with Mr Grieg. After a Protracted Discussion regarding the arraingements for Mr Bright's Meeting it was moved by Mr Monro, seconded by Mr Kennedy, That the address from the Council to Mr Bright be read from where the Delegates are Placed. An amendment was Proposed by Mr Watson,[1] Seconded by Mr Gray, That the address be read from the Platform wether the Delegates were there or not. There voted for the amendment 9, for the motion 17. It was agreed that the Council would meet again next night, the Secretary to communicate the Discision of the Council to Mr Grieg. Mr Burn then introduced the Letter sent to *The Scotsman* by Mr Scott and strongly denied the right of Mr Scott to use his official Position in the Public Press without the Consent of the Council. After a Long and Stormy Debate the Question was ajourned until another meeting.[2]

4 November 1868

The ajourned Meeting of Council took place, Mr Gunn in the chair. The Secretary gave in a report of what had passed between him and

[1] Either Robert Watson, moulders, or John Watson, blacksmiths.
[2] George Scott, glasscutters, treasurer of the trades council, claimed in his letter to the *Scotsman* of 2 November 1868 that the council had not spontaneously asked John Bright to receive an address but had been got to do so by a deputation from the Independent Liberals.

Mr Grieg stating also that Mr Grieg had agreed to wait Personally
on the Council. Mr Greig entered and immediatly laid before the
Council the whole of his arraingments expressing his regret that
anything he had done had not met with thier approval. But as it
was out of his Power to alter the arraingments which had been come
to he hoped the Council would see thier way to agree to them. Mr
Grieg then retired. A Debate took Place as to the competency of the
Council Discussing the Motion carried Last night, When the Chairman Put it to the meeting and it was carried by a considerable
majority that it was Perfectly competent. It was then moved by
Mr Watson,[1] Seconded by Mr Horn, that in consequence of the
arraingments being complete and the impossibility of getting re-
served seats, our office Bearers Present the address from the Platform.
Mr Scott moved an amendment, seconded by Mr Kennedy, that
we adhere to the original Resolution of Council, Mr Grieg having
used the Council unfairly in assigning Platform Tickets to strangers
and ignoring us as working men. The motion was carried by a
majority of 14 against 5.[2]

10 November 1868

The Secretary read two Letters he had recieved from the Secretary
of the Glasgow Working Men's Association for Political and Social
Reform. A Letter was also read from the Secretary of the Tin
Plate Workers anent the annual report and other matters, when after
some Explainations by Mr Lawson it was moved by Mr Monro,
seconded by Mr Burn, That the Secretary write to Mr Robin and
call his attention to the Laws of the Council. Agreed to. Mr Todd
gave in a report of the Labourers Meeting which was approved of.
    The Secretary of the Leith Bakers Association was then introduced
to the Council and gave in a report of his correspondence and inter-
views with the Candidates for the Leith Burghs and read over the
answers given by Mr Millar[3] to the Questions Drawn up by the
Council some weeks ago.[4] After recieving the thanks of the Council

[1] Either Robert Watson, moulders, or John Watson, blacksmiths.
[2] Bright was duly presented with a lengthy address from the trades council at the
Corn Exchange meeting on 5 November. *Scotsman*, 6 November 1868.
[3] William Miller, Radical M.P. for Leith.
[4] Above, pp. 225, 228.

Mr Robertson retired. It was moved by Mr Todd, seconded by Mr Gunn, that a copy of these Questions be sent to Mr D. McLaren and Mr John Miller,[1] requesting an answer in two Days. An amendment was Proposed by Mr Burn, seconded by Mr Scott, that a Deputation wait on the above named gentlemen with the Questions. The amendment was carried by a Large majority. The following members was then appointed to form the Deputation: Mr Burn, Mr Scott, Mr Kinlay, Mr Watson.[2] The Secretary was requested to communicate with Mr McLaren and Mr Millar requesting them to meet the Deputation and suggest Saturday afternoon as the most convenient time.

Mr Burn then formally read the annual Report Drawn up by him when it was agreed that the Council meet to consider the same on next Tuesday night. Mr Gunn tabled the following motion: That no Business be taken up by this Council But by written Documents through our Secretary and that no verbal statement be acted or Depended on for the future. Mr Horn also Tabled the following Motion: That this Council come to some resolution to Prevent members from Publishing in the Newspapers any matter whatever under the title of Trades Delegates, unless by Consent of Council.

17 November 1868

A Special Meeting was held. The Secretary read the correspondence he had had with D. McLaren, M.P., regarding the deputation appointed by the Council to wait on him. Mr Burn then gave in a report of the Deputation's interview with Mr McLaren which was approved off and a vote of thanks Passed to the Members. Mr Burn tabled a number of copies of the Statistical report drawn up by Mr McLaren of the attendence of Scotch Members of Parliament and how they voted, same copies being a Donation from Mr McLaren to the Council. On a motion of Mr Gray, seconded by Mr Horn, a vote of thanks was awarded to Mr McLaren for his Gift. Mr Gray then intimated that if any Party had tickets which were not Duly honoured at the meeting in honour of Mr Bright in the Corn Exchange they would have them cashed by handing

[1] John Miller of Leithen was elected with Duncan McLaren on 16 November 1868 as Radical M.P. for Edinburgh and sat till 1874.
[2] Either Robert Watson, moulders, or John Watson, blacksmiths.

them over to him. The annual report drawn up by Mr Burn was then read when after considerable Discussion it was carried by a majority that the first Portion of the report relating to the reorganisation of the Trades Council be approved of, the remaining Portion to be taken up at next meeting. Mr Dewar[1] tabled a motion on the factory act.

23 November 1868[2]

Mr White, Vice President, in the Chair. The Secretary read the Minutes of Previous ordinary and special meetings. Objection was taken to the Minute recording a vote of thanks to Duncan McLaren, M.P., for his Donation of copies of Statistical attendance of Scotch Members in the house of Commons. The objection was overruled and the Minutes approved off by a Large Majority. Certificates were then read from the Secretary of the Labourers' Society intimating the appointment of Patrick Duffy and Hugh Lundy as Delegates to represent there Body at the Trades Council.

The annual report was taken up. It was moved by Mr Monro that the same be refered to a Select committee. Mr Scott moved an amendment that the report be gone into by the whole Council. Mr Monro's motion was carried. The following Gentlemen were then Elected to form said Committee: Mr Todd, Mr Monro, Mr Scott, Mr White, and Mr. Gray. The Motion Previously Tabled by Mr Gunn was then taken up: That no business be taken up by this Council But by written Documents through the Secretary, That no verbal statement be acted or Depended on for the future and that the Council arrainge all its important affairs and not to rely on the Discretion of its office Bearers. The same was agreed to. Mr Horn then introduced the motion he had tabled on the Previous Meeting and briefly stated his objections to members of Council rushing into the Public Press without first consulting the Council. The general opinion was that it would be left to the honour of the members to abstain from writing in the Press on subjects which ought to be settled by the Council alone.

The following motion was tabled by Mr Scott: That the attention of Council be drawn and a Vigilance Committee appointed to take

---

[1] Andrew Dewar, blacksmiths.
[2] The date should probably read 24 November 1868.

notice of the action of the Association for improving the Condition of the Poor[1] as to keeping a list of unemployed for the use of Employers of Labour. Mr Gunn tabled the following Motion: That Mr Bright's address be considered at next Meeting. Motion by Mr Lawson: That the Council take no active part in any Public or Political Matter without the Previous Sanction of thier Respective Trades the Majority of which shall Determine what action shall be taken.

8 December 1868

The Secretary read two Letters he had recieved from George Robertson, late Secretary of the Leith Bakers Society, anent the holding of a Public Meeting to establish a Trades Council in Leith.[2] A letter was also read from The Secretary of Journeymen Upholdsters' Society wishing information regarding the Constitution, Composition and Qualifications of Trades Council Membership, with a Copy of Rules, with a view of Joining the Council. The Secretary was instructed to answer and furnish the same.

Mr Lawson then took up the motion tabled by him on the previous meeting. Mr Moore seconded the same. It was lost by a majority of 10 against 3, Three members not voting. Mr Dewar introduced the motion on the factory act he had previously given notice of. Mr Todd seconded the motion. It was unanimously agreed to appoint a committee to draw up a petition to be presented to the Town Council by members of that body who would be afterwards selected. A Committee was then appointed consisting of the Office Bearers and Mr Todd, all Powers to arrainge Business being left to them, also that a Special Meeting be held on Friday 11 inst to hear thier Report. Mr Todd then read a Heading he had Prepared for the Memorial which the Council unanimously agreed to.

The Report of the Committee was read by Mr Monro stating the Progress they had made with the Annual Report. The Council having heard the same it was left to the standing committee to have the Report Printed by next ordinary meeting. Mr Scott refered to certain monies paid to him after the auditing of the books and asked

[1] Above, p. 221, n. 2.
[2] If a meeting was held no report of it has been found.

whether he would be allowed to enter the same in the report. Agreed that the same should be entered.

Mr Gunn then called the attention of the Council to some Business connected with the Infirmary and requested that a Special Meeting be held to consider the same. Agreed that a Special Meeting be held on Tuesday 15th inst. The Chairman then read the following notices of motion. Moved by Mr Lawson, That this Council request some member of Parliament to introduce a Bill in behalf of Trades Unions in Scotland into Parliament having for its object the right to Pursue and be Pursued at the Civil Court by a Trust, also the right to refuse his Services at the end of his Contract on any Ground he may think Proper. Moved by Mr Dewar, That this Council take up the question of reducing the hours of Labour with the view of instituting a national agitation for the adoption of 50 hours as a week's work. Moved by Mr Gray, That this Council enters its Solemn Protest against the Demolition of the houses of the Working Classes under the City improvement act[1] and the Building of Middle Class houses in thier Place, Thereby inflicting a serious injury on the Poorer Portion of the community by crowding them into Places that is already overcrowded. Mr Todd then moved, and Mr White seconded, that Mr Marwick, City Clerk,[2] be communicated with regarding the rents of the houses Proposed to be built, the number of Persons Evicted, and the number of houses to be erected. The motion was unanimously agreed to. Mr Todd tabled a motion asking the Council to Elect three Honorary Presidents, Proposing James Moncrieff, Esq., Lord Advocate, Mr E. Grant Duff[3] and Duncan McLaren, Esq., M.P., as such.

11 December 1868[4]

A Special Meeting was held. Mr Gray gave in a report of the Deputation appointed to wait on Councillor David Lewis,[5] stating that

---

[1] The Edinburgh Improvement Act, 30-31 Victoria c. 44.

[2] Sir James David Marwick, 1826-1908, town clerk of Edinburgh 1860-73, and of Glasgow 1873-1903.

[3] Mountstuart Elphinstone Grant Duff, 1829-1906, Liberal M.P. for Elgin Burghs 1857-81, under-secretary of state for India 1868-74.

[4] In the MS. this minute is preceded by that of 15 December.

[5] David Lewis, 1823-1909, a journeyman shoemaker who set up a chain of bootshops throughout Scotland; active prohibitionist and author of temperance publications. For

Mr Lewis was highly Pleased with the action of the Council in supporting his motion on the appointment of Local Inspectors to carry out the Provisions of the Factory acts in the Town Council. He would be very Glad to delay his motion until a Future Meeting of the Town Council in order to give us time to have our Petitions ready to be presented. Mr Todd then Tabled the Printed Memorials and Name Sheets which were distributed to the various Delegates.

15 December 1868

A Special Meeting was held on Infirmary business. Mr Gunn made some remarks regarding the Position of the Council with regard to the Expenses connected with the appointments of Mr Todd and Mr Gray as Superintendents, complaining of Mr Gray recieving Payment for his Labour on Gathering subscriptions for rebuilding the Medical Hospital. Mr Gray then gave in a report of his connection with that work which was recieved with every satisfaction by the Council. Mr Watson[1] moved, Mr Gray seconded, that a committee be appointed to look over the accounts and report, Mr Watson, Mr Dewar, Mr Gunn and Mr White to form said committee.

22 December 1868

Mr White, Vice President, in the Chair.[2] Proof Sheets of the annual Report were Laid on the Table. It was agreed to That the Report be read over and considered before going into any other Business. Mr Todd then went over Minutely the various questions mentioned in the Report. Mr Watson[3] moved and Mr Croall seconded That the report as read be approved of, which was unanimously agreed to. Mr Gunn moved a vote of thanks to the Committee which was duly accorded. It was unanimously agreed to that 500 copies be

---

some time editor of the *Reformer*, Lewis was an Independent Liberal town councillor 1863-73, but declined nomination for the lord provostship in 1872 on temperance grounds, since he disapproved of the provision of alcohol at civic ceremonies. *Scotsman*, 14 April 1909.

[1] Both references to Watson in this minute may be to either Robert Watson, moulders, or John Watson, blacksmiths.

[2] Kinlay, the president, was evidently present later.

[3] All three references to Watson in this minute may be to either Robert Watson, moulders, or John Watson, blacksmiths.

printed. Mr Kinlay asked if there was to be a Title Page added to the Report. Mr Monro stated that no title page was intended. Mr Kinlay then moved, Mr Kenneddy seconded, that a Title Page be added. But on a Division the Motion was lost by a Large Majority. The Memorial to the Town Council was then taken up. It was moved by Mr Watson and seconded by Mr Gillis that a Deputation be appointed to Present the Memorial to the Town Council on Tuesday 29th inst., the same being agreed to. The following Gentlemen were then Elected members of Deputation: Mr Gunn, Mr Watson, Mr Lawson, Mr Scott, Mr Laing, Mr Gillis, Mr Crighton,[1] Mr Shankie and Mr Gray, with power to add to thier number. It was also arrainged that a Special Meeting of Council be held on Monday Evening, 28th inst., at which all Memorial Sheets were to be handed in.

Mr Gray then intimated that owing to his being out of a Situation and the Possibility of him having to Leave the Town he had to tender his resignation of the Secretaryship and requested that at next meeting the Council would Elect a Successor in his Place. Mr Monro requested that the 3s. 6d. struck out of the Report be entered in the Minutes. Agreed to.

28 December 1868

A Special Meeting was held. The Secretary read the correspondence he had with Mr Marwick, City Clerk, regarding the Memorial to the Town Council. It was arrainged that the members of Deputation appointed at Previous Meeting meet at 2 oclock on Tuesday to Proceed to the Council Chambers to present the Memorial and no member to be later than a Quarter Past 2 oclock. It was also unanimously agreed to that all members of Deputation be Paid for the time they are engaged in Presenting the Memorial. The Memorial Sheets with Signatures was then Handed in and Joined together in Proper form for Presentation. 500 copies of the Annual Report was then laid on the Table. It was agreed that the allocation of Copies to the various Trades be at the ratio of 8 Per Cent.

[1] David Crighton, slaters.

1869-1873

Banner of the Tinplate Workers' Union, probably carried at the Edinburgh demonstration of 23 August 1873 to protest against the Criminal Law Amendment Act and other statutes (see above, page xxxiv)

1869

12 January 1869

Mr Scott introduced the motion he had Previously given notice of calling the attention of the Council to the action of the Association lately organised for the improvement of the condition of the Poor.[1] He stated that a roll was kept of men who were in the receipt of support from said association with a view of Providing Employers of Labour with hands at a reduced wage and if the reciepients would not work for any wage they might be offered they were immeadiatly Deprived of the support which they had Previously recieved. He considered that such a Policy was very Detrimental to the interests of Working Classes Generally and would tend in a great measure to reduce wages Generally. It was unanimously agreed to that the whole Council form themselves into a Vigilance Committee to watch the Proceedings of said Association and report. Mr Gunn then Brought forward his motion on the Bright address,[2] asking for a report of Expenditure on the same. The Secretary stated that all the Expenses he was aware of was 5s. 6d. for Vellum and 2s. 6d. for the case. Mr Monro inquired if the money had all been paid for the Tickets. Mr Gray stated that all Ticket Money had been Paid by all Delegates and that he had settled the account for the whole 1,200 and had the reciept which he would lay on the table at next meeting. It was then Proposed that a testimonial be presented to Mr Todd for his services in connection with the getting up of the address. Various members approved of the proposition. But Mr Todd distinctly refused to accept anything, stating that any services he had given were purely done in appreciation of Mr Bright's character. The subject then dropped.

The Secretary then called on the Council to elect a successor in

[1] Above, pp. 233-4. [2] Above, p. 234.

Q

his place as from the uncertain Position in which he was Placed he could not hold the office. If he was called away the Council would be left at a day's notice without a Secretary because the Assistant Secretary[1] was away from the Council Board altogether. Various members were then proposed but refused. Mr Dewar moved that as Mr Gray was not sure when he would leave the City, if they elected an Assistant Secretary it was all that was required and proposed Mr George Hills, Bookbinder, as such. Mr Monro seconded the motion which was unanimously agreed to.

Mr Todd then introduced the motion he had tabled at a previous meeting asking the Council to elect Three Honourary Presidents and naming J. Moncrieff, Esquire, Lord Advocate, Edward S. Gordon, late Lord Advocate,[2] and Duncan McLaren, M.P., as such. He dwelt on the advantages the Council would possess by adopting such a motion. The motion was agreed to. The Secretary was then instructed to forward Copies of the Report to various Members of Parliament. Mr Dewar thought that as there were a large amount of Business in the hands of the Council a Special Meeting should be held on Tuesday next to take up Mr Lawson's motion and the one he had tabled on the fifty hours movement. The suggestion was unanimously agreed to. Mr Scott stated that as the Half year accounts would likely be coming in he wished the Council to elect two auditors. Mr White, vice President, and Mr Dewar were then appointed and it was agreed that they meet an hour previous than usual on next meeting night.

19 January 1869

A Special Meeting was held. Mr Lawson introduced the motion previously tabled by him asking the Council to consider the propriety of having a bill introduced into Parliament by some Scotch member, having for its object the Legalising of Trades Unions, etc.[3] The motion was seconded by Mr McDonald. But the Council seemed to be of opinion that the motion was premature seeing that the whole question was soon to be Brought before the House of Commons by the Government. The motion was accordingly with-

---

[1] James Horn, joiners.
[2] Todd's original choice had been M. E. Grant Duff, above, p. 235.
[3] Above, p. 235.

drawn. Mr Todd moved that the Secretary be instructed to write to Mr D. Maclaren, M.P., requesting him to furnish the Council with Printed Copies of the *Report of Royal Commission on Trades Unions*. If Mr McLaren failed to do so, to write to the Lord Advocate. The motion was agreed to. Mr Dewar then introduced his motion on the Reduction of the hours of Labour,[1] delivering an able and Lenthy address on the Whole Subject. Mr Ferguson[2] seconded the motion. An excellent and animated Debate was then entered into by the Whole Council at the Termination of Which Mr Dewar's motion was unanimously agreed to.

Mr Gray then formally introduced a motion Prepared by the Secretary of the Tailors Union to the following effect: That the office Bearers of the Respective Societies in Edinburgh now met in Council to Deliberate upon the short time movement agree to recommend thier decisions to the favourable consideration of the respective Trades Unions in Scotland, and that with a view of furthering the object under consideration they request an expression of opinion from the various Trades as to whether they would unite into one Great Body for the Purpose of carrying out the resolution as submitted and approved of by this meeting. The motion was seconded by Mr Lawson. An amendment was Proposed by Mr Dewar to the effect that the word 'Scotland' be struck out and 'United Kingdom' inserted. The same being seconded, the Chairman put it to the vote when the amendment was declared carried by a Large Majority. It was also agreed that the resolutions should be Published in the newspapers.

26 January 1869

The Secretary read Letters he had recieved from Mr Gladstone, Mr Bright, Mr Lowe,[3] Mr Wilkinson,[4] Mr Miller, M.P.,[5] Mr McLaren, M.P., acknowledging the reciept of Copies of Report sent. Letters were also read from J. Moncrieff, Esq., Lord Advocate,

[1] Above, p. 235.
[2] Not identified.
[3] Robert Lowe, Viscount Sherbrooke, 1811-92, Liberal M.P. for Kidderminster 1852-9, Calne 1859-67, London University 1868-80; chancellor of the exchequer 1868-73 and home secretary 1873-4.
[4] Not identified.
[5] John Miller of Leithen, Radical M.P. for Edinburgh.

Edward S. Gordon, late Lord Advocate, accepting the office of Honorary Presidents of the Council. The Secretary was then instructed to write to these Gentlemen and convey the thanks of the Council to them. A Letter was also read from D. McLaren, M.P., declining the office of Honorary President, after which it was unanimously agreed to request E. Grant Duff, Esq., Under Secretary for India, to accept the office in room of Mr McLaren.

Letters were then read from Mr Smellie,[1] Secretary, Working Men's Association, Glasgow, and Alexander McDonald, Miners President, Holytown,[2] anent the short time movement and the nessessity of calling a Conference on that and other subjects. Mr Watson[3] moved that a Special Meeting be held to Further Consider the whole subject with a view of coming to a definite Descision as to what further steps the Council would take on the subject and that the officers of the various Societies be invited to attend. Mr Dewar seconded the motion, which was agreed to. Tuesday 2nd February was agreed to for holding said meeting. Mr Monro then moved that as special meetings were summoned by Letter, thereby causing a considerable amount of extra labour to the Secretary, that printed circulars should be got for calling said meetings. Mr Todd seconded the motion which was unanimously agreed to. Mr Scott, Treasurer, then read a report of the Financial Position of the Council which had been certified correct by the auditors. The same was approved of. Mr Dewar moved that Mr John C. Burn be elected Honorary member of the Council. Mr Todd seconded the motion which was unanimously agreed to.

2 February 1869

A Special Meeting. Mr John Watson[4] briefly stated his reasons for calling this meeting. In his opinion the Council should Lose no time in calling a Public Meeting to inaugurate the short time movement in Edinburgh. Mr Dewar moved that the Council take into consideration the nessessity of holding a public meeting on the

---

[1] George Smellie, a brassfounder. *Reformer*, 10 October 1868.
[2] Alexander McDonald, 1821-81, president of the Miners' National Union 1863-81, Lib-Lab M.P. for Stafford 1874-81.
[3] John Watson, blacksmiths.
[4] All other references to Watson in this minute are presumably to him, and not to Robert Watson, moulders.

shortime movement at the earliest opportunity. Mr Watson seconded
the motion. Mr Gray then moved an amendment that a conference
of representatives of the various Trades be held in Edinburgh to
consider the short time movement in all its Bearings and if Possible
to consider those other Questions refered to by the Gentlemen who
had communicated with them. Mr Todd seconded the amendment.
A Long and animated Disscussion then took Place on the whole
Question, after which Mr Gray withdrew his amendment and Mr
Dewar's motion was agreed to. Mr Watson then moved that a
committee be appointed to Draw up Resolutions and arrainge for the
Public Meeting and report, the motion being seconded and agreed
to. The following members were appointed: Mr Dewar, Mr Watson,
Mr Laing, Mr Hills, Mr Kinlay, Mr Fergusson, Mr White, Mr
Gunn, Mr Kenneddy and Mr Gray, to meet on Saturday and
report at next meeting of Council. The Secretary was then instructed
to answer the Letters he had recieved anent a Conference, stating
the opinion of Council.

9 February 1869

The Secretary Read certificates from the Leith Bakers Society,
appointing Mr Alexander Black and Mr George Robertson Delegates to the Council in Room of James Wright and Alexander
Miller, resigned.[1] Certificate was also read from the Joiners Society,
West Branch, appointing Mr James Bartie in room of Mr Croall
as thier Delegate to the Council. A Letter was Read from Mr
Urquhart, Treasurer to the Peoples Union, accompanied with 150
Copies of Report of a meeting of that Body in the Phenix Hall
which were Distributed amongst the members.[2] The Secretary was
instructed to acknowledge Reciept and the Letter was ordered to
Lie on the Table till next meeting when its consideration was to be
gone into. Letter was then read from Secretary of Horseshoers'
Society asking a Deputation to address that Body at thier meeting
same night on the advantages to be Derived from entering the
Council. Mr White and Mr Todd were Deputed to attend said
meeting, but when they went the meeting had Dispersed, it being
near ten oclock. Letter was also read from Henry Rankin, Secretary

[1] There is no previous mention of Miller.
[2] No press report of this meeting has been found, Urquhart has not been further
identified, and no other information about the People's Union has been discovered.

of Earnest Jones Memorial Committee, asking the Council to send a deputation to assist that Committee in the furtherance of that movement.[1] Mr Todd moved that as the Council do not understand the Position of that Committee we decline in the meantime taking part in that movement. The motion being agreed to the Secretary was instructed to communicate the same to Mr Rankin.

The Secretary then Read the Report of Committee on Public Meeting. The following Resolutions were then submitted to the Council for adoption: Resolved that in the opinion of this meeting the adoption of 50 hours Per week is the only Practical method of Giving employment to our Surplus Labour and thereby enabling the Workmen to influence the Labour Market in thier favour so as to secure a more reasonable share of the wealth which thier Labour Produces and thus Prevent the Working Population of this country from being reduced to the condition of Paupers. 2nd, Resolved That in order to establish Permantly the short time movement as embodied in the first Resolution we recommend that the movement should be of a national Character. Mr Todd moved to add the following Rider to the 2nd Resolution, viz., Believing that it will enable the Working Classes more thoroughly to embrace opportunities of Self-improvement which are essential not only to Individual but also to National Life. 3rd, Resolved that it be remitted to the United Trades Council to Draw up a Circular in the name of thier Constituents embodieing these Resolutions along with other ascertained facts Relating to the Reduction of the Hours of Labour, the same to be issued to all organised Bodies of men in the United Kingdom asking thier co-operation in carrying out this movement to a successfull issue. On the motion of Mr Dewar, seconded by Mr Monro, the resolutions were adopted. Mr Dewar then moved that a Special meeting be held on Tuesday 16th inst to further arrainge about the Public Meeting. The motion was agreed to and the secretary was instructed to advertise the same in *Scotsman* and *Reformer*,[2] inviting all office Bearers of Societies to

---

[1] Ernest Jones had died on 26 January 1869. For some biographical information about Henry Ranken, who became a delegate to the trades council from the upholsterers on 9 March 1869, see above, p. xxiv.

[2] A radical weekly published in Edinburgh from August 1868 until February 1875, with Councillor David Lewis as editor and with George Potter among its regular contributors.

attend. The[1] Secretary then stated that he had drawn up the account
of Council Expenses incurred in holding meetings on the Infirmary
Business and had forwarded the same to the Treasurer who had
returned it stating that it was not his Business to draw the account.
Various members of the Council stated that Mr Scott was the only
authorised Person the Council had for that Purpose and as such it
was his Duty to go and have the account cashed. Mr Scott then left
the Council stating that he would not draw it and Distinctly Refused
to furnish the Secretary with funds to carry on the Business of the
Council although requested to Do so. There being so few members
Present the matter was Left over till next meeting.

16 February 1869

A Special Meeting was held. Mr White, vice President, in the chair.
The Secretary read a Letter from the Secretary of Working Men's
Association, Glasgow, approving of the course the Council had
taken up on the short time movement. The Chairman then called
on the Secretary to read the resolutions agreed to on the former
meeting. A Lenthened Debate took Place on the first resolution,
as to whether 50 hours or 51 should be stated in the resolution.
Mr Watson[2] moved, seconded by . . . , that the number 50 should be
struck out and 51 inserted. Mr Dewar moved that the resolution
stands as it is. Mr Dewar's motion was not seconded and consequently
fell to the Ground and Mr Watson's motion was Declared carried.
It was then unanimously agreed to strike out the last sentence of the
resolution and insert: 'and thus Prevent the Working Classes from
Drifting into these Processes of Social Deterioration which will
eventually subvert the Best interests of the Community'. Second
and third Resolutions were then agreed to as read. Mr Todd moved
that a representative of the Masons be invited to move the first
resolution, a representative of the Joiners to second, and a representative of the Plasterers to support the same. The motion was agreed to,
it being Left to the executive committee of each Society to select
said representative. Mr Dewar was then appointed to move the

[1] The remainder of this paragraph was later deleted from the minutes. See below,
p. 248.
[2] Either Robert Watson, moulders, or John Watson, blacksmiths.

second resolution, Mr McWhinnie[1] to be invited to second the same, and Mr Wilson, Engineer,[2] to support it. There was no arraingment made with regard to the third resolution.

Mr Watson then called the attention of the Council to the Division in the town Council and moved that as the names of those who had voted for and against the appointment of inspector under the Workshop act had not been Published that the Secretary be instructed to write to the City Clerk for a List of the Division. The Secretary was authorised to write accordingly. Mr Todd then called the attention of Council to the statements made by Councillor Colston at the meeting of Town Council regarding the memorial Presented to that Body by this Council on the factory act. The Secretary and Mr Todd was instructed to reply to the same in the Public Press.[3]

23 February 1869

The Minutes of Previous ordinary and Special Meetings were Read. Objection was taken to the Last Minute of ordinary meeting. After an explanation by the Secretary it was agreed that it be scored out. The Minutes were then approved of on the motion of Mr Monro, seconded by Mr White. The Secretary explained the Position the Council was in regarding the Infirmary Business expence account. It was agreed that the Secretary forward the account to the acting committee, the Treasurer to look after the cashing of the same. The attention of the Council was then called to the fact that through the abscence of the Treasurer at last meetings various Delegates who had Brought money to Pay over to the Treasurer had to take it away again. It was absolutely necsessary to Elect an assistant Treasurer, whereupon Mr James Bartie was unanimously Elected to the office.[4]

Mr Moore stated that a deputation from the People's Union was

[1] John McWhinnie, tailors.
[2] Probably William Wilson, who became a delegate to the trades council on 14 December 1869.
[3] Colston had declared many of the signatures on the memorial were forged or in the same handwriting. The trades council admitted a number were in the same hand but explained that to save time the men's workshop officials had with their permission signed for them. *Reformer*, 27 February 1869.
[4] Below, p. 251.

waiting outside and wished to be admitted in order to confer with the Council on the Position taken up by the Town Council that Day on the Workshop Act. The Council agreed to recieve said Deputation. Mr Moore then introduced Mr Barret, Mr Jackson, and Mr Barton, members of the Executive Council, Peoples Union,[1] who Briefly stated that as the Town Council had that day refused to appoint an inspector under the Workshop Act by a majority of 19 against 12, they thought that a Public meeting should be held to express thier Disapprobation of the Town Council's Proceedings and urged on the Trades Council to join with them in the movement. A Lenthened Conversation then took Place on the whole Question. The Council did not see thier way to a Public Meeting on the subject at Present but stated that they would be Glad to Give every assistance in thier Power should a meeting be convened by the Peoples Union on the subject. The Deputation then withdrew after recieving the thanks of the Council. Mr Todd then moved that Mr McLaren, M.P., Be Communicated with to Direct the attention of the Government to the Position of the Workshop Act in the City of Edinburgh and Scotland Generally, and to ascertain thier opinion on the enforcement of the act in the House of Commons. The motion was unanimously agreed to. Mr Todd stated that as the Council would Likely have to reply to some of the strictures of Councillor Colston in the Public Press he thought they should empower the Chairman's Committee to do so. Agreed to.

The Secretary read Letters from Lord Advocate and Edward S. Gordon Granting Liberty to Publish thier Letters of acceptance of Honorary Presidents in the Papers. Letter was also read from E. Grant Duff, M.P., Declining the office of Honorary President on the Ground of Pressure of Business. Letter was also read from the Secretary, Earnest Jones Memorial Committee, which was ordered to Lie on the table till next meeting. Letter was also read from Mr Marwick, City Clerk, enclosing an official List of Division in the Workshops Act in the Town Council. Certificate was then read from the Secretary of Edinburgh Branch, Glassmakers Society, appointing Mr Joseph Hall and Mr Robert Gray Delegates to the Council for the next twelve months.

---

[1] None of the three men has been further identified.

9 March 1869

The Chairman stated that as the Public Meeting on the short time movement was to be held on the succeeding night it would be nessessary to take up the Business connected with said meeting in Preference to any other, and moved that no Disscussion be gone into on the Minutes. The motion being unanimously agreed to, the Secretary then read Certificates from the following Societies appointing Delegates to the Council: Upholdsterers, Mr Henry Rankin and Mr Gabriel Wallace;[1] Tailors, Mr John McWhinnie and Mr James Taylor; Joiners Society, West Branch, Mr Alexander Strachan as second Delegate.

The Chairman then gave in a report of the arraingments come to at the committee meeting anent the Public Meeting. The Secretary was to communicate to Mr Edward Strathern Gordon, Honorary President, to know whether he was going to Preside at the meeting. Failing him Doing so to call on Councillor Cranston[2] and ask him, and if he could not come to invite Mr Charles Scott, Esq., Advocate.[3] The Report having been approved of the final arraingments were then gone into for the Public Meeting in Queen Street Hall: Mr Kinlay to move Mr Scott to the Chair; 1st Resolution moved by Mr Andrew Dowie, Mason, seconded by Mr Adam Anderson, Plasterer, supported by Mr Paterson, Central Corresponding Secretary, Joiners Union;[4] 2nd Resolution moved by Mr Andrew Dewar, Blacksmith, seconded by Mr Cobb, Tailor, supported by Mr Wilson, Engineer; 3rd Resolution moved by Mr R. Gray, Secretary of Council, seconded by Mr Cameron, Plumber; Vote of thanks moved by Mr William White, Joiner.

The Letter of Mr Rankin, Secretary, Earnest Jones Memorial

---

[1] For some biographical information about Wallace see above, pp. xxiv-v.

[2] Robert Cranston, 1815-92, former Chartist, founder of a chain of temperance hotels, an Independent Liberal town councillor in Edinburgh 1868-87 and 1889-90. E. Mein, *Through Four Reigns, The Story of the Old Waverley Hotel and its Founder* (Edinburgh, n.d.), 1.

[3] Charles Scott (1819-92) in the event presided at the meeting. He was an active Conservative, had been editor of the *Fife Herald* and two other newspapers in the 1840s, was an unsuccessful parliamentary candidate at Perth in 1874 and Kirkcaldy Burghs in 1880, and was a clerk of justiciary 1874-92. *Scotsman*, 11 March 1869; *The Faculty of Advocates in Scotland 1532-1943*, ed. Sir Francis J. Grant (Edinburgh, 1944), 186.

[4] William Paterson, general secretary.

Committee, was then taken into consideration. Mr Dewar moved the following Resolution: That this Council Publish a resolution recommending the various trades to Subscribe towards the fund now being raised for the widow and family of the late Earnest Jones, and that a Committee be appointed from this Council to co-operate with the existing Committee, urging them to call a Public Meeting on the Subject. Mr Monro Seconded the Resolution, which was Unanimously adopted. The following members were then Elected to form said Committee: Mr John Gunn, Mr Gabriel Wallace, Mr G. Robertson, Mr Robert Gray.

23 March 1869

Certificates were read from the Glasscutters Society Reappointing Mr George Scott and Mr Donald Moore Delegates to the Council for the next 12 months. Letter was also read from the Secretary, International Working Men's Association, London,[1] anent the short time movement. It was agreed that the Letter should be Published in the *Scotsman* and *Reformer*. A Letter was read from Alexander McDonald, Miners Secretary, requesting to be furnished with address of the Secretary of the Trades Council, Dundee. The Secretary intimated that he had acknowledged reciept but was unable to furnish the information required. He was then instructed to communicate with Mr Lancaster, Dundee, and Mr Taylor, Aberdeen, requesting these Gentlemen to furnish the Council with the addresses of Secretaries of Trades Council in thier Respective Towns.[2] The Minutes of Meeting held on 23rd February were then taken up and read by the Secretary. Mr Scott took objection to the 2nd Minute refering to the Election of Mr Bartie as Assistant Treasurer. It was ruled that the word 'Assistant' be scored and 'Pro tem' inserted. It was also agreed that in the abscence of the Treasurer The President was authorised to receive and Grant Reciepts for all money Paid into the Council.

The operation of the Workshop and Factory Acts was then taken into consideration. Mr McWhinnie Detailed various cases of infringment which he had brought under the notice of the authorities,

---

[1] Johann Georg Eccarius, 1818-89, a German emigré tailor in London, secretary of the International from 1867 to 1871.
[2] Neither Lancaster nor Taylor has been identified.

the results being highly favourable and which he had no doubt would ensure a better observance of the Provisions of these acts. Mr Todd moved that a sub Committee be appointed to collect every information regarding the operation of these acts and Report. The motion having been agreed to, the following members were appointed to said Committee: Mr Lawson, Mr Kennedy, Mr Todd, Mr McWhinnie.

The 3rd Resolution approved of at the Public Meeting on the Short time Movement was then taken into Consideration.[1] Mr Rankin thought the night to far advanced and suggestted that it should be Delayed till next meeting. Mr Dewar then moved that a Special Meeting be held on Tuesday next, 30th March, to consider the Question, the same to be advertised in the *Reformer* on Saturday. Mr Todd seconded the motion, adding that all office Bearers of Trades Societies be specially invited to attend. The motion was unanimously agreed to. Mr Lawson then tabled the following motion: That Mr Charles Scott, advocate, be Elected Honorary Vice President of this Council.

30 March 1869

A Special Meeting was held. The Chairman requested that the third resolution adopted at the meeting in Queen Street Hall should be read. The Secretary having read the same, the Chairman introduced the Business of the meeting by stating that it had been called in order to ascertain as much information as Possible relating to the working out of the nine hours movement with a view of emboding the same in the circular that would have to be issued. After a Long Discussion on the Subject of the Best Means to carry out the movement to a Successfull issue, Mr Dewar moved that the Council immeadiatly collect the statistics bearing on the Question from the Trades already working under the nine Hours Movement. Mr Fergusson seconded the motion, which was unanimously agreed to. Mr Watson[2] then moved that a Committee be appointed to agitate the Short time Movement in all Trades not working under that movement and also to draw up the Circular. Mr Dewar

[1] See above, p. 246.
[2] Both references to Watson in this minute may be to either Robert Watson, moulders, or John Watson, blacksmiths.

seconded the motion, which was cordially approved of. The following Gentlemen were then appointed Members of Committee: John McWhinnie, Mr Kinlay, Mr Dewar, Mr McVie,[1] Mr Burn, Honorary member, Mr Paterson, Secretary, Joiners' Association, Mr Todd, Mr Bartie, Mr Rankin, Mr Watson and Mr Gray, with Power to add to thier number. Those marked with a Cross[2] belong to the Committee elected under Mr Dewar's motion.

6 April 1869

A Special Meeting was held. The Chairman intimated that the meeting had been called to take into consideration the Present Position of the factory and workshops acts and hear the Report of Committee Previously appointed. It was stated that as the Committee had never been called together they had not Drawn up any formal report. Mr Dewar moved that the whole Council form themselves into Committee and that a Deputation be appointed to wait on the inspector to get information regarding the working of these acts. The Motion having been agreed to, Mr Todd moved that a Deputation also wait on the Lord Advocate, Mr Kinlay to be Convener of Committee; also that Secretaries be invited from Glasgow to hear his Lordship's opinion thereon. Mr Lawson Seconded the Motion, which was agreed to.

The Bill Drawn up by Mr Macdonald, Miners Secretary, anent injury to workmen was then taken into consideration.[3] It was agreed to instruct the Secretary to write to Mr Macdonald and ask him in what form he would have the Council to act so as to assist him in Getting the Bill brought before the house of Commons. Mr Todd then read some Letters from the *Typographical Circular* in answer to some Letters that appeared in the *Scotsman*.[4] But as

[1] Almost certainly John McVie or McVey, a plasterer. He may not have been a delegate to the trades council at this time but is probably the same man mentioned below between 9 November 1869 and 23 September 1870.

[2] The names of McWhinnie, Kinlay, Dewar and Gray are so marked in the MS.

[3] The Bill provided for compensation to employees for non-fatal injuries at work. After much delay in presentation it was withdrawn in August 1872 at its second reading. G. Howell, *Labour Legislation, Labour Movements and Labour Leaders* (London, 1905 edn.), 226-7.

[4] The *Scottish Typographical Circular* was founded in 1857 by the Edinburgh branch of the Scottish Typographical Association and conducted on behalf of the Association

the night was too far advanced to take up the Subject it was agreed to Leave the matter over till next meeting.

13 April 1869

The Secretary read a Letter from Alexander Macdonald in answer to one sent him anent the Bill drawn up by him on the Subject of making Masters Responsible for the Lives and Limbs of thier Workmen. It was agreed to instruct the Secretary to send copies of the Bill to the following Members of Parliament, viz., D. McLaren, John Miller, Sir Alexander G. Maitland,[1] and Robert A. McFie, the member for Leith.[2] Mr Lawson then took up the Motion tabled by him at a Previous meeting which was that the Council Elect Charles Scott, Esq., Advocate, as Honorary Vice President. Mr Watson[3] moved an amendment that the Council disapprove of the Motion. There voted for the motion 5, for the amendment 7.

A Discussion Took Place as to what further action the Council should take regarding the Earnest Jones Memorial fund. It was unanimously agreed that the former resolution of Council should be again advertised in the *Reformer* with the following addition, viz., that all office Bearers of Trades would be supplied with subscription Books through thier Delegates. Those not represented at the Council would be supplied by applying at the Committee rooms, Buchanan's Hotel, every Thursday Evening. A Discussion then arose concerning the Properiety of advertiseing all Special Meetings and inviting all office Bearers of Trades Societies to them. It was agreed that the meetings should be advertised.

26 April 1869[4]

The Secretary having read the Minutes of Last Meeting Mr Gunn mentioned that there was a Slight ommission with reference to the

---

by the branch until 1908. It is not certain which letters are referred to, but probably they concerned either piece work or the nine hours question. S. Gillespie, *A Hundred Years of Progress 1853-1953* (Glasgow, 1953), 130-1; *Scottish Typographical Circular*, March 1869, 141-2, and April 1869, 153-4.

[1] Sir Alexander Charles Ramsay-Gibson-Maitland, 1820-76, Liberal M.P. for Edinburghshire (Midlothian) 1868-74.

[2] Robert Andrew Macfie, 1811-93, Radical M.P. for Leith Burghs 1868-74.

[3] Either Robert Watson, moulders, or John Watson, blacksmiths.

[4] The date should probably read 27 April 1869.

advertising of Special Meeting.[1] The Secretary was instructed to insert the same. The Minutes were then approved of on the motion of Mr Kennedy, Seconded by Mr Rankin.

The Secretary then read Letters he had recieved from the following Gentlemen: Mr George Potter,[2] Mr Frederick Harrisson,[3] James Moncrieff, Esq., Lord Advocate, John Millar, Esq., M.P., William Yule, Secretary, Trades Council, Dundee. Certificate was also read from the Secretary of Amalgamated Engineers intimating the appointment of Mr Alexander Forbes and Mr Duncan Drummond Delegates to Represent thier body at this Council. A Discussion then took Place as to whether it was understood that all Trades were to be called upon to Pay 2nd Subscriptions in order to meet the Expence of agitating the Nine Hours Question. Mr Todd moved that a 2nd call be made on all Trades. Mr Gunn seconded the motion. Some members having objected to the motion it was withdrawn and the Subject dropped.[4]

The Trades Union Bill by Mr Thomas Hughes was then taken into consideration.[5] Mr Dewar moved that a Special Meeting be called to consider the Whole Bill. The motion having been agreed to it was arrainged that the Meeting be held on Friday Evening, 30th inst. and that all Delegates invite thier office bearers to said meeting. In answer to the Chairman the Secretary stated that he had recieved a Letter from Mr Paterson, Secretary, Joiners Society, regarding his Presence at a meeting of Council. But having some conversation with Mr Paterson on the subject he was of opinion that Mr Paterson did not wish his note to be read and Just allow the matter to Drop. But if any member wished the Letter to be Laid on the table he would do so on next meeting night. Mr Todd then Tabled the following Motion to be taken up next meeting, viz., That this Council Consider the Policy

---

[1] There is no indication in the MS. of any omission.
[2] The London trade union leader.
[3] Frederic Harrison, 1831-1923, positivist, a middle-class defender of trade unionism and a member of the royal commission of 1867-9.
[4] This motion was subsequently considered carried, below, p. 256.
[5] Thomas Hughes, 1822-96, author of *Tom Brown's Schooldays*, christian socialist, Radical M.P. for Lambeth 1865-8 and Frome 1868-74. The Bill, introduced by Hughes on 10 April, had been drafted by Frederic Harrison on the basis of the minority report of the royal commission on trade unions.

and aim of the Permissive Bill, whether it is worthy of Public Support.[1]

30 April 1869

A Special Meeting was held. The Chairman stated that he was sorry to see so few members Present as the meeting had been convened specially to consider the Trades Union Bill now before the House of Commons which was of the Greatest importance to us all, and asked whether it would be better to adjourn the consideration of the Bill until another meeting. It was agreed to go on with the subject but that no Discision be arrived at at this meeting. The Bill was then gone into Clause by Clause, various members objecting to the Bill. Mr Watson[2] moved that a Committee be appointed to Draw up a report on the Bill and Submit the same to a Special Meeting called at the Earliest opportunity. Mr Gray seconded the motion, which was agreed to. The following Gentlemen were then Elected members of committee: Mr Dewar, Mr Paterson, Mr Burn, Mr Cobb, Mr Strachan, Mr White, and Mr Kinlay. It was also arranged to meet on Tuesday Evening 4th May to draw up said report. In Consideration of the short time the Committee had to Draw up thier report it was finally arrainged that the Report be submitted at next ordinary meeting, the same to be advertised in the *Reformer* of Saturday 8th May.

11 May 1869

The Secretary read the Minutes of Previous Meeting. Mr White moved the approval of the Minutes, with the alteration that Mr Todd's motion be considered carried. Mr Dewar seconded the motion, which was unanimously agreed to. Certificates were then read from the Operative Bakers Society intimating the appointment of James Marshall and James McAurther to represent thier Body at this Council. Some Discussion then took Place as to Whether the Motion of Mr Todd on the Permissive Bill or the Committee's Report on the Trades Union Bill be first taken up. It was ruled by the Chairman that the Trades Union Bill should be first considered.

[1] The Permissive Prohibitory Liquor Bill had been introduced in February by Sir Wilfrid Lawson, Radical M.P. for Carlisle, and was refused a second reading in May.
[2] Either Robert Watson, moulders, or John Watson, blacksmiths.

Mr Paterson then submitted the Report of Committee on the Bill, detailing the various amendments which they had made and also showing the various Parts they had struck out. The Report of the Committee was unanimously agreed to. Some remarks then were made as to what further Proceedings the Council would take with a view of Bringing the Bill as amended before the Country. It was agreed that the amendments on the Bill should be Published in all the newspapers and if Possible to get a few slips Published and send them to the Secretaries of Trades Councils.

25 May 1869

The Chairman stated that as there was so few members Present he thought the meeting should be adjourned. Mr White stated that as Mr McLaren, M.P., was in the City a Deputation should be appointed to wait on him regarding the Trades Union Bill as soon as Possible, as before next meeting he would be away. It was finally agreed that the Deputation be sent on Thursday Evening, 27th inst., the Secretary to communicate the same to that Gentleman. The following members were then Elected to form said Deputation: Mr White, Mr Bartie, Mr Dowie,[1] Mr McWhinnie, Mr Kinlay, Mr Gray. Before the meeting seperated it was arranged that a Special Meeting be held on Tuesday June 1st to hear the Report of the Deputation, the same to be advertised in the *Reformer* of 29th inst.

1 June 1869

A Special Meeting. The Secretary read a Letter from Mr Millar, M.P., on the Trades Union Bill. Mr White then gave in the Report of the Deputation that waited on Mr McLaren, which was approved of. Some Discussion then took Place as to the Propereity of retaining certain minor amendments. Mr Gray moved the withdrawal of the amendment on the Preamble. Mr Bartie seconded the motion. Mr Paterson moved an amendment that the amendment stands as it is. Mr Paterson's amendment was carried. It was then unanimously agreed to withdraw the amendment on Clause 8 on the condition that the Registrar's maximum time for retaining the Books be not more than ten Days. The amendments on other Clauses still to stand

---

[1] Andrew Dowie, mason.

R

good. On the motion of Mr White, seconded by Mr Paterson, it was agreed to send for 24 Copies of the Bill, the Secretary to write the amendments on the margin as Recommended by Mr McLaren. The same to be sent to such members of Parliament as shall afterwards be selected.

8 June 1869

The Secretary read a certificate from the Associated Carpenters and Joiners Society appointing Mr William Paterson Delegate to represent them at this Council in room of Mr Alston, resigned.[1] Letters were also read from the following Gentlemen: John Miller, Esq., M.P., John G. Eccarrius, Secretary, International Workmen's Association, London, and William Yule, Secretary, United Trades Council, Dundee.

The Secretary then stated that he had sent for and recieved the 24 Copies of the Trades Union Bill from Mr Applegarth and he wished the Council to name what Members of Parliament they wished copies to be sent to.[2] The following Gentlemen were then Selected: John Bright, Sir R. Anstruther,[3] John Miller, Home Secretary, Mr Bruce,[4] Messrs Anderson,[5] Graham,[6] and Dalglish,[7] Lord Advocate,[8] Mr Disreala, Sir A. G. Maitland, and Mr Gladstone, and any others that the Secretary thought fit. Mr Yule's Letter was then taken into Consideration. It was moved by Mr Rankin that an answer be sent to Mr Yule intimating our Willingness to meet a Deputation of the Dundee Council at Cupar or any other town between Edinburgh and Dundee which may be suggested by the Dundee Council, and that if Practicable said conference to be held on a Saturday Afternoon and that we elect two Delegates to repre-

---

[1] There is no previous mention of Alston.

[2] Robert Applegarth, 1834-1925, general secretary of the Amalgamated Society of Carpenters and Joiners 1862-71, and a leading member of the 'Junta'.

[3] Sir Robert Anstruther of Balcaskie, 1834-86, Liberal M.P. for Fife 1864-80 and for St Andrews Burghs 1885-6.

[4] Henry Austin Bruce, first Baron Aberdare, 1815-95, Liberal M.P. for Merthyr Tydfil and Aberdare 1847-52, Merthyr Tydfil 1852-68 and Renfrewshire 1869-73; home secretary 1869-73.

[5] George Anderson, 1819-96, Radical M.P. for Glasgow 1868-85, master of the mint in Melbourne 1885-96.

[6] William Graham, 1817-85, Liberal M.P. for Glasgow 1865-74.

[7] Robert Dalglish of Kilmardinny, 1808-80, Radical M.P. for Glasgow 1857-74.

[8] James Moncreiff.

sent us at said Conference. Mr White seconded the motion, which was unanimously agreed to. Mr Kinlay and Mr Paterson were then appointed Delegates to the Conference in the event of it taking Place.

22 June 1869

Vice President in the Chair.[1] Mr Gray intimated to the Council that as he had got settled in a situation away from his own Trade he was under the nessessity of Placing his resignation of the office of Secretary in the hands of the Council. He also stated that owing to the great Difficulty in which his Trade was Placed with regard to the attendance of thier Delegates they had been oblidged to withdraw from the Council altogether. He also read a letter from the Glassmakers Society intimating in a very informal manner the same. It was agreed to accept Mr Gray's resignation, the assistant Secretary to Perform the Duties until the Election of office Bearers in the Second Meeting in July.[2] Certificate was read appointing William Rae and John Waddel Delegates to Represent the Amalgamated Slaters at this Council. Letters were read from the following Gentlemen acknowledging Reciept of Trades Union Bills and Letters sent them: The Right Hon. John Bright, M.P., the Right Hon. the Lord Advocate, The Right Hon. The Home Secretary, The Right Hon. W. E. Gladstone, D. McLaren, M.P., John Miller, M.P., W. Graham, M.P., G. Anderson, M.P. Letter was then read from the Secretary, United Trades Council, Dundee anent the Proposed Conference, intimating that as that Body had agreed to Support the Trades Union Bill as it stands it would be of no use for the Conference to be held at Present. Letter was read from the Secretary, Glasgow Working Men's Association, anent the strike at Preston. It was ordered to Lie on the Table.[3] The Secretary laid on the table a copy of the Mines Regulation Bill that he had recieved from Mr McLaren, M.P.[4] The Secretary was instructed to thank that Gentleman in acknowledging reciept.

[1] William White, joiners.
[2] The other glassmakers' delegate was Joseph Hall, above, p. 249. Until 27 July inclusive the minutes continued to be written by Gray.
[3] The Preston cotton operatives had evidently asked for financial assistance. *Reformer*, 10 July 1869.
[4] The Bill had been introduced by Bruce, the home secretary, on 15 April 1869 but was withdrawn on 19 July.

Mr Todd then called the attention of the Council to the Endowed Hospitals Bill and entered Largely into the Provision of the same, controverting the statements made by Dr Lyon Playfair regarding these Hospitals and urged upon the Council to consider the whole subject.[1] After a Lenthened Conversation the subject Dropt. Mr Dewar Brought under the notice of the Council a Letter that had appeared in the *Reformer* on the Trades Union Bill from G. Smellie, and asked the Council to appoint a Committee to answer the same. The request having been agreed to Mr Paterson read a Draft Reply that he had drawn up for the approval of the Council. It was agreed that the same be inserted in the *Reformer* of Saturday.[2] The Chairman then intimated that as the Earnest Jones Memorial subscription fund was about to close all members having Books were requested to return them as soon as Possible.[3]

13 July 1869

Mr Rankin in the Chair. Certificates was read from Brassfounders Society appointing John McDonald and John Scott Delegates to represent that Trade at this Council. Letter was read from Mr Applegarth, Secretary to the Amalgamated Trades, London, inviting the Council to send a Delegate to the Deputation that was to have an interview with the Home Secretary on 1 July anent the Trades Union Bill. It was agreed that as the Bill had been withdrawn for the Present Session we take no further steps in the matter. Letter was also read from John Miller, Esq., M.P., anent the 2nd Reading of the Trades Union Bill. Mr Todd moved that the Secretary be instructed to write to Mr Miller thanking him very kindly for his Letter to the Council and to express to him that they will have Great Pleasure in meeting him at any future time that will be convienent.

[1] Sir Lyon Playfair, first Baron Playfair of St Andrews, 1818-98, professor of chemistry at Edinburgh 1858-69, Liberal M.P. for Edinburgh and St Andrews Universities 1868-85 and for South Leeds 1885-92. He had criticised in the Commons the relative paucity of scholars at Scottish endowed schools and the quality of their education. *Scotsman*, 19 June 1869.

[2] Smellie supported the Bill and rejected the view that unions should be allowed to sue and be sued by their members. The trades council's reply, signed by Kinlay and Gray, described the Bill as deserving 'the most strenuous opposition'. *Reformer*, 19 and 26 June 1869.

[3] At least £101 was raised in Edinburgh for the fund. *Reformer*, 17 July 1869.

Letter was read from Mr Wilkie, Secretary, Edinburgh Lodge, Operative Masons Association, intimating that the masons had resolved to have an annual holiday, the first to be held on 7 August this year and the first Saturday of the same month every year afterwards, and urging the Council to Consider the Subject with a veiw to Co-operate with them in making the movement General among the Trades in Edinburgh. Mr Dewar moved that the Secretary write to Mr Wilkie stating this Council would be very glad to have the whole Question brought before them by the Delegates from the Masons Society. Mr McDonald seconded the motion, which was agreed to. Mr Ranken then Brought under the notice of the Council the Question of the renumeration of the office Bearers, stating that he thought that before electing office Bearers it should be settled what renumeration should be given. The subject was left over till next meeting and in the interval it was agreed to that 2 auditors should be appointed to examine the Books and Accounts and report the finiancial Position of the Council at next meeting.

Mr Todd then Drew the attention of the Council to the Highland and agriculture Show in the West Meadows, stating that the show had been erected on a Peice of ground belonging to the public. Therefore he thought they were entitled to be admitted to the Exhibition at a reduced rate and in order to see what could be done he would move that a committee be appointed to wait on Mr Menzies, the Secretary, for that purpose.[1] Mr Ranken moved an amendment that the Council take no action in this matter. Mr Dewar seconded Mr Todd's motion which on being put to the vote was carried by a majority of 10 against 3. The following Committee were then appointed to wait on Mr Menzies: Mr White, Mr Paterson, and Mr Todd. The Delegates from the Brass founders then stated that their Trade was intending to hold a meeting for to support the nine hours movement and would like a Deputation from the Council to attend the same. The subject was handed over to the agitation committee who was to be communicated with through the Secretary. The Delegates stated that they would report at next meeting how far the arraingments for said meeting were completed.

[1] Fletcher Norton Menzies, secretary of the Highland and Agricultural Society 1866-92.

27 July 1869

Letters were read from the following Gentlemen: D. McLaren,
M.P., J. Miller, M.P., and Sir R. Anstruther on the Trades Union
Bill. Mr Todd moved that the Secretary be instructed to write to
Sir R. Anstruther stating that they thank him for the communication
and that this Council will be glad at any future time to communicate
with him. The motion was unanimously agreed to. Mr Scott,
Treasurer of the Council, gave in the finiancial Report. The auditors
were instructed to meet again and audit the accounts and consider
the Best means of recruiting the funds of the Council. Mr Monro
then moved that all Trades that had given a Donation to the Council
in support of the nine hours agitation be not asked for any further
subscription provided said donation covered second subscription
for the year now finished. Mr Gunn seconded the motion, which
was agreed to.

Mr Todd and Mr Paterson then gave in a report of their interview
with the Secretary of the Highland Society's Show, stating what
arraingments had been made and the result of the Committee's
Labour which had been highly successful. Mr Paterson moved that
a vote of thanks be awarded to the Directors and the Secretary for
arraingments they had made. The motion was unanimously agreed
to. Mr Gunn stated that the Deputation who had waited on the
Directors of the Highland Society's Show deserved the thanks of
this Council and also that they should be paid for the time they were
engaged on that Business. Therefore he would move accordingly.
The motion after some remarks was agreed to. Mr Scott, Brassfounder, Drew the attention of the Council to the agitation in his
trade for the nine hours system. The subject was handed over to the
agitation Committee – Mr Dewar, Convener.

The Salary of the office Bearers of the Council for the Last year
was Brought before the Council by Mr Hills. Mr Gunn moved and
Mr Kenneddy seconded that the subject be Left over for a month.
The motion was agreed to. The Election of office Bearers for the next
twelve months was then gone into when the following members
were Elected: President, Mr Dewar; Vice President, Mr White;
Treasurer, Mr Scott; Secretary, Mr Bartie. The election of assistant
Secretary was left over.[1] Mr Monro and Mr McWhinnie were then

---

[1] None seems to have been appointed until 1871.

Elected auditors. Mr Todd moved a vote of thanks to the retiring office Bearers. Mr Gunn seconded the motion which was unanimously agreed to. Mr Paterson called the attention of the Council to the Conference that was soon to be held at Manchester, stating that some member should Draw up a paper on some Trades subject.[1] After some conversation the subject dropt. Mr Dewar gave in a report of the measures which had been adopted in his trade to secure the nine hours, stating that as far as present appearances went the movement was very Likely to be successfull. Mr Paterson[2] also reported the progress the Cabinet Makers were making in the same movement. Mr Dewar called the attention of the Council to the Circular on the nine hours movement. Mr Paterson stated that the Circular was ready but the subject was Left over.

10 August 1869

When the Minutes of previous meeting were read Mr Munro moved that some errors which he pointed out be corrected, which was agreed to.[3] Mr Scott[4] gave notice that the Deligates who were appointed to wait on the Secratary of the Highland and Agricultural Society at a former meeting had refused payment for the time they had lost. Mr McWhinnie said that seeing that it was a standing rule in the Council that deputations loosing time during work hours receive payment, therefore for the benifit of those who may be similarly engaged in the future, he moved that the said deputation be paid, which was unanimously agreed to.

The Secretary read certificates from the Edinburgh Union Society of Journeymen Bookbinders appointing Messrs William Weir and Alexander Gunn as their representatives in room of Messrs William Kinlay and George Hills, who had resigned. Mr Todd asked if letters of acknowledgement had been sent to Messrs McLaren and Millar, also to Sir Robert Anstruther, as was agreed to at last

---

[1] This conference has escaped identification, unless 'Manchester' should read 'Birmingham', where the second T.U.C. was held from 23 to 28 August 1869.

[2] Probably William Paterson, joiners.

[3] Two insertions were consequently made in the MS.: in the first paragraph, line 12, the phrase 'provided said donation covered second subscription', and 'Brassfounder' in the second paragraph, lines 11-12. In paragraph three, line 8, the words 'till next meeting' were deleted after 'was left over'.

[4] Presumably George Scott, glasscutters, treasurer of the council.

meeting. In the absence of Mr Gray[1] the Chairman could not answer the question. But it was agreed that the Secretary asertain and if it had not been done that he answer the same. Also that he write to the Secretary of the Highland and Agricultural Society thanking him and the Directors for the courtesy with which they received the deputation and the consideration which they gave their sugestions.

The Auditors were next asked for their report. Mr White read the financial report of past year, stating that Mr Dewar and himself had examined the Books and Accounts and found them Correct. But he was of opinion that the present rate of subscription was altogether inadequate to meet the requirements of the Council and that some alteration would require to be made. Mr Dewar in a few remarks substanciated the statements of Mr White. Mr Todd moved that a Committee be appointed to consider the Financial Position and the best means of placing on a sound basis the Council of Trades Delegates, securing the co-operation of the Edinburgh Trades with power to wait upon Trade Officials and to report. This was carried unanimously. The following members were appointed: Messers McWhinnie, White, Dewar, Todd, J. Scott, Shearer,[2] and Bartie. The Secretary was instructed to keep a check of the Income and Expenditure of Council and it was also agreed that Deligates should bring up at next meeting the names and addresses of their respective Trade Secretaries for the use of the Secretary, and when any change occured always to give intimation of the same. Mr Todd then drew the attention of the Council to the case of Scavangers and the Town Council, the Town Council having refused their requist of a shilling advance on their weekly wage, which he considered inconsistant. Therefore he moved that the Secretary be instructed to write to Mr Marwick, Town Clerk, asking him for the division list on the above case. Mr McWhinnie seconded the motion, which was carried unanimously. Mr Paterson gave notice of his intention to bring up a motion next meeting with a view to a national conferance of Trades Deligates to consider the question of a Bill to legalise Trades Unions.

[1] Robert Gray, glassmakers, late secretary of the council.
[2] George Shearer, tinplate workers.

17 August 1869

The Committee met on this date. The members proceeded to draw up a list of the Edinburgh Trades. It was agreed to select the unrepresented and divide them amongst the members of Committee with a view to discover the addresses of their Secretaries and place the Council in communication with them so that we might get them to send Delegates to the Council. A Deputation also waited on the Farriers but found that they had just left. They then waited on the Plumbers who promised to have their Deligates in attendance with more regularity than had been the case for some time back.

24 August 1869

The Secretery stated that he had written to the City Clerk and the Secretary of the Highland and Agricultural Society as requisted, but had only received a letter of acknowledgment from the lattar which was read to the meeting. Mr Gray's report of past year was next taken up when it was moved by Mr Munro and seconded by Mr Gunn[1] that it be read, which was agreed to, and accordingly done. It was then moved and seconded that it be remitted to a committee to examine and correct which was also agreed to, and the following members were ellected: Messers Paterson, McDonald, Strachan, Dewar, and J. Gunn. Mr Paterson's notice of motion was taken up, when he read the following motion: That a committee be appointed with instructions to assertain the opinions of the various trade organisations throughout Scotland upon the propriety of holding a conference during the ensuing Winter regarding the future legislation upon Trades Unions. After a great deal of discussion it was unanimously carried. The following members were then ellected: Messers Paterson, McDonald, Alexander Gunn, and J. Bartie. The Secretary was then authorised to write to the various trade Councils in Scotland and other parties that the Council had corrispondence with informing them of our change of secretary.

14 September 1869

The Vice President[2] in the Chair. On the roll being called fourteen answered to their names. The Secretary called the attention of the

[1] Probably John Gunn, painters, but could be Alexander Gunn, bookbinders.
[2] William White, joiners. Andrew Dewar, the president, was present later.

Council to the fact of his having received no answer nor acknowledgment from the Town Clerk to the letter previously sent to him. On the motion of Mr Todd and Mr Millar[1] it was agreed that he be again written to requesting an answer. A Certificate was read from the Painters stating that Mr John Gunn and Mr John McKay had been duly ellected to represent their society at the Council. A letter was read from Mr Gray stating that he expected some acknowledgement before this time from the Council for his services as Secretary during the past year. Mr McWhinnie moved, seconded by Mr W. Wallace,[2] that he receive the same renumeration as his predicessor, viz., £3. Mr Munro moved as an amendment seconded by Mr Strachan that he only receive £2 as the present libillities of the Council considered would not justify more. It was finally agreed that the Treasurer be authorised to pay to Mr Gray £2 10s, the Secretary to notify him of the decision arrived at, and the Treasurer to receive the same as usual, viz., £0 10s for his sallary. After some conversation on the financial condition of the Council the Treasurer was instructed to draw up a list of the Trades in arrears with their contributions and the Secretary to write to them after next meeting.

The committee appointed with regard to a national conferance was next asked if they had a report to give. Mr Paterson stated that owing to the illness of one member and the non attendance of another we had failed to get a meeting as yet. Mr Gunn[3] handed in some books that had been used in collecting subscriptions for rebuilding the Royal Infirmary. Mr Munro moved, seconded by Mr Paterson, that we take nothing to do with the books seeing that the money was not paid through the Council. Mr Todd moved as an amendment that we minute receipt of the books as returned by Mr Gunn, seconded by Mr Scott.[4] 9 voted for the amendment and 2 for the motion. Mr Paterson then read the anual report as corrected, which was unanimously agreed to on the motion of Mr

[1] This and all subsequent references to a delegate of that name appear to be to Gilbert Miller or Millar, Edinburgh bakers.
[2] Not identified. May be an error for G. Wallace, upholsterers.
[3] This and subsequent references to Gunn in this minute may be to either Alexander Gunn, bookbinders, or John Gunn, painters.
[4] Either George Scott, glasscutters, or John Scott, brassfounders.

McWhinnie and Mr Dewar, subject to some additions sujested by Mr Todd.

Mr McWhinnie called the attention of the Council to the case of 3 Miners who had left the employment of the West Calder Oil Company without giving proper warning and were tried before a Justice of the Peace, and sentenced with the utmost severity. Mr Todd moved That this Council of Trade Delegates regard the decision in the case of the West Calder Oil Company and Thomas Nicolson, William Gordon, and John Gordon as one of great hardship and oppression reviving all the oppressive hardships of the combination laws and calculated to weaken the relations which should exist between employers and employed, and direct the attention of the Home Secretary and the Miners Association to the peculiarities of the case. The same to be incerted in the newspapers, which was unanimously agreed to.[1] Mr Gunn gave notice of a motion for next meeting, viz., That this Council take into consideration and devise means of establishing courts of arbitration between employers and employed. Mr Dewar gave notice of the following: That this Council take up the question of the best means of organising Trade Societies and the best form of organisation. Mr Paterson also gave notice of motion: That this Council take into consideration the propriety of taking action in the ensuing municipal elections.

28 September 1869

On the roll being called sixteen answered to their names. A letter was read from the secretary of the Masons association, Mr Allan,[2] acknowledging receipt of Circular sent with view to a national conference, stating that their executive Committee highly approve of a conferance and that they would lose no time in bringing it before their society and let us know the result. A letter from the Town Clerk was also laid before the Council stating that we would

[1] The three men were convicted on 8 September of absenting themselves from the service of the company on 23 August without giving the six working days' notice required by its rules. Each was fined £2, with £1 10s costs; warrant was granted to point, and failing payment within forty-eight hours the men were to be imprisoned for thirty days. *Scotsman*, 9 September 1869.

[2] Matthew Allan, 1825-83, central corresponding secretary of the Scottish United Operative Masons' Association 1867-83. R. W. Postgate, *The Builders' History* (London, 1923), 256.

get the division list of the Town Council in an extract from the minutes at the usual terms. It was agreed to on the motion of Mr Taylor, seconded by Mr J. Scott, that failing getting the division list otherwise, that we pay for it so as to have it before the November ellections, which was agreed to. In answer to a question the Secretary stated that he had received no letter on the miners case. Mr Todd then moved, seconded by Mr Taylor, that we write to the Lord Advocate[1] on the above case. Mr Ranken moved as an ammendment that we let the matter lie over seeing that we had already applyed at the proper quarter in writing to the Home Secretary. 5 voted for the ammendment and 7 for the motion.

Mr Gunn[2] then in accordance with previous notice moved the following: That this Council take into consideration and devise the best means of establishing courts of arbitration and conciliation between employers and employed. Mr Todd seconded and supported the motion in a able speech. Mr Taylor moved, seconded by Mr McWhinnie, the previous question. Mr Paterson moved as an ammendment that it be remitted to a committee to consider and report on the subject. Mr White seconded. 5 voted for Mr Taylor's and 6 for Mr Paterson's ammendment. It being now past 10 Oclock Mr McWhinnie moved that we adjourn the meeting till this night week, the Secretary to summon all absent members, which was agreed to.

5 October 1869

An adjourned meeting was held. On the roll being called 16 answered to their names. Mr Paterson's notice being reckoned of most importance, he was called upon for his motion when he moved the following: That this Council take into consideration the propriety of taking action in the ensuing municipal ellections. Mr McWhinnie seconded. After several members had expresed their opinion in favor of taking action in the elections it was put to the vote and carried unanimously. Mr Paterson then moved that this Council resolves to use its best endevours to secure the direct representation of Labour in the Edinburgh Town Council. Mr J. Gunn seconded. It was also carried unanimously. With the view of

[1] James Moncreiff.
[2] Either Alexander Gunn, bookbinders, or John Gunn, painters.

carrying out the foregoing resolutions it was then moved and seconded that a committee be appointed to consider Candidates already in the field and others likely to come foreward, said committee to have power to add to their number, and to report at next meeting of Council. Agreed too. The following members were then elected: Messers McWhinnie, Paterson, J. Gunn, Dewar, Shearer, Lawson and Millar. Mr Dewar then moved, seconded by Mr Todd, That this Council take up the following question: What is the best means of organising Trade societies and the best form of organisation? After some discussion he agreed, seeing the great ammount of business before the Council, to let his motion lie over till after the elections in November. Mr Gunn[1] also agreed to let his motion lie over at present.

A conversation then took place regarding the appointment of an inspector of workshops. The general opinion expressed by the members pointed at a report widely prevalent throughout the City that a large proportion of the Councillors were already pledged to the support of two candidates before the situation had been advertised in terms of the remit on Bailie Lewis's motion. The President was also authorised to give Mr McWhinnie a recommendation from the Council in the event of his applying for the situation as it considers him thouroughly qualified for the Office of inspector of workshops. Mr Paterson handed in the division list of the Town Council on the Scavangers case, stating that he had got the same in the *Review* Office. Proofs of the annual report were also laid before the meeting but owing to the lateness of the hour it was not taken up but left over till next night, with a vote of thanks to Mr Paterson for his labour in compilling the report.

12 October 1869

On roll being called 22 answered to their names. Certificates were read from the Leith Bakers appointing James Wilson in room of George Robertson, who had resigned; and from the Upholsters appointing William Ferguson in room of Gabriel Wallace, who had also resigned. Mr Ferguson handed in 7s 6d stating that it had been voted by the Upholsters as a donation to the Council for

---

[1] Either Alexander Gunn, bookbinders, or John Gunn, painters.

general purposes. A letter was read from the Home Secretary in answer to our communication on the Miners case. Mr Rankin moved, seconded by Mr Todd, that a committee be appointed to reply as we consider the answer very unsatisfactory. The following members were then appointed: the Secretary, Messers McWhinnie, Paterson and Todd. A letter was also read from the Secretary of the International Workingmen's Association (with an enclosed letter from the Paper Stainers Society giving notice of a strike in that trade in New York) requisting us to make the contents known where ever we could, also that he would esteem it a great favour if we would get it published in the Edinburgh papers. After several members had expresed their disapproval of advertising, stating that they considered it would do more harm than good owing to the disorganised state of that trade here, Mr McWhinnie moved that the Secretary acknowledge receipt of the letter stating our reasons for not publishing it, which was unanimously agreed to.

The proofs of the Anual report of the Council were then taken up and after several alterations and corrections were made, approved of and ordered to be printed. The committee appointed to consider the candidates for town Council gave in their report. Mr Rankin moved seeing the lateness of the hour that we adjourn the meeting till Friday night so that we may have time thouroughly to consider the report of the committee and devise what steps we intend to take in the ensuing municipal elections. Mr Paterson seconded, on the condition that part of the evening be devoted to the Workshops Act, which was unanimously agreed to. The Secretary was instructed to summon all absent members.

15 October 1869

An adjourned meeting was held. On the roll being called 15 answered to their names. After some conversation on municipal affairs Mr Lawson stated that he was authorised to state by a certain Party, who was willing to furnish the Council with funds to contest a ward, that if we would fix on a working man as a candidate and name any ward that night, subject to their approval, the money would be forthcomming by next night of meeting.

During the temporary absence of two members the conduct of the Town Council with regard to the appointment of an Inspector under the workshops act was reviewed. After several statements had been made by members of facts that had come under their notice relating thereto, Mr Paterson moved, seconded by Mr Lawson, That this Council have received full authentication of the statement made that a number of certificates and applications were circulated amongst the Town Councillors for the office of Inspector of Workshops previous to the vacancy being advertised. This Council hold that the person appointed should have the confidence of the working classes and experience of the working of the Acts, and as Mr John McWhinnie posseses both these qualifications this council resolves to recommend him to apply for the Office and authorise the chairman and secretary to sign a certificate to Mr McWhinnie in name of the United Trades of Edinburgh as represented at this Council. It was carried unanimously.

The municipal bussiness was again resumed when Mr John Gunn moved that as the Canongate was almost altogether a working man's ward we contest it. Mr Yorston seconded.[1] 9 voted in favor of the motion, which was declaired carried, the rest declining to vote. Mr McWhinnie then moved, seconded by Mr Yorston, that we requist Mr Paterson to stand as our candidate. Unanimously agreed to. The following members were then appointed as a committee to get up a requisition: Messers McWhinnie, Gunn,[2] Lawson, Dewar and Scott.[3]

19 October 1869

A special meeting was held. 14 members were present. After the bussiness had been briefly stated Mr Lawson was asked if he had anything further to state in reply. He said that everything was quite favourable as far as he knew but he expected a message shortly. After some conversation Mr Paterson said that the decession he had come to was that he could not go into the contest as he doubted that he was not qualified, not having been 12 months resident in the City at this time, and also that his duties would not permit him. At this time Baillie Lewis was introduced to the Council and briefly stated the possition of Broughton Ward. If we would

---

[1] Cornelius Yorston, blacksmiths. In some minutes his name is spelt Yorkson.
[2] Probably John Gunn, painters, but could be Alexander Gunn, bookbinders.
[3] Either George Scott, glasscutters, or John Scott, brassfounders.

appoint a man to contest the ward with Baillie Millar the Indipendent Liberals would take our candidate on their card with Mr Robertson[1] and unseat the Baillie, for it was a shame to have a man playing fast and loose as he had been doing.[2] After strongly urging the Council to consider what he had said Baillie Lewis took his leave. After some consideration Mr Paterson was prevailed on still to stand as our candidate on Mr McWhinnie offering to fill the breach rather than that we should want a man to represent the working classes in the event of Mr Paterson being disqualified.

Mr Lawson was asked in the event of the Council contesting another ward to that first named would the Party still be willing to advance the money. He replied that he did not think it would make any differance whatever as the only condition was that we should have reasonable hopes of success so that the money would not be thrown away. Mr McWhinnie then moved, seconded by Mr White, that we withdraw our opposition to Mr Buchanan in the Canongate Ward[3] in the meantime and devote all our energies to return a member for Broughton Ward. On the understanding that as many of the members as could get would be present at Broughton Ward meeting the following night, the meeting adjourned.

22 October 1869

A special meeting was held. On the roll being called 21 answered to their names. The Secretary stated that he had called the meeting in accordance with the wishes of eight members. Messers McWhinnie and Paterson then laid their statement before the meeting – how Baillie Millar had returned to the Independent Liberals and how they had taken him back in preferance to our candidate, Mr Lawson also stating that the money promised was not now forthcomming as we had indentified ourselves with a political party. After fully considering our position the following was moved and unanimously

[1] Thomas Robertson, of Oliphant and Co., publishers and booksellers, South Bridge. Robertson was unsuccessful at the election; Millar and a moderate Liberal were elected.
[2] 'Bailie [Peter] Millar had made himself specially obnoxious to the working classes by his gross reflections upon the character of the electors in the poorer districts of the city, and his anti-liberal tendencies for some months past have offended a large number of his former supporters.' *Reformer*, 23 October 1869.
[3] James Buchanan, of Buchanan's Hotel.

agreed to: That in consideration of the overtures addressed to the Trade Council wishing a coalition for the purpose of ousting Baillie Millar and representing labour, this Council were induced to go forward in the contest for Broughton ward, and in consideration of the lateness of the session and their political jugglery this Council resolves that the whole question of labour representation and organisation be remitted to the various Trade Societies for council and consolidation. Before seperating the meeting agreed that 500 Copies of the Anual Report be printed.

26 October 1869

On the roll being called 24 answered to their names. A certificate was read from the Secretary of Type Founders Society, appointing Messers Robert Brown and John McAllen as their representitives at this board. After a statement had been made to the effect that Mr Buchanan had declined to stand as a Candidate for the Canongate Ward, and that Mr McWhinnie had been nominated at the Ward meeting the preceeding evening, the general opinion was that we should adjourn the meeting, and devote what time was yet at our disposal in endeavouring to return Mr McWhinnie for the ward. Before adjourning the meeting Mr McWhinnie moved in accordance with previous notice, seconded by Mr Gunn,[1] That this Council in future connect itself with none of the present pollitical Parties but confine itself to the representation of labour. It was carried unnanimously.

9 November 1869

On the roll being called 18 answered to their names. Certificates were read from Painters Society appointing Hercules Anthony as their representitive, also from the Tinplate Workers appointing Peter Lawson and George Shearer to act again as their representitives, and from the Joiners, Central Branch, appointing Peter McDonald in room of William White, who had resigned. Several Letters were read from Trade Societies that had been communicated with on the subject of proposed Conference on Trades Union legislation, all with one exception agreeing in the necessity and promising to

[1] Either Alexander Gunn, bookbinders, or John Gunn, painters.

S

send deligates to said conference in the event of it being held. The Secretary was instructed to answer the letter from the Masons Society. A letter on the same subject was also read from the Dundee Trades Council signifying their hearty approval of the scheme and offering their aid in making it successful.

The attention of the Council was directed to a notice of motion by Mr Hope[1] in the Town Council to alter the Polling day for the municipal elections to Saturday and to extend the hours till six in the evening for the convenience of Working Men electors.[2] After consideration it was agreed to on the motion of Mr Todd, seconded by Mr J. Scott, That a deputation be appointed to wait on Mr Hope to consider how we could best assist him in carrying his motion seeing that it is of so great importance to us as Working Men. On being put to the meeting it was carried unanimously. The following members were then appointed: Messers McVey, Todd, Scott,[3] McWhinnie, and Bartie. Mr Todd moved, in accordance with a previous motion, that a committee be appointed to draw up an address to submit to our trades on the Subject of labour representation, which was unanimously agreed to. The following were then appointed: Messers Dewar, McDonald,[4] Munro, Millar, and Paterson.

23 November 1869

In the absence of the President Mr Todd was called to the chair.[5] 20 members were present. A certificate was read from the Edinburgh South Branch of the associated Carpenters and Joiners of Scotland, appointing Messers Alexander Forbes and Edward Jeffery as their representitives at this Council. Mr Gunn[6] then called the attention of the meeting to the financial condition of the Council, and moved

---

[1] John Hope, w.s., 1807-93, temperance advocate, philanthropist, militant Protestant, a leader of the local Rifle Volunteer movement, and Conservative town councillor 1857-89.
[2] Under existing arrangements polling day was a Tuesday, and the polls were open from 8 a.m. until 4 p.m.
[3] Presumably John Scott, brassfounders, but could be George Scott, glasscutters.
[4] Probably John McDonald, brassfounders, but could be Peter McDonald, joiners.
[5] Dewar, the president, was present later.
[6] All references to Gunn in this minute may be to either Alexander Gunn, bookbinders, or John Gunn, painters.

the following, seconded by Mr McDonald,[1] That the Committee appointed consider and report progress to next meeting on the financial condition of the Council and that in the mean time the Treasurer . . . the first Anual report due. Agreed to. Mr McDonald stated in answer to a question that owing to non attendance of members the Labour representation Committee had no report.

The correspondence was taken up which consisted of several letters from Mr Hope with regard to his motion in the Town Council with a view to altering the polling day for municipal elections. Also one from the Hairdressers Philanthropic Society wishing to know the present position of the Trades Council with the view of becoming connected. The Secretary was instructed to answer. Mr Dewar asked permission to make a statement to the Council of the position of the Iron Trades with regard to the short time movement, after hearing which Mr Paterson moved that the Secretary be instructed to communicate the following motion to the various Trade Councils of Scotland: That this Council of Trade Delegates, considering the Appeal of the Iron Trades on the Short Time Movement, thoroughly approve of their endevours to limit the duration of the working day, and earnestly desire to call the attention of Trade Councils and Trade Unions of Scotland to the vital nature of the struggle, in the belief they will assist their fellow workmen in a struggle that will further the interests of the whole community. Mr Yorston seconded and the motion was unanimously agreed to.

Mr Todd then reported the proceedings of the deputation that was appointed to wait on Mr Hope with regard to his motion, stating that the deputation comprised Messers McVey, Bartie, and Todd. After a lengthened conversation it was agreed that the resolution stand as altered: That the polling day be Saturday from 8 a.m. till 6 p.m. The deputation, having thanked Mr Hope, withdrew. The Secretary also supplimented the report by stating that owing to the unexpected treetment by the Town Council of Mr Hope's motion[2] he had had further communication with Mr Hope on that

[1] Both references to McDonald in this minute are probably to John McDonald, brass-founders, but could be to Peter McDonald, joiners.
[2] During the debate on Hope's motion at the town council meeting on 16 November, it was discovered there was no longer a quorum and the council adjourned until 30 November. By that date Hope had deleted from his original motion the proposal to

subject. Mr Hope stated that he thought it would be advantagious to have a deputation from the Trades Council seeing the treetment the motion was likely to receive at next meeting of Town Council. The report being approved of, Mr Yorston moved that we send a deputation to memorialize the Town Council in support of Mr Hope's motion at their next meeting as we consider an alteration in the day and hours of polling for municipal elections of the utmost importance. Seconded by Mr Scott.[1] Mr Gunn moved as an amendment, seconded by Mr Rae, that considering the manner in which a former deputation had been treeted by the Town Council that none be sent. 4 voted for the amendment and 10 for the motion. The following members were ellected: Messers Todd, Yorston, Bartie.

The subject of Technical Education was briefly laid before the Council by Mr Gunn, and the protection of Trade funds by Mr Paterson. The Secretary then stated that Mr Hope had desired him to call the attention of the Council to the movement on foot for the removal of the Powder Magazine which had been erected by him for the use of the Third Edinburgh Rifle Volunteers in the Hunters Bog, seeing that it was a question where the intrest and convenience of a number of Working men was likely to be sacrifised simply to gratify a whim of Sir George Harvey,[2] Mr James Ballantine,[3] and the members of the Scottish Academy. Mr Yorston then moved, seeing the lateness of the hour, that Mr Hope's letter be not read till next meeting, when the subject be taken up and fully considered. The motion was seconded by Mr McArthur and agreed to. Copies of a pamphlet on the national Education question were also distributed among the members present.

14 December 1869

18 members were present. A certificate was read from the Edinburgh Branch of the Amalgamated Engineers Society appointing Messers William Wilson and Andrew Scott to represent them at this

extend the hours of polling from 4 to 6 p.m. *Reformer*, 20 November 1869, 4 December 1869.
[1] Either George Scott, glasscutters, or John Scott, brassfounders.
[2] Sir George Harvey, 1806-76, president of the Royal Scottish Academy 1864-76.
[3] Evidently an error for John Ballantyne, 1815-97, R.S.A. 1860.

Council. On the motion of Mr Todd, seconded by Mr McWhinnie, Mr Taylor was appointed Vice President in room of Mr White, who had retired. As agreed to at last meeting Mr Hope's letter was read and considered. Mr McWhinnie moved, seconded by Mr Wilson,[1] That the Secretary be instructed to write to Mr Hope stating that we have heard his letter read and, considering it not trade bussiness, do not see what action we can take in the matter. But in the event of things coming to the worst believe that he will have the unanimous support of the Working Classes in keeping the Magazine in its present Site. Mr Rankine moved as an ammendment, seconded by Mr W. Wilson, That the Secretary be instructed to write Mr Hope stating that we have heard the letter read but considering it not trade bussiness decline to take any action in the matter. Mr Yorston seconded, Mr Munro moved also as an ammendment that the Secretary be instructed to write to Mr Hope expressing our sympathy with him and promising him our hearty support in keeping the magazine where it is. On being put to the vote there voted for Mr Rankin's ammendment 3, Mr Munro's 7, and the motion 6. Mr Munro's ammendment and the motion were then voted on, when there voted for ammendment 8, and for the motion 9.[2]

A letter was then read from the Secretary of the International workingmens association stating that the Stone Masons of Vienna were contemplating forming a co-operative Building Society and having heard of a Society of that kind in Edinburgh[3] were desirious of obtaining a copy of the rules and other documents of kindred societies in Scotland along with a statement of the rate of wages in the Building Trades in Edinburgh. The Secretary stated that he had procured the necessary documents along with other information required but wished to consult the Council before posting them. The Council approved of what had been done and instructed the Secretary to requist a similar statement from them regarding the hours wrought and the rate of wages in the Building Trades in Vienna. The finance committee stated that they had met, and

[1] Presumably James Wilson, Leith bakers.
[2] Hope subsequently won his battle to retain what its critics described as 'Hope's Hut' or 'The House that Jack built'. Rev. D. Jamie, *John Hope* (Edinburgh, 1907, abridged edn.), 213-6.
[3] The Edinburgh Co-operative Building Company Ltd, above, p. 54, n. 3.

considering that a number of the unrepresented Trades had as yet failed to answer our appeal the Committee in the meantime recommend the Deligates to appeal to their respective trades for assistance. After a good deal of discussion Mr McWhinnie moved, seconded by Mr Paterson, that the committee again meet and that the Treasurer be requested to attend said meeting so that the Committee may be able to give in full report by next usual meeting. Mr Taylor was also added to the committee in room of Mr White, who had resigned.

The Deputation who were appointed to wait on the Town Council relitave to Mr Hope's motion were then asked for their report. Mr Todd submitted the following: November 27th, 1869 – The committee appointed to take action regarding Mr Hope's motion to the Town Council, anent alteration of day and hour of polling, met of this date when a draft memorial was read and approved of. The Secretary was requested to read the same at the meeting of Town Council on Tuesday first. There being no other bussiness the Committee adjourned. November 30th, 1869 – Of this date the Committee appointed to take action in accordance with resolution of Trade Council waited on Edinburgh Town Council. After the Secretary had read the memorial and supported the same in a few observations the other members of the deputation were heard in support of the same. A few questions being asked and answered, the deputation, having thanked the Council for their courtisy, withdrew. On a further disscussion of the question it was agreed from a division that the subject be remitted to the Lord Provost's Committee. In view of this division we recommend that a deputation wait upon the Lord Advocate[1] and press the question on his attention with the addition that the polling day be the first Saturday of November for municipal elections, between the hours of 8 a.m. and 4 p.m. After hearing the report, it was moved by Mr Rankin and agreed to that it be engrosed in the minutes. It was also agreed that we take no further action in the meantime untill the representatives at the proposed Trade Conference have an oppertunity of expressing their oppinions on the subject.

The night being far advanced it was found impossible to take up

George Young, Lord Young, 1819-1907, lord advocate 1869-74, Liberal M.P. for Wigtown Burghs 1865-74, a judge of the court of session 1874-1905.

all the bussiness on the programe. Mr Dewar therefore moved, seconded by Mr Paterson, that this meeting be adjourned till this night week to consider the advisability of holding the proposed Trade Conferance, which was unanimously agreed to.

21 December 1869

A special meeting was held, Vice President in the chair.[1] On the roll being called 21 answered to their names. After the reason for calling the meeting had been stated Mr Dewar called on the Secretary to read the correspondence on the subject. Mr Dewar moved, seconded by Mr Ranken, That the number of favourable answers we have received warrant us in calling the Conferance together. Mr Todd moved, seconded by Mr Bartie, That said conferance be not held as we have not a sufficient number of favourable answers to the circular to warrant us in calling it together, but that a deputation be appointed from this Council to wait on the Lord Advocate on the subject together with representitives from those Trades who were agreeable to take part in the deputation. There voted for Mr Dewar's 14, Mr Todd's 2. It was also moved and agreed to that said conferance meet on the 8th day of February 1870 in Buchanan's Temperance Hotell, Edinburgh. Mr Paterson and the Secretary were instructed to draw up a circular in accordance with this agreement to be issued again to the Trade Societies of Scotland. After settling about advertising the conference in the Newspapers and agreeing to ellect delegates at next meeting the Council adjourned.

28 December 1869

A report being asked from the financial Committee the Secretary stated that owing to the nonattendance of the members of committee there had been no meeting, consequently there was no report. After some discussion it was agreed the matter be recommitted to the committee. Mr Paterson then breefly reported the progress that had been made in the getting up of the circular calling the Conference, which was approved of. In accordance with agreement at last meeting Mr Rankin moved that 4 Delegates be elected to represent

[1] James Taylor, tailors. Presumably Dewar, the president, vacated the chair to move his resolution.

this Council at the proposed Trade Conference. Mr Todd seconded, which was agreed to. Mr Ranken proposed the following leet, seconded by Mr Yorston, viz., Messers Todd, Dewar, McVey, and McWhinnie, which was unanimously agreed to. The Secretary was instructed to write to Edward Strathearn Gordon, Esq., M.P., asking him to deliver a lecture any evening the conference was siting, either on the 8, 9, or 10 of February. Mr Paterson then stated that he had received a letter from Mr Millar, M.P.,[1] on the subject of the Workingmen's International Exibition, enclosing a letter from the Lord Provest[2] in which it was stated that he would call a public meeting on the subject on a requision from a committee of working men. The President and Secretary were instructed to draw up a memorial requisting the Provest to call a public meeting.[3]

Mr McVey then stated that General Cary, a U.S. member of Congress, had offered to deliver a lecture to the Workingmen of Edinburgh under the auspices of the Trade Council should he return to Edinburgh.[4] Mr W. Wilson moved that the Secretary write to General Cary asking on what conditions he would be willing to come and deliver a lecture, which was agreed to. Mr William Wilson submitted the following motion before adjourning: That the Trade Council of Edinburgh heartly concur with the working men of Southwark in choosing Mr Odger as a fit and proper candidate to represent the rights of Labour in parliment and that this resolution be forwarded to the Trade Council of London. Unanimously agreed to.[5]

[1] John Miller of Leithen, M.P. for Edinburgh.
[2] William Law, 1799-1878, lord provost 1869-72.
[3] The exhibition was held in London from 16 July to 1 November 1870.
[4] General Samuel Fenton Cary of Cincinnati, Ohio, temperance reformer, had addressed a public meeting in the Music Hall on 15 December 1869. *Scotsman*, 16 December 1869.
[5] George Odger, 1820-77, a shoemaker, a leader of working class radicalism, secretary of London trades council 1862-72 and one of the 'Junta'; president of the International Working Men's Association 1864-7. At the Southwark election as the candidate of the Labour Representation League he came a close second to the Conservative. *Minutes of the General Council of the First International 1866-8* (Moscow and London, 1964), 431; G. D. H. Cole, *British Working Class Politics 1832-1914* (London, 1941), 56-7.

1870

Twenty members were present. An answer was read from Edward S. Gordon, Esq., M.P., stating that he would be unable to deliver an address on the 8 February as he required to be in London previous to that date. Mr Ranken moved that the Secretary be instructed to write to Charles Scott, Esq., Advocate, asking him to receive a deputation on Tuesday evening the 18th January, who should be instructed to requist him to deliver an address on the same conditions as Mr Gordon had been asked. Mr McWhinnie seconded. There voted for the motion 10, against 2. The following members were then appointed to wait on Mr Scott: The President, Secretary, Mr McWhinnie, Mr Gunn,[1] Mr Wilson,[2] and Mr Ranken. An Answer from General Cary was also read in which he stated that his return to Scotland would depend on the number of engagements to Lecture which he received.

A Note from Mr Todd was also laid before the meeting in which, while acknowledging the honor, he declined to stand as a representitave of the Council at the Trade conference in February. Mr John Gunn was then unanimously elected in room of Mr Todd. After several other letters relitave to the Trade Conference had been read it was unanimously resolved that Mr Wilson[3] be requisted to deliver an address on one of the nights of the conference. Mr Dewar having also intimated that he would be agreeable to deliver a short address, Mr Todd moved that Mr Wilson's essay and Mr Dewar's be read on Wednesday night the 9th February 1870, before a public meeting in the presence of the Delegates appointed to take part in the conference. Mr Ranken seconded the motion which was unanimously

[1] Either Alexander Gunn, bookbinders, or John Gunn, painters.
[2] Either William Wilson, engineers, or James Wilson, Leith bakers.
[3] William Wilson, engineers.

agreed too. It was also agreed that financial committee should meet on Friday the 14th January in order to be able to report at next meeting.

25 January 1870

25 members were present. Mr Dewar gave in report of deputation that waited on Mr Charles Scott, stating that Mr Scott would be most happy to deliver an address on Trade Unionism as required. Mr Rankin moved approval of Committee report, Mr Lawson seconded. Agreed to. Mr Ranken and Mr Lawson then moved that a sub-committee be appointed to make the necessary arrangements for the Public meetings. The following members were appointed: Mr McArthur, Mr Paterson, Mr McWhinnie, and Mr George Scott. It was agreed that Mr Dewar take the Chair at the meeting and the Secretary to write to Mr Scott as soon as they get fixed about a Hall. Mr McWhinnie gave in report from finance Committee showing the financial position of the Council. Messers Paterson and Ranken moved approval, which was agreed to. After considering report it was agreed that those Trades in arrears pay up to be clear in July and that the contributions in future be doubled. Mr Paterson then moved that the Treasurer prepare accounts of amount due the Council by each Society represented, also that they be requisted to clear up to July. The accounts to be ready by next meeting. Agreed to. It was also agreed that the Treasurer pay the Printer £4 to account. The Treasurer then stated that the duties of his office encroached so much on his leasure time that he had resolved to resign, but was prevailed upon to continue in office till after the Conference.

Letters were then read from Mr C. Scott intimating that he would be happy to receive the deputation from the Council. Also from the Edinburgh Temperance Electoral association[1] wishing a meeting with representitaves from the Council for the purpose of endevouring to come to some understanding in reference to future Electoral action, when it was agreed that it lie on the table till our

---

[1] 'The Edinburgh Temperance Electoral Association supports election of those candidates for Parliament or Town Council whose return will promote prohibition of liquor.' Membership, at a subscription of at least 1s per annum, was open to all citizens. *Reformer*, 22 August 1868.

meeting on the second Tuesday of February. Several letters relitave to the Trade Conference were also read. Before seperating Mr Paterson moved that the subcommittee be instructed to engage the Craggie Hall[1] or a place similar for Mr Scott's meeting. Mr Yorston moved, seconded by Mr Ranken, that the Queen Street Hall be engaged, which was carried by a majority of 14 to 8. It was then moved that the Council meet this night week to make the necessary arrangments connected with the Trade Conference, which was agreed to.

1 February 1870

A special meeting was held. 22 members were present. The Committee having been asked what arrangments they had made for Mr Scott's Lecture, Mr Paterson stated that he had not been successful in getting Brighton Street Chapel but had secured Queen Street Hall for Wednesday night the 9 inst. Mr Gunn[2] then moved that the addresses by Mr W. Wilson and Mr Dewar be read on Thursday the 10th inst., seconded by Mr Lawson and agreed to unanimously. The Committee were then instructed on a motion by Mr Todd to secure Brighton Street Chaple Tabernical, Cockburn St Hall, or Phoenix Hall for that purpose. Mr Laing[3] then moved, seconded by Mr Todd, That we instruct our delegates attending Conference to move that report of proceedings be printed, including the addresses delivered during the sitting of Conference, which was agreed to.[4] The Delegates were then instructed to bring the following subjects before the Conference, viz., the legalisation of trade unions, the shortening of the hours of Labour, and the necessity of Labour representation. Mr Gunn[5] intimated that owing to a change with regard to his Employer he would be unable to attend the conference as a Delegate from this Council. The question of remuneration for delegates was then considered when it was agreed to allow 5s. with 2s. of expences per day on the motion of Messers Todd and Munro.[6] Mr Wilson gave in the subject of his address as

---

1 The Craigie Hall was at 5 St Andrew Square.
2 Either Alexander Gunn, bookbinders, or John Gunn, painters.
3 Not identified, but possibly David Laing, plasterers.
4 If the proceedings were printed no copy has been found. There is no report of such a motion in the press accounts of the conference.
5 John Gunn, painters.   6 Identity uncertain.

The progress and principles of Trade Unions. It was agreed that a special meeting be again held on Saturday 5th inst. at 6 oclock evening to instruct the Delegates appointed to attend Conference.

5 February 1870

A special meeting was held. 16 members were present. The several subjects were taken up and considered and the delegates instructed in accordance with decision arrived at. Some conversation also took place on the subject of General Holidays and Free Public Libriaries but nothing definate was arrived at. The Secretary was instructed to write to Mr Cobb[1] and invite him to be present at the meeting of Conference for the purpose of taking a shorthand report. It was also agreed the regular meeting be posponded for a week so as not to interfere with Trade conference meeting that day.

15 February 1870

26 members were present. A Letter was read from the Aberdeen Trade Council wishing this Council to take up the question of the repeal of the game Laws and bring the matter before the public as much as possiable. The letter was also accompanied by a packet of reports for distribution of a meeting on that subject held in Aberdeen.[2] The Secretary was instructed to answer.

Mr McWhinnie gave in report of Trade Conference stating that he had been elected Chairman and had filled that office and that the conference had lasted four days. Mr Dewar also stated the reason why he had been unable to attend. Mr Wilson[3] asked an explination of a clause that had been introduced into the Trades Union Bill as prepared by the Conference by Mr Inglis, Secretary for Blacksmiths' Society.[4] A long discussion ensued when the majority of the Council seemed unfavourable to the clause. Other parts were also discused

---

[1] Presumably Cobb, tailors.

[2] The meeting had been held in Aberdeen on 3 February 1870, with Lord Provost Leslie in the chair. 'The present stagnation in trade' was said to be closely related to the game laws. *Reformer*, 12 February 1870.

[3] Either William Wilson, engineers, or James Wilson, Leith bakers.

[4] John Inglis, 1834-1910, general secretary 1863-1910 of the Associated Blacksmiths' Society and a member of the parliamentary committee of the T.U.C. 1877-85, 1887-9 and 1891. It is not clear which clause is referred to. W. H. Marwick, *A Short History of Labour in Scotland* (Edinburgh, 1967), 33.

but nothing definate arrived at. The letter from the Edinburgh
Temperance Electoral association was also taken up, when Mr
Yorston, seconded by Mr Todd, moved as the night was so far
advanced that the Letter lie over till next meeting but that it come
up as first bussiness then, which was agreed to.

22 February 1870

The letter from the Edinburgh Temperance Electoral Association
was read. Mr Paterson moved, Mr Jeffery seconding, That this
Council resolve to appoint a deputation of five for the purpose of
conferring with the Edinburgh Temperance Electoral Association
upon municipal elections and that the deputation report to this
Council before they take any steps or give any pledges or assurances.
Mr Wilson[1] and Mr Millar moved as an ammendment: That as the
Temperance party are pledged to support Temperance men as
Town Councilors we cannot co-operate with such parties in as much
as we consider that the right men for Councilors are those who will
represent the rights of labour, whether temperance men or not.
There voted for the motion 10, for the ammendment 4. The follow-
ing Gentlemen were appointed as a deputation: Mr Yorston, Mr
Paterson, Mr Weir, and the President and Secretary.

After hearing a sujestion from Mr Dewar wishing the Council to
take some action in regard to the Bakehouse Act some referance
was made to the financial possition of the Council. It was agreed to
remit the matter to the committee appointed lately to make arraingments for public meeting then held, with powers to borrow money
to liquidate the debt at present pressing on the Council.

8 March 1870

In the absence of the President and Vice president Mr William
Wilson was called to the Chair. 20 members were present. A
certificate from the Cabinet and Chair Makers Society was read
appointing Mr James Sinclair and Mr John Shedden as their representitives at this board.

Mr Paterson then gave in report from deputation that was
appointed to confer with deputation from the Temperance Electoral

---

[1] Either William Wilson, engineers, or James Wilson, Leith bakers.

Association, when as had been agreed to the following was submitted for approval: I. That a mutual understanding be arrived at
beforehand so that the Edinburgh United Trades Council and the
Edinburgh Temperance Electoral Association shall not be found
contesting the same wards in opposition to each other. II. To
reciprocate such mutual support as can be afforded without inter-
feering with the indipendent action of either party. III. It is not
required that either party addopt the oppinions or platform of the
other. After some discussion Mr Todd moved that the report lie
on the table so that the deligates might have an opportunity of
laying the matter before their Trades. Mr Yorston seconded. Messers
William Paterson and Peter McDonald moved the approval of
the report. 10 voted for Mr Todd's motion and 4 for Mr Paterson's
motion.

The subject of overcrowding in the dewellings of the poorer
Classes was then brought under the notice of the Council. The
following motion, moved by Messers Todd and Paterson, was
unanimously agreed to: That a special meeting of Council be held
on Tuesday first the 15 March for consideration of this question
before the Council takes public action in it. Before seperating Mr
Paterson called the attention of the Council to the advisibillity of
endevouring to get the Royal Scottish Academy's Exhibition opened
at reduced rates for the benifit of the Working Classes. The following Gentlemen were appointed as a deputation to wait upon the
directors for that purpose, viz., Messers Todd, Forbes, Andrew Scott,
Wilson[1] and Bartie.

15 March 1870

A special meeting was held. Mr D. Munroe occupied the chair. 16
members were present. A letter from the Secretary of the Royal
Scottish Academy was read wishing a definite proposal from the
Council, after hearing which the committe was reappointed with
powers to answer the letter. A letter from Councilor Hope was also
read in which he stated that as he presumed the Edinburgh United
Trades Council would be raising subscriptions in aid of Joiners of
Glasgow during their strike for the short time movement, he would
be happy to send £10 to the Secretery to be forwarded to them for

[1] Either William Wilson, engineers, or James Wilson, Leith bakers.

that purpose. After some consideration the position and prospects of the Glasgow Joiners strike was deemed of such importance as to warrant the united action of the Scottish and English Trade Councils. Messers Todd and Lawson then moved: That a special meeting of delegates and Trade officials be held on Friday for the purpose of considering what means should be addopted to afford the Glasgow joiners substancial support. Unanimously agreed to. The Secretary was instructed to invite Mr Hope to be present.[1] It was also agreed that seeing the night was so far advanced to leave the bussiness of the meeting till our next regular meeting.

18 March 1870

A special meeting of Council and Trade officials was held, the President in the chair. The Secretary was requisted to read Mr Hope's letter. Mr Wilson[2] then oppened the proceedings by moving the following, seconded by Mr Todd, That as the various trades of Edinburgh and Leith have repeatedly expressed their oppinions respecting the benifits which would result from a reduction of the hours of labour, and seeing the determination displayed by the Glasgow joiners to work no longer under the old system this Council respectfully requists the various workmen of Edinburgh and Leith to take immediate action in every workshop for the raising of weekly subscriptions to assist and enable our brethren in the West to bring their present dispute to a successful and satisfactory issue. It was carried unanimously. Messers Todd and Lawson then moved: That this meeting of Edinburgh Trades Council and Trade Union officials respectfully requists the English and Scotch trade councils and societies to consider the present position of the Glasgow joiners with regard to the nine hour movement. Also unanimously agreed to. It was also agreed that a finance [committee] be appointed to receive subscriptions and carry out the foregoing resolutions. The following members were appointed: The Chairman, Secretary, Mr Todd, Mr A. Scott, and Mr Sinclair. A hearty vote of thanks having been awarded to Mr Hope for his liberal subscription, the meeting seperated.

---

[1] The Glasgow joiners' strike had begun on 1 March for an increase of $\frac{1}{2}$d an hour and a reduction of hours to nine a day. Most of the employers had granted the men's demands by 18 April. *Glasgow Sentinel*, 5 March 1870; *Scotsman*, 19 April 1870.
[2] Probably William Wilson, engineers, but could be James Wilson, Leith bakers.

22 March 1870

22 members were present. A certificate from the Leith Branch of the Amalgamated Society of Engineers was read appointing William Reid to represent them at this Board. The letter was read from the Secretary of the Royal Scottish Acedemy wishing a specific proposal to lay before their Council from this board. Mr Todd then read a letter in reply which he proposed to send. The same was agreed to on motion of Mr Lawson and Mr Alexander Munro.[1]

Mr Todd then opened the bussiness of the meeting, viz., the overcrowding in the dewellings of the poorer classes, by giving some instances that had come under his own observation that called for some action being taken, and moved that the secretary be instructed to write to the society for improving the condition of the poor for the purpose of obtaining statistics. Mr Lawson seconded and also gave some very important facts on the same subject. After several other members had expressed their opinions it was agreed to adjourn the meeting, the same subject to come up as first bussiness at next meeting. Mr McVey intimated that he would be unable to stand as Treasurer, being otherwise engaged, and some difficulty being experienced in getting a member to fill that office Mr McAllen agreed to act as Treasurer for a night or two, which was agreed to. Mr Paterson then gave notice of motion for next meeting on the wages arrestment Bill.

12 April 1870

23 members were present. The following resolutions, moved by Mr Scott,[2] seconded by Mr Wilson,[3] were unanimously agreed to:

THE[4] OVERCROWDING OF THE DWELLINGS OF THE POORER CLASSES

1. Judging by practical experience and daily intercourse with the working classes, also after hearing from time to time the general

---

[1] Not identified.
[2] Probably Andrew Scott, engineers, but could be John Scott, brassfounders, or George Scott, glasscutters.
[3] All references to Wilson in this minute are probably to William Wilson, engineers, but could be to James Wilson, Leith bakers.
[4] From here to '. . . with powers' in line 16 of next page is a press cutting pasted into the minute book.

statements and almost inexhaustible statistics by the various delegates
anent the miserable condition of the poor for want of proper house
accommodation, this Council unanimously agrees that if suitable
and more commodious houses are not speedily built for the working
classes, to reduce the evils of 'overcrowding', and to advance the
social, moral, and physical wellbeing of the poor, those who are
entrusted with the city improvements will contract a deep moral
guilt, which neither sophistry nor *self-interest* shall remove.

2. That the overcrowded dwellings at exorbitant rents in Edinburgh are particularly inadequate, in respect of (1) insufficiency of
space, (2) light, (3) cleanliness and want of water, (4) ruinous
rents – necessitating a pinching of fuel, food, and clothing. That
some of these evils would be mitigated by erecting houses in place
of hovels, and placing part of the *trust*-money to the erection of
those houses which *should* be erected.

Remit to Special Committee, with powers, the following gentlemen being appointed as committee: Messers Lawson, McWhinnie,
Wilson, Paterson, Andrew Scott, Shedden, McArthur, McDonald,[1]
Weir, John Gunn, and Jeffrey. The Secretary Conveener. A vote of
thanks was awarded to Dr Murray[2] for attendance and for the interest
taken by him in the subject.

On the motion of Mr Todd the following was unanimously
[carried]: That[3] this Council of Trade Delegates support Mr
Anderson's Wages 'Original' Arrestment Bill,[4] so far as regards
the limitation to 30s., for the following reasons: 1. That the
principle of the bill will prevent the present unhealthy credit
system, reduce the power of the improvident to injure the fair
trader, and ultimately prove beneficial to buyer and seller. 2. That
the present law of arrestment has been used as a powerful stimulant
and backing to the tally system and money usurer, and ruinous to
the domestic peace and comfort of the poorer classes. 3. That the
law of arrestment, in many cases, inflicts serious irreparable personal
injury, even where the alleged debtor is unaware of any debt having

[1] Either John McDonald, brassfounders, or Peter McDonald, joiners.
[2] David Murray, M.D., Edinburgh 1862.
[3] From here to '. . . next session' in line 23 of next page is a press cutting pasted into
the minute book.
[4] George Anderson, Radical M.P. for Glasgow. The Bill was enacted on 9 August 1870
as the Wages Arrestment Limitation (Scotland) Act.

T

been contracted. 4. That the objections of merchants to the ready-money system, and of yearly society officials to the passing of this Act, proceed from the circumstances of the present obscuring what must be in the law of the future. Resolve to support Mr Anderson's bill, and to petition in its favour as a Trade Council.

A letter being read from the *Beehive* newspaper, the following was agreed to on the motion of Messers Todd and Wilson: That this Council, touching the letter received from the proprietors of the *Beehive* newspaper wishing the patronage and support of trade unionists and trade societies, learn with regret that the office in which the *Beehive* newspaper is printed is worked on the excessive turnover apprentice system, and that the same was objected to by the officials of the London Typographical Society, but without practical effect. Resolve that this Council cannot consistently encourage directly or indirectly the promotion of the cause of trade unionism in this manner; and further state that the various trade societies are in the habit of inquiring at the proper officials, so that the recognised houses in the printing trade receive all trade union work or contracts.

A letter was read from the secretary of the Royal Scottish Academy intimating that the request of the Council, that greater facilities should be afforded the working classes for admission, would be considered previous to the opening of next session. A letter was also read from the Labour Representation League wishing the Council to help forward the cause of direct labour representation by forming a branch of the league and asking a reply.[1] It was agreed that the letter lie on the table. Mr Munro[2] then brought forward the financial statement when it was agreed that the Secretary meet with auditors and report.

26 April 1870

17 members were present. Mr Todd stated on behalf of the overcrowding committee that they had met on the 21st inst., Councilor Gowans being present at the meeting, at which it was agreed that

[1] The Labour Representation League had been formed in London in September 1869 to organise the working class vote and secure the election of working men to parliament, but also to support other sympathetic candidates. G. D. H. Cole, *British Working Class Politics 1832-1914* (London, 1941), 50.
[2] Identity uncertain.

the Tron district be inspected by the committee and reported so as
to be supplied with statistics to prove the real state of matters.
Several of the members then gave in their report of the progress
made in the division alloted to them. It was agreed still to prosecute
the inspection untill the whole district had been gone over.

10 May 1870

In the absence of the President, Mr Todd was called to the chair.
Dr Murray and Mr Gowans[1] being present, it was agreed to take
up the overcrowding question. After hearing report from Councilor
Gowans and several members of committee, it was unanimously
agreed, on the motion of Mr McDonald[2] and Mr McAllen, that as
the best means of bringing the matter before the public a public
meeting be held. The begining of June was fixed for the meeting,
Mr Gowans to make arrangements for a Hall and to be communicated with as to date after next meeting of Council. Before
withdrawing Mr Gowans brought the subject of establishing courts
of conciliation and arbitration before the council for consideration,
deploring that Lockouts and strikes should exist between Employers
and Employed as was at present the case. He also offered to draw up
a form for a basis for the establishment of said Courts and submit
it to the Council. Agreed to unanimously. Dr Murray and Mr
Gowans then withdrew.

The correspondence was then taken up. Credentials were read
from Edinburgh Bakers stating that James Malcom and Andrew
Drysdale had been elected in room of James McArthur and Gilbert
Millar, resigned. Also from the Leith Bakers appointing Alexander
Turnbull in room of James Wilson, resigned. Also a letter from
E. S. Gordon, Esq., M.P., stating that he had presented our memorial
in favour of Mr Anderson's Wages arrestment abolition Bill and in
Mr Anderson's absence had got it passed through committee. Also
letters from the Edinburgh Branch of the National Society for

[1] James Gowans, 1821-90, architect, railway engineer, builder of the Synod Hall,
'Rockville' (his architecturally notable residence in Napier Road, Edinburgh), and
houses for the working classes. A town councillor from 1868 to 1880, he oscillated
between Independent Liberals and Conservatives; knighted for promotion of the
Edinburgh international exhibition of 1886. *Scotsman*, 27 June 1890.
[2] Either John McDonald, brassfounders, or Peter McDonald, joiners.

Women's Suffrage accompanied by petition forms.[1] Several members having expressed their oppinion as opposed to the Society on the ground that it would create great facilities for faggot voting and would almost disenfranchise the Working classes by putting it within the power of the Monied class of obtaining votes for the female members of their families, the discussion was closed by Mr Yorston moving that the subject lie over till next meeting, which was agreed.

Information was then asked regarding the Treasurer's Book. It was stated that it was still in Mr Scott's possession and had never been audited. It was also stated that Mr Dewar had promised to call and get it. It was then agreed that the Secretary write to Mr Dewar in case he should have forgot, and ask him to call on Mr Scott and get the book and the money he had in hand so that we might get the trade conference expence made up.

24 May 1870

16 members present. Mr Todd moved and Mr Wilson seconded that the meeting on overcrowding be delayed for settlement till this night fortnight, the Secretary to communicate to Mr Gowans this decission. Notice of Motion from Mr McVey that Sir Wilfred Lawson's Prohibitory Liquor bill be discussed by this Council at next meeting.[2] The correspondence from the Edinburgh branch of the National Society for Women's Sufferage was then brought up. Mr Todd moved, Mr Wilson seconding, that the correspondence on this subject lie on the table for 6 months. Mr McVey moved, seconded by Mr Jeffrey, that the Secretary be instructed to communicate the sympathy of the Trades Council to the Edinburgh Branch of the Society for Women's Sufferage on the rejection of the Women's dissabillity Bill.[3] There voted for Mr Todd's motion 11, for Mr McVey's 3.

[1] The Edinburgh Society had been formed in 1867 and became a branch of the National Society the following year. Miss Agnes McLaren, daughter of Duncan McLaren, M.P., was secretary of the branch. *Reformer*, 29 August 1868; C. Rover, *Women's Suffrage and Party Politics in Britain, 1866-1914* (London, 1967), 6, 56.

[2] Sir Wilfrid Lawson, 1829-1906, Radical M.P. for Carlisle 1859-65 and 1868-85, Cockermouth 1886-1900 and 1906, and North West Cornwall 1903-06. See above, p. 256, n. 1.

[3] A Bill to remove the electoral disabilities of women. It was lost at its second reading on 12 May by 220 to 94 votes.

A report on the alteration of the Polling day for Parlimentery
and Municipal Elections with a table showing the hours wrought
by the various trades and how unsuitable the present day of the
week was for polling, was read by Mr Todd. It was approved and
the Secretary authorised to send a copy to the Lord Advocate[1] and
requist him to endevour to get Her Majesty's Government to
insert a clause in accordance with the report in the Ballot Bill.[2]

7 June 1870

A special meeting was held. Mr Yorston moved that a public
meeting [on overcrowding] be held, which was agreed to, it being
left in the hands of a subcommittee consisting of President, Secretary
and Mr Todd to make arrangements. The Secretary was also
instructed to transmit to Mr Charles Scott, Advocate, a copy of
the Rules of the Caledonian Rubber Works which had been brought
before the Council by a delegate, stating that a deputation had been
appointed to wait upon him to hear his opinion as to the legality
of said rules. The deputation appointed consisted of Mr Dewar, Mr
Yorston and Secretary.

14 June 1870

23 members present. A letter from Mr Charles Scott was read
wishing to know the particular rule we wished his opinion upon,
also stating that he would receive the deputation on Wednesday
evening the 15th inst. The Secretary was instructed to answer. A
letter was also read from the Lord Advocate acknowledgeing receipt
of report on alteration of the Polling day, stating that the subject
would have his attention. Two delegates were then introduced to
the Council from the Coach Makers: Mr William Henderson and
Mr Allen Scott. Mr McVey's motion on the Permissive Bill being
the first bussiness on the minutes was taken up, but it was agreed to
let it lie over untill he was present himself. Arrangements were then
made with regard to auditing the Treasurer's book, Mr Strachan
being appointed auditor in room of Mr McWhinnie in case he did
not attend. The committee gave in report on Public Meeting on
Overcrowding and City Improvements, which was approved of.

[1] George Young.
[2] The Bill had been published on 18 May.

Mr McVey then moved that the further arrangements be left in the hands of the Committee, which was agreed to. The following Gentlemen were added to the Committee: Messers Paterson, Strachan, and McVey.

On account of some information laid before the Council by a member of the finance committee the deputation appointed to wait on Mr Scott were instructed to wait on Mr Bridgeford and report.[1] Mr McVey then moved that Sir Wilford Lawson's Prohibitory Liquor Bill be discussed by this Council, seconded by Mr Paterson. Mr Yorston moved as an ammendment, seconded by Walter Clark,[2] that it be remitted to our Trades, which was carried by a majority of one, 7 voting for the ammendment and 6 for the motion. Mr Paterson gave notice of motion: That the Council take up the question of general holidays at next meeting.

28 June 1870

The President being absent, Mr Andrew Scott was called to the chair. 16 members were present. A letter from D. McLaren, M.P., was read acknowledgeing receipt of report on the alteration of the polling day and stating that he would be glad to consider all the plans that may be proposed. A letter from Dr Alexander Wood was also read stating that he would be happy to move the resolution assigned to him at the meeting on overcrowding on the 29th.[3] A Certificate was also read from the Painters Society appointing Mr Alexander Brian and Mr James Aitken as their representatives pro tem. The Secretary then submitted report from the deputation that waited on Mr Charles Scott relitave to rules of the Caledonian Rubber Works, which was approved of. With the consent of the Council Mr Paterson's motion was allowed to lie over to admitt of arraingments being made for the Public Meeting on the 29th. After the arraingments that had been made with regard to the 3 first resolutions were submitted and approved of, Mr Jeffery and Mr Reid were appointed to move and second the 4th, and Mr

[1] David F. Bridgeford, s.s.c., an active Conservative. *Reformer*, 29 May 1868.
[2] Slaters.
[3] Alexander Wood, M.D., 1817-84, sanitary reformer, a founder and leading member of the Edinburgh Association for Improving the Condition of the Poor (see above, p. 221, n. 2). Rev. Thomas Brown, *Alexander Wood* (Edinburgh, 1886), 3, 145, 152, 202.

Dewar to propose a vote of thanks to the Chairman.[1] Mr Todd moved that a special meeting of Council be held this night week to consider the factory Act and proposed modifications thereon. Agreed to.

5 July 1870

A special meeting was held. Mr Todd opened by showing the necessity for the meeting as the Master Printers of Edinburgh had entered into communication with the Home Secretary with the view of getting the Factory Act modified in its restriction of the working hours of apprentices in that Trade. Mr Todd, Mr Munro[2] and the Secretary were then appointed to write to the Home Secretary asking him to delay the consideration of the subject until he had heard both sides of the question. Mr Todd and Mr Paterson then moved the following resolutions which were unanimously agreed to: The[3] Council having learned with extreme regret that the provincial master printers of England propose a modification of the Factory Acts Extension Act 1867, respectfully request the Right Hon. the Secretary of State for the Home Department to delay granting any modification of the same until both sides of the question have been fully laid before him, and remit the matter to a special committee, with powers. Also That this Council express surprise that no report has been laid before the public relative to the operations of the inspector under the Workshop Act in Edinburgh, and that the same should be published for the information of the community at the instance of the Edinburgh Town Council.

12 July 1870

Certificates were read from the Edinburgh and Leith Brassfounders Society appointing Mr James Laidlaw and reappointing Mr John Scott as their representitaves at this board for the ensuing 12 months. Also from the Bakers Society appointing as their representative Mr Peter Victory. A letter from Mr Bridgeford was again read that had

---

[1] The meeting was held in St Mary's Hall, with Sheriff Cleghorn in the chair. *Scotsman*, 30 June 1870.
[2] Probably Daniel Munro, printers, but possibly Alexander Munro or A. Munro, trade(s) unknown.
[3] From here to the end of the minute is a press cutting pasted into the minute book.

been read previously at special meeting when the deputation was instructed to wait upon him as he expressed his willingness to receive them. Mr Yorston as a member of the deputation gave in report stating that after Mr Bridgeford had been informed of the bussiness the deputation had called on he informed them that he still had £10 which he was prepared to pay as a donation to the Trades Council funds without any restriction whatever if the Council would send for the money. The President and Secretary were then appointed for that purpose on the motion of Mr Todd, seconded by Mr Malcom.

Mr Todd intimated that the members appointed to write to the Home Secretary had met and drawn up a memorial against any modification in the restrections on the working hours of young persons engaged in the letterpress printing which he submitted to the Council. After some consideration as to the best means of bringing it before the Home Secretary, Mr Scott,[1] seconded by Mr Yorston, moved its addoption and that it be sent to Edward S. Gordon, Esq., requisting him to present it to Mr Bruce, which was unanimously agreed to. After some conversation on the Holidays for Edinburgh as proposed in Mr Paterson's motion of a previous meeting, Mr Todd moved, Mr Laidlaw seconding, That this Council, recognising the importance of the question of general annual Holidays, remit the question to our constituents for their consideration. Mr Reid also brought up the question of establishing courts of arbitration, and moved that the Secretary be instructed to write to Mr Gowans on the subject, which was unanimously agreed to. Before seperating Mr Dewar gave notice of motion for next night of meeting, viz., That this Council consider the propriety of taking action in the ensuing Municipal Elections.

26 July 1870

18 members were present. The Secretary stated that he along with Mr Yorston, in room of Mr Dewar, had waited on Mr Bridgeford on the 16 inst. at the time fixed but found that he was away from home. Therefore they had not seen him or received any message. Mr Paterson and Secretary were instructed to see about the issuing of

[1] Uncertain whether Andrew Scott, engineers, Allen Scott, coachmakers, or John Scott, brassfounders.

Trades Conference accounts. The election of office bearers was then proceeded with. Mr Dewar was re-elected as president on the motion of Mr Allen Scott and Mr Brian; Mr E. Jeffery was elected as vice President; Mr Brian, Treasurer, on the motion of Mr Todd, seconded by Mr Jeffery; Mr Andrew Scott, Secretary, on the motion of Mr James Bartie, seconded by Mr Malcom. Mr Munro[1] and Mr Malcom were unanimously elected as Auditors for the ensuing year.

Mr Dewar's motion being the only bussiness, he left the chair and moved the following: That this Council consider the propriety of taking action in the ensuing Municipal Elections. Mr Paterson seconded the motion, Mr Malcom also supporting. The night being far advanced Mr Brian moved that we adjourn the debate, which was unanimously agreed to. Before leaving Mr Paterson gave notice of the following motion for next meeting, viz., The propriety of considering the present possition of West Princes Street Gardens.[2]

9 August 1870

15 members were present. The attention of the meeting having been called to the circumstance that Mr Brian, the newly elected Treasurer, was only appointed interim representative of his trade up till August, Mr Todd moved and Mr Malcolm seconded the approval of the minutes, which was agreed to. The Secretary then intimated that he had written to Mr Bridgeford intimating the desire of the deputation to wait upon him to receive the promised donation of £10 but no acknowledgement had been received. The following motion moved by Mr Allen Scott and seconded by Mr C. Yorkson[3] was adopted: That a deputation be appointed to wait upon Mr McWhinnie and ask an explanation on the subject. Mesers Dewar, Weir, Strachen and Andrew Scott were appointed to form the deputation. The adjourned debate on the municipial elections was postponed, as was also the motion in reference to the opening of Princes Street Gardens.

Mr Yorkson intimated that he had been requested by the Black-smiths Society to make a complaint at this Council against a member

---

[1] Identity uncertain.
[2] See below, p. 307.
[3] Cornelius Yorston, blacksmiths.

of the Engineers Society who it is asserted had refered to some of the Blacksmiths Society's rules in harsh terms at one of the meetings of his Society. The Council in taking the complaint into consideration failed to discover any symptoms of a direct or definite accusation, and consequently refrained from taking any steps in the matter untill the following motions be carried into effect, moved by Mr Paterson and seconded by Mr A. Munro[1]: That this council reccomends the Blacksmiths Society to communicate with the Engineers Society in order to obtain information on the subject. Mr Paterson also gave notice that at next meeting he would move, That this council Take into consideration the propriety or impropriety of the Blacksmiths Society prosecuting its members who fall into arrears. It was also moved and agreed to, That the Secretary be instructed to forward a copy of the above resolutions to the Blacksmiths Society.

23 August 1870

16 members were present. A letter was read from the Secretary of the Edinburgh branch of the Amalgamated Engineers intimating the appointment of Messers McBride and Scott[2] to represent the above branch at this Council. The following letters were also read: From Mr Bridgeford, intimating his convenience to receive the deputation appointed by the Council for the reception of the £10 donation; from the Secretary of the Blacksmiths Society, declining to entertain the motions forwarded to them from last meeting of Council; and from Mr Wilson,[3] removing the cause of complaint lodged at last meeting of Council by Mr Yorkson. It was proposed by Mr Paterson, seconded by Mr Todd, and agreed to, That the motion, notice of which was given at last meeting, anent the Blacksmiths Society's rules, should be the first business on the table. After a very interesting and animated discussion the following motion was moved by Mr Paterson, seconded by Mr Allen Scott, and unnanimously agreed to: That in the opinion of this Council it would be desirable for the Blacksmiths Association to modify the prosecution of arrears to the period the members are entitled to benefit under the rules.

[1] Not identified.
[2] Alexander McBride and Andrew Scott.
[3] Presumably William Wilson, engineers.

The deputation appointed to wait upon Mr Bridgeford reported that they had received the sum of ten pounds, being the donation presented to the Council by Mr Scott, Advocate, through Mr Bridgeford. The Secretary handed the money over to the treasurer. It was moved by Mr Paterson, seconded by Mr Munro,[1] and unnanimously adopted, That this Council record their thankful acknowledgement of the donation from Messers Bridgeford and Scott of £10 and desire the Secretary to communicate with Messers Bridgeford and Scott accordingly.

After some conversation upon the accusation against the Engineers Society by the Blacksmiths, the following motion was moved by Mr Todd and seconded by Mr Paterson: That this Council dismiss the case as we have only hearsay evidence to consider. The continued absence of the Treasurer having been brought under notice of the Council, it was deemed expedient to appoint another, and Mr Strachen was elected accordingly. The motions in reference to the municipial elections and Princes Street Gardens were again postponed.

13 September 1870

Mr Jeffry, vice president, occupied the chair. 17 members were present. Credentials were presented from the Painters Association intimating the appointment of Messers James Nicol and Andrew C. Wilson; from the Joiners, Edinburgh South Branch, certifying the election of Mr James White in room of Mr A. Forbes; and from the Blacksmiths, intimating the appointment of Messers John Wilson and Cornelius Yorkson to represent their respective Societies.

The following letters were read: From the Leith Branch, Operative Bakers National Association, intimating the necessity they are under of withdrawing their representative from the Council in consequence of some difficulties experienced in procuring one to fill the office during winter. From the Blacksmiths Society, stating that the resolutions presented to them by the Council were duly considered at last meeting and a conclusion arrived at to the following effect, That the Council should have gathered all possible information previous to discusing the subject, which would doubtless have prevented the adoption of said resolutions. And from the

[1] Identity uncertain.

committee in behalf of the Sick and Wounded, informing the Council that a deputation would wait upon them tonight, to consider the best means of enlisting the cooperation of the working classes in subscribing for the sick and wounded in the present war.

The first business on the minutes being the motion anent municipial elections, the subject was freely discussed but in consequence of the Deputation from the Committee in behalf of the Sick and Wounded making their appearance at this stage of the proceedings, the discussion was adjourned untill a future meeting. Baillie Cousin and Mr Murray being introduced to the Council the former explained the nature of the present war on the Continent and expressed a desire that the Council should endeavour to lend a helping hand in sending aid to the wounded. The following resolutions were adopted, moved by Mr McWhinnie and seconded by Mr Yorkson: That subscription sheets be issued to the various trades and all money subscribed be handed over to the Treasurer at next ordinary meeting of Council. That the Secretary be instructed to forward subscription sheets to delegates who are absent. And that the Treasurer and Secretary meet half an hour earlier next meeting night for the purpose of receiving subscriptions. The Deputation then retired.

In consequence of Mr Dewar, President, having resigned his seat at the Council it devolved upon the members to elect his successor to the chair. Mr Jeffry was accordingly elected President and Mr D. Munro Vice President for the ensuing year. Mr Paterson moved and Mr Masson[1] seconded the following resolution: That a special meeting be held this night week to take up the busness on the minutes, and that the Secretary notify the same to absentees.

20 September 1870

A Special meeting was held. 17 members were present. Mr Paterson having made a few pithy and well timed remarks upon the municipial elections submitted to the meeting the following motion: That this Council considers it expedient to endeavour to return working men's representatives to the Edinburgh Town Council at the ensueing elections. Mr McWhinnie, in seconding the motion,

---

[1] Not identified.

urged upon the Council the necessity of going immediatley to work feeling assured that the results would be highly successful. The motion was unanimously adopted. The following motion was also moved by Mr Paterson and seconded by Mr Wilson[1]: That a public meeting of working men be held during the present month for the purpose of taking action in the municipial elections, and that the expenses of said meeting be meantime defrayed by the Council. Mr Strachan moved an ammendment: That no meeting be held untill the Council find a working man's candidate who will stand for election. The ammendment was seconded by Mr McBride. Two voted for it and 16 for the motion. Messers Jeffery, Strachan, and Scott[2] were appointed a committee to engage a hall and call the meeting, etc.

23 September 1870

A Special meeting was held. 20 members were present. The Chairman stated that in consequence of an advertisement which appeared in the *Scotsman* and *Review*[3] of the 22 inst. requesting the Delegates or Representatives of each of the Trades to meet the Convener of the Trades in Mary's Chapel, High Street, on the 24 inst. to make preliminary arrangements for taking part in the proceedings regarding the laying of the Foundation Stone of the New Infirmary,[4] this meeting had been convened for the purpose of considering what steps might be taken in the matter. The following motion was moved by Mr McVey and seconded by Mr Paterson: That this Council refuses to recognise the advertisement of the so called convener of the Trades; at the same time it deems it avisable that the Representatives of the Trades should attend that meeting to watch over the interests of their respective bodies. An amendment was moved by Mr Yorkson and seconded by A. Scott,[5] That this Council refrains from recognising the advertisement of the so called

[1] Either John Wilson, blacksmiths, or Andrew Wilson, painters.
[2] Uncertain whether Andrew Scott, engineers, Allen Scott, coachmakers, or John Scott, brassfounders.
[3] The *Daily Review*, 1861-86, Independent Liberal, founded by members of various churches but regarded as a Free Church paper. W. Norrie, *Edinburgh Newspapers Past and Present* (Earlston, 1891), 25-6.
[4] The foundation stone was to be laid on 13 October 1870.
[5] Either Allen Scott, coachmakers, or Andrew Scott, engineers.

convener of the Trades, and resolve to take no action in the matter in any aspect at present. Ten voted for the motion and four for the ammendment.

27 September 1870

20 members were present. A letter from the Tailors Association was read intimating the appointment of Mr William Jenkinson as their representative in room of Mr Taylor. A letter was also read from Mr Dewar explaining the cause of his retiring from the Council. The Secretary was instructed to present him with the thanks of the Council for his services in the past, etc. The Committee appointed to arrange for the Public Meeting intimated that the Phoenix Hall had been engaged for Friday night. It was agreed that the Committee meet tomorrow night to draw out resolutions for Public meeting.

A letter was also read from the Secretary of the Edinburgh Central Branch of the Joiners Association enquiring after the number of meetings Mr Paterson their Delegate had been present at and how many absent during the past year. After consideration the following resolution was unnanimously adopted: That the Secretary be instructed to comply with the request of the Edinburgh Central Branch of Associated Joiners, and also to give expression to the feelings of satisfaction which prevail in the Council not only as regards Mr Paterson's attendance but also the untiring zeal and admirable skill which characterises all his efforts in promoting the best interests of the Council. It was moved by Mr Wilson[1] and seconded by Mr Munro.[2]

The Secretary intimated that a deputation had just waited upon him from the Independant Liberal Committee for the Cannongate ward expressing a desire that this Council should elect a deputation with powers for the purpose of comming to a mutual understanding in connection with the comming Municipal Elections. It was agreed to appoint a deputation after the public meeting. It was moved by Mr Paterson and seconded by Mr Malcolm that Mr Bartie, late Secretary, should receive £2 10s as salary for past year.

[1] Either John Wilson, blacksmiths, or Andrew Wilson, painters.
[2] Identity uncertain.

PUBLIC MEETING[1]

Phoenix Hall
Melbourne Place
30 September 1870

A meeting of working men, convened by the Trades Delegates, was held to consider what action ought to be taken by them at the coming municipal elections. Mr Edward Jeffrey, President of the Trades Council, was called to the chair.

Mr McWhinnie, who was called upon to move the first resolution, read as follows: That in the opinion of this meeting it is of the utmost importance that immediate action be taken so as to secure the return of *bona fide* working men representatives to the Edinburgh Town Council at the ensuing November election. Mr Wilson, blacksmith, seconded the motion, which was carried. Mr McNeill, builder,[2] proposed the second resolution: That this meeting, recognising the importance of securing the return of working men to the Edinburgh Town Council, resolves to appoint a large committee, with full powers. Mr Malcolm, baker, seconded the resolution, which was unanimously passed.

Mr Scott, secretary of the Trades Council, proposed the following resolution: That, in order to ensure the successful carrying out of the foregoing resolutions, this meeting authorise the committee to issue subscription-lists and raise funds to defray the necessary expenses. Mr Strachan, joiner, seconded the resolution, which was passed unanimously. Mr Paterson proposed: That a deputation be appointed to wait upon the Edinburgh Town Council, and urge upon them the propriety of changing the hour of meeting from twelve to six o'clock p.m. Mr Yorkston, blacksmith, having seconded the motion, it was carried. The meeting then appointed its committee. The proceedings closed with a vote of thanks to the chairman.

---

[1] This report is a press cutting pasted into the minute book.
[2] Presumably Peter McNeill, manager of the Edinburgh and Leith Joiners' Building Company Ltd. (formed in May 1868, with membership restricted to joiners), and secretary of the Edinburgh branch of the Reform League at the time of John Bright's visit to Edinburgh in November 1868. *Reformer*, 29 August 1868; *Scotsman*, 6 November 1868.

3 October 1870

The Committee appointed at the Public meeting held on the 30th September met tonight. Mr Paterson was called to the chair. A deputation was appointed to wait upon the Town Council to support Ballie Lewis' motion anent the changing of the hour of meeting from 12 noon to half past six. A very limited number of the committee being present, it was agreed upon to adjourn the meeting to the 6th inst., the Secretary having received instructions to call a special meeting of Council, and invite the Officebearers of Trades.

6 October 1870

A[1] meeting of the Trades Council and the committee appointed at the working men's meeting on Friday night was held. Mr Edward Jeffrey, president of the Council, who was called to the chair, stated that the object of the meeting was to take immediate steps to bring forward working men as candidates for municipal honours at the forthcoming municipal election, and to fix upon what wards such candidates would be likely to contest most successfully. After some discussion in regard to the wards which should be contested, Mr McWhinnie moved the following resolution: That in the opinion of this meeting Mr William Paterson, corresponding secretary to the Joiners' Association, and Mr Peter McNeill, secretary to the Edinburgh and Leith Joiners' Building Association, are proper candidates to contest the Canongate and George Square Wards at the election in November next. Mr Laing[2] seconded the resolution, which was adopted. Some conversation afterwards took place as to whether these gentlemen – who were said to be fully employed by the societies with which they were connected – would be allowed by their directors to act as Town Councillors in the event of their being elected, and the following resolution, on the motion of Mr Burns, seconded by Mr Hilson, was ultimately agreed to: That deputations be appointed to wait upon the Edinburgh and Leith Joiner's Building Company, and also at the various branch committees of the Associated Carpenters and Joiners' Society, in

---

[1] From here down to '. . . contest St Giles' Ward', line 5 of next page, is a press cutting pasted into the minute book.
[2] Almost certainly David Laing, plasterers.

order to impress upon them the necessity of allowing Messrs
Paterson and McNeill to stand as working men's candidates at the
forthcoming municipal election.[1] A resolution was subsequently
passed, nominating Mr J. H. Waterston as a working men's
candidate to contest St Giles' Ward.[2]

The following were the members composing the deputations:
Messers Wallace,[3] Fairburn, and Burns[4] for the Building company;
Messers McWhinnie and Dewer[5] for the Joiners Central Branch;
for the North Branch, Messers Antonio[6] and Malcolm; for the
South, Messers Hilson[7] and Makay; and for the West, Messers
Wallace and Waterston. It was agreed that the above deputations
resolve themselves into one deputation and wait upon the Independant Liberal Committee for the Canongate to negotiate with them
in order to arrive at a mutual understanding in connection with the
Canongate Ward. Mr Wallace and Mr Waterston were also
appointed to confer with the Temperance Electoral Committee.

Mr W. Fairburn having intimated that Ballie Lewis was willing
to introduce his motion for the alteration of the hour of Town
Council meeting, provided the Working Men's Committee would
support him, it was agreed that a memorial should be presented to
the Council in support of the change. It being also agreed that
subscription sheets should be issued to the Secretaries of the Trades,
Messers McNeill, Paterson, Waterston, Fairburn and Scott[8] were
appointed as committee to frame the memorial and issue the subscription lists. Mr Waterston was appointed convener of the
committee.

It was moved by Mr McNeill, seconded by Mr Fairburn, and
unanimously agreed to, that this meeting be called The Trades

---

[1] McNeill did not in fact stand at the election.
[2] James H. Waterston, evidently an itinerant temperance lecturer. At the election he
actually stood in St Cuthbert's Ward and was defeated by 383 to 847 votes for his
Liberal opponent. *Scotsman*, 1 and 2 November 1870.
[3] Almost certainly Gabriel Wallace, upholsterers.
[4] J. C. Burn, blacksmiths.
[5] Andrew Dewar, blacksmiths.
[6] Not identified.
[7] Presumably Matthew Hilson, blacksmiths, a delegate to the trades council from 24
January 1871.
[8] Uncertain whether Andrew Scott, engineers, Allen Scott, coachmakers, or John
Scott, brassfounders.

U

Council Municipal Election Committee. The Secretary was instructed to write the City Clerk and appologize for the non-appearance of the Deputation appointed to wait on the Town Council.

11 October 1870

A meeting of the United Trades Council Municipal Election Committee was held. 20 members were present. The Chairman stated that the Trades Council having resolved itself into a Municipal Election Committee, it would be neccessary for the ordinary buisness of Council to lie over in the meantime. To carry out the operations of the committee the following office bearers were then appointed: Mr Andrew Dewar, Chairman; Mr John Wilson, Treasurer; and Messers George Macdonald[1] and J. C. Burns, Secretaries. The Buisness was accordingly transfered.

8 November 1870

The ordinary meeting of Council was held tonight. 18 members were present. The minutes of special meetings held on the 30th September and the 6th and 11th October were read. In consequence of some of the members questioning the propriety of minutes of such meetings being recorded in the Minute Book seeing that the only buisness was the municipal elections a lively discussed ensued, which ultimately closed in the following motion and ammendment being put to the meeting. Moved by Mr Common, and seconded by Mr Laidlaw: That all minutes since the 27th September be expunged from the minute book. Ammendment moved by Mr Paterson and seconded by Mr Allen Scott: That the whole of the minutes as they stand in the minute book be adopted. There voted for the ammendment 12 and for the motion 3. The correspondence then read consisted of credentials from the Edinburgh Typographical Society, appointing Mr J. S. Common as successer to Mr Tod, who resigned, and colleague to Mr D. Munroe in the representation of their Society at this Board; and from the Bakers' Association, intimating the appointment of Mr Charles McKinnon, in place of Mr Malcolm, retired.

---

[1] Should probably read John McDonald (brassfounders). See below, p. 310.

Mr J. Scott in bringing under the notice of the Council the late contest in George's Square Ward, expressed himself dissatisfied with the reccommendation presented by the Trades Council Municipal Election Committee to Mr Tait, the defeated candidate. And knowing it to be to a great extent the belief of the Public that that reccommendation proceeded from the Trades Council, he moved the following, seconded by Mr Reid: That this Council disclaims having any connection with the certificate granted to Mr Tait by the Trades Council Municipal Election Committee. The motion was agreed to.[1]

Mr Reid expressed a desire that the Council should again take into consideration the establishing of Courts of Arbitration, and moved to the following effect: That the subject of the establishment of Courts of Arbitration be taken up at next meeting, and that the Secretary be instructed to write Mr Gowans reminding him of the offer he made as recorded in minutes of the 10th May. The propriety of taking immediate action in endeavouring to secure the opening of Princes Street Gardens was then considered. It was moved by Mr Paterson and seconded by Mr Wilson,[2] That a memorial be drawn up and presented to the Town Council soliciting their attention to the opening of Princes Street Gardens. The motion was adopted and Mr Paterson was appointed to frame the memorial.[3]

22 November 1870

The President and vice president being absent, Mr Allen Scott occupied the chair. 13 members were present. The correspondence read consisted of credentials from the Associated Iron Moulders, appointing Messers Thomas Blackie[4] and George Young as the

---

[1] George Tait, an Independent Liberal and merchant tailor and outfitter. The Trades Council Municipal Elections Committee on 26 October had publicly recommended working class electors to vote for him, although he had received some notoriety at the previous election for having fined a girl in his employment. *Scotsman*, 30 October 1869, 29 October 1870.

[2] Either John Wilson, blacksmiths, or Andrew Wilson, painters.

[3] West Princes Street Gardens remained in private hands until 1876 when ownership passed to the town council and the gardens were opened to the public. D. Robertson, *The Princes Street Proprietors* (Edinburgh, 1935), 1-61.

[4] Spelt Blaikie in some subsequent minutes.

representatives of their body at the Council. Copy of report by a subcommittee of the Streets and building committee as approved of by the Town Council on resolutions and memorial adopted at the public meeting held in St Mary's Hall on the 29th of June on the subject of overcrowded dwelling houses was read. Consideration was left till next meeting. Some disscussion took place concerning the contributions of the Brassfounders and Iron Moulders, further consideration of which was also left over till next meeting. The Secretary intimated that he had acted in accordance with instructions received at last meeting, and had written to Mr Gowans upon the subject of conciliation and arbitration, but had received no reply. After some remarks the subject was laid on the table for future consideration.

The motion anent the establishing of General Holidays in Edinburgh was taken into consideration,[1] and after a very animated discussion the following motion and ammendment were put to the meeting. Moved by Mr Common, seconded by Mr J. Scott: That a circular be issued to the Trades directing attention to the subject of a general holiday, and requesting their views as to the steps which should be taken to secure that object. Ammendment moved by Mr Strachan and seconded by Mr Weir: That the Secretary be instructed to request the absent delegates to submit for the consideration of their Trades the question concerning the establishing of general holidays in Edinburgh, and report at the second meeting in February 1871. 5 voted for the motion and 6 for the ammendment.

13 December 1870

Fourteen members were present. The missunderstanding anent the Brassfounders contributions was again taken into consideration, when Mr J. Scott produced receipts for all contributions due by his trade up to the 23rd August 1870. The Council adopted the following motion moved by Mr Common and seconded by Mr Allen Scott: That the Treasurer be instructed to cancel the claim dated 10th August 1869.

The Arbitration question was briefly discussed, a motion to the

1 Above, p. 296.

following effect being adopted, moved by Mr Miller[1] and seconded by Mr J. Scott: That the Secretary be instructed to collect statistics and submit them to the Council. It was moved by Mr J. Scott, seconded by Mr Millar, and agreed to that 500 post cards be printed for the summoning of special meetings. The other business in the minutes was left over till next meeting. Mr Millar having given notice of his intention to bring before the Council at next meeting, the propriety of taking steps for the holding of a public meeting to sympathise with the French Republic, the meeting closed.

27 December 1870

12 members were present. A letter was read from the Bakers' Association intimating the appointment of Gilbert Miller as their representative at the meeting of Council. A letter was also read from the Trades Council Municipal Election Committee thanking the Trades Council for the interest they had taken in the origin of that body, etc. It was moved by Daniel Munroe, seconded by Gilbert Miller, that the letter be minuted. The motion was adopted. The Secretary was instructed to forward to the Moulders Society all information regarding their contributions. In accordance with previous intimation Mr Miller submitted the following resolution: That the Council consider the desirability of calling a public meeting to express sympathy with the suffering French in the present aggressive war. Mr A. Munroe[2] seconded the Resolution. Allen Scott, seconded by Thomas Blaikie, moved the following amendment: That under present circumstances it is inexpedient to call a public meeting. After considerable discussion the amendment and motion were put to the meeting when the former was carried by a majority. Mr Weir brought under the notice of the Council the disgraceful system of overtime, etc., at present indulged in by the employees of Mr Grieg, Printer, Browns Square,[3] and Mr White, Stationer, North St David Street. The Secretary was instructed to write to Mr Inglis, Inspector of workshops, on the subject.[4]

[1] Gilbert Miller or Millar, Edinburgh bakers.
[2] Not identified.
[3] Greig had been an Independent Liberal councillor for George Square ward until shortly before this date.
[4] George Inglis, appointed inspector in Edinburgh earlier that year.

54 St Mary's Street
December 26, 1870

Gentlemen,

I am instructed by the Trades Council Municipal Election Committee to convey their thanks to you for your initiation of the proceedings which brought that committee into existence. Being convinced that a permanent organisation will ensure ultimate success to their cause, they by public meeting established the Scottish Reform Union as an advocate of their political rights of labour.[1]

In thus ending the duties devolving on them, the Committee thinks the best means have been taken to further the objects the Trades Council has at heart and they hope that both bodies may be always united in action to better the social and political condition of the working classes.

Allow me to be in name of Council,
Yours gratefully,
John McDonald
Secretary

[1] The Union met weekly at Buchanan's Hotel; its prospectus appeared in the *Reformer* of 17 December 1870.

1871

Nine members were present. An Intimation was given by the Cabinetmakers of the appointment of Mr Thomas Barrett as their representative in place of Mr Shedden, who has left the town. In consideration of the insignificant number of members present Mr Allen Scott moved that the meeting be adjourned and on the Secretary being instructed to summons all absent members to next meeting, the motion was carried into effect.

In the President's absence the Vice president[1] took the chair. 12 members were present. Credentials from the Blacksmiths Society were read announcing the appointment of Walter Fairbairn[2] and Matthew Hilson as their delegates to the Council. A letter from Mr Inglis was read acknowledging receipt of Secretary's letter anent the working of overtime in the establishments of Mr Greig, Brown Square, and Messers A. Whyte and Son, North St David Street, and promising to inquire into the matter. A letter was also read from Mr Applegarth, intimating the sudden death of his wife as the cause of delay in sending information upon the Arbitration question. He also requested the Secretary to wait upon Mr Torrens, M.P., who is desirous of making the acquaintance of our class in Edinburgh.[3] Mr Reid moved that a deputation be appointed for that purpose. Mr Hilson seconded the motion, which was agreed to, and Messers Paterson and the Secretary were appointed accordingly. Mr Paterson submitted to the meeting a draught of the

---

[1] Daniel Munro, printers.
[2] In some minutes spelt Fairburn.
[3] William Torrens McCullagh Torrens, 1813-94, Radical M.P. for Dundalk 1847-52, Yarmouth 1857, and Finsbury 1865-85.

memorial to the Town Council refferring to the opening of
Princes Street Gardens. On the motion of Messers McWhinnie and
Reid the memorial was approved off and the President and Secretary
authorised to sign it and forward it to the Town Council.

Some discussion took place about the delay that had taken place
in preparing the Anual Report and Mr Paterson moved, seconded by
Mr Munroe,[1] That no report be issued in the meantime, but that
it lie over till next July. This motion was agreed to. The report
from the Town Council Committee on the petition anent the overcrowding question was read and after due consideration the subject
was dismissed. The Secretary was instructed to write to Mr Marwick,
City Clerk, and ask him if the Inspector of workshops intended
issuing a report. The Treasurer was also instructed to discharge an
account against the Council for printing of post cards, amount
£1 8s. 6d.

14 February 1871

14 members were present. Credentials were read from the Engineers
Society intimating the appointment of Mr James Blair in place of
Alexander McBride as delegate from there society. A letter was
read from Mr Marwick acknowledging receipt of the Secretary's
last letter, and promising to bring it before the first meeting of the
Town Council. The Deputation appointed to wait upon Mr Torrens,
M.P., gave in a report of the interveiw. The question upon Boards of
Conciliation and Arbitration was again taken into consideration.
The Secretary was instructed to request Mr Odger, Secretary to the
London Trades Council, to forward any statistics relating to the
question. And pending further information on the subject the
following motion was moved by J. S. Common and seconded by
Allen Scott: That the subject lie over for further consideration. This
motion was agreed to.

A circular from the Trades Council in London was laid on the
table intimating that a Congress is to be held in London to watch
over the interests of unionists in the Trades Union Bill at present
before Parliment and inviting delegates from the various Trades.[2]

---

[1] Identity uncertain.
[2] This congress was the Trades Union Congress of 1871 which opened in London on
6 March. The Bill, which was introduced in February by the government, was split

The Council considered the intimation to be too late, refrained from taking action in the matter, and instructed the Secretary to forward a copy of the Trades Union Bill prepared at the conference held in Edinburgh last year.[1] Some discussion took place upon the action the Council should take in connection with the bill at present before Parliment. Mr Hilson moved that the Secretary request Mr McLaren, M.P., to forward a copy of the bill to the Council, and on the reception of which to call a special meeting and also invite officebearers and all trades' representatives by means of advertisment. Mr Munroe[2] seconded the motion, which was agreed to.

23 February 1871

A special meeting was held. The Secretary intimated that in accordance with instructions received at last meeting he had written to Mr McLaren, requesting him to forward a copy of the Trades Union Bill. The letter was duly acknowledged and the Bill forwarded, on the receipt of which the meeting was summoned. After a long discussion upon several clauses of the Bill, and without any definite resolutions being passed, it was agreed to adjourn the deliberations till next ordinary meeting of Council. Mr Paterson announced his intention to bring before next meeting of Council the desirabillity of again applying for the opening of the Royal Scottish Academy's Exhibition at reduced rates for the benefit of the working classes.[3]

28 February 1871

Mr Allen Scott occupied the chair. 14 members were present. It having been agreed upon to allow the ordinary business lie on the table, the meeting proceeded to consider the various clauses of the Trades Union Bill. After a considerable amount of discussion it was moved by Mr Fairbairn, seconded by Mr Paterson, and agreed to, that a committee of five be appointed to consider the Bill and report. Messers Fairbairn, Common, Paterson, Sinclair, and Wilson[4] were appointed members of committee. It was agreed to hold a special meeting of the Council on Tuesday the 7th March to consider the

---

into two parts which were enacted as the Trade Union Act and the Criminal Law Amendment Act.   [1] Above, p. 284.

[2] Identity uncertain.   [3] Above, p. 290.   [4] Possibly Andrew Wilson, painters.

committee's report, and the Secretary was instructed to advertise said meeting in the *Reformer*. He was also instructed to open communication with the Secretary of the Royal Scottish Academy upon the opening of the exhibition at reduced rates for the benefit of the working classes.

7 March 1871

A special meeting was held. Mr[1] W. Fairbairn in the chair. The subcommittee appointed at last meeting reported on the Trades Union Bill now before Parliament as follows: (1) That the third clause be expunged; (2) that the fifth clause be also expunged, unless considerably amended; (3) that a circular be prepared for transmission to the Home Secretary, members of Parliament, and trades societies; (4) that a draft petition, containing the above resolutions, be framed and submitted to the various unions for signature and presentation to Parliament. The recommendation of the committee with regard to clause three, which refers to the criminal provisions of the bill, was unanimously adopted. In regard to clause five, it was agreed that it ought to be amended so as to provide that all agreements between trades unions and their members should be enforceable, except as regards fines. The Council also agreed to endeavour to remove the restriction as to the amount of land tenable by a trades union, which under the present bill is restricted to one acre; and also to secure the trial of any cases connected with unions before a Sheriff and not before a Justice of Peace or magistrate as provided for in the bill. A committee was appointed to prepare a circular and issue the forms of petition to the different societies for signature. Messers Common and Thomson[2] were the committee appointed. After resolving to hold another meeting of Council to distribute the letters, 300 of which were to be printed, the meeting closed.

14 March 1871

Mr Allen Scott occupied the chair. 12 members were present. The following letters were read: from Mr George Hill, Secretary to

[1] From here down to the end of the third last sentence of the minute, '. . . societies for signature', is a press cutting pasted into the minute book.
[2] Identity uncertain; perhaps Alexander Thomson, printers, who became a delegate to the trades council from 25 July 1871.

the Iron workers in the west, soliciting the attention of the Council to the present lock-out. A circular also accompanied the letter giving a clear definition of the circumstances connected with the struggle, etc.[1] The letter was dated the 6th February but had unfortunately undergone a delay in delivery. The meeting instructed the Secretary to acknowledge the receipt thereof, at the same time to appologize for the delay that had occured, and also request Mr Hill to send a number of circulars for distribution among the Trades in Edinburgh. From Mr Marwick, City Chambers, acknowledging receipt of letters of the 11th and the 15th ultimo[2] and intimating that the magistrates had submitted the same to the Lord Provist's committee for consideration. From Mr Applegarth, giving some usful hints on the result of the establishment of Boards of Conciliation and arbitration. Also a circular containing the result of the deliberations of the Anual Trades Congress on the Trades Union Bill and requesting the secretary to forward the addresses of the Trades in Edinburgh in order that he might send to each secretary a copy of the Trades Union Bill. The secretary was instructed to act in accordance with his request.

From the Secretary of the Royal Scottish Academy, informing the Council that after full consideration of the question of reduced rates of admission at the Evening Exhibition they do not see their way to lower the present rates. It was agreed that this letter lie over for further consideration. From Mr Edward Jeffries, President, intimating that in consequence of his leaving the locality he was under the necessity of tendering his resignation to the Council. The secretary was instructed to inform him of the Council's acceptance of his resignation and also in acknowledgement of his past services to present him with an expression of gratitude. From the secretary of the Edinburgh Branch of the Scottish National Association of Operative Tailors intimating the appointment of Messers Troupe[3] and Ward as delegates to represent their Society at this Board; and from the United Brassfounders of Edinburgh and Leith intimating

---

[1] A strike against a reduction of wages had begun in January in Lanarkshire and Glasgow and became a lockout on 6 March. There was soon afterwards a return to work on the employers' terms. *Reformer*, 21 January, 11 and 18 March 1871.

[2] Concerning publication of the workshops inspector's report.

[3] Presumably William Troup, former president of the trades council.

the appointment of Mr David Allan as the representative of their body in place of Mr John Scott who had to retire in consequence of ill-health.

The General Holiday question was then taken into consideration. The following reports were given in by the delegates. The Blacksmiths reported in favour of the adoption of general Anual Holidays and recommended the last Thursday, Friday and Saturday of July as the most suitable. The Moulders, Engineers, Bookbinders, Cabinetmakers, Joiners, West Branch, and Slaters all reported in favour of the movement and recomended two or three days in the last week of July. The Coachmakers are also unanimous in favour of anual general Holidays, but reccomend no particular time. After some discussion the following motion, moved by Andrew Scott, seconded by Alexander Munroe,[1] was put to the meeting: That this Council in considering the reports given in by the various delegates, all of which are in favour of the establishment of general Anual Holidays in Edinburgh and Leith, deems it expedient to take immediate steps in order to secure the accomplishment of this end. The motion was unanimously adopted and the Secretary was instructed to advertise in next two issues of the *Reformer* the meeting of Council to be held on the 28th March to consider the question, requesting all interested to attend. Before seperating, the letters and copies of petition drawn up by the committee appointed for that purpose were circulated amongst the delegates and the secretary was instructed to forward a letter to all the Scotch M.P.s and Trades Societies.[2]

28 March 1871

Mr Munroe, vice president, occupied the chair. 12 members were present. In accordance with the advertisement in the *Reformer* several strangers were present to consider the Holiday question. The following motion was moved by Mr Strachan and seconded by Mr A. Munro[3]: That this Council take the necessary steps for calling a public meeting in order to bring the subject before the working classes. The time being up ere the question was fully discussed it was agreed to adjourn the meeting.

[1] Not identified.
[2] The petition concerned the Trade Union Bill.   [3] Not identified.

11 April 1871

Mr Allan Scott presided. 14 members were present. Credentials were read from the Painters Association appointing Messers R. S. Law and George Black to represent their trade at the Council. The discussion on the Holiday question was resumed. The Bakers reported in favour of the holidays and recomended a day in the last week of July. The Brassfounders also reported in favour of and recomended the last Friday and Saturday of July. Mr Paterson intimated that his Society was in favour of Anual Holidays and recomended 3 days in the last week of July. Mr Paterson moved the following resolution: That this Council approves of three holidays being held in the month of July in each year and reccomends the same for general adoption by the working classes of Edinburgh and Leith. This motion was seconded by Mr Blaikie and agreed to. It was also moved by Mr Sinclair, seconded by Mr Munroe,[1] and unanimously carried: That this Council take the necessary steps for calling a public meeting in order to bring the subject before the public. It was moved by Messers Munroe and Law that five of a committee be appointed to arrange for holding the Public meeting. This motion was also carried, and the following committee was appointed: Messers Alexander Munroe, R. S. Law, James Sinclair, Alexander Strachan, and Michial Ward. The Secretary was instructed to write Councilor Cranston asking particulars relating to the letting of his hall for the public meeting. He was also instructed to advertise the said meeting in Saturday's *Scotsman* and *Reformer*, and by Bills, 600 of which to be printed. The following resolution was also adopted, moved by Messers Laidlaw and Blaikie: That the Secretary be instructed to communicate with the Grocers and Drapers Early Closing Association and request their co-operation in the movement.[2]

Andrew Scott then brought under the notice of the Council the efforts made by the Sunderland engineers to obtain the nine hours day, and proposed the following resolution: That this Council having always manifested a desire to promote the success of any movement calculated to secure a reduction of the hours of labour

[1] None of the three references to Munroe in this minute have been identified.
[2] The Association had been formed in the early 1850s. W. H. Marwick, *Economic Developments in Victorian Scotland* (London, 1936), 156.

in all trades, hail with great satisfaction the efforts now being made by the Engineers in Sunderland to secure the nine hours system. The Council would urge upon all trades in the United kingdom to use all means financial and moral to support the men in their present dispute and thereby advance the interests of the nine hours movement. The resolution was seconded by Mr George Black and unanimously adopted. The Secretary was instructed to forward the same to the men on strike and also to get it inserted in the local newspapers. The Secretary[1] then intimated that as he was about to leave the country he was compelled to give in his resignation. His resignation was accepted and the election of another was left off till next meeting.

25 April 1871

Mr Allen Scott in the chair. Eight members were present. The Secretary read correspondence from the Sunderland Engineers on the dispute regarding the reduction of the hours of labour, and from Mr Cranston in reference to the letting of the New Waverley Hall for public meeting. Mr Scott stated that as he intended leaving the country, he could not be present at next meeting. It was therefore necessary to appoint a Secretary immediately. Upon the motion of the Chairman a hearty vote of thanks was awarded to Mr Scott for the very creditable and energetic manner in which he had discharged the duties of Secretary. Mr Sinclair being proposed by Mr Blair and seconded by Mr Alexander Munroe[2] was ellected interim Secretary. Mr Andrew Scott, convener of committee, gave in the report on the Progress of the Holiday Movement, which was adopted and the committee reappointed with instruction to take a Hall for a public meeting and carry out all the neccessary arrangements. Mr T. Barrett was added to the committee.[3]

The reply from the Engineers of Sunderland on strike for the nine hours-day was taken up. Mr Scott[4] moved that the Council ellect a committee for the purpose of opening subscriptions to aid

[1] Andrew Scott, engineers.
[2] Not identified.
[3] The public meeting was held on 4 May in Phoenix Hall. *Scotsman*, 5 May 1871.
[4] This and the reference in the following sentence are presumably to Allen Scott, coachmakers.

the Sunderland Engineers in the present struggle, and also to recommend the movement to the support of the Trades in Edinburgh and Leith, which was seconded by Mr Munro[1] and agreed to. Messrs Blair, Strachan, Scott and Blackie were appointed as a committee to carry out the foregoing resolution. Mr Alexander Munro moved, seconded by Mr Masson,[2] that Mr Scott be paid the usual salary for the time he had been secretary. It was therefore agreed to give Mr Scott £2 for his services.

9 May 1871

Mr Blair, Engineer, in the Chair. The Secretary read correspondence from the Sunderland Engineers, and from the Grocers and Drapers Early Closing Association. Upon the motion of Mr R. S. Laws the Secretary was instructed to communicate with the grocers and request them to endeavour to have their holdiay within the three days which were agreed on at the Public meeting, viz., the last Saturday of July and the two preceeding days. Mr H. Finlay, from Mr George Bertram's Works,[3] reported that the workmen in that establishment were favourable to having general annual Holidays. After considerable discussion as to the way in which the Council were to proceed in getting general annual Holidays established in Edinburgh and Leith, it was moved by Mr Strachan and seconded by Mr Masson: That the committee ascertain as far as possible the feeling in the various shops in regard to holidays, and wait upon the Railway Companies to see what facilities they would give, then call a public meeting. It was also moved by Mr James Laidlaw and seconded by Mr Hilson: That the Council appoint a committee to wait upon the Railway Companies to ascertain what facilities they would give, and to put these facilities before the public either by advertisement or otherwise. There voted for the first motion two, for the other motion six. Messrs R. S. Laws, J. Laidlaw, W. Fairbairn, H. Finlay, and J. Gifford[4] were appointed as a committee to carry out the resolution.

The Council agreed to record their sympathy with the House

[1] Identity uncertain.
[2] Not identified.
[3] Engineers and millwrights, West Sciennes, Edinburgh.
[4] James Gifford, engineers.

Painters in their present struggle for a rise of wages. Mr Laws called attention to the neccessity of having the certificates of the appointment of delegates stamped.

23 May 1871

Mr James Gifford in the Chair. Twelve members present. Correspondence was read from the grocers association, and from the Sunderland Engineers, also a letter from the Manager of the Caledonian Railway Company offering to meet a deputation from the Trades Council. The committee appointed to make arrangements for annual holidays reported that they had waited on the manager of the North British Railway Company and that the Company were willing to grant return tickets to the various stations on their lines, to be available for eight days commencing 26th July; but not having had an interview with the Caledonian Company they could not proceed any further in the movement. The report was adopted, and the committee instructed to carry out the resolution of former meeting.

13 June 1871

Mr Daniel Munro, Vice president, in the chair. 12 members present. Mr Strachan, the Treasurer, stated that £5 13s 6d had been collected for the Sunderland engineers which had been remitted to their Committee, and as the strike was at an end before the subscription sheets went round numbers did not subscribe that otherwise might have done so. The Secretary laid before the meeting a statement of the short time movement in Newcastle and Gateshead which he had received from two delegates from the Engineers then on strike for the 9 hours day. Mr Fairbairn moved that the Council make an appeal to the various trades in behalf of the workmen now on strike in Newcastle and Gateshead, which was seconded by Mr Strachan and unanimously agreed to. Messrs James Gifford, James Laidlaw and James Blair were appointed as a committee to receive subscriptions every Monday evening from 8 to 9 o'clock in Buchanan's Hotel. It was agreed to print 300 subscription sheets with the Engineers statement as a heading.

It was moved by Mr James Laidlaw and seconded by Mr Thomas Blaikie: That this Council petition the house of Lords in favour of

the Edinburgh and District Water Bill (St Mary's Loch Scheme[1])
and that the Secretary communicate the above to the Lord Provost
of Edinburgh and the Provosts of Leith and Portobello.[2] Mr R. S.
Law moved the previous question, seconded by Mr Wilson[3]. Mr
Fairbairn moved that the motion be discussed at this meeting, which
was seconded by Mr M. Hilson. 8 voted for Mr Law's amendment
and 6 for Mr Fairbairn's motion. Mr James Laidlaw then gave
notice that he would bring it up at next meeting of Council.

27 June 1871

Mr James Blair in the Chair. 14 members present. Correspondance
was read from the North British Railway Company trying to get
clear of their engagment for return tickets during the Holidays.
The Secretary read a letter he sent to the Railway Company holding
them to their former agreement. A letter was read from the grocers
association stating that they had fixed their anul Holiday for thursday
27 July. The Secretary then intimated that he would have to leave
the meeting in consqunce of illness at home. Matthew Hilson was
appointed to take the Secretary's place till he could attend.

James Laidlaw reported that he had sent £7 to the Newcastle
Nine Hours League. Mr Gifford interduced a deputition from the
Newcastle Nine Hours League who addressed the meeting on the
present position of the men on the Tyne and urged their claims on
the members of the council as being worthy of their support.
Sevarl of the members expressed their sympathy with the men now
on strike for a reduction of the hours of labour and hoped that the
trades would give them every support in their power. James Laidlaw
then withdrew his motion on the water Bill.

11 July 1871

Mr James Blair in the Chair. 12 members present. A disscussion
took Place on the Holidays and the return ticket, when the Former
holiday Committee, viz., W. Fairbairn, R. S. Laws, James Gifford,

[1] The Bill was a controversial proposal by the Edinburgh and District Water Trustees
to bring water from St Mary's Loch in Selkirkshire. It was rejected by a committee
of the House of Lords in July 1871.
[2] Respectively William Law, James Watt and Thomas Wood.
[3] Identity uncertain.

X

J. Laidlaw and James Sinclair were appointed to go to the North British Railway Company on the following Friday night, if no Bills were out before that time, to try and keep them to their former agreement. Owing to both the Auiditors Having left the council Mr Peter Wilson[1] and R. S. Laws was appointed auiditors to auidit the Book and take an inventry of the Box before next meeting. A Letter was read from the Brassfounders stating that David Allen and David Fraser were appointed delegates for the ensueing twelve months.[2] It was agreed to sumin the next meeting as it was the Election of Officebearers, and the secretary was instructed to write to the different secretarys where their members Had not been attending the Council meeting for some time back.

25 July 1871

Mr W. Fairbairn in the chair. 18 members present. A Letter was read from the Typographical Society intamiting that James Petrie and Alexander Thomson was their repersentivates for the ensueing twelve months. R. S. Laws gave in the Holiday committee's report of their interview with the Manager of North British railway Company. After considerable trouble he agreed to keep to there former arrangements about return tickets. The auidtors' report was delayed till next meeting. Mr Gifford gave in the report of the sub committee in connection with the Newcastle strike. He stated they had sent £35 to Newcastle and he was sorry to say that there was no prospect of a settlement, that a conference had been held between the masters and men but that nothing had come out of it. Affairs seemed to look as bad as at the commencement of the struggle. It was agreed to put an advertisment in the different papers calling attention to the necesity for keeping up the subscriptions in behalf of men.

Messrs T. Knox and T. Usher[3] appeared as a deputition from the Scot centenary celebration committee to try and get the trades to get up a demonstration in honer of late Sir Walter Scot. They both urged the properity of the trades taking an active share in the cele-

[1] Not identified.
[2] Allen had been a delegate to the trades council since 14 March 1871.
[3] Thomas Knox and Thomas Usher, the brewer, who was secretary of the Scott Centenary Committee.

beration of the Scot centenary. The depution then withdrew, when
R. S. Laws moved that we take no action in matter, seconded by
George Mackay.[1] An amendment was moved by W. Noble,[2]
seconded by G. Black, that the subject be remited to trades, re-
comending them to get up a demonstration in honor of the late
Sir Walter Scot. 12 voted for the motion, 3 for the amendment.
Mr Paterson then moved that the secetary write to the Secretary of
the Scot Centenary Committee informing them of the disicesin of
the council, which was agreed to.

The council then proceeded to the election of officers when the
following was elected: President, Walter Fairbairn, on the motion
of Peter Wilson, seconded by Alexander Blair[3]; Vis President,
R. S. Laws, on the motion of A. Blair, seconded by D. Fraser;
Secretary, M. Hilson, on the motion of Mr Weir, seconded by
Thomas Blaikie; Assistant Secretary, James Petrie, on the motion
of Mr Weir, seconded by T. Blaikie; Treasurer, Thomas Blaikie,
on the motion of M. Hilson, seconded by Peter Wilson. M. Hilson
moved the following committee to prepair the anual report:
Alexander Strachan, P. Wilson, R. S. Laws, and M. Hilson, which
was agreed to.

8 August 1871

The Vice President[4] in the Chair. 8 members present. A letter was
read from the Manchester and Salford Trades Council in reference
to a letter that appeared in the *Typographical Circular* casting
reflections on this council for extreme political proclivities.[5] It was
agreed that the Secretary answer said Letter, and send a copy of our
laws along with it. The annual reports was then taken up when
owing to the smallness of the meeting it was agreed to Hold a
special meeting on tuesday 15th August to consider Proof of said
report. A sucgestion [was made] to hold a Public Meeting in
favour of the men on strike in Newcastle. It was agreed to take it
up at special meeting.

---

[1] Probably a typefounder; below, p. 329.
[2] Probably a delegate from one of the iron trades.
[3] Not identified.
[4] R. S. Laws, painters.
[5] The letter appeared in the issue of July 1871, and was signed by 'o.k.'.

15 August 1871

A special meeting was held. The annual reports was taken up and discussed, when after some slight alterations they were agreed to unanimously. The consideration of public meeting in aid of the men on strike at Newcastle was taken up when after considerable discussion it was agreed not to hold a meeting in the meantime but that the members do everything in their power to aid the cause.

22 August 1871

The vicepresident in the chair. 9 members present. Letters was read from the Bookbinders intimating that they had withdrawen their members from the council; and from the Glasgow Trades Council asking the cooperation of this council in obtaining the Federation of all the trades of Scotland and all other matters of general interest to the Industerial Classes. The Secretary was to acknowledge both letters and to state to the bookbinders that the council hoped they would reconsider the subject and send back their delegates to the council board; and to say to the Trades Council of Glasgow that this council would be happy to correspond with the Glasgow Trades Council in all matters to advance the social condition of the Industrial classes.

A Letter signed O.K. in the *Typographical Circular* was then taken up. It was agreed to take no notice of said letter further than sending a copy of our annual report to the Editor, asking him to take notice of said report in his *Circular* as early as possible. The Secretary was further instructed to send a copy of report to all the papers with a notice accompaning them asking the Editor to publish them if possible. Mr James Blair then gave in a report from the sub committee in charge of the subscriptions for the men on strike in Newcastle. The subscriptions were graduly falling off and the men had as much need for money as ever. He hoped the members would do everything in their power to help there Brethern in their present struggle.

12 September 1871

8 members were present. Letter was read from the moulders intimating that Robert Turner was their delegate in room of George

Young, and From the Bookbinders acknowledging letter from Secretary. Mr Blair then gave in a report on the Newcastle strike when he informed the council that the Engineers was geting up a concert in behalf of the men out on strike. The Council formaly agreed to give them there support. The attendance of Council was then taken up. Mr Alexander Thomson moved that a committee be appointed to wait on the trades not represented at the Council Board to urge upon the different trades to send delegates, seconded by T. Blakie. The Following was appointed: Messers Fairbarn, R. S. Law, A. Thomson, T. Blakie, and the secretary. The secretary was instructed to write to the different Trades requesting permission for a deputition to wait on them.

26 September 1871

The Vice President in the chair. 9 members present. Mr J. Blair stated that the concert in aid of the Newcastle men cleared £14. Mr Alison, delegate from Newcastle nine Hours League, was then interduced to the meeting when he addressed the council and laid the claims of the men before the meeting and also urged the necesity for holding a public meeting in aid of the men on strike. James Blair moved that the united Trades Council get up a public meeting as early as possible, seconded by M. Hilson. Agreed to. The following committee was appointed: R. Turner, R. S. Law, J. Blair, and Secretary.

3 October 1871

A special meeting was held. The Vice President in the Chair. 14 members present. The public meeting in support of the men on strike in Newcastle was taken up when the resolutions was agreed to be moved at the public meeting. Mr Burnet, President, Nine Hours League,[1] being present addressed the meeting on the strugle now going on in Newcastle. He informed the Council that Mr Mundella, M.P., had been in Newcastle and tryed to get an agreement but he had failed.[2]

[1] John Burnett, chairman of the Newcastle Nine Hours League formed 2 May 1871, general secretary of the Amalgamated Society of Engineers 1874-86. J. B. Jefferys, *The Story of the Engineers* (London, 1945), 86, 110.
[2] Anthony John Mundella, 1825-97, Nottingham hosiery manufacturer, Radical M.P. for Sheffield 1868-85 and Sheffield Brightside 1885-97.

PUBLIC MEETING[1]

St Mary Hall
Lothian Street
5 October 1871

A crowded meeting of working men was held to hear a deputation from the engineers now on strike at Newcastle. Mr Fairbairn occupied the chair and introduced the deputation.

Mr Burnet, president of the Nine Hours League, said that misrepresentations had been made regarding the position of the men, and gave an account of the affair from its origin till the present day, in the course of which he was several times loudly cheered. The statements of both parties had been made public and the decided feeling which had sprung up in favour of the Nine Hours League was sure evidence of who had right on their side. When the strike commenced the subscriptions were small but now each was in receipt of 12s. per week and 1s. for each child. They had now been idle for 18 or 19 weeks, but they considered they were engaged in the noblest work they had ever taken in hand. It was not only for themselves they were fighting, but for the working men throughout the whole country. (Applause.) The masters knew that and they had asked and obtained support from masters in all parts of the country. It was for the meeting to say whether it would support the men in this struggle of labour against capital. (Applause.) He compared the strikers to men making an engine which they were determined should not leave the shop until it was quite complete. When it was complete it would go out over the whole of the land. The engine was for Edinburgh workmen as well as Newcastle ones. He expected it would go like a parliamentary train – stop at all stations. (Applause and cheers.) It would come to Edinburgh, Glasgow, and other places, taking up passengers at every point, until all were riding safely in the nine hours train. (Loud and prolonged cheering.)

Mr Alison, Newcastle, next addressed the meeting. He said from the reception he had got in Scotland he had no doubt but that Edinburgh and Glasgow would cope with the great trade centres

[1] This report is a press cutting pasted into the minute book.

in England in their support of the present movement. Many of the trades in Glasgow were already contributing large sums weekly, and the Trades' Council of Edinburgh was making regular remittances. The working men everywhere should resolve to give a small sum weekly, and when the strike came to a successful termination they would have the satisfaction of having aided in a great national work.

Mr William Paterson was called upon to move the first resolution as follows: That this meeting, having heard the deputation from Newcastle, sincerely regrets the position the employers have assumed in the present dispute, and deeply sympathises with the men in their noble endeavours to obtain the nine hours day. He congratulated the engineers of Newcastle upon the happy hit they had made in sending Mr Burnet to Edinburgh, and expressed a wish that there was a Mr Burnet in every town and trade. The nine hours system would soon be universal. He urged thorough combination as the only means of obtaining their ends. The strike had become national, and every working man in the country should take an interest in it and assist the men to bring it to a successful termination. The real working day was eight hours, but until the Newcastle men had got the nine hours it would be useless for men in other trades to try to get their working day reduced to eight. Mr Dewar[1] seconded the motion of Mr Paterson. He said that the question of the machines standing idle was very easily solved. If a man had twelve machines going, and the working hours were reduced from ten to nine, all the master had to do was to get another machine and his productive power would be the same. (Applause.)

The Chairman – Sympathy is all very good, but it is very cheap. Now there is something of a more practical nature to come before you. He then called upon Mr Gifford to move the next resolution. At this point Mr Burnet said he had received a telegram desiring him to return to Newcastle by the night train. He then left the meeting amid tremendous cheers, the audience rising and waving their hats. Mr Gifford then moved: That, in consequence of the position taken up by the employers of Newcastle and district against the men on strike, it becomes a national duty to aid and assist the men both by our sympathy and money, and this meeting pledges

[1] Andrew Dewar, blacksmiths.

itself to do all in its power to attain that end. (Applause.) Mr Arnot[1] seconded the motion.

It was then proposed to form a committee for the purpose of carrying out the foregoing resolutions. A voice – Let the meeting form itself into a branch of the Nine Hours League. Mr Colville[2] said the proposition just made was a good one; that the Trades' Council, which was at present taking in subscriptions for the men on strike, did not possess the confidence of the working men of Edinburgh. (Hisses.) Mr Paterson said that the large meeting which had come together at the call of the Trades' Council was a pretty good proof they did possess the confidence of the trades. (Applause.)

Various other proposals were made, after which the Chairman said the best plan would be for those who wished to get sub-scription-sheets to wait after the meeting broke up, or to go to the meeting of the Trades' Council Committee in Buchanan's Hotel, on Monday evening next, and get them there. Mr Alison made a few additional remarks, in the course of which he said that the balance-sheets of the Nine Hours League showed that they had already had £14,000 through their hands. That was an example of what small things would do, and he urged them all to do a little. The meeting then broke up.

10 October 1871

16 members present. Letters was read from the Joiners, Centeral Branch, intimating that James Kirk was their delegate at the councill Board; from the Joiners, West Branch, that James Hunter and Thomas Montgomery were delegates for their Branch; and from the Masons stating that a deputation would be recived from the Council on Monday the 9th October at 8.30 p.m.

The Nine Hours Movement was then taken up. Alexander Thomson moved: That this meeting instruct those delegates whose Trades are not in the enjoyment of the nine hours day to adopt means to arrive at a sence of their trade on the subject and report, and in the event of such report being favourable to the short time movement the council take measures to have the movement brought publicly before the trades and other wise give them every assistance

---

[1] Not identified.   [2] Not identified.

in there power. Seconded by James Wightman[1] and agreed to. Mr Blair[2] then moved that the secretary be instructed to open a correspondence with Glasgow Trades Council urgeing on them the necesity of their Board agitating for the nine hours day as it was only by united action that we would have any chance of success. Seconded by Thomas Blaikie and agreed to. The secretary was then instructed to send a letter of congratulation to the nine hour League of Newcastle on the end of their strugle.

24 October 1871

Mr Thomson in the Chair. 9 members present. W. Noble reported that the Iron Trade were agitating for nine Hour. It was agreed to hold a special meeting the following Tuesday and the secretary was instructed to summon the members.

31 October 1871

A special meeting was held. Mr Alexander Thomson in the Chair. Mr George Mackay reported that the workmen of Millar and Richard, Typefounders, was to ask the nine hours next day. A deputation from the Nine Hours League was then interduced and addressed the meeting. After some discussion David Allan moved the council get up a public meeting as eraly as possible on the nine hour movement. The following committee was appointed with full powers to get up the meeting: W. Fairbarn, A. Thomson, T. Blaikie, J. Kirk and the secretary.

14 November 1871

14 members present. A letter was read from Nottingham asking the council to send a delegate to the anual Trades congress to be held in Nottingham. Mr J. Taylor moved that the subject lie over till next meeting which was agreed to. Certificates was read for the Joiners, West Branch, that Walter Chisholm was appointed delegate in room of James Hunter, resigned; from the Bakers that James Trodden was appointed delegate in room of Gilbert Millar; and from the Tailors that James Taylor was appointed their delegate.

[1] Edinburgh bakers.
[2] Either James Blair, engineers, or Alexander Blair, trade unknown.

The Public Meeting was then taken up when the following motions was agreed to be moved at a Public Meeting to be held in the New Waverly Hall on Friday the 17 inst. at 8 p.m., Councillor Gowans to take the chair. 1st Resolution: That the meeting, beliving the shortening of the Hours of labour to be the next and direct road to the amelioration morally and physically of the working classes and that the recognised hours should not exceed nine hours per day, heartly sympathises with and pledges itself to promot and further the nine hour movement. To be moved by G. Goodfellow, seconded by James Balmain,[1] and supported by Councillor Cranston. Second Resolution: That this meeting views with Plesure the growing tendency on the part of the General public in favour of a reduction of the hours of labour and solicits their countance and support on behalf of the working classes in their endeavours to obtain such reduction. Moved by Alexander Thomson, seconded by John Marshall,[2] and supported by Councillor Bladworth.[3] 3rd resolution: That this meeting call upon all working men to support the different associations whose object is the reduction of the hours of labour in their efforts to make the 51 hours per week an accomplished fact throughout the whole kingdom.

28 November 1871

Mr A. Thomson in the chair. 14 members present. The Trades congress was taken up. It was agreed that the delegates present lay the subject before there trades and report at next meeting. The secretary was instructed to write to absent delegates to lay the matter before their trades and report at next meeting and to see if they would pay the expenses.

The Nine Hours Committee report on behalf of the Newcastle Strike was then taken up when Mr D. Allen moved, seconded by D. Fraser, that James Laidlaw be paid his lost time when remiting money to Newcastle. Agreed to. Mr James Blair moved that whatever surplus was left after Paying all expenses be handed over to the Nine Hours League of the Iron Trade. Seconded by James Kirk and agreed to. Mr Turner reported that the Moulders had given

---

[1] Goodfellow was a joiner and Balmain an engineer. *Scotsman*, 18 November 1871.
[2] A joiner. *Scotsman*, 18 November 1871.
[3] Richard Bladworth, wholesale ironmonger, an Independent Liberal.

notice to their employers that they wished to adopt the 9 hours. A
Testimonial to the leaders of the Nine Hours League of Newcastle
was then taken up when James Blair moved that owing to the
present position of trades we take no action in the matter. Mr Blair
gave notice of motion to be taken up at next meeting that the council
take action in behalf of the trades now moving for the nine hour
day.

12 December 1871

10 members present. It was agreed not to send a delegate to the
Nottingham Trades Congress. The Chairman brought before the
Council the altered plans of the new Royal Infrimary. It was agreed
to summon a meeting to consider the subject and a Notice of Motion
by R. Turner regarding the Engineers dispute. The council then
proceeded to elect a Vice President in room of Mr R. S. Law,
withdrawn. Mr Wightman, Baker, was elected. Mr Walter Chisholm was elected assistant secretary in room of Mr Petrie, who has
left town.

19 December 1871

A special meeting, the Vice President in the Chair. 15 members
Present. A deputation from the Associated Bakers was interduced
to the meeting by the chairman who laid before the Council the
position of there trade.[1] It was agreed to give them every support
within the Power of the Council. It was then agreed to send a paragraph to the Press. A deputation from the Iron Trades Nine Hours
League was then interduced consisting of Messrs Gifford,[2] Munro,[3]
and Cornielus Yorston. They addressed the council and urged the
Claims of the Iron Trades. Mr Hutton[4] moved that the council issue
subscriptions sheets in support of the men on strike as eraly as Possible and that a Committee be appointed to carry out the same.
Messers Chisholm, Turner and Grant[5] was appointed Committee.

[1] Thirty bakers were reported to be on strike in twelve shops where employers had
refused to accept new agreed hours of work and a minimum wage of 22s a week.
Scotsman, 25 December 1871.
[2] James Gifford, engineers.
[3] Not further identified.
[4] R. Hutton, printers.
[5] Probably John Grant, tailors. See below, p. 336.

1872

10 January 1872[1]

Mr Blair[2] was appointed secterary pro tem owing to the absence of the secretary through indisposition.[3] 11 members present. Mr Wightman, Baker, brought up the question relating to the movement among the Bakers for the reduction of the Hours of Labour, etc. Having given a short review of their movements, the several conferences they had with their employers and the result of such, he intimated that some of the masters had failed to implement the agreement come to by the conference, namely, that on the first five days of the week all work shall begin at 5 a.m. and end at 4 p.m., and on Saturday from 5 till 2 p.m. Overtime only to be wrought in cases of emergency, for which time and half shall be paid, and the minimum wage to be twenty two shilling per week. Also a court of arbitartion has been established composed of seven employers and seven operatives at which all matters may be settled amicabley, the decisions of such court being binding on all parties. The following resolution was agreed to: In view of such agrement being departed from by some the Trades Council express their sympathy with the bakers and regreets that those employers should have failed to adopt the whole of the instructions in the forgoing circular, and advises the Bakers to adopt every lawfull meanes to obtain their ultimate purpose.

A deputation interduced from the bookbinders, who are out on strike on the short time question, explained that it was their first intention to go in for the 51 hours but seeing that the printers had accepted the 54 hours to their demand it was thought on their part

[1] The date should probably read 9 January 1872.
[2] Either James Blair, engineers, or Alexander Blair, trade unknown.
[3] The minutes nonetheless continue in the handwriting of Hilson, the secretary, although on 23 January he is said to have smallpox.

not to be advisible to press for more than 54. Having accepted such the dispute culminated on the arrangement of the hours. The masters proposed to start work at 8.30 a.m. and drop at 7 p.m. 3 nights a week and start same time and drop at 7.30 p.m. 2 nights and saturday at two, having only one meal hour. The men's demands are that they start at say 6.30 a.m. and drop at 4.p.m. or not later than 6 p.m. This not being acceded to by the masters hence the dispute. The council at the request of the deputation resolved that subscription sheets be issued by the bookbinders under the Trades Council authority. A vote of sympathy was also accorded to the Dundee Iron Workers now on strike for the 51 hours and that a paragraph be sent to the local Journals.

23 January 1872

Mr Wightman in the Chair. 10 members present. A letter was read from the secretary stating he was precluded from attending owing to being subjected to an attack of smallpox. Letter and circular was read from the Miners Association regarding the mines regulation bill about to be interduced into Parliment and asking the support of the Council in recommending their circular to our M.P.s, asking them to support the same.[1] Some little discussion ensued upon the merits of the Circular when the previous question was moved by Mr Turner, seconded by Mr Grant, that we adjourn the debate till next ordinary meeting. A counter motion was moved by Mr Trodden, seconded by Mr Blaikie, that we continue the debate. Majority of one in favour of the motion. Report from the subscription committee to the effect that owing to the successfull termination of the strike[2] they had actually no report to give. They were to advertise for the subscriptions which had not been received by them as also for the sheets which was distributed by them.

30 January 1872

A special meeting was held. 8 members present. A deputation from the Operative Bakers stated in detail the correspondence regarding

[1] The Bill was enacted in August 1872 as 35-36 Victoria, c. 77.
[2] In the iron trades.

short time movement and the desirability of Holding a Public meeting for the purpose of laying before the Public their grievances and requesting the council to co-operate with them in geting up the meeting. They also stated there were 40 men on strike provided for and that their were 60 shops Black who had failed to adopt the resolutions of the conference of December 3rd, 1871, these masters employing about 140 men. It was moved by Mr Blaikie, seconded by Mr Thomson and carried unanimously that a public meeting be held at as eraly date as possible for the above Purpose under the auspices of the Trades Council. A committee was appointed consisting of Blaikie, Thomson, and Blair,[1] to act in conjunction with the Bakers Committee to make arrangements for the meeting.[2]

20 February 1872

A special meeting was held. The Vice President in the chair. 16 members present. A deputation from the operative Bakers was interdoucded when they stated that their was no improvement in their dispute since last meeting. The following motion was agreed to: That the council issue the revised list of employers who have acceded to the demands of the men through their various Trades, and further urge upon the bakers to do every thing in there Power to get the trade better orginised. The tresurer was instructed to Pay the St Marys Street Hall for Public Meeting.

A deputation of saw millers of Edinburgh and Leith was then admitted. They stated that they had sent circular to their employers requesting the 51 hours per week. They were requested to attend next meeting and report. A deputation from the Marble and Slate Masons of Edinburgh and Leith was then heard. They explained to the meeting that they were endeavouring to get the 51 hours per week and that their employers had refused there demand. They had given in their warning that unless the 51 hours was granted they would strike on Saterday first. John McAllen asked the deputation what were their present hours when they replied 57 hours. The exception was Field & Allen: their hours was $59\frac{1}{2}$. It was resolved to give them every support within the power of council.

[1] Either James Blair, engineers, or Alexander Blair, trade unknown.
[2] No press report of this meeting has been found.

27 February 1872

11 members present. A deputation from the bakers asking the council to issue subscriptions sheet in behalf of the members of their trade now on strike. Agreed to, and the following committee was appointed to take charge of the subscriptions: James Kirk, D. Paterson,[1] James Wightman, and James Trodden, and the council further urged upon the Bakers the necesity of them trying every means within their power to get the non-members to join their society. Mr Chisholm then asked the deputation on what condition the bakers would work overtime. Mr Bennet[2] stated overtime could be wrought in the afternoon but must be paid time and half, but on no condition could it be wrought in the morning. A deputation from the Marble Masons was then heard when they stated that they were all out on strike with the exception of one shop, namely, Mr Lightbody, Lothian Road, which had granted their request. The council agreed to do everything in their power to assist them in their struggle. A deputation from the saw millars reported that three of their employers had granted their request, viz., the 51 hours: Bailie Pentland, Leith, Lindsay, Cannon Mills, and Millons, Fountain Bridge, and that the men was to give in their warning on Saterday first if no settlement was come to.

The Education bill was then taken up.[3] D. Paterson moved that it lie on the table, seconded by W. Chisholm. M. Hilson moved an amendment that a special meeting be called this night week to consider the bill. Seconded by J. Kirk. 6 voted for the motion and 6 for the amendment. The Chairman gave his casting vote in favour of the amendment, and the secretary was instructed to summon absent members.

12 March 1872

Mr Blair[4] in the Chair. 9 members present. Correspondence was read from the Operative Bakers, thanking the council for the assistance they had given them in their struggle to shorten their Hours of Labour. A circular was read from the Flax operatives of Leeds when

---

[1] Not identified.

[2] Probably John Bennet who had been a delegate to the trades council in 1868.

[3] The Bill was passed in August 1872 as the Education (Scotland) Act.

[4] Either James Blair, engineers, or Alexander Blair, trade unknown.

after some discussion it was agreed to let it lie on the table.[1] The masters and workmen wages bill was then taken up when it was agreed to summon next meeting to consider the Bill.[2]

26 March 1872

12 members present. A Letter was read from the Cabinet and Chair-makers stating that James Paterson and James Inglis had been duly elected delegates to the United Trades Council. Mr Bennet, Baker, then reported that the Bakers would be obliged to give in owing to the men not geting support. The master and workmen Bill was then read when after a long discussion James Wightman moved that the United Trades Council Petition the House of commons in favour of the bill. Seconded by R. Turner and agreed to. Alexander Thomson and secretary was appointed to draw up a petition and forward it to J. Millar, Esq., M.P., for presentation to the house of commons.

9 April 1872

Mr Blair[3] in the Chair. 11 members present. A Letter was read from the Tailors Society intimating that John Grant and Neil McLean[4] was their delegates at the Council Board and that they had voted their anual contribution to the funds of the council. A paragraph in the daily papers of Monday last was then brought under the notice of the Council about a meeting to be held in Glasgow on the 11 June for the purpose of federating the Trades of Scotland. The secretary was instructed to write to Glasgow asking an explanation about the meeting.[5]

23 April 1872

11 members present. A circular was read from Mr Howel, London,[6] asking the council to give their support to the masters and workmen

---

[1] A strike by the flax operatives had begun at Leeds on 5 March for a reduction of hours to nine a day. *Scotsman*, 5 March 1872.
[2] Presumably the Payment of Wages (Truck) Bill introduced by the government on 22 February but withdrawn in July after mutilation. G. Howell, *Labour Legislation, Labour Movements and Labour Leaders* (London, 1905 edn.), 222-4.
[3] Either James Blair, engineers, or Alexander Blair, trade unknown.
[4] For a few items of information about McLean see above, p. xxiv.
[5] The meeting was called by Glasgow trades council.
[6] George Howell, 1833-1910, secretary 1871-5 of the parliamentary committee of the Trades Union Congress.

wages Bill. After a good deal of discussion Mr McLean moved that we wait on the members for the City asking them to support said Bill in its orignal form, seconded by J. Wightman. The confederation of trades unions for Scotland was then taken up. Mr Thomson moved that it be remitted to the various trades for their consideration and the delegates to report at next meeting. The secretary was instructed to write to absent members and others. Mr Blaikie gave notice of motion anent the annual holiday.

28 May 1872

14 members present. A letter was read from the slaters society stating that John Purves had been elected their delegate in room of Thomas McKenize,[1] who had gone to America. The minutes of former meeting was read, when James Kirk objected to no notice be taken of the report submitted by the secretary of the attendance of members at the council which was disapproved of on account of sum of the members thinking they had been oftener present. The secretary stated he could not be responceable for members coming in after the roll was called. The minutes was then approved of on the motion of J. Inglis, seconded by J. Paterson.

The Chairman asked if their was any report to give about the conference to be held in Glasgow on the 11 June. The cabinet makers intimated that their trade was going to send two delegates, the tin Plate Workers League was to send 2 delegates, the Blacksmiths and Moulders was to be represented by their centreal Boards. The Engineers and Tailors was to take no action in the matter. A letter was read from the masons stating that they as a local Branch was to take no action but [it was in] every way likely they would be represented from the centreal Board.

The Holiday question was then taken up. Thomas Blaikie brought forward his motion: That a Committee be appointed to confer with the Railway Companies in regard to the Anual Holidays to bring about some definet arrangement. Seconded by James Kirk. Mr Noble moved an amendment that the council simply intimate to the Railway Companies that the Holidays take place on the 25, 26, and 27 of July, leaving them to make their own arrangements. Seconded

---

[1] There is no previous mention in the minutes of 'McKenize' or McKenzie.

Y

by N. McLean. 12 voted for the motion and 2 for the amendment. The following Committee was appointed: Messers Kirk, Thomson, Inglis, Blaikie, and the Chairman and Secretary. The Secretary was then instructed to write to J. Millar, Esq., M.P., asking information about amending the Criminal Law amendment act of last session.

11 June 1872

Mr James Paterson in the Chair. 9 members present. Certificates was read from the Tinplate workers intimating that John Holburn[1] and John Jack had been elected to represent them at the council; and from the Coopers that Alexander Mackay and James McKenize was elected to represent them at the council. The Secretary then gave in report of the deputation that had waited on the Railway companies. Messers Fairbairn, Inglis, Blaikie and himself waited on Mr Irons, superintendent, Caledonian Railway. He stated that he could give us no definate information till he communcatied with his superior in Glasgow but what he would reccomend, and he was certain it would be their terms, that they would issue their ordinary return tickets from Wednesday the 24 July up to Wednesday 31st July. The Secretary also reported that Mr Inglis and himself waited on Mr McLaren, North British Railway, but they had made no satisfactory arangements. It was then agreed to remit the subject back to the committee to push Mr McLaren for an answer.

The criminal Bill was then read when it was agreed to let it lie over till next meeting. Mr Paterson, Bookbinder, brought under the notice of council the bookbinders strike in Toronto when he moved that the United Trades council deeply sympathise with the Bookbinders of Toronto in their present strugle to shorten their hours of Labour from 60 to 54 hours per week, and that a paragraph be sent to the papers stating the same. Seconded by Walter Chisholm and agreed to.

25 June 1872

9 members present. A certificate was read from the Joiners, West Branch, intimating that John Welsh had been appointed delegate to represent them at the Council Board. The Secretary then gave

---

[1] For some biographical details of Holburn see above, p. xxv.

in the report of the Holiday Committee when the subject was
remited back to the committee to try to get better terms from the
railway companies. George Mackay was added to the committee.
The Criminal Law amendment act was then taken. Mr Blaikie
moved that the council petition the House of Commons for the
total repeal of said act as the Common law of the country was quite
sufficient of itself for all classes of offenders. Seconded by J. Kirk
and agreed to. The President, Secretary, Chisholm and Blaikie was
appointed to draw up petition. Extension of the hours of polling
was then taken up when Mr J. Purves moved: That we petition the
House of Commons, Praying them to extend the hours of polling
to eight o'clock in evening. Seconded by G. Mackay and agreed to.
The former committee was instructed to draw up petition.

5 July 1872

A special meeting was held. 14 members present. Mr Thomson
gave the report of the Holiday Committee. The only alteration the
Railway Companies was disposed to make was that of an extension
of the Ordinary return tickets for one whole week. Great dissatisfaction was expressed at the very illiberal [terms] offered by the
companies. Mr Thomson moved that the council reluctantly agree
to recommend the acceptance of the Companies offer to the various
Trades and that the Holidays be held on the last Saturday and two
preceeding days as usual. Seconded by George Mackay and agreed
to.

A sugestion to petition House of Lords, Praying for the extension
of the Hours of polling to Eight O'clock in the evening, was then
taken up. The secretary read a draft petition which was adopted.
On the motion of James Kirk, seconded by Mr Thomson, Mr
Thomson was then appointed to assist the secretary to draw up
annual report and Mesers Chisholm and Inglis was appointed
Auditors.

9 July 1872

13 members present. A Letter was read from Leith Branch of Joiners
asking information about the Holidays. The secretary was instructed
to give them all the information possible and to send a few circulars.
The secretary was instructed to get 700 circulars and send them to

the various trades as soon as possible. The President then brought the case of the Flour and Meal Millers of Edinburgh, Leith and Vicinety before the council. It was unanimously agreed to send a paragraph to the Press sympathizeing with them in their Endeavors to get the nine Hours. Mr T. Blaikie gave notice of motion for next meeting: to take up the rules of the Confederation of the United Trades of Scotland.[1]

16 July 1872

A Special meeting was held. 20 members present. A Letter was read from the Brassfounders stating that John Adams and John Graham had been elected delegates to the council for the ensueing twelve months.

The Annual report was then read. J. McAllen moved its adoption, seconded by R. Turner and agreed to. The Secretary then read a report of the attendance of members. J. McAllen moved that the report be sent to the various secretarys connected with the Council. M. Hilson moved it be not sent, seconded by Mr Welsh. 4 voted for the motion and 14 for the amendment. On Mr A. Thomson, delegate for the Printers, riseing to leave the meeting, M. Hilson moved that the council give Mr Alexander Thomson a vote for his able services to the council during the past year, which was unanimously agreed to. The Chairman then thanked Mr Thomson in the name of Council. The income and expenditure was then taken up. It was agreed that the financial statement be Printed along with the report after the Book is audited and found correct. Mr Inglis reported that he had waited on Mr Irons, Superentendent, Caledonian Railway, as instructed by the secretary. Mr Irons asked the council to get up excursion to Glasgow on the 27 July when he would make the tickets 2s. 6d., with 7½ per cent off. Mr J. Holburn moved that seeing it was against the princapels of the council to recoginise excursions we decline Mr Irons' offer with thanks. Seconded by George Mackay and agreed to.

23 July 1872

14 members present. The President intimated that M. Hilson and himself had been relected delegates to the Council for the ensueing

[1] This subject seems not to have been raised again until 26 November 1872.

Twelve months.[1] The Election of officebearers then took place. Walter Fairbairn was relected President on the motion of James Inglis, seconded by J. Adams. Matthew Hilson was relected Secretary on the motion of John Welsh, seconded by J. Graham. John Holburn was elected Vice President on the motion of John Jack, seconded by R. Turner. Walter Chisholm was relected assistant secretary on the motion of James Paterson, seconded by R. Turner. James Inglis was elected Treasurer on the motion of Robert Turner, seconded by Thomas Blaikie. John Jack, John Graham, and Alexander McKay was elected Trustees on the motion of M. Hilson, seconded by James Inglis.

The President having to leave, Mr Welsh was moved to the Chair. The following motion was given notice of for next meeting: that Rule 7, page 6, first line be altered so as to read 'above five pounds', instead of 'one' as at present. The propriety of adjourning the meeting of council for a month was then taken up. J. Jack moved that the Council stand adjourned till the 10th September, seconded by J. Graham and agreed to. The secretary was instructed to let absent delegates know and to send the annual report to all the trades as soon as Possible.

27 August 1872

A special meeting was held. 18 members present. Letter from Greenock was first taken up asking the Council to agitate for the repeal of the criminal Law amendment act. Mr Holburn moved that a committee be appointed to draw up a report on said Act, seconded by George Mackay and agreed to. The following members was appointed a Committee, to report as eraly as possible: Messers Fairbairn, Holburn, Grant, Chisholm and Wilson.[2]

The *Scotsman* strike was then taken up.[3] The members was instructed to take the subject to their Trades and to do everything

[1] For the blacksmiths.
[2] Not identified.
[3] The strike began on 24 July when four or five of the journeymen printers including, the clerk of their chapel, were dismissed for 'misconduct and neglect'. Some sixty other employees then struck in protest. Basically the dispute was caused by the management allocating more work to apprentices than to journeymen. As a result of the dispute the *Scotsman* became a non-union establishment. MS. Minutes of Edinburgh Typographical Society, 26 July 1872 (National Library of Scotland, Acc. 4068); *Scotsman*, 21 August 1872.

in their power to keep their members from supporting the *Scotsman* in any way. Mr Fergie[1] here read the following resolution from the Edinburgh Typographical Society:

27 August 1872 – At a meeting of the Executive Committee of the Edinburgh Typographical Society held last night the following resolution was unanimously agreed to: That this meeting in name of the Printers of Edinburgh tender its hearty thanks to the United Trades council of Edinburgh and Leith for the sympathy manifested towards their Brethren now on strike resisting an infringement of Trade prices, and for the active co-operation of that body in promoting and prosecuting to so successful an issue the Public meeting held in the Music Hall on the 20th curt.; that especial [thanks] are due and are hereby tenderd to the President and Secretary (Messers Fairbairn and Hilson) and to the various office-bearers for the ability, efficiency and zeal displayed in the performance of their several self-imposed duties, and that the delegates of the Edinburgh Typographical Society be instructed to lay this resolution before the Council at its first meeting. By order of Committee, William Tod, assistant secretary.

The letter from Aberdeen was then taken up. It was in reference to the poor Law. It was agreed to take no action in the matter as it did not come within our laws. The circular from Mr Howell was ordered to lie on the table till next meeting.

Mr Fergie moved: That the Trades Council having had their attention called to certain decisions lately given in the law courts of Edinburgh with regard to men leaving their employments, and considering such decisions as unjust and one-sided, Resolve that it be remited to the several delegates to bring the subject before the first general meeting of their Trades with the view of adopting the following recommendation of the council, viz., that warnings be abolished, employers having the Power to dismiss on the spot and men having Power to leave at once; and that the delegates report the decision come to at said meetings to the next meeting of the council following thereafter. Seconded by W. Chisholm, agreed to.[2]

---

[1] Robert Fergie, printers.

[2] A compositor had been fined £5 plus three guineas expenses at Edinburgh sheriff court on 22 August for leaving his employment before his notice had expired. The case arose out of the printers' strike on the *Scotsman*. *Scotsman*, 20 and 23 August 1872.

10 September 1872

9 members present. A certificate was read intimating that Andrew Munro had been elected to represent the Engineers at the council. A Letter was read from the secretary of the Iron Trades nine Hour league intimating that a deputation of that body would wait on the council to invite them to the Platform in the new Waverly Hall on the 12th September. The deputation was then interduced when Mr Reid addressed the meeting and invited the Council to a public meeting in the Waverley Hall when Mr Borrowman, the Treasurer of Scottish Co-operative Iron Works, Glasgow, would deliver a lecture on Productive co-operation.[1] It was agreed to accept the invitation and the secretary was instructed to summon absent members. Mr Grant moved that in Rule seventh, Page six, first line, read 'above five pounds' instead of 'one pound' as at present. Seconded by Mr Holburn and agreed to.[2] Mr Holburn gave notice of motion for next meeting.

24 September 1872

Mr Wilson[3] in the Chair. 17 members present. A circular was read from Mr Howell, secretary of the Trades Union Congress Parliamentary Committee, when it was agreed to let said Circular lie over till next meeting and the Secretary was instructed to write for a few more copies.

The *Scotsman* dispute was then taken up. Mr Hilson moved, seconded by G. Mackay, that the United Trades Council put the following advertisement in the Paper: Municipal Elections – Candidates for Municipal honours are requested to Advertise the *Reformer, Daily Review*, and *Courant*[4] as the only organs which the working class support. Unanimously agreed to. Mr Grant then

[1] James Borrowman, died 1898, manager 1868-74 of the Scottish Co-operative Wholesale Society Ltd; a son of John Borrowman, a former president of Edinburgh trades council. The iron works was founded in 1872 and collapsed in 1875. William Maxwell, *History of Co-operation in Scotland* (Glasgow, 1910), 249-58, 324.
[2] Under the existing rule all funds of the trades council over £1 had to be deposited in a bank 'or other proper investment'.
[3] Not identified.
[4] *Edinburgh Evening Courant*, 1705-1886, a daily from 1860 when it became definitely Conservative. W. Norrie, *Edinburgh Newspapers Past and Present* (Earlston, 1891), 10-15.

moved: Whereas great expense has been incurred by the Typographical Society in carrying on the dispute in connection with the
Scotsman newspaper, and whereas all who have taken any interest
in the matter cannot but see that it is intended as a representative
struggle, being a blow aimed it is concieved at Trades Unionism
in general, and will if successfull be followed by other employers in
other Trades, Resolved That we the United Trades Council of
Edinburgh and Leith viewing it in this light solicit the support of
all trades unionists on behalf of the Printers, confidently expecting
that it will be heartly tendered autherore.[1] Subscriptions sheets to
be issued to the various Trades for that purpose and so enable the
printers to carry on the struggle unembarrassed and bring it to a
successful issue. Seconded by M. Hilson and agreed to. The following committee was appointed to issue sheets and draw in subscriptions: Messers Grant, Holburn, Chisholm, and Wilson.[2]

12 November 1872

Mr Walter Chisholm in the Chair.[3] 14 members present. A deputation from the Printers Society laid the cause of their dispute before
the council. Mr Holburn moved that this Council give them every
support in their Power both moraly and materialy, and that we
issue subscriptions sheets in support of the men out on strike.
Seconded by Mr Grant and unanimously agreed to. Mr Grant,
Chisholm and Wilson[4] was appointed to recive subscriptions. A
letter was then read from the Glasgow trades Council about starting
a working man's newspaper.[5] The secretary was instructed to write
for information. A letter was read from the Nine hour Factory
association, Dundee,[6] complaining about D. McLaren, M.P. A deputation was appointed to wait on McLaren, viz., Holburn, Welsh
and Hilson.

---

[1] Meaning not known.   [2] Not identified.

[3] Holburn, vice-president, was present.   [4] Not identified.

[5] The proposal came to nothing since it was advanced again a year later. *Glasgow Herald*, 18 September 1873.

[6] Little seems to be known about this Dundee Association except that it sent its
chairman, a Mr Middleton, to London in the summer of 1873 during the consideration
of A. J. Mundella's Nine Hours Bill, a petition in favour of which had been signed by
over 30,000 people in Dundee in 1872. *People's Journal*, 10 February and 3 June 1872;
Scotsman, 5 August 1873.

26 November 1872

16 members present. The deputation appointed at last meeting reported that they had waited on D. McLaren, M.P., in reference to a letter recived from the nine hours factory association, Dundee. He stated he had no remberance of a deputation meeting him in London from said association, that he never in his life said the Hours was to short already, and that he had been in favour of short hours all his life. He further refered the deputation to his own firm in the High St. They were the first in the trade to give the Saturday half Holiday. Mr McLaren was extremely courtous to the deputation and went fully into the matter to the entire satisfaction of the Committee. Mr McLean moved that the secretary write to Dundee and inquire when and where their deputation saw Mr McLaren and whither they made any arrangements as to time and place of meeting and let them know what the council had done in the matter. Seconded by Mr Purves and agreed to.

The Printers dispute was next taken up. Mr Thomson, a deputation for the Printers Society, reported that their was no change in their affairs since last meeting and they had every appearance of having a very protracted struggle, and urged on the members to do everything in their power to support them in there hour of need. It was agreed that the Committe meet every Monday evening to recive subscriptions. The Confederation of Trades was then taken up. The Secretary read the Rules of the Confederation of the United Trades of Scotland. Mr Welsh moved the adjournment of the meeting which was agreed to.

10 December 1872

14 members present. A Certificate was read from the Bookbinders Society intimating that W. Weir and Thomas Reikie had been elected delegates to represent their trade at the Council Board. The Trades Union Congress was taken up. J. Welsh moved that we as a council take no action in the matter. Seconded by J. Holburn and agreed to. The committee in charge of the subscriptions to the Printers reported that they had drawn £8 12s. 7d. on the 2nd December and £17 10s. 8d. on the 9th. The adjourned debate on the confederation of Trades was then

taken up. Mr Welsh moved that we as a Council can take no part in this Confederation unless the rules are so altered that no Trade can come out on strike unless the majority of the members give them power to do so. Seconded by W. Chisholm. Mr Reikie moved the following amendment: That this Council recommend the various Trades here represented To consider the rules of the confederated Trades of Scotland with a view to joining that body, and would especialy draw attention to the main object aimed at by such federation, namely, the ablotion of eloemosynary aid in the case of strikes and lock outs, a complete system of federation rendering such unnecessary, and the establishing of a spirit of independence among its members. Mr Holburn seconded the amendment. After some discussion the subject was left over till next meeting. Mr Wilson, Printer,[1] asked the council to send circulars to all trades Councils throughout the Kingdom pressing the claims of Printers before their members. The secretary was instructed to give Mr Common[2] power to issue said circulars in name of the Council.

24 December 1872

17 members present. A Certificate was read from the Typefounders intimating that W. Nisbet and J. McAllen had been elected delegates to represent them at the council. A Certificate was also read from saddlers intimating that John Brown had been elected in room of Mr Johnston, resigned.[3]

A Circular and letter was then read from the Framework Knitters of Hawick asking the assistance of the council to support their men now on strike. Mr Purves moved: That this council, while fully recognising the claims of the Frame Work Knitters of Hawick for our sympathy and support at there Present Juncture, and expresing a hope that they may be successfull in their efforts to do away with the undoubted Greivances under which they have been laboured, yet deem it inadvisable to issue subscription sheets on their behalf seeing their is subscription sheets going round the trades on behalf

[1] It is uncertain whether Wilson was a delegate to the council or merely a deputation from the printers.
[2] J. S. Common, secretary of the Edinburgh Typographical Society.
[3] There is no previous mention of Johnston in the minutes.

of the Printers. Seconded by M. Hilson and agreed to.[1] The debate on federation was then resumed. After a protracted discussion the amendment was carried, 15 voting for the amendment and 1 for the motion. Mr Fergie then gave notice of motion for next meeting.

[1] The Hawick strike had begun on 28 October against offtakes from wages for seaming, oil, and light. *Scotsman*, 28 October 1872.

1873

14 January 1873

Eleven members present. Mr Fergie brought forward his motion which he gave notice of last meeting: That the Trades Councill of Edinburgh and Leith having had their attention called to the recent decision by Mr Justice Brett in the case of the Gas stokers of London and considering such decision contrary to justice, dictated in a spirit of revenge, and if further carried into practice totally subversive of the freedom of speech and liberty of action of all Trade Unionists, resolve that this Council instruct the delegates imeadately to bring the matter before their several Trades, and order a petition to be at once drawn up and signed in the name and on behalf of the United Trades Council of Edinburgh and Leith, to be presented to the Right Honourable H. A. Bruce, Home Secretary, for the object of mitigating the sentences thus passed and geting an imeadate abolition of such a one-sided and tyranical law. Seconded by Mr J. Holburn and agreed to. The Chairman, Secretary, Holburn and Fergie was appointed to draw up the memorial and send it off.[1] The secretary was instructed to write Mr T. Hughes, M.P., requesting him to give an address to the working men of Edinburgh on Capital and Labour.

28 January 1873

11 members present. A certificate was read from the Masons Society intimating that James Wood and James Walker[2] had been appointed to represent them at the Council Board. The secretary

[1] Six gas stokers had been sentenced on 19 December 1872 to twelve months' imprisonment for conspiracy. The case arose from a threatened strike against victimisation. The sentence was later commuted to four months. G. Howell, *Labour Legislation Labour Movements and Labour Leaders* (London, 1905 edn.), 237-53.
[2] Later references show that Walker's first name was Thomas, not James.

read a letter he had recived from Thomas Hughes, Esq., M.P., in reply to a invitation to give a lecture to the working men of Edinburgh on the question of Capital and Labour, declining the invitation owing to the want of time at his disposal; and also a letter from the home secretary acknowledgeing receipt of the memorial on behalf of the imprisoned Gass stokers of London.

A deputation from the printers on strike was then introduced who gave a statement as to how the strike was proceeding, the prospects of its termination and the means the employers were taking to defeat the movement. It was again stated that the reports appearing in the daily newspapers was as a rule intended to damage the cause of the men and tend most materially to lessen the sympathy of other trades on their behalf, and they asked the council if they would suggest some other method whereby the help of other trades might be increased and true statment of there position laid before the public. On the withdrawal of the deputation a discussion took place as to the best means which should be adopted to support the printers in their struggle. It was generally maintained that they fully deserved the support of every trades unionist for the manner in which they had conducted the struggle and the way they had resisted the efforts and offers of the employers, efforts unequalled in any former struggle no matter whatever trade. Elements of pressure had been put upon them, enormous sums of money had been expended, rare inducements had been held out, untruths had been circulated, even religion had been abused and brought to play on purpose to shake the men, and yet after all these means had been expended and an income verging on starvation the men had remained as firm as at first. To bring their case properly before the public could only be done, it was maintained, by a public meeting which should be held as eraly as possible. This was unanimously agreed to and committee appointed to carry it out.

11 February 1873

10 members present. A letter was read from the Home Secretary, in reply to memorial from the council on behalf of the Gass stokers of London sentenced to twelve months imprisonment by Justice Brett, that their punishment had been mitigated to four months imprisonment. The Council on considering the whole matter

agreed to rememorialise the Home Secretary for the immediate release of the gas stokers in prison.

A resolution was unanimously carried protesting against the funds of Heriot's Hospital being diverted to uses different to those indicated in the founder's Will. A copy of said resolution was ordered to be sent to the Endowed Schools Commision.[1]

A Deputation was appointed to wait upon the returning officer for the City of Edinburgh under the Education Act after the appointment of official has been made by the Town Council, with the view of impressing on that Gentleman the necessity of fixing the election day upon a Saturday so that the working men may have an opportunity of recording their votes before four o'clock – the limitation of such an hour for closing of the Poll being strongly condemned by the Council as unwise and contrary to the wishes of the great body of the constituents.

22 February 1873

A Special Meeting was held. 18 members present. The Secretary read letters from Ralph Richardson, w.s., Convener of the Committee on Technical Education,[2] asking a conference with the Council on the above subject and also the preliminary report of said Committee. After a good deal of discussion it was agreed to invite reporters to be present at the conference. The deputation was then interduced when Mr Cousins, architect,[3] referred to the previous meeting which was held in the Council Chambers lately to consider the subject of technical Education and said the present meeting was called to ask the opinion of the Council and in order to get the view of the working Classes. Mr Ralph Richardson, w.s., read Mr Cousins' paper on the subject in which he referred to the kind of schools proposed to be erected with the surplus funds of Heriot's Hospital. Bailie Cousins[4] asked to have the views of the council and on being asked he briefly gave a history of the increase of the funds. The money was left for decayed Burgesses of the city and it had now

---

[1] The Endowed Schools and Hospitals (Scotland) Commission had been appointed in September 1872 and its reports were issued in 1873-5.
[2] Ralph Richardson, w.s., 1845-1933, son of James Richardson (see above, p. 81, n. 1).
[3] David Cousins, the city architect.
[4] Bailie George Cousin, partner in a firm of surveyors and valuators.

overgrown itself, and was close upon £20,000 a year. Heriot provided an Education far in advance of the general Education of his age and they were now proposing to carry out the spirit of George Heriot, supplying a Higher education than was provided by Government. Mr Common[1] said they [had] no reason to object to the establishment of a technical college but if the money should be diverted for the purpose of such a school the Industrial Classes feared that by and bye it would miss the mark and the middle classes would be the only parties that would get the advantage of it. That thought was encouraged by the fact that when the Hospitals were opened up for the benefit of the working classes the fees rose to such an extent as to put the education out of the reach of the industrial classes. What they feared was that although the schools were erected exclusively for the benefit of the working classes they would eventualy slip out of their Hands. After several of the deputation had expressed their views on the subject it was agreed to adjourn to Tuesday first.

25 February 1873

18 member present. A certificate was read from the Brassfounders League intimating that James Mitchel and Crawford Campble had been appointed to represent them at council board. The final arrangements [were made] for the lecture on Capital, Labour, and Wages, to be delivered by Bailie Lewis in Brighton Chaple on Wednesday the 26 February. M. Hilson moved that we advertize the lecture in the *Review* and *Courant* and the *Craftsman*[2] and *Reformer*, and also to employ 3 men with boards to walk in the High Street and Bridges, which was agreed to. Mr Fairbairn was appointed to move that C. Cranston take the chair,[3] Mr Holburn to move a vote of thanks to the lecturer, and Mr Grant to move a vote of thanks to the chairman.

The adjourned debate on the technical College resumed. The following motion was moved by Mr Walker, mason: That this

[1] J. S. Common, printers.
[2] The *Craftsman*, originally titled *Out on Strike*, issued weekly by the Edinburgh printers during their strike in 1872-3 and ceased publication in June 1873. W. Norrie, *Edinburgh Newspapers Past and Present* (Earlston, 1891), 15; S. Gillespie, *A Hundred Years of Progress 1853-1953* (Glasgow, 1953), 119-20.
[3] Councillor Robert Cranston.

Council having considered the statements and report of the deputation and seeing that the main source of revenue for establishing a technical College is proposed to be taken from the Heriot Fund, Resolve that they oppose by every legitimate means the appropriation of said funds for such a purpose. This motion was seconded by Mr Holburn, tinplate worker, and after several members had expressed in strong terms their condemation of the proposed scheme as unfavourable to the object contemplated, namely a Higher class education for the Children of the working classes, it was unanimously carried. The following motion was then unanimously agreed to: That this Council, having considered the scheme brought forward by Mr Cousin and his party, and disapproving of the same, appoint a committee to draw up a report on the other two schemes, namely, that formerly by the Governors and that proposed by Mr Duncan McLaren. The following committee was appointed: President, Secretary, Mesers Walker, Reikie, Fergie, Grant, Jack, and Holburn.

THE MEMORIAL OF THE EDINBURGH TRADES COUNCIL[1]

Sheweth – That your petitioners represent the workmen composing the trades of this city, and are therefore deeply interested in the maintenance of the means of education existing within the city specially intended and adapted for the class to which they belong. That your memorialists are specially concerned to see that the funds of George Heriot's Hospital are not diverted from their legitimate object, viz., their application towards the education of the children of the humbler classes of the city of Edinburgh. Any movement in that direction they would consider a great injustice, and one which they would consider themselves bound by every legitimate means to resist. Your memorialists believe that conclusive evidence can be submitted to prove that the appropriation of the Heriot funds for different objects than those to which they are at present applied would most seriously prejudice the cause of education in this city; and they most respectfully crave that the fullest inquiry and consideration may be bestowed upon the subject by the Commission. – Signed in name and by authority of the Edinburgh Trades Council,

[1] A press cutting pasted into the minute book.

in meeting assembled, at Edinburgh, the 20th day of February 1873.
– Walter Fairbairn, Chairman, Matthew Hilson, Secretary.

7 March 1873

A special meeting was held. 11 members present. A deputation from the Joiners out on strike was recived by the council when they laid their case before the meeting. The following motion was agreed to: That this meeting sympathizes with Joiners out on strike and recommend to their fellows to reconsider their decision.[1]

Bailie Lewis attended the council by request of the committee appointed at last meeting to get information about Heriot's Hospital. He gave in a report of his evidence before the Endowed Schools Commission. He thought the only way to improve Heriot's Hospital was to break up the monastic system and convert the Hospital into a large middle class school for Technical and the other branches of Higher Education, and to board out all the orphans with respectable people who had accomadation for them. Bailie Lewis was then asked by the Council through chairman to allow himself to be nominated for the School Board. Almost Every Member pressed him very urgently to stand. He stated he was exceedingly sorry it was not in his power to comply with their request owing to want of time to attend to the duties properly and that so much Brain Work was telling on his Health. Mr Grant moved a vote of thanks to Bailie Lewis for his valueable information.

11 March 1873

17 members present. A letter was read from Greenock Trades Council urging the necessity of a general agitation throughout the country for a thorough revision of the laws affecting employers and employed. It was unanimously agreed to co-operate with the Greenock and other Trades Councils throughout the country in their endeavours to get the one-sided laws affecting trades unionists abolished.

The Secretary then read a letter from Simon Laurie, Esq.,

[1] Some 300 joiners in Edinburgh and Leith had struck work on 28 February for an increase of 1d. an hour. On 1 March some of the men evidently agreed to accept the employers' offer of ½d., but half the strikers were not taken back. *Scotsman*, 28 Februayr, 4 and 6 March 1873.

z

Secretary to the Endowed School commission,[1] acknowledgeing reciept of memorial on Heriot's Hospital. A deputation was appointed to meet Mr Laurie at his request to explain more fully the views of the council on the subject. A report on Heriot's Hospital was read but owing to the importance of the subject it was unanimously agreed to hold a special meeting for its consideration on Tuesday first. It was decided to Proceed at once with the Printing in pamphlet form of the lecture 'Capital, Labour and Wages' recently delivered by Bailie Lewis, the manuscript of which was so kindly placed at the disposal of the council by that Gentleman.

18 March 1873

A Special Meeting was held. 17 members present. A certificate was read from the United Kingdom Society of Coach Builders intimating that James Bruce and Archbald Taylor had been elected to represent them at the council Board.

A letter was read from Mr Menizes[2] asking Permission for a deputation on behalf of the Royal Infirmary to wait on the Council. It was agreed to recive the deputation. A letter was read from J. C. Burns wishing the Council to recive a deputation from the Advanced Liberal Association and Citizen Committee.[3] It was agreed to recive the deputation at 9.30 this evening. A letter was read from Mr Bruce, Newtyle,[4] asking whither Bailie Lewis' lecture was published yet. The Secretary was instructed to answer Mr Bruce's Letter.

The discussion on Mr Walker's report on Heriot's Hospital was resumed. It was ultimately agreed to remit the report to a committee to bring up a report on the Hospital. Mesers Reikie, Walker, and Fergie was appointed a committee. The deputation from the Advanced Liberals was then interduced. Bailie Lewis, Mr Sim, Craigmount,[5] and Mr Menizes[6] was the deputation. Bailie Lewis addressed the meeting and urged the claims of their candidates for

---

[1] Simon Somerville Laurie, 1829-1909, educationist.
[2] Presumably T. H. Menzies, evidently a draper, who was active in raising funds for the infirmary. *Report of the Managers of the Royal Infirmary, 1874.*
[3] Burn was a former blacksmiths' delegate to the trades council.
[4] Not identified.
[5] James Sime, M.A., Craigmount House, Dick Place; author and teacher of English at Edinburgh Academy.
[6] Not identified.

the school Board. Mr Sim followed in the same strain. Mr Reikie moved a vote of thanks to the deputation for their information they had given the Council. The deputation then retired when Mr Walker moved: That this Council recommend the following candidates for Election to the School Board, viz., Bailie Wilson,[1] Councilor Gowans,[2] Thomas Ivory, Esq.,[3] J. Carment, Esq.,[4] and W. Mcrie, Esq.,[5] and urge on all working men to give 3 votes to each of the above candidates. Unanimously agreed to. Mr Blaikie moved that we recommend a Holiday from ten o'clock on the day of Election, seconded by M. Hilson. Mr Fergie moved the Previous question, seconded by D. McAllen.[6] The motion was carried by a large majority.

25 March 1873

19 members present. Before entering into the Business of the meeting Mr Mences, Clerk to the Infirmary,[7] requested that the deputation from the infirmary appointed to meet the council be delayed till next meeting. Mr D. McAllen moved that we hold a special meeting this night week to recive the deputation, seconded by A. Taylor and agreed to. The minutes of former meeting was then read when Welsh moved the disaproval of that Part of the minutes refering to the Election of school Board, seconded by Mr Holburn. Mr Reikie moved the aproval of the minutes, seconded by Mr. Walker. Their voted for the approval of minutes 13, for the disaproval 4.

Mesers Walker, Reikie and Fergie reported that they had met the secretary to the Endowed Schools Commision in place of Mesers Fairbarn and Grant. They gave in a repport of their interview. Mr Grant moved that this Council give the deputation a hearty vote of thanks for the able way they represented council and expressed his entire confidence in the deputation. Seconded by Mr Taylor and unanimously agreed to. Mr Fergie then read the sub committee on

---

[1] Bailie John Wilson, merchant, Liberal M.P. for Edinburgh Central 1885-6, and unsuccessful Unionist candidate in 1886.
[2] James Gowans.
[3] Thomas Ivory, 1818-82, advocate, son of Lord Ivory the judge.
[4] John Carment, S.S.C., 1817-1901, an active Free Churchman and supporter of Y.M.C.A., chairman 1874-99 of the board of examiners under the Law Agents Act. Scotsman, 11 December 1901.
[5] William M'Crie, head of a firm of paperstainers.   [6] Donald McAllen, tailors.
[7] T. H. Menzies, not clerk to the infirmary, but to its fund-raising committee.

Heriot's Hospital report. Mr Holburn moved the approval of the report, seconded by Inglis, and unanimously agreed to. The Secretary said he had seen Bailie Lewis and he thought that they ought to get a publisher to Publish the lecture he delivered on Capital, Labour and Wages. Mr Holburn moved that the secretary get a Publisher to issue said pamphlet, seconded by Mr Reikie and agreed to.[1]

REPORT ON THE PROPOSED FUTURE MANAGEMENT OF GEORGE HERIOT'S HOSPITAL[2]

Gentlemen, – In presenting this report on the proposed future management of Heriot's Hospital and how the surplus funds should be administered, your committee desire the Council to bear in mind the extreme cautiousness which is necessary before absolutely deciding upon any given point, for two reasons – first, the great sums of money which are at stake; and secondly from the extreme desire of several parties to have an interest in these funds, and their wish, both expressed and avowed, to have them turned from what your committee consider their proper channel – namely, the education and to a certain extent the clothing and feeding of the children of the poorer classes of the community.

Your committee consider in the first place that it was not so much the wish of George Heriot to turn out great, and learned, and shining men, as to raise up a respectable, thinking, able class of artizans or citizens, and to do so more especially by helping those who had not the means to help themselves – to assist first of all 'the faitherless and mitherless bairn', and afterwards those whose parents through sickness or reverse of fortune needed a helping hand to bring up their children decently and honestly. To attain these ends your committee consider are the main purposes of George Heriot's will; and it is only when the whole poor of Edinburgh are fully and amply provided for that your committee conceive the notion should be entertained of diverting the funds to University or any other purpose whatsoever.

To carry out these views and to give the benefits of the Hospital

---

[1] See below, p. 371. No other details of publication have been found.

[2] The report is a press cutting pasted into the minute book.

funds to as many as possible, your committee consider that the
extension of the outdoor schools should be warmly approved of.
They consider that those which are already established have been
of immense benefit to the working and artizan class of Edinburgh,
and that, the Education Act notwithstanding, great benefits would
accrue from the establishment of the four or five schools proposed at
the present time to be erected.

Your committee, in connection with the out-door schools, would
draw the attention of the Council to the proposal that has been
mooted in some quarters to levy fees from the children. It is maintained by some that if fees were levied more money would come
from the Imperial treasury to Edinburgh, that the schools could be
further extended, that consequently the benefits would be considerably increased, and a considerable diminution be made on the
school-rate. Your committee consider that such arguments do not
and ought not to weigh with those advanced against the levying of
fees. Your committee consider that the levying of fees is contrary
to the will of George Heriot; that the fees will never amount to
anything like a sum to compensate for the bad feeling that will exist
in a school composed of paying and non-paying students; and that
if the rates are lessened it will be as great a burden taken off the rich
as the poor, who are not intended to be benefitted.

Your committee have had their attention drawn to what is
popularly known as the monastic system of bringing up children.
They cannot but regret that the attempt made some time ago to
abolish that system proved ineffectual. They hope that another
effort will soon be made, and that a system so universally condemned
will ere long come to a termination; and that the Council will do
everything in its power to help on an end so desirable. Boarding
with their relatives or respectable families is in every sense more
beneficial and commendable.

While your committee are of opinion that it was not so much
the wish of George Heriot to turn out great men as to raise good
citizens, as before stated, they still conceive that every aid should
be given to promising children, in order to develope their talents.
Your committee are of opinion that every working man's child in
Edinburgh should have within his or her reach a thorough university
training, to fit either for any of the higher professions, provided

he or she show the talents, the energy, and determination to fit him or her for such a sphere of life. They recommend that, should the present inmates of Heriot's Hospital be boarded out, the hospital should be turned into a secondary school, the scholars of which should be drafted from the various primary schools in Edinburgh, and after the age of fourteen receive a bursary equal to what is generally earned by boys or girls of that age. They recommend also that great care should be taken in the selection of these scholars; that they be recommended by their formers teachers as possesing considerable talents; that they undergo an examination or examinations, whether competitive or otherwise, as may afterwards be determined; and that in undergoing such examinations consideration should be given to the advantages or disadvantages under which a boy or girl has laboured in the prosecution of his or her studies, more especially the amount of help derived from parents or others. It is considered that from this school, and from this alone, boys and girls should be drafted for university training, always providing they show the necessary aptitude for learning, and that bursaries should be granted for their continued maintenance.

Your committee are of opinion that night classes should be established, free of any charge, on purpose that apprentices desiring further knowledge than that given at the primary schools, may have facilities afforded them for gaining such; and as a further inducement to promising pupils in the Heriot primary schools, it is thought that the Watt Institution might be supplemented £200 or £300 per annum, and tickets to that amount retained and distributed among the more deserving pupils who may wish to attend any of the School of Arts classes after leaving the primary schools.

Lastly, your committee having considered the question as to how the full benefits could be extended, recommend that the Town Council should be petitioned to lower the price of the burgess ticket to £2, thereby bringing the acquisition of such a ticket more within the reach of working men; they cannot assent to the definition given that only skilled artisans should have the benefit of outdoor schools, believing that those who pay what was formerly known as scot and lot, or what is now known as taxes, are fully entitled to have their children educated at these schools, the poorest and most needy always receiving a preference.

In conclusion, your committee cannot too strongly urge upon the Council the necessity of bringing these recommendations before their several trades, and organising and taking the necessary steps to make them have their due weight as the recommendations of those to whom the Heriot funds primarily belong, and doing their utmost to get them carried into effect. – In name of the committee, T. Walker, Convener.

1 April 1873

A Special meeting was held. 19 members present. A Deputation from the Royal Infirmary waited on the council to Solicit their aid in favour of raising subscriptions for its suport. The following resolution was unanimously agreed to: That this Council strongly recommend the Different Trades and workmen Generally throughout Edinburgh and Leith to consider the Best Means of raising funds for the Royal Infirmary and that the sum thus raised be entered in the List of contributions in individual names so as to secure adequate representation at the anual meeting for the election of managers, seeing that a contribution of £5 entitles a trade or body of men to one vote provided it is entered in the name of a single individual. A Deputation from the Bakers was also Heard in reference to a dispute which had arisen in Mr Henderson's shop, Fountainbridge, the men having struck work in consequence of an infringment of their agreement. A Resolution was adopted expressing sympathy with the men out on strike.

A Deputation from the Operative Tailors Executive then addressed the meeting. They stated their employers had locked out all the principal Branches in Scotland under the pretence of a refusal on the part of said Executive to confer with the employers. The deputation explained that they had twice asked what was the subject they were to discuss and they were twice refused an answer, the only statment made to them being that the masters were pledged not to submit to such an engagment as was entered into last year, and which was found to work so well both for employers and workmen. After asking questions regarding the numbers locked out, the prospect of dispute, etc., the following Resolution was unanimously agreed to: That the Trades Council having heard the statement made by the deputation warmly sympathise with the Operative Tailors in there dispute, condemn the conduct of the employers and do their utmost by raising subscriptions or otherwise to assist the workmen in their present difficulties to enable them to carry on the struggle to a successful termination.

8 April 1873

The Vice President[1] in the Chair. 19 members present. Mr Grant gave in a report of the Tailors Lock out. The members of council expressed their desire to do every thing in their power to assist the Tailors in their struggle. The desireability of geting the council rules reprinted was taken into consideration. Mr Wood moved that a committee be appointed to correct the rules and report to next meeting.

13 May 1873

17 members present. A Letter was read from Mr Boa, Glasgow,[2] asking the Council to appoint two delegates to attend the Peace Conference to be held in the Lesser City Hall, Glasgow, on the 19th May.[3] Mr Welsh moved that we appoint 2 delegates, seconded by Mr Holburn and agreed to. Mesers Cubie[4] and Holburn was appointed delegates. Mr Grant then reported the state of the Tailors lock out. He Brought the Firm of McLaren and Company under the notice of the council, stating that that firm had refused to sign the agreement. The Secretary was instructed to write to D. McLaren, M.P., on the subject.

27 May 1873

10 members present. A Deputation from the Amalgamated Carpenters and Joiners of England asking subscriptions in behalf of the Joiners on strike in Liverpool.[5] Mr Cubie moved that the

[1] John Holburn, tinplate workers.
[2] Andrew Boa, a stonemason, chairman of Glasgow trades council, member 1874 of the parliamentary committee of the T.U.C., chairman 1875 of the S.C.W.S., emigrated for health reasons to Australia and died there 1877.
[3] The conference was organised by the National Workmen's Peace Association and was attended by delegates from a score of trade unions and trades councils in Scotland. *Scotsman*, 20 May 1873.
[4] John Cubie, cabinetmakers. For a few biographical details of Cubie see above, p. xxiv.
[5] The strike had begun on 1 May for an increase in wages to $7\frac{3}{4}$d. an hour; it ended on 1 September when the men accepted the compromise terms of $7\frac{1}{2}$d. an hour. *The Porcupine* (Liverpool, 1873), xv, no. 23, 355-6.

subject lie over till next meeting, seconded by Mr Taylor and agreed to. A letter was read from Mr McLaren, M.P., in reference to Tailors dispute. The secretary was instructed to . . . McLaren & Company on the subject. The secretary then read correspondence on the criminal Law,[1] and from the Plimsoll Committee on behalf of our seamen.[2] It was agreed to take them next meeting.

10 June 1873

The Vice President in the chair. 15 members present. A certificate was read intimating that D. McNab and James Baldie had been appointed to represent the Saddlers at the council.

A Deputation from the Shoemakers then addressed the meeting on the strike in their trade.[3] It seems they are paid about 5d. per hour, working about 60 Hours per week, and that work is given out in the most irregular manner. After several questions had been put regarding the accuracy of the statements, and general condemnation expressed of the system of making their Houses workshops, the following resolution was unanimiously agreed to, moved by Mr Reikie, seconded by Walker: That having heard the statements made by the operative shoemakers the council express their cordial sympathy with them in their present struggle and earnestly recommend their case to the favourable consideration of their fellow workmen throughout the city and hope that they may soon obtain the advance asked for, beliving as they do it is reasonable and just.

The Council next took up the case of the Tailors who have now been locked out for 11 weeks. Mr Reeves, secretary to the Edinburgh Branch, stated that he had under the Circumstances a most cheering report to lay before the council. Out of between two and three thousand locked out in Scotland only 20 remained on the Books. It was agreed to record a minute expressing the Council's appreciation of the manly, honorable, and successful part which the Tailors

[1] Criminal Law Amendment Act.
[2] Samuel Plimsoll, 1824-98, Radical M.P. for Derby 1868-80, had addressed public meetings in Edinburgh and Leith on 26 May 1873 on seamen's conditions. To arouse public opinion on the question, the Plimsoll Committee had been formed early in 1873, with Lord Shaftesbury as chairman and a broadly based membership. *Scotsman*, 27 May 1873; G. Howell, *Labour Legislation, Labour Movements and Labour Leaders* (London, 1905 edn.), 268-9.
[3] They were reported to have struck on 28 May for a twenty-five per cent increase in wages.

had acted in their dispute, in striking contrast to measures adopted by the employers. The Joiners strike in Liverpool was then taken up. Mr Fergie moved we take no action in matter. Agreed. The Secretary read a letter from Mr Irons, superintendent, Caledonian Railway, enquiring when the anual trades Holidays take place this year. The secretary was instructed to write the North British and Caledonian informing them that the holiday take place as usual on the last Saterday of July and two preceeding days, viz., the 24, 25, and 26th July. It was agreed to hold a special meeting on Tuesday first for consideration of the criminal Law amendment act and other Business.

16 June 1873[1]

A Special Meeting was held. The President asked whither the council would allow Mr Todd to be present to report the meeting in the *Edinburgh Evening News*.[2] It was agreed not to admit reporters. The Criminal Law amendment act was then taken up. Mr Holburn moved that this council petition Parliment for the total repeal of criminal Law Amendment Act, seconded by Mr Reikie, and unanimously agreed to. Mr Dewar[3] then moved that in view of strong opposition which our Friends in Parliment are likely to meet in their endeavours to repeal this tyrannical and one-sided measure this Council resolve to call a Conference of the different Trades of Edinburgh and Leith to consider the advisability of having a Trades Demonstration to protest against the injustice of the Act, seconded by Holburn and agreed to.

Mesers Holburn and Cubie [reported] their proceeding at the Peace Conference held some time ago in Glasgow. It was agreed to send the following petition to J. Millar, M.P., for presentation to the House of Commons: The Honorable the Commons of Great Britain and Irland in Parliment assembled. The petition of the United Trades Council of Edinburgh and Leith showeth that your petitioners have learned with great satisfaction that a motion will shortly be submitted to your honorable house in favour of establishing some Permanent system of international arbitration, and as your

---

[1] The date should probably read 17 June 1873.
[2] Established as an independent daily evening newspaper in 1873 and still in publication.
[3] Andrew Dewar, blacksmiths.

petitioners belong to that class which suffers most from the present barbarous mode of fighting out disputes with nations, and as your petitioners are fully impressed with the belief that if an international Tribunal administering Justice on the basis of international Law were established, it would Gradually supersede the present system of employing Brute force to decide who is right, and that ultimately all disputes arising between nations would be adjusted by Peacefull means, and your petitioners therefore Pray your Honorable House to immediately take the necessary steps for the establishment of such a Tribunal.[1]

Mr Walker than moved that this council petition the Town Council against the removal of the Sinclair Fountain from the west end of Princes Street, which was unanimously agreed to.[2]

24 June 1873

15 members present. A certificate was read from the coopers intimating that Edward Rose and Peter Anderson had been elected to represent them at the Council Board. A letter was then read from the Secretary, Brassfounders League, asking information regarding the number of apprentices in each trade. Out of 12 trades present it was found that only 2 trades had any limitation and their society restricted their number to 1 apprentice to every three Journeymen. Mr Plimsoll's apeal on behalf of our seamen was then taken up. After a good deal of discussion as to how the council could best assist Mr Plimsoll in his noble efforts on behalf of our sailors it was ultimately agreed to remit the subject to conference of Office Bearers for their consideration. It was agreed to hold a conference with the Office Bearers of Trade Societies on Thursday the 3rd July.

Mr Walker and Mr Taylor was appointed to wait on the Joiners executive to try and get them to hold their demonstration on the same day as the Demonstration proposed to be held by the Council.[3]

---

[1] A resolution in favour of an international tribunal of arbitration was moved in the Commons on 8 July by Rev. Henry Richard, Radical M.P. for Merthyr Tydfil, and carried by ninety-eight votes to eighty-eight.

[2] The town council had decided on 3 June to remove the fountain to Haymarket as it was obstructing traffic at the West End. *Scotsman*, 4 June 1873.

[3] The joiners evidently agreed to do so, since groups of them from towns all over Scotland took part in the trades council's demonstration on 23 August.

Mr Fergie and Mr Reikie was appointed to audit the Books and get up the anual report. Mr Fairbairn intimated that next meeting would be his [last] meeting at council.

8 July 1873

The annual meeting was held. 17 members present. A letter was read from the City Clerk intimating that the Town Council had agreed not to remove the Sinclair Fountain from its present site. The Election of Officebearers then took place when the following were elected: President, John G. Holburn; Vice president, John Grant; Secretary, Thomas Walker;[1] Assistant Secretary, Matthew Hilson; Treasurer, John Jack; Trustees, Messers Taylor, Inglis and Cubie. On the motion of Mr Reekie it was agreed to defer the apointments till the usual time for auditing the Books. Mr Reekie then gave in a report in connection with the Demonstration against the Criminal law amendment act which contained very cheering reports from the various trades as to the probability of success.

Mr Blackie then moved, seconded by Mr Reekie, that it be remitted to the Secretary to advertise the Holidays Should the Railways take no steps in the matter. Mr Fergie gave notice of motion on Local Confederation of trades. Messers Fergie and Cubie were apointed a Committee to endeavour to get trades not represented at the Council to send delegates their. Mr Jack moved that Mr Walter Fairbairn be elected an Honorary member. Seconded by Mr Taylor and agreed to.

22 July 1873

12 members present. Mr Walker having declined the office of Secretary, Mr John Cubie was, on the motion of Mr Blackie, elected and Mr Dewar elected trustee in place of Mr Cubie. To a question by Mr Walker as to the position of the shoemakers Mr Watt[2] intimated that the statement in the newspapers was substantially correct[3] but that a statement would possibly be prepaired and

[1] Walker resigned from the secretaryship at the next meeting, and this minute is in the handwriting of John Cubie.
[2] William Watt, formally appointed a shoemakers' delegate to the council on 23 September 1873.
[3] No press statement has been found.

circulated on the subject. Mr Fergie then read the draft annual report, and the different subjects having been taken seperately, several alterations were agreed to and remitted to Mr Fergie. The report, which was a singularly able summary of the Council proceedings during the past year, was on the motion of Mr Dewar approved of and instructions given to print.

12 August 1873

20 members present. A letter was read from Mr Duncan, Secretary to the Milling Trade, duly accrediting Messers Ormiston and Wardlaw as their representitives at the Council. The laws of the Council was then taken up and with several minor alterations the recomendations of the Committee were agreed to. And on the motion of Mr Hilson instruction was given to print 250 copies. The Annual Report was then distributed to the members present for circulation amongst their several trades.

The president then recomended that the next meeting of Council should be adjurned until the first ordinary meeting in September so that members might give their undivided attention to the Demonstration Committee for repeal of Criminal law Ammendment Act, etc.[1] Mr Walker called attention to the position of the Tailors in view of adjurnment. Mr McAllen[2] asked if there was no comunication from the Tailors Committee. The Secretary stated that he had called on Mr Reeves and explained that a special meeting would be called to suit them on notice being given to that effect. Mr Grant made a short statement as to the position of the trade, 2 or 3 more shops being opened. He did not know the reason the deputation appointed to wait on the Council had not come. On the understanding that a special meeting should be called for the Tailors if necessary, the sugestion of the President was agreed to and the Council adjourned for a month.

23 September 1873

20 members present. The Minutes of last meeting was read and Mr McAllen[2] called attention to no notice being taken of a conversation as to the position of the Tailors and a statement as to their

---

[1] The demonstration was held on 23 August.
[2] Donald McAllen, tailors.

present situation. After considerable discussion as to the language used, the secretary was instructed to ammend the minute with which correction they were approved of.[1] A letter of inquiry as to the conduct of Mr Grant from Mr Reeves, Secretary to the Tailors Society, was then read. The Council were unanimously of opinion that he had at all times Faithfully represented and been Zealous in the interest of the Operative Tailors, the Secretary being instructed to answer accordingly. Certificates were read duly accrediting Mr James Hunter and John Welsh to represent the West Branch of Associated Carpenters and Joiners, and John Dickson and William Watt to represent the Operative Shoemakers, and Mr Robert Stevenson the Edinburgh Cabinetmakers Society.

A letter from Councilor McLachlan asking the assistance of Council to secure the opening of the Castle Banks was then submitted to the meeting.[2] After remarks by several members as to the extent of the ground and relation to West Princes Street Gardens the Chairman narrated the steps previously taken by the Council to secure these grounds for the public use. Mr Dewer then moved, seconded by Mr Walker, that the Council take action in support of this matter, and Mr Walker moved, seconded by Mr Dewer, that Messers Holburn, Dewer, Walker and Cubie be appointed a committee with power to act in name of the Council for this purpose. Both motions carried unanimously.

Mr Plimsoll's apeal, which when last before the Council had been remitted to the conferance of Trade Society Officebearers but had not been taken up by them, there time being fully engaged with discussion of the Criminal Law Repeal and proposed Demonstration, was again taken up. The unsatisfactory nature of the Merchant Shiping Act of Past Session,[3] though an improvement on previous Legislation, was dwelt upon as being totally inadequate to the proper security of Life and Property at Sea, and the urgent necessity of a proper load line restriction as to deck cargo and survey of all sea-going vessels amply illustrated. Though strongly sympathysing

---

[1] There is no sign in the MS. of any amendment.
[2] William B. McLachlan, an Independent Liberal. The north castle banks were opened to the public in 1876 along with West Princes Street Gardens. D. Robertson, *Castle and Town* (Edinburgh, 1928), 47.
[3] 35-36 Victoria, c. 73.

with the movement a genneral opinion obtained that the present
was an inopertune time for active assistance and Mr Dewer moved,
seconded by Mr Jack, that the question of supporting Mr Plimsoll
be delayed and that advantage be taken of renewed agitation, which
was adopted.

The Council then agreed to record their sense of the successful
character of the Demonstration on the 23rd August against the
Criminal Law ammendment Act and kindred laws, justifying the
course the Council followed in remiting to the trades and reflecting
the highest credit on the Committee who organised and so skillfully
conducted the arrangements throughout. The ability and clear
logical argument and illustration used by the various speakers in
shewing the invidious and objectionable nature of those laws both
in their constitution and administration has helped to raise the
question to one of great public importance, demanding an early
and satisfactory solution by their removal from the statute Book
where they should never have had a place. It was then agreed to
take up Mr Fergie's motion for Confederation of trades at next
meeting.

7 October 1873

Special meeting held to consider invitation from Endowed Schools
Commission to give evidence in support of memorial on the Heriot
Trust of February last.[1] The letter from the Commission was read
and also the Memorial in question from the minutes of Council,
Mr Walker giving an account of how the matter stood when last
before the council. Mr Jack moved, seconded by Mr Grant, that a
deputation be appointed to give evidence to the Commission. Mr
Mitchell moved, seconded by Mr McAllen,[2] that Messers Holburn,
Fergie, Walker, and Reekie be appointed. Both motions agreed to.

14 October 1873

Mr Dewer, in the absence of the President and Vice President,
being called to the chair, the secretary read minute of previous
ordinary and special meeting when Mr McAllen asked that the
letter to the Secretary of the Tailors Operative Society should be

[1] Above, pp. 352-3.
[2] Either Donald McAllen, tailors, or John McAllen, typefounders.

read, he having understood that notice was to be taken of the words used by Mr Grant as to the position of their society at last meeting and intimating that it was of considerable importance to himself and others in the trade. It was agreed that Mr McAllen might call upon the President or Secretary to give evidence as to language, and the minutes were then unanimously adopted.

The President at this stage taking the chair read letter of invitation to the Council to send representitives to the Demonstration against the Criminal Law ammendment Act, etc., to be held in Glasgow on Saturday 1st November. Mr Watt, in a few words on the propriety of keeping up friendly relations with Glasgow, moved, seconded by Mr Dewer, that representitives be sent, which was adopted. Mr Jack then moved, seconded by Mr Walker, that two be sent, which was also agreed to, the President and Secretary being appointed in accordance theirwith, and that 10s. each be allowed for Expenses.

The Secretary read correspondence received and sent since last meeting. Mr Mitchell introduced the question of trying to secure the services of Professor Hunter to give a lecture in Edinburgh on laws affecting labour and the working classes, imediately after his visit to Glasgow.[1] A general opinion obtained that such lecture might be of great service but that to little time intervened to make the necessary arrangements, but that the Deputation to Glasgow take steps to secure such lecture during the Easter holidays or such other time as might be suitable. Mr Fergie then moved that the Council consider the Propriety of forming a local Confederation of trades represented at the Council. And giving living[2] powers over such trades in cases of dispute, stating the argument for and against such a scheme and narating the experiance of the Printers during their late dispute in support of such a course. Mr Dewer also generally supported the idea of Confederation and spoke as to the proper course to follow in case of strike and moved the adjournment of the discussion until next meeting. The Secretary then called the roll and 15 members present.

[1] William Alexander Hunter, 1844-98, professor of jurisprudence at University College, London, Radical M.P. for Aberdeen North 1885-96. He lectured to a meeting of working men in Glasgow on 30 October. *Glasgow Herald*, 31 October 1873.
[2] Sic. Word should probably be 'levying'.

28 October 1873

Mr Grant, Vice President, in the chair.[1] The Deputation to the
Endowed Schools Commission gave in a report as to their evidence
and reception by the Commission. Mr Holburn, who had been
unavoidably absent from the Deputation, moved that the thanks
of the Council be accorded to the Deputation, which was agreed to
unanimously.[2]

The discussion on Local Confederation was then taken up and in
the absence of Mr Fergie and of Mr Dewer, who had moved the
adjournment, Mr Jack moved that discussion be again adjourned,
seconded by Mr Reekie. Mr Walker opposed the adjournment and
argued against proposed Confederation, believing that it was
hopeless to expect branches of National Societys to join. Mr Watt
continued the discussion in favour of Confederation. Mr Cubie
while aproving of Confederation as a theoretic Principle pointed
out what he considered practical difficulties. Mr Blackie then moved
that the Council do not entertain the proposal of Confederation,
Seconded by Mr Welsh who also urged the hopelesness of getting
branches of National Unions to join, that the difficulties urged had
been avoided rather than replied to, and instanced the failure of the
Manchester Alliance and National Confederation of 1871 in support
of his position.[3] Mr Jack having withdrawn his motion, Mr Reekie
moved that a committee be appointed with Mr Fergie as Convener
to mature a scheme of Confederation to be submitted to the Council,
contending that the discussion was in favour of Confederation and
that the difficulties might not be insurmountable. Seconded by Mr
Wilson.[4] Mr Holburn then moved that it be remitted to the trades
to consider and report by the first of March, urging that however
right in principle the trades were not yet ripe for its adoption, and
that it would be a waste of time on the part of the Council unless
their seemed more prospect of support from the trades themselves.

[1] Holburn, the president, was present.
[2] The members of council who gave evidence before the Commission were John
Cubie, James Mitchell, Thomas Walker and Thomas Reekie. *Endowed Schools and
Hospitals (Scotland) Commission, Second Report* pp. 98-109.
[3] Neither reference is clear. Possibly the first is to the United Kingdom Alliance of
Organised Trades (above, p. 181, n. 1), and the second to the confederation set up in
Scotland in 1872 (above, pp. 336-7).
[4] Not identified.

This was seconded by Mr Hunter but ultimately withdrawn in favour of Mr Reekie's motion. The discussion in which nearly all present had joined was then closed by the Chairman puting the motions to the meeting. Their voted for Mr Reekie's motion 15 and for Mr Blackie's 3. The following members were elected members of committee: Mr Welsh, Mr Reekie, Mr Mitchell, Mr Holburn, Mr Fergie Convener. The roll was then called and 20 members present.

11 November 1873

Secretary read letter from Mr Ralph Richardson approving of the position taken by the Council in connection with the Heriot Trust and the evidence before the Endowed Schools Commission. The Secretary was instructed to answer Mr Richardson, thanking him for his interest in the Council on this subject. An invitation to send delegates to Trade Congress to be held in Sheffield was then read but as the Council considered such a course beyond their ordinary resources agreed to recommend an apeal to the trades, the representitive to explain the purpose and object of the proposed meeting, and that meantime the letter lie on the table. Mr Walker then directed the attention of the Council to the inconvenience of the present hours for registration and gave notice that he would submit a motion on the subject.

The Deputation to the Demonstration against the Criminal Law in Glasgow then gave in their report, agreeing as to the succesful character of the meeting and their courtious reception by the Executive Committee, the thanks of the Council being awarded to the Deputation. A Notice of Motion by Mr Dewar was then given: That the Council communicate with the various Trade Councils for the purpose of ascertaining the feeling with regard to the adoption of eight hours a day for labour. Mr Welsh then introduced the iregularities of the Post Office in the delivery of Post Cards and the propriety of memorialising the Post Office authorities on this subject. The members generally concured in this view but considered that it would be a judicious course to delay until they could substantiate their position by one or more well authenticated instances of such irregularity. 16 members present.

25 November 1873

Mr Fergie read a letter addressed to the Council on the subject of school fees which it was agreed to place on the programme of business for next meeting. The Committee on the Heriot Trust reported that they had read the proof of evidence before the Endowed Schools Commission and returned with a few corrections. It was then resolved to make a further effort to dispose of Lewis' Lecture, reducing the price to one penny, their being over 1,000 copies still on hand.[1] Mr Taggart from Inverness[2] next addressed the meeting, wishing a letter from the Council to the working classes of that neighbourhood. Considerable diversity of opinion existed as to the propriety of such a course, but eventually it was agreed to do so, this being remitted to the Secretary to write and forward. Mr Miller[3] and Mr Lyall being duly accredited as the representitives of the Bakers took their seat at the council. The roll was called and 15 members present.

9 December 1873

Copies of Reports, etc., from the Parlimentary Committee of the Trade Union Congress were laid on the table and answers from the Saddlers, Tailors, Printers, Tinplate workers, and Milling trade stating that they were willing to contribute toward the sending of a Representitive to Sheffield. A letter from the Secretary of the Painters Association was read enclosing tickets for Trade Soiree and requesting the Council to appoint two Delegates to attend it. The Chairman and Secretary were appointed. The Parlimentary Committee of Trade Union Congress having invited reports of cases under the Criminal Law Amendment Act, it was agreed that any member who had any case of importance should draw up a report of the same and the Secretary forward it to Mr Howel in London.

An Invitation to attend the Trade Demonstration to be held in Dundee being the next business, Mr Blackie moved that a Deputa-

---

[1] Above, p. 356.

[2] Presumably C. Taggart, Inverness, who seconded a resolution at a great trade union demonstration at Dundee on 3 January 1874, but not further identified. *Scotsman*, 5 January 1874.

[3] Almost certainly Gilbert Miller or Millar.

tion of two should be sent, which was agreed to and Mr Holburn and Mr J. Mitchell appointed.[1] Mr Blackie then intimated that the discussion on the proposed laying out of the Meadows came up at the next meeting of Town Council and that he was authorised to offer the use of the New Waverly Hall if the Council thought it judicious to hold a public meeting on the subject. The Council, however, thought this was not necessary at this time but agreed to forward a memorial to the Town Council on the proposed opening up of the Centre Walk for Carriage traffic.[2] It was also agreed to summons the next meeting of Council as that of the Members for the City took place on the usual night. 15 members present.

30 December 1873

Answers from the following trades were recieved intimating that they were willing to contribute towards the expense of sending a delegate to Sheffield, viz., Coopers, Coachmakers, Blacksmiths, Ironmoulders, Masons, Slaters. Mr McAllen[3] then moved that, seeing the support promised for this purpose and the probibility of other trades ultimatly contributing, several of them not having meetings at which to decide, the Council should send a representitive to the Congress, which was agreed to unanimously. Considerable discussion then took place as to the payment of the deligate. Ultimately a motion by Mr Blackie that 12s per day be allowed was agreed to. Mr McNab then moved that the Secretary be sent, seconded by Mr Blackie. Mr McAllen moved that the President be elected, remarking that this would be a well merited compliment to him for the interest and ability he at all times displayed in the business of the Council, seconded by Mr Welsh. The Vice President taking the chair for the purpose of putting the motions to the meeting, the President was elected by a majority. Mr Holburn resumed the Chair and returned thanks for his election.[4] 21 members present.

---

[1] The demonstration was held in Dundee on 3 January 1874 to demand the repeal of the Criminal Law Amendment Act, the criminal clauses of the Master and Servant Act and the law of conspiracy. *Scotsman*, 5 January 1874.

[2] A similar proposal by the town council had been made in 1864. See above, pp. 146–7.   [3] Donald McAllen, tailors.

[4] Holburn was unable in the event to attend the Trades Union Congress and his place was taken by Donald McAllen, tailors.

Appendix I

LIST OF OFFICE-BEARERS 1859-73

PRESIDENT

1859 March	John Borrowman, joiners
1859 December 6	William Troup, tailors
1867 August 13	James Donaldson, masons
1868 July 25	William Kinlay, bookbinders
1869 July 27	Andrew Dewar, blacksmiths
1870 September 13	Edward Jeffrey, joiners (resigned 14 March 1871)
1871 July 25	Walter Fairbairn, blacksmiths
1873 July 8	John Holburn, tinplate workers

VICE-PRESIDENT

1859 March	William Troup, tailors
1859 December 6	George Smith, brassfounders
1860 December 4	George Herbert, masons[1]
1861 December 17	John Sheddin, cabinetmakers (re-elected)
1863 January 13	John McDonald, brassfounders
1864 January 26	Thomas Young, cabinetmakers
1865 January 10	James Hart, masons
1866 January 23	? None appointed
1867 August 13	Robert Webster, engineers
1868 July 25	William White, joiners

[1] Herbert had resigned and been replaced by John Sheddin, cabinetmakers, some time before December 1861.

1869 December 14   James Taylor, tailors
1870 July 26   Edward Jeffrey, joiners
1870 September 13   Daniel Munro, printers
1871 July 25   R. S. Laws, painters
1871 December 12   James Wightman, bakers
1872 July 23   John Holburn, tinplate workers
1873 July 8   John Grant, tailors

SECRETARY

1859 March   Alexander Taylor, tailors
1859 October 11   John Iverach, tailors
1860 June 5   Alexander Fraser, blacksmiths
1861 June 4   John Beaton, glasscutters
1864 January 26   Alexander Fraser, blacksmiths
1867 April 16   R. S. Laws, painters (interim; never acted)
1867 May 14   J. C. Burn, blacksmiths (interim)
1867 August 13   J. C. Burn, blacksmiths
1868 July 25   Robert Gray, glassmakers
1869 July 27   James Bartie, joiners
1870 July 26   Andrew Scott, engineers
1871 April 25   James Sinclair, cabinetmakers (interim)
1871 June 27   Matthew Hilson, blacksmiths (interim)
1871 July 25   Matthew Hilson, blacksmiths
1872 January 10   Blair (pro tem.)[1]
1872 July 23   Matthew Hilson, blacksmiths (re-elected)
1873 July 8   Thomas Walker, masons (never acted)
1873 July 22   John Cubie, cabinetmakers

ASSISTANT SECRETARY

1867 August 13   William Todd, printers
1868 July 25   James Horn, joiners (resigned before 12
                    January 1869)

[1] Either James Blair, engineers, or Alexander Blair, trade unknown. Hilson, the secretary, continued, however, to write the minutes.

1869 January 12	George Hills, bookbinders
1869 July 27	None appointed
1871 July 25	James Petrie, printers
1871 December 12	Walter Chisholm, joiners
1873 July 8	Matthew Hilson, blacksmiths

TREASURER

1859 March	James Collins, masons
1859 October 25	William Tait, joiners
1860 May 8	William Caw, joiners
1861 July 30	James Collins, masons
1867 April 16	Alexander Duncanson, joiners (interim)
1867 August 13	George Scott, glasscutters[1]
1870 March 22	John McAllen, typefounders
1870 July 26	Alexander Brian, painters
1870 August 23	Alexander Strachan, joiners
1871 July 25	Thomas Blaikie, moulders
1872 July 23	James Inglis, cabinetmakers
1873 July 8	John Jack, tinplate workers

[1] On 23 February 1869 James Bartie, joiners, was appointed assistant treasurer and on 23 March treasurer pro tem. But Scott apparently resumed the office some time before 27 July 1869, when he was re-elected.

Appendix II

TABLE OF AFFILIATED UNIONS 1859-73

Until 1867, apart from most of the latter half of 1859, the delegates present at meetings of the trades council were formally listed in the minutes, with the unions they represented. The table overleaf is therefore a reliable picture of affiliation to the council from 1859 to 1867. Between the latter date and 1873, however, no such lists were entered in the minutes; consequently that part of the table is not quite so reliable, especially as the unions of some delegates in that period have not been ascertained. Thirty-one separate unions appear to have been affiliated at one time or another between 1859 and 1873. Those that had more than one branch affiliated are indicated in the table. With the inclusion of these additional branches, the trades council evidently had a total of thirty-five, or possibly thirty-six, affiliates.

The following symbols have been used in the table overleaf:

a   affiliated throughout the year
b   became affiliated or re-affiliated
c   ceased to be affiliated, or at least ceased to be represented

	1859	1860	1861	1862	1863	1864	1865	1866	1867	1868	1869	1870	1871	1872	1873
ENGINEERING AND METAL TRADES															
Blacksmiths	a	a	a	a	a	a	a	c	b	a	a	a	a	a	a
Brassfounders	a	a	a	a	a	a	c		b	a	a	a	a	a	a
Engineers[1]*	b?	a	a	a	a	a			b	a	a	a	a	a	a
Ironmoulders[2]				b						b	b	a	a	a	a
Tinplate workers					c					b	b	a	a	a	a
BUILDING AND FURNISHING TRADES															
Joiners[3]	a	a	a	c				b	a	a	a	a	a	a	a
French polishers	a	c													
Masons[4]	c	b	a	a	a	a	a	c?	b	a	a	a?	a	a	a
Plumbers	a	a	c	a						b	?	?	?	?	?
Cabinetmakers			b	a	a	a	a	a	a	c		b	a	a	a
Slaters			b	a	a	a	a	a	a	a	a	a?	a	a	a
Plasterers						b	a	c?		bc?	?	?	a	a	?
Painters									b	a	a	a	a	a	a
Bricklayers									b	bc					
Upholsterers											b	c?			

* For notes see overleaf. p. 380.

	1859	1860	1861	1862	1863	1864	1865	1866	1867	1868	1869	1870	1871	1872	1873
CLOTHING AND LEATHER TRADES															
Tailors	a	a	a	a	a	a	a	a	a	a	a	a	a	a	a
Skinners				b	a	a	c								
Saddlers														b?	a
Shoemakers															b
PRINTING AND ALLIED TRADES															
Printers									b	a	a	a	a	a	a
Bookbinders									b	a	a	a	c	b	a
Typefounders											b	a	a	a	a
FOOD, GLASS AND MISC. TRADES															
Clockmakers	b?	a	a	c											
Glassmakers	b	a	a	a	a	c				b	c				
Glasscutters		b	a	a	a	c			b	a	a	c?	a		
Bakers[5]		b	c	a					b	a	a	a	a	b	a
Coopers			b	a	c				b	c					
Corkcutters			b	a	a	a	c								
Coachmakers												b	a	a	a
Milling trades															b
UNSKILLED WORKERS															
Labourers										bc					

1. Leith branch of the engineers was affiliated in 1870-1, in addition to Edinburgh branch.

2. The ironmoulders affiliated in February 1862 but appear to have disaffiliated from August 1862 until September 1863 and again after Novermber 1863.

3. Between 1867 and 1873 three branches of the joiners were affiliated: central and west each from 1867 to 1873, and south branch in 1869-70.

4. There may have been two groups of masons affiliated in 1859. (See above, p. 17 and *n.*)

5. In addition to Edinburgh branch of the bakers, Leith branch was affiliated in 1861 and from 1868 to 1870.

INDEX[1]

[1] Where the name of a delegate to Edinburgh trades council (TC) occurs frequently throughout many pages, the first and last page numbers only have been shown in the index and the word passim is to be understood. Office-bearers of the TC itself are designated merely as 'secretary', 'treasurer', etc., but office-bearers of other bodies are designated specifically, e.g. 'secretary of corkcutters'.

2C

bility of, 108; numbers of, xix;
sectionalism among, xlii;
victimisation of, xxiii, 15 and
n, 16, 112-14
records of, xi, xii and *n*
Report of Select Committee, 1838,
anent, 144, 146, 147, 199
represented at peace conference,
360 *n*
Royal Commission, 1867-9, on,
xxxii, 189, 190 *n*, 223, 243, 255 *n*
see also anti-trade unionists; Bills
and Acts; 'Junta', the; labour
laws; lectures; master and
servant laws; non-unionists;
Social Science Association;
trades councils; Trades Union
Congress; *and* individual unions,
viz, bakers; Blacksmiths; Boilermakers; Bookbinders; brassfounders; bricklayers; brushmakers; building trades; Cabinet
and Chairmakers; carters; clockmakers; Coachmakers; coopers;
corkcutters; cotton operatives;
curriers; dockers; Engineers; file
trades; flax operatives; framework knitters; french polishers;
gas stokers; Gardeners; glasscutters; Glass Makers; Hairdressers; hatters; horseshoers;
Ironfounders; Iron Moulders;
iron trades; joiners; labourers;
lithographic printers; Masons;
Milling Trade; miners; painters;
paper stainers; Plasterers;
Plate, Spoon and Fork Filers;
plumbers; Railway Servants;
ropemakers; saddlers; sailmakers; saw-grinders; sawmillers; ship-wrights; shoemakers; skinners; slaters; tailors;
Tinplate Workers; typefounders;
Typographical; upholsterers;
weavers

trades councils, xi and *n*, xii and *n*,
xiv, xxvii, xxx, xli, 83, 127, 211,
257, 265, 275, 287, 346, 353,
360 *n*, 370
see also Aberdeen; Birmingham;
Bristol; Dundee; Edinburgh;
Glasgow; Greenock; Kirk-
caldy; Leith; Liverpool; London, Manchester; Sheffield
Trades Union Congress, xxiv, 61 *n*,
284 *n*
and labour laws, xxxiv, 313, 315,
336 and *n*, 371
origins of, xlii, 190 *n*, 211 and *n*
representation of T C at, xii, 263
and *n*, 312 and *n*, 313, 329-31,
342-3, 345, 370-2
Trodden, James, bakers' delegate,
329, 333, 335
Trotter, John, treasurer, 'non-
society masons', 17 and *n*
Troup, George, journalist, 49 and *n*,
54, 55
Troup, William, tailors' delegate
and president, xvi, xx, xxiv,
xxviii, 3-210, 315 and *n*
truck, *see* Bills and Acts, Wages
Tunny, J. G., Independent Liberal,
228 and *n*
Turnbull, Alexander, Leith bakers'
delegate, 291
Turnbull, Mr, engineers' delegate,
71-114, 131, 151-7
Turnbull, Mr, secretary, Lithographers' Society, 204
Turner, Robert, ironmoulders' delegate, 324-33, 336 and *n*, 340, 341
typefounders' union, xxxviii, 145,
273, 329
Typographical Association, Scottish,
xviii, 253 *n*
Typographical Society, Edinburgh,
xviii and *n*, xx, xxiii, 19, 26, 36,
43, 202, 215, 253 and *n*, 323 and
n, 324, 351, and *n*

MEMBERSHIP

*Membership of the Scottish History Society
is open to all who are interested in the history of Scotland.
For an annual subscription of £2 2s. or $7
members normally receive one volume each year.
Enquiries should be addressed to
the Honorary Secretary or the Honorary Treasurer,
whose addresses are given overleaf.*

REPORT

of the 81st Annual Meeting

The 81st Annual Meeting of the Scottish History Society was held in the Rooms of the Royal Society, George Street, Edinburgh, on Saturday, 9 December 1967, at 11.15 a.m. Dr W. Douglas Simpson, President, was in the Chair. The Report of the Council was as follows:

The third volume of the Fourth Series, *Letters of John Ramsay of Ochtertyre, 1799–1812*, edited by Miss B. L. H. Horn, was issued during the year. The Council is glad to note that this volume has been popular with members and has received favourable reviews. The next volume, *Court Books of Orkney and Shetland, 1614–15*, edited by Dr R. S. Barclay, will shortly be ready for printing off and will be issued to members before the end of the year.

The volume for issue in 1968 will be *Minutes of Edinburgh Trades Council, 1859–73*, edited by Mr Ian Macdougall. These minutes record the efforts of a body of working men, representative of various trades, to improve labouring, social and educational conditions in the city. This is the first occasion on which the Society has issued a volume from the Victorian era and these are the first Trades Council records from any part of the United Kingdom to appear in print. The Council hopes that the volume will prove to be of unusual interest to members and that it will advance the study of working class history.

Since 1963 the Council has been giving special attention to the task of securing editions of nineteenth-century historical material, since this period has so far been under-represented in the Society's list of publications. The Council is glad to record that this policy is meeting with success, since five volumes dealing with the nineteenth century are now at various stages of preparation. The Council has recently accepted for publication a volume on *The Dundee Textile Industry, 1790–1885, from the papers of Peter Carmichael*, to be edited by Mrs Enid Gauldie. Carmichael was an outstanding engineer, inventor and captain of industry, who rose to be senior partner in Baxter Brothers, one of the largest businesses in Dundee. These papers consist of his personal letters, linked by a narrative of Carmichael's career written by his nephew. The volume will throw light on a neglected aspect of the linen and jute industry and will contain much that is of social as well as of economic interest. The Council has also accepted for publication a volume on *William Melrose in China: the letters of a Scottish tea merchant, 1848–55*, to be edited by Dr Hoh-Cheung Mui and Mrs Lorna H. Mui. These letters are from the records of Messrs Melroses, the Edinburgh tea merchants, which are almost unique in Britain in their interest and comprehensiveness. William Melrose was a young partner in the firm and his letters to his father, from Canton, Hong Kong and Macao, describe trading conditions in detail and report his purchases and the state of the tea market. These interesting and perspicacious letters will contribute much knowledge to the important but little-studied topic of Scottish economic enterprise in the East.

The Council has been grateful for suggestions received about possible contributions to a *Miscellany* on trade and industry. The Council has decided to confine this volume to industrial material. It will be titled *Scottish Industrial History: a miscellany of documents* and will consist of the following items: 'Selected Scottish building contracts, 1660–90', edited by Mr John Dunbar; 'Heinrich Kalmeter's diary of his travels in Scotland, 1719–20', edited by Dr T. C. Smout (already announced); 'Sederunt book of the Muirkirk Iron Company, 1786–1800', edited by Dr John Butt; 'Notebook of Henry Brown, woollen manufacturer, 1818–19', edited by Mr C. Gulvin (already announced); 'Report by the Committee of Investigation to the Shareholders of the North British Railway Company, 1866', edited by Mr Wray Vamplew; 'The beginning and end of the Lewis Chemical Works, 1858–74', edited by Dr T. I. Rae.

The Council is planning a parallel *Miscellany* volume on the history of Scottish agriculture. This will include the 'Oldcambus Farm Accounts, 1596–7', edited by the Rev. W. E. K. Rankin and Mr Alexander Fenton, which have already been announced. It will also include a remarkable manuscript from the muniments of the Earl of Southesk. This is the 'Kinnaird Farm Stock Book, 1559–93', which records transactions relating to animals, mainly sheep, on the Kinnaird estate in Angus at this unusually early date. The manuscript has the added interest that it was partially written by David Carnegy of Colluthie, who was a Privy Councillor in the 1590s and one of the Octavians. This item will be edited by Mr Alexander Fenton. The Council will be glad to hear from any members who know of suitable historical documents about agriculture from the period prior to the Agricultural Revolution. The Council is particularly anxious to trace any material relevant to agriculture in the seventeenth century.

The Council also takes this opportunity to remind members, and scholars generally, that it is always ready to consider suggestions, either general or specific, for possible publications. Such proposals should be forwarded to the Honorary Secretary.

On account of pressure of other commitments, the Kraus Reprint Corporation has not yet been able to announce reprinting of the Society's First, Second and Third Series, but hopes to be able to do so in January 1968. Production of the reprints will probably commence about the end of 1968.

The Council has decided to accept an invitation to appoint a representative to serve on the British National Committee of the International Congress of Historical Sciences and hopes in this way to spread further afield a knowledge of, and interest in, Scottish historical studies. Professor G. W. S. Barrow, Chairman of Council, has agreed to represent the Society on the Committee.

To assist with the increasing volume of work being undertaken by the office-bearers, Council has appointed Dr Katharine L. Davies, of the Scottish Record Office, to the post of Honorary Assistant Secretary.

Members of Council who retire in rotation at this time are Mr R. J. Adam, Professor S. G. E. Lythe and Dr I. M. M. MacPhail. The following will be proposed to the Annual Meeting for election to the Council: Mr James Halliday, Mrs Rosalind Mitchison and the Rev. Duncan Shaw. The Council is anxious to foster contacts with other countries and will therefore also propose that Professor Maurice Lee, Jr., of Rutgers University, New Brunswick, u.s.a., be elected a Corresponding Member of Council.

During the past year six members have died, eleven have resigned, and two have been removed from the list for non-payment of subscription. Fifty-four new members have joined. The membership, including 199 libraries, is now 559, as against 524 in 1966. The Council is glad to note that membership continues to increase and that a total membership of 600 is now within sight. But the Council wishes to emphasise that a larger membership yet will be necessary to counteract rising costs of printing. Experience during the current year has shown that the most effective means of bringing in new members is through a personal letter. Members are earnestly requested to notify the Honorary Secretary of the names and addresses of interested persons who could be asked to join the Society.

In presenting the Annual Report, Professor G. W. S. Barrow, Chairman of Council, drew attention to the resurgence of interest in Scottish history in many ways and among many people, building up steadily over a number of years, which had brought the membership of the Society to a figure approaching 600. Council intended to meet this varied interest by a widely-

2D

based publications policy. But this could be successful only if supported by a flourishing membership; and he encouraged the Society to aim now at a figure of 700 or 800 members. Professor Barrow announced that since the Annual Report had been printed, the Society had received a gift of £500 from an anonymous donor, which would give much-needed elbow-room in the planning of publications. He was sure that the Council and the Society would wish to express their appreciation of this very generous donation and this statement was received with applause. Professor Barrow then proposed the adoption of the Annual Report. This was seconded by Mrs Rosalind Mitchison and the Report was duly adopted.

Mr R. W. Munro nominated for election as ordinary members of Council Mr James Halliday, Mrs Rosalind Mitchison and the Rev. Dr Duncan Shaw, and as corresponding members of Council Professor Michel de Boüard, University of Caen, Normandy, and Professor Maurice Lee, jr, Rutgers University, City of New Brunswick, New Jersey, U.S.A. These were seconded by Professor E. L. G. Stones and were duly elected.

The President then gave an address entitled 'The siege of Dunyveg Castle, Islay, 1615: a study in combined operations'. The meeting closed with a vote of thanks to the President, proposed by the Chairman of Council.

ABSTRACT ACCOUNT OF CHARGE AND DISCHARGE OF THE INTROMISSIONS OF THE HONORARY TREASURER for the year 1st November 1966 to 31st October 1967

I. GENERAL ACCOUNT

CHARGE

I. Cash in Bank at 1st November 1966:

   1. Sum at credit of Savings Account with Bank of Scotland — £7 5 8

   2. Sum at credit of Current Account with Bank of Scotland — 143 15 2

   3. Sum at credit of Savings Account with Edinburgh Savings Bank — 51 6 3

   4. Sum at credit of Special Investment Account with Edinburgh Savings Bank — 230 19 9

              £433 6 10

II. Subscriptions received — 1,208 19 5

III. Editors' Conference — 51 12 6

IV. Past publications sold (including postages recovered from purchasers) — 310 17 2

V. Interest on Savings Accounts with Bank of Scotland and Edinburgh Savings Bank — 67 10 1

VI. Grants from Carnegie Trust — 500 0 0

VII. Income Tax Refund — 83 17 4

VIII. Sums drawn from Bank Current Account — £3,561 17 10

IX. Sums drawn from Bank Savings Account — £1,400 0 0

              £2,656 3 4

I. Cost of publications during year (*Letters of John Ramsay*)   £1,689 4 5

Postage of volumes   113 19 9

Cost of printing Annual Report, Notices and Printers' postages, etc.   115 16 2

    £1,919 0 4

II. Payments in furtherance of forthcoming publications   146 12 6

III. Miscellaneous Payments and refunds of subscriptions   61 12 0

IV. Editors' Conference   34 13 0

V. Sums lodged in Bank Current Account   £3,699 1 7

VI. Sums lodged in Bank Savings Account   £1,757 1 9

VII. Funds at close of this account:

    1. Balance at credit of Savings Account with Bank of Scotland   20 2 2

    2. Balance at credit of Current Account with Bank of Scotland   137 3 9

    3. Balance at credit of Savings Account with Edinburgh Savings Bank   52 11 9

    4. Balance at credit of Special Investment Account with Edinburgh Savings Bank   284 7 10

    494 5 6

    £2,656 3 4

II. DR ANNIE I. DUNLOP SPECIAL FUND ACCOUNT

CHARGE

I. Cash in Bank at 1st November 1966:

    1. Sum at credit of Savings Account with Bank of Scotland   £747 14 1

    2. Sum at credit of Current Account with Bank of Scotland   19 6 0

                                            £767 0 1

II. Interest on Savings Account with Bank of Scotland   30 3 10

                                            £797 3 11

DISCHARGE

I. Sums lodged in Bank Savings Account   £30 3 10

II. Funds at close of this Account:

    1. Balance at credit of Savings Account with Bank of Scotland   777 17 11

    2. Balance at credit of Current Account with Bank of Scotland   19 6 0   £797 3 11

EDINBURGH, *9th November* 1967. I have examined the General Account and Dr Annie I. Dunlop Special Fund Account of the Honorary Treasurer of the Scottish History Society for the year from 1st November 1966 to 31st October 1967 and I find the same to be correctly stated and sufficiently vouched.

C. T. MCINNES
Auditor

SCOTTISH HISTORY SOCIETY
LIST OF MEMBERS
1967–1968

ADAM, R. J., Cromalt, Lade Braes, St Andrews
ADAMS, I. H., PH.D., 77 Clerwood Park, Edinburgh 12
ADAMSON, Miss Margot R., 100 Handside Lane, Welwyn Garden City, Herts.
AGNEW, C. H., ygr., of Lochnaw, The Lowland Brigade Depot, Penicuik, Midlothian
ALDERSON, J. J., Havelock, Victoria, Australia
ALEXANDER, Joseph, Trust, per J. A. Carnegie & Smith, Solicitors, Bank of Scotland Buildings, Kirriemuir, Angus
ANDERSON, Mrs Marjorie O., West View Cottage, Lade Braes Lane, St Andrews
ANDERSON, Rev. W. J., 16 Drummond Place, Edinburgh 3
ANGUS, Rev. J. A. K., T.D., M.A., The Manse, 90 Albert Road, Gourock, Renfrewshire
ANNAND, A. McK., Magdalen, High Street, Findon, Worthing, Sussex
ANNAND, James K., 174 Craigleith Road, Edinburgh 4
ANTON, Professor A. E., 18 West Chapelton Crescent, Bearsden, Glasgow
ARGYLL, His Grace the Duke of, Inveraray Castle, Argyll
ARKLE, Douglas G., F.S.A. SCOT., Airthrey, 91 Keptie Road, Arbroath, Angus
ARMET, Miss Catherine M., Mount Stuart, Rothesay, Isle of Bute
ARMSTRONG, M., 17 Muirend Gardens, Perth
ASH, Miss Marinell, M.A., Department of Scottish History, The Swallowgate, St Andrews
ASPLIN, P. W., Strathcraig, Loganswell, Newton Mearns, Glasgow

BACSICH, Mrs Anna B., 11 Ashton Road, Glasgow w 2
BAIRD, Kenneth D., 17 Bellevue Crescent, Edinburgh 3
BANNERMAN, John W. M., PH.D., Arrochy Beg, Balmaha, Stirlingshire
BARCLAY, R. S., PH.D., 185 Carrick Knowe Drive, Edinburgh 12
BARLOW, Miss Ethel, 4 Hillside Terrace, Old Kilpatrick, Glasgow
BARR, Mrs A. R., Bonahaven, Colintraive, Argyll
BARROW, Professor G. W. S., Department of Modern History, The University, Newcastle upon Tyne (Chairman of Council)
BAYNE, Mrs Neil, 51 Ann Street, Edinburgh 4
BECKET, Miss Lindsay D., Quaker Cottage, Barcombe, Lewes, Sussex
BECKMAN, Miss Gail McK., LL.B., Faculty of Law, University of Glasgow, 63 Hillhead Street, Glasgow, w 2
BENNETT, Miss Josephine M., B.L., 91 Victoria Road, Dunoon, Argyll
BERNARD, K. N., B.A., F.S.A. SCOT., No. 1 Mews Flat, 3 Sydenham Road, Glasgow w 2
BEST, Professor Geoffrey, 4 Ormidale Terrace, Edinburgh 12
BIGWOOD, Miss A. R., 13 Jackson Street, Inverurie, Aberdeenshire
BONAR, John J., 30 Greenhill Gardens, Edinburgh 10

BRANSTON, Miss A. L., 41 Raeburn Place, Edinburgh 4
BRISTOL, Nicholas M. V., 22 Whitlesey Street, London SE1
BROUN LINDSAY, Lady, Colstoun, Haddington, East Lothian
BROWN, A. L., D.PHIL., History Department, The University, Glasgow W2
BROWN, Commander A. R. P., R.N. (Retd.), Capelaw, 29 Woodhall Road, Edinburgh 11
BROWN, G. W., North Cuan Farm, Isle of Seil, by Oban, Argyll
BROWNING, Professor Andrew, D.LITT., Durie House, 6 West Abercromby Street, Helensburgh, Dunbartonshire
BRYSON, William, 1 Sutherland Avenue, Petts Wood, Kent
BUCHANAN, John, 67 Great King Street, Edinburgh 3
BUIST, Frank J., Fairneyknowe, by Arbroath, Angus
BUIST, J. S., M.A., 55 Dublin Street, Edinburgh 3
BULLOCH, Rev. James, Manse of Stobo, Peebles
BURNS, Rev. Charles, Archivio Segreto, Citta del Vaticano, Roma, Italy
BURNS, David Murray, 60 North Castle Street, Edinburgh 2
BURRELL, Professor Sydney A., A.B., PH.D., Department of History, Boston University, Boston, Mass. 02215, USA
BURROWS, B. S. M., M.A., 2 Kendrick Mews, London SW7
BUTCHART, H. J., Willowwood, 626 King Street, Aberdeen

CAIRD, J. B., D.DE L'UNIV., Department of Geography, The University, Glasgow W2
CAIRNS, Mrs Trevor, B.A., 4 Ashmore Terrace, Sunderland, Co. Durham
CAMERON, Alexander D., 18 Crown Avenue, Inverness
CAMERON, The Hon. Lord, 28 Moray Place, Edinburgh 3
CAMPBELL, Colin, P.O. Box 8. Belmont 78, Massachusetts, USA
CAMPBELL, Lt.-Col. H. Alastair, Altries, Milltimber, Aberdeenshire
CAMPBELL, Ian Burns, LL.B., PH.D., Faculty of Law, University of Liverpool, Liverpool 3
CAMPBELL, J. L., of Canna, D.LITT., LL.D., Isle of Canna, Inverness-shire
CAMPBELL, Peter H., Levensholme, Tyneview Road, Haltwhistle, Northumberland
CAMPBELL, Professor R. H., School of Social Studies, Wilberforce Road, Norwich
CAMPBELL, Rev. William M., The Manse, Barloan, Dumbarton
CANT, R. G., 2 Kinburn Place, St Andrews
CARMICHAEL, Major G. B., Three Ways, Cold Ash, Newbury, Berks.
CARMICHAEL, P. O., Arthurstone, Meigle, Perthshire
CARNEGIE, B. Grant, Willburn, Northmuir, Kirriemuir, Angus
CHECKLAND, Professor S. G., PH.D., Department of Economic History, The University, Glasgow W2
CHEYNE, Rev. Professor A. C., B.LITT., B.D., 11 Tantallon Place, Edinburgh 9
CHRISTIE, William, M.A., 306 Blackness Road, Dundee
CLARK, Ian D. L., PH.D., Bishop's College, 224 Lower Circular Road, Calcutta 17, India

CLAVERING, R. J., Lucarne House, 56 Farnley Road, Menston, Ilkley, Yorks.

COCKBURN, Very Rev. J. Hutchison, 8 Stonehill Road, East Sheen, London sw14

COHEN, Mrs M. C., 8 Norfolk Road, London nw8

COLQUHOUN, Rev. John, Free Presbyterian Manse, Glendale, Skye

CORBETT, Rev. John R. H., b.d., 235 Elizabeth Avenue, City of the Two Mountains, Quebec, Canada

COSH, Miss Mary, m.a., 63 Theberton Street, London n1

COSSAR, James, Lyndale, 10 Craig's Bank, Edinburgh 12

COWAN, Edward J., m.a., Department of Scottish History, William Robertson Building, 50 George Square, Edinburgh 8

COWAN, Ian B., ph.d., 119 Balshagray Avenue, Glasgow w1 (*Honorary Treasurer*)

COWE, F. M., 10 Ravensdowne, Berwick-upon-Tweed

COWIE, Miss Isabella, Glenrinnes, Dufftown, Banffshire

CRAWFORD & BALCARRES, The Rt Hon. The Earl of, Balcarres, Colinsburgh, Fife

CRAWFORD, Iain A., m.a., Nether Kinneddar, Saline, Fife

CRAWFORD, Thomas, m.a., 61 Argyll Place, Aberdeen

CREGEEN, E. R., Eaglesview, Auchterarder, Perthshire

CRORIE, William D., b.sc., 34 Dumyat Drive, Falkirk, Stirlingshire

CROSS, A. R., 13 Grange Road, Edinburgh 9

CURRIE, Rev. D. R., ph.d., St. Cuthbert's Manse, Galashiels, Selkirkshire

CUTHBERT, Alexander, c.a., f.s.a. scot., 27 Cumlodden Avenue, Edinburgh 12

DAICHES, Professor D., Downsview, Wellhouse Lane, Burgess Hill, Sussex

DARRAGH, James, m.a., 103 Deakin Leas, Tonbridge, Kent

DAVIES, Miss Katharine L., ph.d., 198 Dalkeith Road, Edinburgh 9 (*Honorary Assistant Secretary*)

DAVIS, E. D., Craigie College of Education, p.o. Box 17, Ayr

DAWSON, J. P., 2 Highburgh Avenue, Lanark.

DE BEER, E. S., 31 Brompton Square, London sw3

DICKSON, A. Hope, House of Aldie, Rumbling Bridge, Kinross-shire

DICKSON, C. H., 8 Highwood Gardens, Ilford, Essex

DICKSON, D., 20 Lime Grove, Lenzie, Dunbartonshire

DICKSON, Walter, 5 Elcho Terrace, Portobello, Edinburgh 15

DOCHERTY, Rev. Henry, ph.l., St Bartholomew's, Trent Street, Coatbridge, Lanarkshire

DONALDSON, Professor Gordon, d.litt., 24 East Hermitage Place, Edinburgh 6

DONALDSON, Robert, National Library of Scotland, George IV Bridge, Edinburgh 1

DONNELLY, H. H., c.b., ll.b., Highfield West, Claremont Drive, Bridge of Allen, Stirlingshire

DOW, Rev. A. C., ph.d., Stoneywood Church Manse, Bankhead Road, Bucksburn, Aberdeenshire

DRAFFEN, George S., of Newington, M.B.E., Newington House, Cupar, Fife

DRUMMOND-MURRAY, P., Orchard Cottage, New Road, Tylers Green, Penn, Bucks.

DRYSDALE, Charles D., M.B.E., Woodcot, Dollar, Clackmannanshire

DUNBAR, John G., F.S.A., Royal Commission, Ancient & Historical Monuments (Scotland), 52/54 Melville Street, Edinburgh 3

DUNCAN, Archibald, Windward House, Kilcreggan, Dunbartonshire

DUNCAN, Professor Archibald A. M., Scottish History Department, The University, Glasgow w2

DUNLOP, Mrs Annie I., O.B.E., PH.D., D.LITT., LL.D., 73 London Road, Kilmarnock, Ayrshire

DUNLOP, Rev. A. Ian, 11 Bellevue Place, Edinburgh 7

DUNLOP, Professor D. M., D.LITT., 423 West 120th Street, New York, N.Y. 10027, USA

DURACK, Mrs Isabel J., 87 Comiston Drive, Edinburgh 10

DURKAN, J., PH.D., 14 Newfield Square, Glasgow sw3

ELIBANK, The Rt Hon. Lord, 3 Duncan Street, Edinburgh 9

ELRICK, W. J. H., 14 High Street, Strichen AB4 4SR, Aberdeenshire

EWING, Mrs Winifred, M.P., LL.B., 52 Queen's Drive, Glasgow s2

FARQUHARSON, R., 6 Monaro Crescent, Red Hill, ACT 2603, Australia

FENTON, Alexander, M.A., 132 Blackford Avenue, Edinburgh 9

FERGUSON, William, PH.D., Scottish History Department, William Robertson Building, 50 George Square, Edinburgh 8

FERGUSSON, Sir James, of Kilkerran, Bart., LL.D., Kilkerran, Maybole, Ayrshire

FEWELL, Percy C., 1402 Kirby Building, Dallas, Texas, 75201, USA

FILBY, P. W., Assistant Director, Maryland Historical Society, 201 West Monument Street, Baltimore, Maryland 21201, USA

FINLAYSON, Rev. Angus, Free Church Manse, North Tolsta, Stornoway, Isle of Lewis

FINLAYSON, C. P., 17 Granville Terrace, Edinburgh 10

FINLAYSON, G., History Department, The University, Glasgow, w2

FLECK, John M. M., M.A., Ard-Coile, Conon Bridge, Ross-shire

FLEMING, A. M. H., Fasnacloich, Appin, Argyll

FLEMING, Mrs M. J. P., M.B., CH.D., 17 Graham Park Road, Gosforth, Newcastle upon Tyne

FRASER, Mrs Agnes J., D.A., F.S.A. SCOT., 76 Moira Terrace, Edinburgh 7

FRASER, Barclay S., Viewforth, Glebe Road, Cramond, Edinburgh

FRASER, The Hon. Lord, 20 Moray Place, Edinburgh 3

GAFFNEY, Victor, 51 East Trinity Road, Edinburgh 5

GALLOWAY, T. L., of Auchendrane, by Ayr

GASKELL, P., PH.D., Dormers Comberton, Cambridge

GAULD, Miss Mary B., 29 Beechgrove Terrace, Aberdeen

GAULDIE, Mrs Enid, B.PHIL., Waterside, Invergowrie, by Dundee

GESNER, Miss Marjorie E., PH.D., History Department, 402 Morrill Hall, Michigan State University, East Lansing, Michigan 48823, USA
GILFILLAN, J. B. S., Edenkerry, Helensburgh, Dunbartonshire
GILL, Brian H., 23 Redford Drive, Colinton, Edinburgh 13
GILL, W. M., M.A., Woodburn, Cairnryan, Stranraer, Wigtownshire
GILLANDERS, Farquhar, M.A., The University, Glasgow, W2
GLADSTONE, John, Capenoch, Penpont, Dumfriesshire
GLENTANAR, The Rt Hon. Lord, Glen Tanar, Aboyne, Aberdeenshire
GORDON, Edmund von, c/o 5419 Dierdorf, Bez Koblenz, West Germany
GORRIE, D. C. E., M.A., The Knowe, Limekilns, Fife
GOULDESBROUGH, Peter, LL.B., Scottish Record Office, H.M. General Register House, Edinburgh 2
GRAHAM, Norman W., Suilven, Kings Road, Longniddry, East Lothian
GRANGE, R. W. D., Aberdour School, Burgh Heath, nr. Tadworth, Surrey
GRANT, I. D., 5 Crawford Road, Edinburgh 9
GRANT, Miss I. F., LL.D., 35 Heriot Row, Edinburgh 3
GRANT, Ian R., 11 Cumin Place, Edinburgh 9
GRANT-PETERKIN, K., B.A., Invererne, Forres, Moray
GRAY, Alexander L., 131 High Street, Inverurie, Aberdeenshire
GRIEVE, Miss Hilda E. P., B.E.M., B.A., 33 Shrublands Close, Chelmsford, Essex
GUTHRIE, Douglas, M.D., F.R.C.S., 21 Clarendon Crescent, Edinburgh 4

HADDO, The Rt Hon. the Earl of, Haddo House, Aberdeen
HADEN-GUEST, Lady, The University, Glasgow W2
HAIG, Miss Lilian S., 30 Hazel Avenue, Kirkcaldy, Fife
HALDANE, A. R. B., W.S., 4 North Charlotte Street, Edinburgh 2
HALLIDAY, J., 10 Argyle Street, Maryfield, Dundee
HALLIDAY, Rev. R. T., B.D., Holy Cross Rectory, 28 East Barnton Avenue, Edinburgh 4
HAMPTON, Gordon, B.L., c/o Messrs Hastings & Co., 1st Floor, Marina House, 15-19 Queen's Road, Hong Kong
HANNAH, Alexander, The Red Cottage, 37 Abbotswood, Guildford, Surrey
HARGREAVES, Professor John D., 146 Hamilton Place, Aberdeen
HARPER, Colin C., LL.B., c/o Cairns, McIntosh & Morton, W.S., 31 Queen Street, Edinburgh 2
HARRISON, E. S., of J. Johnston & Co., Newmill, Elgin, Moray
HAWS, Charles H., B.A., Department of History, Old Dominion College, Norfolk, Virginia 23508, USA
HAY, Professor Denys, 31 Fountainhall Road, Edinburgh 9
HAY, Frederick G., M.A, Department of Political Economy, The University, Glasgow W2
HAY, George, F.S.A., 29 Moray Place, Edinburgh 3
HAY, Colonel R. A., United Service Club, Pall Mall, London SW1
HEELY, Mrs Muriel S., Norbury House, Alford, Lincolnshire
HENDERSON, Mrs M. I. O. Gore-Browne, Malleny, Balerno, Midlothian
HENDERSON, W. H., Cedar Grove, Dirleton, North Berwick, East Lothian

HENDERSON-HOWAT, Mrs A. M. D., 7 Lansdowne Crescent, Edinburgh 12
HESKETH, Lady, Towcester, Northamptonshire
HILLEARY, Ian, Tayinloan Cottage, Bernisdale, Isle of Skye
HILTON, Miss Margaret, B.A., 10 Lorraine Gardens, Glasgow W2
HOLBOURN, L. A., D.A., The Manse, Foula, Shetland
HOPE, Colonel Archibald J. G., Luffness, Aberlady, East Lothian
HORN, Professor D. B., D.LITT., Department of History, William Robertson Building, 50 George Square, Edinburgh 8
HOUSTON, George, Department of Political Economy, The University, Glasgow W2
HOWDEN, D. G. B., Greenaway, London Road, Balcombe, Haywards Heath, Sussex
HOWE, J. R., Sandene, 106 Somerset Road, Meadvale, Redhill, Surrey
HOWELL, Roger, jr., D.PHIL., Department of History, Bowdoin College, Brunswick, Maine 04011, USA
HUGHES, Miss Elizabeth M., F.S.C.T., 44 Thornwood Avenue, Glasgow W1
HUIE, A. W., 15 Louisville Avenue, Aberdeen
HUME, John R., B.SC., 194 Hyndland Road, Glasgow W2
HUNTER, Mrs Elizabeth M., 7 Dreghorn Loan, Colinton, Edinburgh 13
HUNTER, J. N. W., PH.D., 23 Kaimes Road, Edinburgh 12
HUNTER, R. L., F.S.A., 74 Trinity Road, Edinburgh 5
HUNTER, R. L. C., LL.B., Department of Jurisprudence, Queen's College, University of Dundee, Dundee

IIJIMA, Keiji, B.LITT., 4-34-8 Yayoi-cho, Nakano-Ku, Tokio, Japan
INNES, Rev. George P., B.D., PH.D., South Manse, Skelmorlie, Ayrshire
INNES, Sir Thomas, of Learney, G.C.V.O., Lord Lyon King of Arms, New Register House, Edinburgh 2
IREDELL, Godfrey W., LL.M., PH.D., D.P.A., F.S.A. SCOT., Woodlands, Braithwaite, Keswick, Cumberland

JAMESON, Morley, 57 West Holmes Gardens, Musselburgh, Midlothian
JEFFRIS, Miss Ruth B., B.A., M.A., 602 East Holmes Street, Jamesville, Wisconsin 53575, USA

KATES, G. N., 39 Brimmer Street, Boston, Mass. 02108, USA
KEILLAR, Ian J., 80 Duncan Drive, Elgin, Moray
KEIR, Sir David Lindsay, Hillsborough, Lincombe Lane, Boars Hill, Oxford
KELLY, F. N. Davidson, St Gerardine's, 30 Old Kirk Road, Edinburgh 12
KENNEDY, A., Ardvoulin, South Park Road, Ayr
KENNEDY, F., 20 Constitution Street, Dundee
KENNEDY, James, B.SC., 9 Segton Avenue, Kilwinning, Ayrshire
KERR, Rev. T. A., PH.D., 13 Lady Road, Edinburgh 9
KETELBEY, Miss C. M., 18 Queen's Gardens, St Andrews

KIDD, Matthew P., Coorie Doon, Queen Victoria Street, Airdrie, Lanark-
shire
KILGOUR, Robert M., Messrs Ferguson Reekie & Kilgour, 22 Great King
Street, Edinburgh 3
KILPATRICK, P. J. W., Slipperfield House, West Linton, Peeblesshire
KINNIBURGH, T. C., The Battery, The Bayle, Folkestone, Kent
KIRK, David C., Croft End, 117 Foxley Lane, Purley, Surrey CR2 3HR
KIRKPATRICK, Mrs A., 33 Keir Street, Bridge of Allen, Stirlingshire
KIRKPATRICK, H. S., Strathyre, 2 Marchhill Drive, Dumfries
KNOX, J. M., 57 St Vincent Street, Glasgow C2

LEE, Professor Maurice, jr., Douglass College, Rutgers University, New
Brunswick, New Jersey, USA
LEGGE, Professor M. D., B.LITT., Department of French, David Hume
Tower, George Square, Edinburgh 8
LESLIE, John J., Kantersted Sound, Lerwick, Shetland
LESLIE, The Hon. J. W., East Kintrockat, Brechin, Angus
LEYLAND, Rev. F. Winston, S.SC., B.A., 6 Woodland Road, N. Scituate,
Rhode Island, USA
LILBURN, Alistair J., B.SC., Newlyn, Aboyne, Aberdeenshire AB3 5HE
LILBURN, Gavin G., c/o National Liberal Club, Whitehall Place, London
SW1
LOBBAN, R. D., ED.B., 3 Orchard Terrace, Edinburgh 4
LOCKETT, G. D., M.B.E., Clonterbrook House, Swettenham, Congleton,
Cheshire
LOCKHART, S. F. MacDonald, Newholm, Dunsyre, Carnwath, Lanark-
shire
LOLE, F. P., 54 Whalley Hayes, Macclesfield, Cheshire
LONGMUIR, Right Rev. J. Boyd, B.L., 1 Lygon Road, Edinburgh 9
LORIMER, Hew, R.S.A., Kellie Castle, Pittenweem, Fife
LYTHE, Professor S. G. E., University of Strathclyde, George Street,
Glasgow C2

MACALLISTER, R. B., 9 Holmwood Crescent, Langholm, Dumfriesshire
McALLISTER, R. I., 6 Ogilvie Place, Bridge of Allan, Stirlingshire
MACARTHUR, D., 8 Dempster Terrace, St Andrews
McARTHUR, James M., M.A., 7 Prince Albert Terrace, Helensburgh,
Dunbartonshire
McARTHUR, Neil, Solicitor, Old National Bank Buildings, Inverness
MACAULAY, James M., M.A., 6 Hamilton Drive, Glasgow W2
McCAFFREY, J. F., 109 Canniesburn Road, Bearsden, Glasgow
McCLOSKEY, Miss Phyllis D., 30 Athole Gardens, Glasgow W2
McCOSH, Bryce K., of Huntfield, Quothquan, Biggar, Lanarkshire
MACDONALD, Mrs C., 1 Windsor Street, Edinburgh 7
MACDONALD, J. M., Bruach, Sidinish, Locheport, North Uist
MACDONALD, Rae, 12 Rosemod Court, 333 Musgrave Road, Durban,
South Africa
MACDONALD, Rev. R., S.T.L., St Kierans, Campbeltown, Argyll

MACDOUGALL, A. C., J.P., Cornaigmore Schoolhouse, Isle of Tiree, Argyll

MACFARLANE, L. J., F.S.A., 113 High Street, Old Aberdeen

McINNES, C. T., LL.D., White Cottage, Old Kirk Road, Edinburgh 12

MACINNES, Rev. John, PH.D., D.D., Eastcott, Fortrose, Ross-shire

MACINTYRE, J. Archibald, B.A., M.A., 40 Spring Street, Guelph, Ontario, Canada

MACINTYRE, Robert D., M.B., CH.B., J.P., 8 Gladstone Place, Stirling

MACIVER, I. F., M.A., 17 Balmerino Drive, Stornoway, Isle of Lewis

MACKAY, Miss E. R., B.A., F.S.A. SCOT., Ach na Craobhan, Rhearquhar, Dornoch, Sutherland

MACKAY, Rev. Hugh, M.A., F.S.A. SCOT., The Manse, Duns, Berwickshire

MACKAY, Miss Margaret L., 3 Braid Mount, Edinburgh 10

MACKAY, Rev. P. H. R., M.A., The Manse, Premnay, Insch, Aberdeen AB5 6QE

MACKAY, William, O.B.E., Netherwood, Inverness

MACKAY, William, 1 Pear Tree Cottage, Woodside, Windsor Forest, Berks.

MACKECHNIE, Miss Catherine B., 59 Polwarth Street, Glasgow W2

MACKECHNIE, Donald, Schoolhouse, Bridge of Douglas, Inveraray, Argyll

MACKECHNIE, John P.O. Box 621, Chatham, Ontario, Canada

MACKENZIE, Miss Annie M., PH.D., Celtic Department, King's College, Old Aberdeen

MACKENZIE, Sir Compton, 31 Drummond Place, Edinburgh 3

MACKENZIE, Mrs P. C., The Cottage, Upper Clatford, Andover, Hants.

MACKIE, Professor J. D., C.B.E., M.C., LL.D., 67 Downside Road, Glasgow W2

MACLEAN, Angus, Sea-View, Caolis, Isle of Tiree, Argyll

MACLEAN, Rev. Ewan A., 12 Tantallan Place, Edinburgh 9

MACLEAN, James N. M., ygr., of Glensanda, B.LITT., PH.D., Department of History, William Robertson Building, 50 George Square, Edinburgh 8

MACLEAN, Dr. J., Van Neckstraat 102, 's-Gravenhage 1, Netherlands

MACLEAN, Mrs L. M., of Dochgarroch, The Parsonage, Pitlochry, Perthshire

McLENNAN, Ian, 157 Park View, Whitley Bay, Northumberland

MACMILLAN, Andrew T., C.A., 12 Abinger Gardens, Edinburgh 12

McMILLAN, N. W., LL.B., 160 West George Street, Glasgow C2

McNAB, Rev. J. Strathearn, 2 Broomfield Gardens, Ayr

McNAUGHT, James, Education Offices, Keith, Banffshire

MACNAUGHTON, Mrs Catherine, Oakbank Cottage, St Fillans, Perthshire

McNAUGHTON, D., M.A., 28 Pitbauchlie Bank, Dunfermline

McNEILL, Sheriff Peter G. B., 185 Nithsdale Road, Glasgow S1

McNEILL, William A., 33 Oakfield Avenue, Glasgow W2

McNIE, R. W., M.A., 18 Gartcows Drive, Falkirk, Stirlingshire

McNUTT, Miss Margaret R., LL.B., 384 North Deeside Road, Cults, Aberdeen

MACPHAIL, Angus N., 3 Denton Avenue, Gledhow, Leeds 8
MACPHAIL, I. M. M., PH.DR., Rockbank, Barloan Crescent, Dumbarton
MACPHAIL, W. D., M.A., B.A., Academy House, Fortrose, Ross-shire
MACPHERSON, Captain J. Harvey, F.S.A. SCOT., Dunmore, Newton-
more, Inverness-shire
MACQUEEN, Professor John, English Literature Department, David
Hume Tower, George Square, Edinburgh 8
McRAE, J. A., 230 8th Avenue, Prince Rupert, B.C., Canada
McROBERTS, Right Rev. Monsignor David, S.T.L., F.S.A., Carstairs House,
Carstairs Junction, Lanarkshire
MAGRUDER, Thomas G., jr., Scotland House, 607 South Washington
Street, Alexandria, Virginia 22313, USA
MALCOLM, Colonel George, of Poltalloch, Duntrune Castle, Lochgilphead,
Argyll
MARSHALL, David C., Kilbucho Place, Broughton, Peeblesshire
MARSHALL, Rev. James S., M.A., 4 Claremont Park, Edinburgh 6
MARSHALL, Miss Rosalind K., M.A., 21 Church Street, Kirkcaldy, Fife
MARWICK, W. H., 5 Northfield Crescent, Edinburgh 8
MATTHEWS, Henry McN., 120 East End Avenue, New York City, New
York 10028, USA
MAXWELL, Stuart, F.S.A. SCOT., 23 Dick Place, Edinburgh 9
MICHAEL, James, O.B.E., Achtemrack, Drumnadrochit, Inverness-shire
MILLER, R. Pairman, W.S., 13 St Catherine's Place, Edinburgh 3
MILNE, Miss Doreen J., PH.D., History Department, King's College, Old
Aberdeen
MILNE, J. S. K., 8 Craigcrook Terrace, Edinburgh 4
MITCHELL, Brian, c/o Hood, 20 Guthrie Park, Brechin, Angus
MITCHELL, Miss Rosemary, M.A., 24 Alexander Place, Oban, Argyll
MITCHISON, Mrs R., 6 Dovecot Road, Edinburgh 12
MONCREIFFE, Sir Iain, PH.D., F.S.A., House of Moncreiffe, Bridge of Earn,
Perthshire
MOORE, Edwin, Merry Leazes West, Hexham, Northumberland
MORPETH, R. S., 11 Albert Terrace, Edinburgh 10
MORRISON, Alick, 844 Tollcross Road, Glasgow E2
MORRISON, Dr. H. P., Shawpark, Selkirk
MUI, Hoh-Cheung, PH.D., Department of History, Memorial University,
St John's, Newfoundland, Canada
MULHOLLAND, R., 29 Dores Road, Inverness
MUNRO, Mrs R. W., 15A Mansionhouse Road, Edinburgh 9
MUNRO, R. W., 15A Mansionhouse Road, Edinburgh 9
MURCHISON, Rev. T. M., 14 Kinross Avenue, Glasgow, SW2
MURDOCH, Mrs S. M., The Jaw, Baldernock, Stirlingshire
MURRAY, A. L., PH.D., LL.B., 33 Inverleith Gardens, Edinburgh 3

NAUGHTON, Miss J. M., M.A., 9 Summerside Street, Edinburgh 6
NEIL, J. K., The Viewlands, Blakeshall, nr. Kidderminster, Worcs.
NEILLY, Miss Margaret, R.G.N., 9 Woodmuir Road, Whitburn, West
Lothian

NICHOLAS, Don L., Temple Guiting House, Temple Guiting, nr. Cheltenham, Gloucestershire

NICHOLSON, R. G., Department of History, University of Guelph, Guelph, Ontario, Canada

NICOL, Miss Mary P., M.A., 15 Falcon Road West, Edinburgh 10

NICOLL, Mrs I. M., Westcroft, Wardlaw Gardens, St Andrews

NIMMO, Mrs A. E., 9 Succoth Gardens, Edinburgh 12

NOBLE, Iain A., 1 Albyn Place, Edinburgh 2

NOBLE, John, Ardkinglas, Cairndow, Argyll

NOBLE, R. S. P. C., F.S.A. SCOT., Struan, 7 Medow Mead, Radlett, Herts.

NORBY, Mrs Eunice, 207 Mary Avenue, Missoula, Montana, USA

NOTMAN, R. C., B.L., W.S., 5 Ainslie Place, Edinburgh 3

OLDFIELD, Lady Kathleen, M.A., Woodhall Cottage, Pencaitland, East Lothian

PALMER, Kenneth, 4 Cumin Place, Edinburgh 9

PARTINGTON, T., 38 Vincent Road, Cobham, Surrey

PATERSON, Mrs Mairi M., M.A., Beach House, West Bay, Dunoon, Argyll

PATTULLO, Miss Nan, 29 Ormidale Terrace, Edinburgh 12

PEEL, Robert A., Ardvaar, Helensburgh, Dunbartonshire

PHILLIPSON, N. T., History Department, William Robertson Building, 50 George Square, Edinburgh 8

PIRIE-GORDON, Harry, of Buthlaw, D.S.C., F.S.A., Polesacre, Lowfield Heath, Crawley, Sussex

POLLOCK, Mrs Gladys M., Ronachan, Clachan, Tarbert, Argyll

PORTEOUS, Robert, 8 Burnbank Road, Grangemouth, Stirlingshire

PRAIN, Sheriff A. M., Castellar, Crieff, Perthshire

PREBBLE, John, F.R.S.L., Shaw Coign, Alcocks Lane, Burgh Heath, Tadworth, Surrey

RAE, Alan, Eastnor, School Brae, Cramond, Edinburgh 4

RAE, Miss Isobel, Dunlugas Cottage, Nairn

RAE, Thomas I., PH.D., National Library of Scotland, George IV Bridge, Edinburgh 1

RAMSAY, Alan D. M., Bolland of Galashiels, Selkirkshire

REID, Sir Edward J., 16 Buckingham Terrace, Edinburgh 4

REID, Professor W. Stanford, Department of History, University of Guelph, Guelph, Ontario, Canada

RITCHIE, Alexander, 19 Langside Drive, Kilbarchan, Renfrewshire

RITCHIE, A. G., C.B.E., 102 Polwarth Gardens, Edinburgh 11

RITSON, F. A., J.P., C.A., Easter Lathrisk, Ladybank, Fife

ROBB, George, Inverdee, 14 Westerton Road, Cults, Aberdeen

ROBBINS, Miss Caroline, PH.D., Department of History, Bryn Mawr College, Bryn Mawr, Pa. 19010, USA

ROBERTSON, A. Irvine, T.D., LL.B., The Old Manse, Park Avenue, Stirling

ROBERTSON, James J., LL.B., Faculty of Law, Queen's College, University of Dundee, Dundee
ROBERTSON, Miss Kathleen N., M.A., 120 Albert Road, Gourock, Renfrewshire
ROBERTSON, The Hon. Lord, 49 Moray Place, Edinburgh 3
RODGER, George M., 9 The Cross, Forfar, Angus
ROSEBERY, The Rt Hon. the Earl of, D.S.O., Dalmeny House, Edinburgh
ROSS, Rev. Anthony, O.P., S.T.L., 24 George Square, Edinburgh 8
ROSS, N. P., History Department, Carthage College, Kenosha, Wisconsin 53140, USA
RULE, R. H., 3473 South Leisure World Boulevard, Silver Spring, Maryland 20906, USA
RUSSELL, D. F. O., Rothes, Markinch, Fife
RUSSELL, Miss Florence M., 4A Inverleith Terrace, Edinburgh 3

SALVESEN, Captain Harold K., Inveralmond, Cramond, Edinburgh
SALVESEN, T. Norman F., Kinloch House, Amulree, Perthshire
SANDERSON, Miss Margaret H. B., 28 Highfield Crescent, Linlithgow, West Lothian
SANDISON, William, Lythburn, Hempmill Brook, Market Drayton, Salop.
SCOTLAND, James, M.A., M.ED., 67 Forest Road, Aberdeen
SCOTT, David, Glenaros, Isle of Mull, by Oban
SCOTT, P. H., c/o Foreign Office, London SW1
SCOTT, R. Lyon, Braeside, Loanhead, Midlothian
SCOTT, Thomas H., 32 Couston Street, Dunfermline, Fife
SCOTT, William W., 7 Hill Road, Brentwood, Essex
SEFTON, Rev. H. R., PH.D., Manse of Newbattle, Easthouses, Dalkeith, Midlothian
SELLAR, W. H. D., 76 Blairbeth Road, Burnside, Glasgow
SEMPLE, Walter G., Longways, 4 Neidpath Road West, Giffnock, Glasgow
SERVICE, Commander Douglas, of Torsonce, 16 Redington Road, Hampstead, London, NW3
SHARP, Buchanan, B.A., M.A., 1380 Ardmore Drive, San Leandro, California, USA
SHAW, Major C. J., of Tordarroch, M.B.E., T.D., D.L., Newhall, Balblair, Conon Bridge, Ross-shire
SHAW, Rev. Duncan, PH.D., 4 Sydney Terrace, Edinburgh 7
SHEAD, N. F., 16 Burnside Gardens, Clarkston, Glasgow
SHEARER, J. G. S., M.A., 14 Manse Crescent, Stirling
SHEPHERD, James P., M.A., The Schoolhouse, Biggar, Lanarkshire
SIMPSON, Eric J., M.A., F.S.A. SCOT., 6 Frankfield Road, Dalgety Bay, Dunfermline, Fife
SIMPSON, Grant G., PH.D., F.S.A., Scottish Record Office, H.M. General Register House, Edinburgh 2 (*Honorary Secretary*)
SIMPSON, John M., Scottish History Department, William Robertson Building, 50 George Square, Edinburgh 8
SIMPSON, S. M., 60 Orchard Brae Gardens, Edinburgh 4

SIMSON, Mrs Annie, Balmanno, Laurencekirk, Kincardineshire
SINCLAIR, Alexander, M.A., DIP.M.S., A.M.B.I.M., 16 Kensington Drive, Bearsden, Glasgow
SINCLAIR, John N., Glengarth, 10 Ronald Street, Lerwick, Shetland
SLADE, H. Gordon, T.D., A.R.I.B.A., 15 Southbourne Gardens, London SE12
SMITH, David B., LL.B., 30 Great King Street, Edinburgh 3
SMITH, J. A., B.ED., 108 Queen Victoria Drive, Glasgow W3
SMOUT, T. C., PH.D., 93 Warrender Park Road, Edinburgh 10
SOUTHESK, The Rt Hon. The Earl of, K.C.V.O., Kinnaird Castle, Brechin, Angus
STENHOUSE, B. A., 11 Learmonth Park, Edinburgh 4
STEVENSON, Michael, M.C., 18 Royal Circus, Edinburgh 3
STEVENSON, William, 27 Ferguston Road, Bearsden, Glasgow
STEWART, H. C., Netherton, Wellside Road, Falkirk, Stirlingshire
STIRLING, Matthew, 20 Westbourne Terrace, London W2
STONES, Professor E. L. G., PH.D., F.S.A., History Department, The University, Glasgow W2
STOREY, Miss Patricia J., 30 Garscube Terrace, Edinburgh 12
STRACHAN, M. F., M.B.E., 7 Napier Road, Edinburgh 12
STRAWHORN, John, PH.D., 2 East Park Avenue, Mauchline, Ayrshire
SUNTER, J. R. M., M.A., 30 March Road, Blackhall, Edinburgh 4
SUTHERLAND, The Countess of, Uppat House, Brora, Sutherland
SWAINSTON, Mrs A. Y. Imrie, 8 Sheldon Avenue, London N6
SYNGE, A. M., Plas Draw, Ruthin, Denbighshire

TAYLOR, David B., M.A., F.S.A. SCOT., Delvine, Longforgan, by Dundee
TAYLOR, W., PH.D., 25 Bingham Terrace, Dundee
THOMPSON, F. G., 17 Viewfield Road, Culcabock, Inverness
THOMS, David, Strathview, Trinity Road, Brechin, Angus
THOMSON, A. G., PH.D., 14 Regent Terrace, Edinburgh 7
THOMSON, A. McLay, F.R.H.S., 94 Baldwin Avenue, Glasgow W3
THOMSON, J. A., Summerhill House, Annan, Dumfriesshire
THOMSON, J. A. F., D.PHIL., History Department, The University, Glasgow W2
THOMSON, J. B., 30 Kingsway, Tarbert, Argyll
THOMSON, James M., The Farm House, Auchincruive, Ayr
THOMSON, W. O., 14 West Castle Road, Edinburgh 10
THURSO, The Rt Hon. the Viscount, of Ulbster, Ulbster Estates Office, Thurso East, Thurso, Caithness
TODD, J. M., Redbourn House, Main Street, St Bees, Cumberland
TRAILL, Miss M., Lower Pendents, Winchelsea, Sussex
TROUP, J. A., 2 Manse Park, Stromness, Orkney
TURNER, Professor A. C., College of Letters & Science, University of California, Riverside, California 92502, USA

URQUHART, Kenneth T., ygr., of Urquhart, 353 Vinet Avenue, New Orleans, La. 70121, USA

VEITCH, Rev. Thomas, F.S.A. SCOT., St Paul's and St George's Rectory, 53 Albany Street, Edinburgh 1

VON GOETZ, Richard B., 16B Lady Wynd, Cupar, Fife

WADDELL, W. A., Fairport, Ayr

WALKER, Professor David M., Q.C., PH.D., LL.D., 1 Beaumont Gate, Glasgow W1

WALLS, Andrew F., M.A., B.LITT., Department of Church History, King's College, Old Aberdeen

WALTON, Mrs P. M. Eaves, 55 Manor Place, Edinburgh 3

WATSON, Miss Elspeth G. Boog, 24 Garscube Terrace, Murrayfield, Edinburgh 12

WATT, Donald E.R., Department of Medieval History, St Salvator's College, St Andrews

WEBSTER, Bruce, F.S.A., 5 The Terrace, St Stephens, Canterbury, Kent

WEDGWOOD, Miss C. V., 22 St Ann's Terrace, London NW8

WEIR, Thomas E., B.D., PH.D., R.A.F. Station, Edzell, nr. Brechin, Angus

WHITEFORD, Rev. D. H., Q.H.C., B.D., PH.D., 16 Mostyn Road, Bushey, Herts.

WHYTE, Donald, 4 Carmel Road, Kirkliston, West Lothian

WILLIAMSON, John, New Grunnasound, Bridge End, Shetland

WILLOCK, Professor I. D., Department of Jurisprudence, Queen's College, University of Dundee, Dundee

WILLS, Mrs Peter, 26 Howard Street, Bantasken, Falkirk, Stirlingshire

WILSON, Miss Florence Eva, 164 Forest Avenue, Aberdeen

WILSON, Sir Garnet, LL.D., St Colmes, 496 Perth Road, Dundee

WILSON, Miss Isabel J. T., 2 Segton Avenue, Kilwinning, Ayrshire

WILSON, John, 16 Goff Avenue, Edinburgh 7

WISHART, Edward McL., O.B.E., M.A., Trebor, Garngaber Avenue, Lenzie, by Glasgow

WITHRINGTON, D. J., M.ED., History Department, King's College, Old Aberdeen

WOOD, Miss Wendy, 31 Howard Place, Edinburgh 3

WOTHERSPOON, Robert, Solicitor, Inverness

WRIGHT, James M. B., of Auchinellan, Ford, Lochgilphead, Argyll

YOUNG, Douglas, Makarsbield, Tayport, Fife

YOUNG, Mrs Janet G., 114 Mearns Road, Clarkston, Glasgow

YOUNG, Kenneth G., LL.B., W.S., Dunearn, Auchterarder, Perthshire

YOUNG, Miss Margaret D., 13 Craiglockhart Drive North, Edinburgh 11

YOUNG, R. M., Treetops, 120 Boundary Lane, Congleton, Cheshire

YOUNG, Miss V. C., Castlehill, Dalbeattie, Kirkcudbrightshire

YOUNGSON, Professor A. J., D.LITT., Department of Economics, William Robertson Building, 50 George Square, Edinburgh 8

Aberdeen Public Library
Aberdeen University Library
Aberystwyth, National Library of Wales
Adelaide, University of, Barr Smith Library, Australia
Alabama, University of, USA
Arbroath Public Library
Argyll County Library, Dunoon
Auckland University College, New Zealand
Ayr, Carnegie Public Library
Ayr, Craigie College of Education

Baltimore, Peabody Institute, USA
Bedford Park, Flinders University of South Australia
Belfast Library and Society for Promoting Knowledge (Linenhall Library)
Belfast, Queen's University
Birmingham, Public Libraries
Birmingham University Library
Blackburn, Stonyhurst College, Lancashire
Boston Athenaeum, USA
Boston Public Library, USA
Boston University Libraries, USA
Bristol University
British Columbia, University of, Vancouver, Canada
Brunswick, Bowdoin College Library, USA
Buffalo, Lockwood Memorial Library, State University of New York, USA

California, Los Angeles Public Library, USA
California University Library, Berkeley, USA
California, University of, Riverside, USA
California, University of California Library, Los Angeles, USA
California, University of Southern California Library, Los Angeles, USA
Cambridge, Harvard College Library, USA
Cambridge University Library
Canberra, National Library of Australia
Capetown, University of, South Africa
Cardiff Free Library
Cardross, St Peter's College, Dunbartonshire
Chicago, E. M. Cudahy Memorial Library, Loyola University, USA
Chicago, Newberry Library, USA
Chicago University Library, USA
Cincinnati, The General Library, University of Cincinnati, USA
Cleveland Public Library, USA
Coatbridge, Carnegie Public Library
Copenhagen, Royal Library, Denmark

Glasgow, City Archives
Glasgow, Mitchell Library (The Moir Fund)
Glasgow, University Library
Glasgow University, Scottish History Class Library
Glasgow University, Scottish History Departmental Library
Goteborg, City and University Library of Goteborg, Sweden
Guelph, University of, Ontario, Canada

Haddington, Sancta Maria Abbey, Nunraw
Hague, The, Netherlands Royal Library, Netherlands
Houston, University of, USA
Hull, University Library

Indiana University Library, USA
Inverness County Library
Inverness Public Library
Iowa, State University of Iowa Libraries, USA

Kilmarnock, Public Library
Kirkcudbrightshire County Library, Castle Douglas
Kirkintilloch, Public Library
Kirkwall, Orkney County Library

Lancaster, University of
Latrobe, St Vincent College, USA
Laurinburg, St Andrews College, USA
Leeds Reference Library
Leeds, University of Leeds, Brotherton Library
Lerwick, Zetland County Library
Liverpool, The University of Liverpool
London, Bailliere, Tindall and Cassall Limited
London, Corporation Library, Guidhall
London, Institute of Historical Research
London, Lambeth Palace Library
London, London Library, St Jame's Square
London, London School of Economics and Political Science
London, National Central Library
London, Public Record Office
London, Queen Mary College (University of London)
London, Society of Antiquaries
London, Society of Genealogists
London, University College
London, University of London Library
Louvain, Bibliothèque de L'Université, Belgium
Lund, Universitets Bibliotheket, Sweden

Manchester, John Rylands Library
Manchester, Public Library

Manchester, University Library
Maryland, University of, McKeldin Library, USA
Melbourne, State Library of Victoria, Australia
Melbourne University, Australia
Michigan State University Library, East Lansing, USA
Michigan University, General Library, Ann Arbor, USA
Mills Memorial Library, McMaster University, Canada
Minnesota, Library of University of Minnesota, USA
Missouri, University of, General Library, Columbia, USA
Montreal, McGill University, Redpath Library, Canada
Montreat Historical Foundation of Presbyterian Reformed Churches, USA
Morpeth, Northumberland County Library
Motherwell Public Libraries

Nashville, Joint University Library, USA
Nebraska, University of, Lincoln, USA
Newcastle upon Tyne, Public Library
Newcastle upon Tyne, The University of Newcastle
New England, University of, Armidale, Australia
New Jersey, Princeton Theological Seminary, USA
New Jersey, Princeton University Library, USA
New York, Columbia University Library, USA
New York, Cornell University, Ithaca, USA
New York, Library of the General Theological Seminary, USA
New York, Public Library, USA
New York, State Library, Albany, USA
New York University Libraries, USA
Notre Dame, University of Notre Dame, Indiana, USA
Nottingham Free Public Library

Ohio State University, Columbia, USA
Oregon University Library, Eugene, USA
Ottawa, National Library of Canada, Canada
Oxford, All Souls College
Oxford, Balliol College
Oxford, Bodleian Library
Oxford, Worcester College

Paris, Bibliothèque Nationale, France
Pennsylvania, Historical Society of Pennsylvania, USA
Pennsylvania, University Library, Philadelphia, USA
Perth and Kinross County Library
Perth, Sandeman Public Library
Pittsburgh, University Library, USA

Reading, University Library
Rochester University Library, New York, USA

St Andrews, Hay Fleming Library
St Andrews, University Library
St Louis, Washington University Libraries, Missouri, USA
San Francisco Public Library, USA
San Marino, Henry E. Huntington Library and Art Gallery, USA
Sheffield, Free Public Library
Sheffield, University Library
Stanford University Library, USA
Stirling County Library
Stirling High School
Stirling Public Library
Stirling University Library
Stockholm, Royal Library, Sweden
Sydney, New South Wales Library, Australia
Sydney, New South Wales, Australia, The Society of Australian Genealogists

Texas Technological College Library, Lubbock, USA
Texas, University of, Austin, USA
Toronto Reference Library, Canada
Toronto, University Library, Canada

Uppsala, Royal University Library, Sweden
Urbana, Illinois University Library, USA
Utrecht, Historisch Genootschap, Holland

Vaticana Biblioteca Apostolica, Citta del Vaticano, Italy
Virginia State Library, Richmond, USA

Washington, The Folger Shakespeare Library, USA
Washington, Library of Congress, USA
Washington, University Library, Seattle, USA
Wellington, Victoria University of Wellington, New Zealand
Wick, Carnegie Public Library
Williamsburg, The Library, College of William and Mary, USA
Wisconsin, University of, The General Library, Madison, USA

Yale University Library, USA

Copies of the Society's publications are presented to the British Museum,
London

PUBLICATIONS

Volumes marked with an asterisk are no longer obtainable

FIRST SERIES

*1. BISHOP POCOCKE'S TOURS IN SCOTLAND, 1747-1760. Ed. D. W. KEMP. 1887.

*2. DIARY AND ACCOUNT BOOK OF WILLIAM CUNNINGHAM OF CRAIGENDS, 1673-1680. Ed. Rev. JAMES DODDS. 1887.

*3. GRAMEIDOS LIBRI SEX: an heroic poem on the Campaign of 1689 by JAMES PHILIP of Almerieclose. Trans. and ed. Rev. A. D. MURDOCH. 1888.

*4. THE REGISTER OF THE KIRK-SESSION OF ST ANDREWS. Part I, 1559-1582. Ed. D. HAY FLEMING. 1889.

*5. DIARY OF THE REV. JOHN MILL, Minister in Shetland, 1740-1803. Ed. GILBERT GOUDIE. 1889.

*6. NARRATIVE OF MR JAMES NIMMO, A COVENANTER, 1654-1709. Ed. W. G. SCOTT-MONCRIEFF. 1889.

*7. THE REGISTER OF THE KIRK-SESSION OF ST ANDREWS. Part II, 1583-1600. Ed. D. HAY FLEMING. 1890.

*8. A LIST OF PERSONS CONCERNED IN THE REBELLION (1745). With a Preface by the EARL OF ROSEBERY. 1890.

Presented to the Society by the Earl of Rosebery

*9. GLAMIS PAPERS: The 'BOOK OF RECORD', a Diary written by PATRICK, FIRST EARL OF STRATHMORE, and other documents (1684-89). Ed. A. H. MILLAR. 1890.

*10. JOHN MAJOR'S HISTORY OF GREATER BRITAIN (1521). Trans. and ed. ARCHIBALD CONSTABLE. 1892.

*11. THE RECORDS OF THE COMMISSIONS OF THE GENERAL ASSEMBLIES, 1646-47. Ed. Rev. Professor MITCHELL and Rev. JAMES CHRISTIE. 1892.

*12. COURT-BOOK OF THE BARONY OF URIE, 1604-1747. Ed. Rev. D. G. BARRON. 1892.

*13. MEMOIRS OF SIR JOHN CLERK OF PENICUIK, BARONET, 1676-1755. Ed. JOHN M. GRAY. 1892.

*14. DIARY OF COL. THE HON. JOHN ERSKINE OF CARNOCK, 1683-1687. Ed. Rev. WALTER MACLEOD. 1893.

*15. MISCELLANY OF THE SCOTTISH HISTORY SOCIETY. Vol. I. 1893.

*16. ACCOUNT BOOK OF SIR JOHN FOULIS OF RAVELSTON, 1671-1707. Ed. Rev. A. W. CORNELIUS HALLEN. 1894.

*37. PAPAL NEGOTIATIONS WITH MARY QUEEN OF SCOTS DURING HER REIGN IN SCOTLAND. Ed. Rev. J. HUNGERFORD POLLEN. 1901.

*38. PAPERS ON THE SCOTS BRIGADE IN HOLLAND, 1572-1782. Ed. JAMES FERGUSON. Vol. III. 1901.

*39. THE DIARY OF ANDREW HAY OF CRAIGNETHAN, 1659-60. Ed. A. G. REID. 1901.

*40. NEGOTIATIONS FOR THE UNION OF ENGLAND AND SCOTLAND IN 1651-53. Ed. C. STANFORD TERRY. 1902.

*41. THE LOYALL DISSUASIVE. Written in 1703 by Sir ÆNEAS MAC-PHERSON. Ed. Rev. A. D. MURDOCH. 1902.

*42. THE CHARTULARY OF LINDORES, 1195-1479. Ed. Right Rev. JOHN DOWDEN, Bishop of Edinburgh. 1903.

*43. A LETTER FROM MARY QUEEN OF SCOTS TO THE DUKE OF GUISE, Jan. 1562. Reproduced in Facsimile. Ed. Rev. J. HUNGERFORD POLLEN. 1904.

Presented to the Society by the family of the late Mr Scott of Halkshill

*44. MISCELLANY OF THE SCOTTISH HISTORY SOCIETY. Vol. II. 1904.

*45. LETTERS OF JOHN COCKBURN OF ORMISTOUN TO HIS GARDENER, 1727-1743. Ed. JAMES COLVILLE. 1904.

*46. MINUTE BOOK OF THE MANAGERS OF THE NEW MILLS CLOTH MANUFACTORY, 1681-1690. Ed. W. R. Scott. 1905.

*47. CHRONICLES OF THE FRASERS; being the Wardlaw Manuscript. By Master JAMES FRASER. Ed. WILLIAM MACKAY. 1905.

*48. PROCEEDINGS OF THE JUSTICIARY COURT FROM 1661 TO 1678. Vol. I, 1661-1669. Ed. Sheriff SCOTT-MONCRIEFF. 1905.

*49. PROCEEDINGS OF THE JUSTICIARY COURT FROM 1661 TO 1678. Vol. II, 1669-1678. Ed. Sheriff SCOTT-MONCRIEFF. 1905.

50. RECORDS OF THE BARON COURT OF STITCHILL, 1655-1807. Ed. CLEMENT B. GUNN. 1905.

51, 52, 53. MACFARLANE'S GEOGRAPHICAL COLLECTIONS. Ed. Sir ARTHUR MITCHELL. 3 vols. 1906-8.

*54. STATUTA ECCLESIÆ SCOTICANÆ, 1225-1559. Trans. and ed. DAVID PATRICK. 1907.

*55. THE HOUSE BOOKE OF ACCOMPTS, OCHTERTYRE, 1737-39. Ed JAMES COLVILLE. 1907.

56. THE CHARTERS OF THE ABBEY OF INCHAFFRAY. Ed. W. A. LINDSAY, Right Rev. Bishop DOWDEN and J. MAITLAND THOMSON. 1908.

*57. A SELECTION OF THE FORFEITED ESTATES PAPERS PRESERVED IN H.M. GENERAL REGISTER HOUSE AND ELSEWHERE. Ed. A. H. MILLAR. 1909.

58. RECORDS OF THE COMMISSIONS OF THE GENERAL ASSEMBLIES, 1650-52. Ed. Rev. JAMES CHRISTIE. 1909.

59. PAPERS RELATING TO THE SCOTS IN POLAND. 1576-93. Ed. A. FRANCIS STEUART. 1915.

20. HIGHLAND PAPERS. Vol. III. Ed. J. R. N. MACPHAIL. 1920.

THIRD SERIES

1. REGISTER OF THE CONSULTATIONS OF THE MINISTERS OF EDINBURGH. Vol. I. 1652–1657. Ed. Rev. W. STEPHEN. 1921.

2. DIARY OF GEORGE RIDPATH, MINISTER OF STITCHEL, 1755–1761. Ed. Sir JAMES BALFOUR PAUL. 1922.

3. THE CONFESSIONS OF BABINGTON AND OTHER PAPERS RELATING TO THE LAST DAYS OF MARY QUEEN OF SCOTS. Ed. Rev. J. H. POLLEN. 1922.

4. FOREIGN CORRESPONDENCE WITH MARIE DE LORRAINE, QUEEN OF SCOTLAND (BALCARRES PAPERS). Vol. I, 1537–1548. Ed. MARGUERITE WOOD. 1923.

5. SELECTIONS FROM THE PAPERS OF THE SIR WILLIAM FRASER. Ed. J. R. N. MACPHAIL. 1924.
Presented to the Society by the Trustees of the late Sir William Fraser, K.C.B.

6. PAPERS RELATING TO THE SHIPS AND VOYAGES OF THE COMPANY OF SCOTLAND TRADING TO AFRICA AND THE INDIES, 1696–1707. Ed. GEORGE P. INSH. 1924.

7. FOREIGN CORRESPONDENCE WITH MARIE DE LORRAINE, QUEEN OF SCOTLAND (BALCARRES PAPERS). Vol. II, 1548–1557. Ed. MARGUERITE WOOD. 1925.

*8. THE EARLY RECORDS OF THE UNIVERSITY OF ST ANDREWS, 1413–1579. Ed. J. MAITLAND ANDERSON. 1926.

9. MISCELLANY OF THE SCOTTISH HISTORY SOCIETY. Vol. IV. 1926.

10. THE SCOTTISH CORRESPONDENCE OF MARY OF LORRAINE, 1543–1560. Ed. ANNIE I. CAMERON. 1927.

11. JOURNAL OF THOMAS CUNINGHAM, 1640–1654. CONSERVATOR AT CAMPVERE. Ed. ELINOR JOAN COURTHOPE. 1928.

12. THE SHERIFF COURT BOOK OF FIFE, 1515–1522. Ed. WILLIAM CROFT DICKINSON. 1928.

13, 14, 15. THE PRISONERS OF THE '45. Ed. Sir BRUCE SETON, Bart., of Abercorn, and Mrs JEAN GORDON ARNOT. 3 vols. 1928–9.

16. REGISTER OF THE CONSULTATIONS OF THE MINISTERS OF EDINBURGH. Vol. II, 1657–1660. Ed. Rev. W. STEPHEN. 1930.

17. THE MINUTES OF THE JUSTICES OF THE PEACE FOR LANARKSHIRE, 1707–1723. Ed. C. A. MALCOLM. 1931.

18. THE WARRENDER PAPERS. Vol. I, 1301–1587. Ed. ANNIE I. CAMERON, with Introduction by Principal ROBERT S. RAIT. 1931.

19. THE WARRENDER PAPERS. Vol. II, 1587–1603. Ed. ANNIE I. CAMERON, with introduction by Principal ROBERT S. RAIT. 1932

20. FLODDEN PAPERS. Ed. MARGUERITE WOOD. 1933.

21. MISCELLANY OF THE SCOTTISH HISTORY SOCIETY. Vol. V. 1933.

22. HIGHLAND PAPERS. Vol. IV. Ed. J. R. N. MACPHAIL, with Biographical Introduction by WILLIAM K. DICKSON. 1934.

50. MISCELLANY OF THE SCOTTISH HISTORY SOCIETY. Vol. IX. 1958.
51. WIGTOWNSHIRE CHARTERS. Ed. R. C. REID. 1960.
52. JOHN HOME'S SURVEY OF ASSYNT. Ed. R. J. ADAM. 1960.
53. COURT BOOK OF THE BURGH OF KIRKINTILLOCH, 1658-1694. Ed. G. S. PRYDE. 1963.
*54, 55. ACTA FACULTATIS ARTIUM UNIVERSITATIS SANCTI ANDREE, 1413-1588. Ed. ANNIE I. DUNLOP. 2 vols. 1964.

FOURTH SERIES

1. ARGYLL ESTATE INSTRUCTIONS (Mull, Morvern, Tiree), 1771-1805. Ed. ERIC R. CREGEEN. 1964.
2. MISCELLANY OF THE SCOTTISH HISTORY SOCIETY. Vol. X. 1965. (Memoir of Dr E. W. M. Balfour-Melville, by D. B. HORN; Bagimond's Roll for the diocese of Moray, ed. Rev. CHARLES BURNS; Accounts of the King's Pursemaster, 1539-40, ed. A. L. MURRAY; Papers of a Dundee shipping dispute, 1600-4, ed. W. A. MCNEILL; A Scottish liturgy of the reign of James VI, ed. GORDON DONALDSON; List of Schoolmasters teaching Latin, 1690, ed. D. J. WITHRINGTON; Letters of Andrew Fletcher of Saltoun and his family, 1715-16, ed. I. J. MURRAY; Sir John Clerk's Observations on the present circumstances of Scotland, 1730, ed. T. C. SMOUT; A Renfrewshire election account, 1832, ed. WILLIAM FERGUSON.)
3. LETTERS OF JOHN RAMSAY OF OCHTERTYRE, 1799-1812. Ed. BARBARA L. H. HORN. 1966.
4. THE COURT BOOKS OF ORKNEY AND SHETLAND, 1614-15. Ed. ROBERT S. BARCLAY. 1967.
5. THE MINUTES OF EDINBURGH TRADES COUNCIL, 1859-73. Ed. IAN MACDOUGALL. 1968.

In preparation

1. THE SWEDISH PAPERS OF JAMES SPENS, 1606-31. Ed. ARCHIBALD DUNCAN and the late JAMES DOW.
2. TYNINGHAME KIRK SESSION MINUTES, 1615-50. Ed. D. J. WITHRINGTON.
3. LETTERS OF POPES CLEMENT VII AND BENEDICT XIII CONCERNING SCOTLAND, 1378-1418. Ed. Rev. CHARLES BURNS. 2 vols.
4. PAPERS ON SUTHERLAND ESTATE MANAGEMENT, 1780-1820. Ed. R. J. ADAM and A. V. COLE. 2 vols.
5. CALENDAR OF SCOTTISH SUPPLICATIONS TO ROME. Vol. III. Ed. ANNIE I. DUNLOP.
6. ESTATE RECORDS OF THE RAMSAYS OF BARNTON, 1788-1865. Ed. J. S. K. MILNE.
7. RECORDS OF THE KNIGHTS HOSPITALLERS IN SCOTLAND. Ed. the late ANGUS MACDONALD.
8. SCOTTISH INDUSTRIAL HISTORY: A MISCELLANY OF DOCUMENTS.

RULES

1. The object of the Society is the discovery and printing, under selected editorship, of unpublished documents illustrative of the civil, religious and social history of Scotland. The Society will also undertake, in exceptional cases, to issue translations of printed works of a similar nature which have not hitherto been accessible in English.

2. The affairs of the Society shall be managed by a Council, consisting of a Chairman, Treasurer, Secretary, and twelve elected Members, five to make a quorum. Three of the twelve elected Members shall retire annually by ballot, but they shall be eligible for re-election.

3. The Annual Subscription to the Society shall be two guineas or seven dollars. The publications of the Society shall not be delivered to any Member whose Subscription is in arrear, and no Member shall be permitted to receive more than one copy of the Society's publications.

4. The Society will undertake the issue of its own publications, *i.e.* without the intervention of a publisher or any other paid agent.

5. The Society normally issues one volume each year.

6. An Annual General Meeting of the Society shall be held at the end of October, or at an approximate date to be determined by the Council.

7. Two stated Meetings of the Council shall be held each year, one on the last Tuesday of May, the other on the Tuesday preceding the day upon which the Annual General Meeting shall be held. The Secretary, on the request of three Members of the Council, shall call a special meeting of the Council.

8. Editors shall receive 20 copies of each volume they edit for the Society.

9. The owners of Manuscripts published by the Society will also be presented with a certain number of copies.

10. The Annual Balance Sheet, Rules, and List of Members shall be printed.

11. No alteration shall be made in these Rules except at a General Meeting of the Society. A fortnight's notice of any alteration to be proposed shall be given to the Members of the Council.

✱